Facing History and Ourselves

The Jews of Poland

Facing History and Ourselves National Foundation, Inc.
Brookline, Massachusetts

For permission to reproduce the following photographs and maps in this book, grateful acknowledgement is made to the following:

p. 46: Courtesy of YIVO Institute for Jewish Research. 50: From *Image Before My Eyes*, by Lucjan Dobroszycki and Barbara Kirshenblatt-Gimblett. Schocken Books, 1977. 57: Courtesy of YIVO Institute for Jewish Research. 62: Courtesy of YIVO Institute for Jewish Research. 63: A. Kacev, Taurogen (YIVO Institute for Jewish Research). 82: From *Image Before My Eyes*, by Lucjan Dobroszycki and Barbara Kirshenblatt-Gimblett. Schocken Books, 1977. 83: Vilna/Gustav Eisner Collection (YIVO Institute for Jewish Research). 89: Forward Collection (YIVO Collection for Jewish Research). 96: Alter Kacyzne/Raphael Abromovitch Collection (YIVO Institute for Jewish Research). 99: Courtesy of YIVO Institute for Jewish Research. 102: Prof. Leopold Pfefferberg-Page. Courtesy of USHMM Photo Archives. 109: Courtesy of YIVO Institute for Jewish Research. 125: From *The Atlas of the Holocaust* by Martin Gilbert. © Martin Gilbert 1982. 131: Courtesy of YIVO Institute for Jewish Research. 133: From *In Memory of Polish Jews*, Warsaw, 1987. 142: From *In Memory of Polish Jews*, Warsaw, 1987. 148: From *In Memory of Polish Jews*, Warsaw, 1987. 168: Courtesy of YIVO Institute for Jewish Research. 171: Courtesy of YIVO Institute for Jewish Research. 191: Yad Vashem Photo Archives, courtesy of USHMM Photo Archives. 197: From *In Memory of Polish Jews*, Warsaw, 1987. 209: From *In Memory of Polish Jews*, Warsaw, 1987. 213: Yad Vashem Photo Archives, courtesy of USHMM Photo Archives.

Acknowledgment of the many quotations included in each chapter of this book may be found at the end of the chapter. Every effort has been made to trace and acknowledge owners of copyrighted materials, but in some cases that has proved impossible. Facing History and Ourselves would be pleased to add, correct, or revise any such acknowledgments in future printings.

Facing History and Ourselves
16 Hurd Road
Brookline, MA 02146
(617) 232-1595

Printed in the United States of America.

ISBN 0-9615841-8-1

CONTENTS

Preface   vi

Overview   viii

Guide to Related Books and Videos   ix

Chapter 1: In Search of Identity   **1**
1. Behind Closed Doors   2
2. Three Definitions of Jewishness   6
3. Reaching Back in Time   9
4. Mistaken Identity   13
5. Being Jewish   16
6. "I'm Not Really Jewish"   18
7. Belonging   21
8. Religious Stereotyping   24
9. The Roots of Religious Stereotyping   26
10. Jewish by Choice   29

Chapter 2: Outsiders in Eastern Europe   **33**
1. Strangers in a New Land   35
2. We and They   39
3. On the Edge of Time and Space   42
4. The Pull of Hasidism   44
5. The Lure of the Modern World   48
6. Choices in a Modern World   52
7. Separated   56
8. Jewish Pride   60
9. Hatred   67
10. Traveling Third Class   69

Chapter 3: At the Crossroads   **72**
1. Nationalism and "Race"   73
2. Nationalism and European Jews   76
3. A Matter of Loyalty   78
4. "Only So Many Jews"   81
5. Protecting Minorities   86
6. Uniting a Nation   89
7. Winds of Change   93
8. Tradition and Change   95
9. A Yearning to Belong   98
10. Two Separate Groups   101
11. Economic Competition   104
12. Building Bridges in Changing Times   106
13. Explosions of Violence   108
14. The Doors Close   111

Chapter 4: In Time of War   **116**

  1. On the Eve of War   117
  2. The Siege of Warsaw   119
  3. Flight   122
  4. The Star   125
  5. Collective Responsibility   128
  6. Terror and Humiliation   131
  7. Jewish Self-Help   133
  8. Self-Defense   136
  9. Resistance   138
  10. Adjustments   140
  11. The Walls Rise   142

Chapter 5: The Warsaw Ghetto   **146**

  1. No Exit   148
  2. Hunger   151
  3. Germans and Germans   153
  4. For Those I Loved   155
  5. The Jewish Police   158
  6. The Limits of Healing   160
  7. In the Heart of Europe   162
  8. The Rush for Papers   165
  9. The Great Aktion   167
  10. Buried Treasure   171
  11. Fateful Choices   173
  12. Treblinka Means Death   177
  13. Let the World Know!   181

Chapter 6: The Warsaw Ghetto Uprisings   **187**

  1. Finding Common Ground   189
  2. Building a Movement   191
  3. In Search of Hiding Places   195
  4. A Turning Point   199
  5. In Search of Weapons   201
  6. The Limits of Persuasion   204
  7. On the Eve of Passover   206
  8. The Ghetto in Flames   209
  9. Polish Responses   213
  10. The World Is Silent   216
  11. For Your Freedom and Ours   218

Chapter 7: Legacies   **223**

  1. The Persistence of Hatred   224
  2. Faith and Dialogue   228
  3. "And You?"   232

4. Judgment 234
5. Education and Memory 237
6. Monuments and Memorials 241
7. Politics and Memory 244
8. Reclaiming a Heritage 246
9. Restoring the Life That Was 250
10. Imagination and Possibility 254
11. The Importance of Not Coming Too Late 256
12. Education and the Future 260

Glossary **263**
Index **266**

Maps

Partitioned Poland, 1815-1918 50
The Second Polish Republic 1921-1939 82
The German-Soviet Partition of Poland, September 28, 1939 125
The Warsaw Ghetto 146

For over twenty years, Facing History and Ourselves has been teaching about the events that led to the destruction of democracy in Germany in the 1930s, the rise of the Nazis, and ultimately the Holocaust. Over the years we have often been asked how much history students need in order to understand what happened and, more importantly, why it happened. For many teachers, such questions are compounded by a concern that a study of the Holocaust may be the only Jewish history their students ever learn. They fear that without a more complete picture of Jewish life, students will have only the Holocaust experience to define Europeans Jews. Jewish educators have been particularly troubled by their students' lack of a broader perspective.

In response to these concerns, Facing History and Ourselves asked the Covenant Foundation to support an effort to present a more comprehensive view of Jewish life before the Holocaust. It is a history that is not covered in our Resource Book nor is it addressed in the many other books in our library. The project began to take shape when Jan Darsa brought us the results of her work in Israel as a Jerusalem Fellow. The materials she developed on the Jews of Poland during her leave of absence helped us find a focus, but we quickly discovered that we still had much to learn. As we studied the history of the Jews of Poland, we found that it raised powerful questions about identity, membership, and belonging. It also taught us much about courage, caring, and compassion. As we uncovered a history that complicated our understanding of human behavior, we began to reexamine our assumptions, revise our thinking, and reevaluate our questions.

With Phyllis Goldstein's attention, those questions were translated into a resource book. Her unique talents for scholarship and original research and her ability to work closely with me, Jan, and others at Facing History have resulted in what I believe to be an extraordinary gift to educators. It is a book that respects the complexities of Jewish history, engages readers, and provides a lens with which to examine the vibrancy of Jewish life before, during, and after the Holocaust. The scholars and educators who reviewed the work have recognized this unique achievement. After reading the manuscript, Dr. Michael Berenbaum offered the resources of the Survivors of the Shoah Visual History Foundation in order to create a video supplement to the book. It contains the testimonies of Holocaust survivors from Poland.

While the book was in development, Jan, with the guidance of Program Director Marc Skvirsky, began an extraordinary outreach effort to Jewish educators. As a result of their work, a number of educators in Jewish schools have attended our institutes. There they not only learned Facing History's content and methodology but also reviewed portions of the new book. Many of them later piloted the materials and offered suggestions for improvement. We are grateful for their enthusiastic support.

I am grateful too for all of the help provided by the Facing History staff. I would particularly like to acknowledge the following individuals: Mary Johnson who thoughtfully critiqued the book; Tracy O'Brien who handled permissions and photo research; Joe Wiellette and Jenifer Snow who designed and laid out the book; and Cathy McCarney who proofread the manuscript. I would also like to thank Seth Klarman, our chair, for his careful review of the book and his enthusiasm for its contents.

Margot Stern Strom
Executive Director
Facing History and Ourselves

My work on *Facing History and Ourselves: The Jews of Poland* has taken me on an incredible journey—one that could not have occurred without the help and support of many individuals and groups. The journey began as an outgrowth of my work at Facing History and Ourselves. Over the years, many of my colleagues have expressed a concern that in a study of the Holocaust, one often loses sight of who the victims were and how they responded to events. Too often the Holocaust is taught without a real understanding of the rich and vibrant culture that was lost. I shared those concerns and often wondered how we as an organization could address them.

Then in 1988, I took a leave of absence from Facing History to become a Jerusalem Fellow. While in Israel, I hoped to develop a companion to the Facing History and Ourselves Resource Book. It would be book that would focus on Jewish history before, during, and immediately after the Holocaust. During the two years I spent studying with Israel's leading scholars in the field, my ideas began to take shape. Under the guidance and with the encouragement of my tutor, Ze'ev Mankowitz, I thought deeply about what the content of the book and what its pivotal questions would be.

I chose to focus on Warsaw, Poland, which had the largest Jewish community in Europe. In the 1930s, Jews made up over 30 percent of the city's population. I believed that as students became aware of the richness of life in Jewish Warsaw, they would begin to understand the impact of the destruction. In addition to confronting the enormous loss of individual lives, they would see the devastation of a distinctive way of life. By looking intensively at life in one community, students would gain important insights into the legacies of this history and reflect on a number of larger questions: What does it mean to live as a Jew in the Diaspora? How is a Jewish identity formed? What has this history meant to people everywhere and to Jews in particular?

When I returned from Jerusalem, I shared my ideas for a new study guide with Margot Strom and Marc Skvirsky. With their support, Facing History and Ourselves applied for a grant from the Covenant Foundation in New York. The funding that the foundation provided allowed for outreach to the Jewish community as well as the development of a new book. I was therefore able to travel around the country meeting with leaders in Jewish education. I spoke at national and regional conferences like the annual CAJE (Conference on Alternatives in Jewish Education); offered workshops in each of Facing History's regions; and met with teachers, principals, parents, and religious leaders.

Wherever I went, I encountered enthusiastic educators eager to try out the materials in a variety of settings. It was becoming increasingly evident that the book was not just of interest to Jewish educators but also to teachers in public and private schools. I particularly valued the opportunity to try out lessons in their classrooms as well as piloting a course of my own at Prozdor, the program for high school students at Hebrew College in Boston.

I am also grateful for the help I received from my very special Facing History colleagues, my fellow Jerusalem fellows, and the many teachers and students with whom I have worked. I would particularly like to thank Josie Fisher from Gratz College and CAJE in Philadelphia who brought together a group of talented educators who spent a year reading, piloting, and critiquing early chapters. I also wish to acknowledge the important experience I had with the Jerusalem Fellows, while I lived with my family in Jerusalem. They encouraged me and I owe them and my family my thanks.

Jan Darsa
Senior Program Associate
Facing History and Ourselves

Facing History and Ourselves: The Jews of Poland considers the ways Jews and their non-Jewish neighbors in Poland and other parts of Eastern Europe responded to questions of identity, membership, and difference at various times in their shared history. Students explore this history by reading autobiographies, diaries, official documents, literary works, and other sources. Each helps them "draw conclusions from what we see to what we do not see" and "recognize themselves in the past, on the steps to the present."

Like other Facing History publications, Facing History and Ourselves: The Jews of Poland is a resource book. It provides a meaningful but flexible structure for examining complex events and ideas. Teachers are encouraged to select the readings that are most appropriate for their students and match the objectives of their curriculum. They are also encouraged to choose the questions and activities that further those objectives from a section entitled "Connections." It appears at the end of every reading and contains suggestions for class discussions, writing assignments, and research projects. Many of the questions encourage students to investigate key concepts and issues, prompt perspective taking, and offer opportunities to explore connections between historical events and their own lives.

Adolescence is a time of major developmental transitions. Students need to think about their thinking in order to become aware of their moral development. Facing History seeks to foster cognitive growth and historical understanding through content and methodology that continually complicate students' simple answers to complex questions. The readings and the Connections that follow them also stimulate students to think about the complexities of good and evil, the choices they have as individuals, the consequences of those decisions, and their responsibilities to self and others.

This book, which is divided into seven chapters, is organized in much the way a Facing History course is. The first chapter introduces key concepts and ideas. It engages students in thinking about human behavior and the connections between individuals and the society in which they live. In the next five chapters students focus on what a Jewish identity meant in Poland at various times in history.

Chapter 2 examines questions of membership and belonging in Poland under Polish and later Russian rule. Chapter 3 looks at membership in the early 1900s, a time of heightened nationalism. Chapters 4, 5, and 6 explore the impact of the Nazi occupation of Poland by examining one community in great detail: Warsaw, Poland's capital. Because it was home to more Jews than any city in Europe, its people have come to symbolize for many the plight of all of Europe's Jews. Its history raises important questions about the way individuals and nations defined their "universe of obligation" as the Nazis segregated, isolated, and ultimately annihilated European Jews. It is in these chapters that students come to understand why Cynthia Ozick warns that "when a whole population takes on the status of bystander, the victims are without allies; the criminals unchecked are strengthened; and only then do we need to speak of heroes."

In the last chapter, students move from thinking about the past to questions of judgment and then to action. Many of the readings return to themes developed in the first chapter. They explore how individuals, groups, and nations remember the past and the ways those memories shape the present. Other readings consider what it means to be a good citizen in the world today in Poland and the United States.

A variety of books, videos, and other materials may be used to supplement, enrich, or extend ideas developed in *Facing History and Ourselves: The Jews of Poland*. These materials have been organized by chapter and often by reading. Three works are of particular importance to the concepts and themes developed in this book.

A special video has been created by the Survivors of the Shoah Visual History Foundation to accompany *Facing History and Ourselves: The Jews of Poland*. The film is divided into five parts, each keyed to themes and content developed in Chapters 3 through 7 of the book. Each part contains excerpts from the testimonies of Polish Jews who survived the Holocaust. Archival footage is used to provide a visual context for their stories. The first two segments offer a picture of Jewish life in Poland before World War II and help students understand how that way of life changed as soon as the war began. The next two segments describe living conditions in the Warsaw Ghetto and express the exhilaration, pride, fear, and sadness many experienced during the Warsaw Ghetto uprisings. In the final segment, survivors share their experiences after the war. Although many of their memories are difficult and often painful to relate, each has chosen to speak so that others can learn and remember what happened.

Each chapter in this book is correlated to Facing History and Ourselves' primary resource book, *Holocaust and Human Behavior*. Based on the latest scholarship, it explores the consequences of discrimination, racism, and antisemitism by holding up "the tarnished mirror of history" to one of the most violent eras in the recent past-the 1930s and 1940s. Students read and reflect on the forces that undermined democracy in Germany, betrayed a generation of young people, and ultimately led to the Holocaust. The book connects that history to the moral questions students confront in their own lives. It also helps students discover how their decisions can make a positive difference in their community, nation, and the world.

A number of readings are keyed to *Elements of Time*, a guide to Facing History's videotape collection of Holocaust testimonies. It is the result of a five-year joint effort between Facing History and Ourselves and the Fortunoff Video Archive for Holocaust Testimonies, Yale University. It contains background information on the videos and guidelines for using survivor testimonies in the classroom. Supplemental essays and readings from scholars and resource speakers provide additional perspectives.

A number of materials highlighted in this guide can be borrowed from the Facing History Resource Center. These materials are set off with a special symbol (☑).

Key Concepts: identity, heritage, membership, stereotyping, prejudice
Chapter 1 enriches and extends concepts developed in Chapter 1 of Holocaust and Human Behavior

The Jews of Boston, WGBH Boston (video, 60 min., color). The opening segment of the film (approximately 10 min.) focuses on the ways some Jews regard "being Jewish."(Use with the **Introduction** or **Readings 1-3**.)

☑ *A Jew Is Not One Thing*, Jewish Museum (video, 28 min., color). The film adds an international dimension to discussions of Jewish identity by including interviews with Jews from many different parts of the world. (Use with **Introduction** or **Readings 1-8**.)

☑ *the bear that wasn't* by Frank Tashlin (1946, reprint, Dover Publications). Even as we struggle to define our identity, others may attach labels to us that differ from those we would choose for ourselves. *the bear that wasn't* uses words and pictures to describe that process. Discuss why it becomes harder and harder for the bear to maintain his identity as he moves through the bureaucracy of the factory. What is Tashlin suggesting about the relationship between the individual and society? An abridged version of the story appears on pages 2-7 of *Holocaust and Human Behavior*. (Use with **Readings 4-7**.)

☑ *Names Can Really Hurt Us*, Anti-Defamation League (video, 24 min., color). Teenagers in an ethnically diverse New York City junior high school share their anger at being stereotyped and their guilt for the times they hurt others with thoughtless or cruel remarks. According to an old children's rhyme, "sticks and stones can break my bones but names can every hurt me." Is it true? What power do the labels others place on us have on the ways we see ourselves? (Use with **Reading 8**.)

☑ *A Boy of Old Prague* by Sulamith Ish-Kishor (out of print). A novel set in the 1500s in what is now the Czech Republic describes the effects that the separation of Jews and Christians had on a young Christian boy. Tomas was taught to be suspicious and even fearful of Jews. When his master sends him to work for a Jew, the frightened boy is convinced that the Jew will kill him and drink his blood. That notion resulted from stories that claimed Jews murdered Christians for religious purposes. Tomas's terror shows the power of these stories and how they can lead to hatred and violence. In time, Tomas learns that Jews are not demons but people much like himself. *Only individual copies of the book are available. An excerpt appears on pages 294-296 of* Holocaust and Human Behavior. (Use with **Reading 9**. May also be used with **Readings 1-3** in **Chapter 2**.)

Books for Further Reading: The following books may be helpful to students interested in learning more about a Jewish identity in the 20th century.

David, Jay, ed. *Growing Up Jewish: An Anthology.* Morrow, 1996. *Noted Jewish writers reflect on their childhood and adolescence.*
Frommer, Myrna K. and Harvey Frommer, eds. *Growing Up Jewish in America.* Harcourt, 1995. *Brief interviews with Jews from cities across the nation.*
Hautzig, Esther. *Remember Who You Are.* Crown, 1990. *A memoir.*

Chapter 2: Outsiders in Eastern Europe

Key Concepts: membership, identity, universe of obligation, separation, tradition, change, discrimination, violence, assimilation, hatred

Chapter 2 correlates to concepts developed in Readings 7, 8, 9, and 11 of Chapter 2 in Holocaust and Human Behavior *(pages 86-94, 97-99). These readings can be used to compare and contrast ideas about membership in Russian-occupied Poland with those in Western Europe.*

☑ *A Boy of Old Prague* by Sulamith Ish-Kishor (out of print). A novel set in the 1500s. *See Chapter 1 for a full description.* (For use with **Readings 1-3**.)

☑ *Image Before My Eyes*, Ergo Media, Inc. (video, 90 min., color). The film is divided into four parts that range in length from 15 to 30 minutes. Each uses photographs, drawings, home movies, music, and interviews to portray Jewish life in Poland from the late 19th century through the 1930s. Part One entitled "The Setting: Poland Before 1919" (approximately 30 min.) describes Jewish life in Poland in the late 1800s. Although many of the home movies included in the segment were made in the 1920s and early 1930s, they suggest what traditional Jewish life in Poland was like in the late 1800s. (For use with **Readings 5-10**.)

Books for Further Reading: The following books may be helpful to students interested in learning more about the history and culture of Eastern European Jews.

Aleichem, Sholem. *Tevye the Dairyman and the Railroad Stories*, trans. by Hillel Halkin. Shocken, 1987. *A book of short stories.*

Chagall, Bella. *First Encounter*, trans. by Barbara Bray and illus. by Marc Chagall. Schocken, 1983. *Memoirs of Jewish life in Vitebsk, a small town in the Pale of Jewish Settlement. It was the childhood home of both Bella and Marc Chagall.*

Dawidowicz, Lucy S., ed. *The Golden Tradition: Jewish Life and Thought in Eastern Europe*. Holt, 1967. *Readings that document Jewish life in the late nineteenth century.*

Dobroszycki and Barbara Kirshenblatt-Gimblett. *Image Before My Eyes: A Photographic History of Jewish Life in Poland Before the Holocaust*. Schocken, 1977. *A print supplement to the video highlighted above.*

Howe, Irving and Eliezer Greenberg, eds. *A Treasury of Yiddish Stories*. Meridian, 1958. ____, eds. *Voices from the Yiddish*. University of Michigan Press, 1972.

Meir, Golda. *My Life*. Putnam, 1972. *The autobiography of the first woman to become prime minister of Israel. Her story parallels many events described in this book.*

Meltzer, Milton. *A History of Jewish Life from Eastern Europe to America*. Jason Aronson, Inc., 1996. *An overview of modern Jewish history for young readers.*

Rubin, Ruth. *Voices of a People: The Story of Yiddish Folksong*. Jewish Publication Society of America, 1979.

Szymborska, Wislawa. *View with a Grain of Sand: Selected Poems*, trans. by Stanislaw Baranczak and Clare Cavanagh. Harcourt, 1995. *More poems by the Nobel-prize-winner Polish poet.*

Wiesel, Elie. *Souls on Fire: Portraits and Legends of Hasidic Masters*. Random House, 1972.

Chapter 3: At the Crossroads

Key Concepts: nationalism, citizenship, democracy, "race," antisemitism, membership, identity, tradition, change, discrimination, violence

Chapter 3 correlates to Chapters 3, 4, 5, and Readings 1-10 in Chapter 6 of Holocaust and Human Behavior. *These chapters look at Germany during the the 1920s and early 1930s, the years covered in Chapter 3.*

☑ *Image Before My Eyes*, Ergo Media, Inc. (video, 90 min., color). Part Two, "To the Stars" (approximately 30 min.), describes Jewish life in Poland during and immediately after World War I. (Use with **Readings 1-5**.) Part Three, "Among the Organized" (15 min.), focuses on the wide variety of political, social, and cultural groups within Poland's Jewish communities between the wars. Among those featured are the Zionists, Bundists, and Agudat Israel. (Use with **Readings 6-9**.) Part Four, "Darkening Clouds" (15 min.), covers the years between Jozef Pilsudski's death in 1935 and the start of World War II on September 2, 1939. (Use with **Readings 10-14**.)

☑ *Facing History and Ourselves: The Jews of Poland.* The Survivors of the Shoah Visual History Foundation (video, 35 min., color). The film features the testimonies of Holocaust survivors. Part 1:"At the Crossroads," (approximately 7 min.), recalls life in Poland just before World War II. The narrators were all students during those years and their testimonies paint a vivid picture of what it was like to be a young Jew in Poland during the 1930s. (Use with **Readings 10-14**.)

☑ *Jewish Life in Poland*, National Center for Jewish Film (5 videos, 10 min. each, black/white) Warsaw, Bialystok, Krakow, Lvov, and Vilna are each the focus of one of the five travelogue. The producers hoped the films would encourage tourism to Poland, but the Nazis invaded Poland soon after the they were completed. Narrated in Yiddish with English subtitles, the films offer important images of daily life in Jewish communities just before the Nazi invasion. (Use with **Readings 10-11**.)

Books for Further Reading: The following books may be helpful to students interested in learning more about Jewish life in Poland between the two wars.

Dobroszycki and Barbara Kirshenblatt-Gimblett. *Image Before My Eyes: A Photographic History of Jewish Life in Poland Before the Holocaust.* Schocken, 1977.

Fluek, Toby Knobel. *Memories of My Life in a Polish Village: 1930-1949.* Knopf, 1990. *The author recalls her childhood through words and paintings.*

Lifton, Betty Jean. *The King of Children.* Farrar, Straus, and Giroux, 1988. *A biography of Henryk Goldszmit.*

Singer, Isaac Bashevis. *A Day of Pleasure: Stories of a Boy Growing Up in Warsaw.* Farrar, Straus and Giroux, 1969.

Tene, Benjamin. *In the Shade of the Chestnut Tree*, trans. by Reuben Ben-Joseph. Jewish Publication Society, 1981. *Reminiscences of life in Warsaw in the years between World War I and World War II.*

Vishniac, Roman. *A Vanished World.* Farrar, Straus, and Giroux, 1983. *A book of photographs taken in Eastern Europe just before World War II.*

Chapter 4: In Time of War

Key Concepts: war, universe of obligation, choice, terror, discrimination, violence, identity
Chapter 4 correlates to Readings 11-22 in Chapter 6 (pages 278-305) of
Holocaust and Human Behavior. These readings deepen understanding of
how the war affected individuals and groups in other parts of Europe.

☑ *Facing History and Ourselves: The Jews of Poland*. The Survivors of the Shoah Visual
History Foundation (video, color) Part 2, "In Time of War" (approximately 7 min.),
recalls life in Poland, particularly Warsaw, during the first year of the war. Many of the
survivors interviewed describe the sights and sounds of the invasion as well as the choices
they and their families made soon after the war began.

☑ *Witness to the Holocaust*, Cinema Guild (video, 7 parts, approximately 20 min per
segment black/white). In this series, Holocaust survivors narrate documentary footage
and photographs. The first segment details the rise of the Nazis and the beginnings of
World War II. (Use with **Readings 1-3**.)

☑ *Survivors of the Holocaust*, The Survivors of the Shoah Visual History Foundation
(video, 60 min., color). In this documentary produced by Steven Spielberg, the stories
of survivors are placed in historical context through the use of historical films, photographs, and artifacts. The first 15 minutes of the film bridges Chapters 3 and 4. The
accompanying study guide, produced by Facing History, includes a timeline, background
information, and questions for use prior to seeing the film and after viewing it. (Use
with the **Introduction** and **Readings 1 and 2**.)

☑ *The Hangman*, CRM (video, 12 min., color). A poem written by Maurice Ogden
and narrated by Herschel Bernardi provides the script for this short animated film. It is a
parable in which the people of a town are hanged, one by one, by a mysterious stranger
who erects a gallows in the center of the town. The remaining townspeople find a ratio-
nale for each hanging, until the hangman comes for the last survivor, who finds no one
left to speak up for him. (Use with **Reading 11**.)

Books for Further Reading: The following books may be helpful to students interested in
learning more about Jewish life in Poland during the war. The authors of these memoirs
were all students when the war began. They look at the events of the day from a young
person's perspective. *Brief excerpts from their books appear in Chapters 4-6.*

Bauman, Janina. *Winter in the Morning: A Young Girl's Life in the Warsaw Ghetto and
   Beyond*, 1939-1945. Free Press, 1986.
Birenbaum, Halina. *Hope Is the Last to Die*, trans. David Welsh. Twayne, 1971.
Gray, Martin. *For Those I Loved*. Little Brown, 1971.
Meed, Vladka. *On Both Sides of the Wall: Memoirs from the Warsaw Ghetto*, trans. by
   Dr. Steven Meed. Holocaust Library, 1979.
Rotem, Simha. *Memoirs of a Warsaw Ghetto Fighter: The Past Within Me*, trans and
   ed. Barbara Harshav. Yale University Press, 1994.
Swajger, Adina Blady. *I Remember Nothing More*, trans. Tasja Darowska and Danusia
   Stok. Pantheon, 1990.

Chapter 5: The Warsaw Ghetto
Chapter 6: The Warsaw Ghetto Uprisings

Key Concepts: war, universe of obligation, choice and choiceless choice, terror, courage, resistance, rescue

Chapters 5 and 6 correlate to Chapters 7 and 8 in Holocaust and Human Behavior. *These chapters focus on the choices made by the perpetrators, victims, and bystanders once the Holocaust began. They also explore acts of courage, resistance, and rescue.*

☑ *Facing History and Ourselves: The Jews of Poland*, The Survivors of the Shoah Visual History Foundation. (video, color). Part 3, "The Warsaw Ghetto" (approximately 7 min.) describes the experiences of a few survivors of the Warsaw Ghetto. In Part 4, "The Warsaw Ghetto Uprisings," survivors recall what the ghetto was like during the uprisings. Several were active members of resistance groups.

☑ *Witness to the Holocaust*, Cinema Guild. (video, approximately 20 min per segment, b/w)   The segments entitled "Ghetto Life," "Deportations," "Resistance," and "The Final Solution" relate to important themes in **Chapters 5 and 6**.

☑ *Through Our Eyes: Children Witness the Holocaust.* Social Studies School Service (Video, 30 min.) Young people read aloud from diaries written by children during the Holocaust. The story is told through archival photos and film as well as interpretive drawings. (Use with **Chapter 5, Readings 2-6**.)

☑ *I Promised I Would Tell* by Sonia Weitz. (Facing History and Ourselves, 1993). Poet Sonia Weitz has created a vivid tapestry of her years in Poland-first her childhood in Krakow, then the years she spent in concentration camps, and finally her time at a displaced persons camp. A 30 min. video is also available. (Use with **Chapter 5**.)

☑ *Heil Hitler: Confessions of a Hitler Youth*, Ambrose Video Publishing, (video, 30 min., b/w and color). An in-depth interview with a high-ranking member of the Hitler Youth. He discusses the way peer pressure and propaganda encouraged him and millions of other German children to participate in the "war effort." Some were as young as twelve years old. (Use with **Readings 3 and 5** in **Chapter 5**.)

☑ *Imagining the Unimaginable*, Facing History and Ourselves (video, 23 min., color). This montage conains video testimonies that suggest the near-impossibility of anticipating the Holocaust. Professor Lawrence Langer introduces each survivor, provides background information, and discusses questions raised by the testimony. (For use with **Readings 9-13** in **Chapter 5** and **Readings 1-10** in **Chapter 6**.)

☑ *Schindler's List*, MCA/Universal Home Video (video, 197 min., b/w and color) This Academy Award-winning film by Steven Spielberg presents the story of Oskar Schindler, a war profiteer who saved the lives of over 1,100 Jews in Poland during the Holocaust. Due to the length of the film, special scheduling may be required. Facing History has prepared a study guide to accompany the film. (Use with **Chapters 5 and 6**.)

☑ *So Many Miracles*, Alternative Pictures, Inc. (video, 48 min., color). Accompanied by their son, Saul, the Rubineks visit Poland after a 40-year absence. The film relates their story and that of the Polish couple who hid them for two years during the Holocaust. (Use with **Reading 3** in **Chapter 6**.)

☑ *Courage to Care*, Anti-Defamation League of B'nai B'rith (video, 30 min., color). A profile of individuals who helped save Jews in France, the Netherlands, and Poland. The film raises importation questions about what motivated rescuers. (Use with **Reading 3** in **Chapter 6**.)

☑ *America and the Holocaust: Deceit and Indifference*, PBS Video, (video, 81 min., b/w and color). A documentary that examines the role of the United States in the Holocaust. It looks at such issues as American antisemitism, apathy in the State Department, and the deliberate suppression of information that European Jews were being murdered. Facing History has written a study guide to accompany this film. It contains suggestions for using portions of the film to illustrate key concepts. (Use with **Reading 13**, **Chapter 5** and **Reading 10**, **Chapter 6**.)

☑ *Elements of Time: Portraits*, Facing History and Ourselves, (video, times vary, color).Each tape focuses on the experience of one individual:
—**Jan Karski**, who worked as a courier for the Polish underground during the war, describes his efforts to inform Allied leaders of what the Nazis were doing to Jews in occupied Poland. (Use with **Reading 13, Chapter 5**.)
—**Nechama Tec** from Lublin explains how she and her sister "passed" as Christians with a Polish family in order to survive the Nazi occupation of Poland. (Use with **Reading 3, Chapter 6**. The film may also be used as a bridge between **Chapters 1** and **2**.)
—**Rena Finder** from Krakow explains how the industrialist Oskar Schindler helped protect her and other Jews at Plaszow and Brunnlitz. (Use with **Readings 3 and 6** in **Chapter 6**.)
—**Helen K.** relates her experiences in the Warsaw Ghetto uprisings. (Use with **Readings 3-8** in **Chapter 6**.)

Books for Further Reading: The memoirs highlighted in the bibliography to Chapter 4 may be used with these chapters. The following books may also be helpful to students interested in learning more about how Jews and non-Jewsresponded to the Holocaust.

Block, Gay and Malka Drucker. Rescuers: *Portraits of Moral Courage in the Holocaust.* Holmes and Meier, 1992.

Browining, Christopher. *Ordinary Men: Reserve Police Battalion 101 and the Final Solution in Poland.* HarperCollins, 1992. *A look at the perpetrators.*

Hilberg, Raul. *Perpetrators, Victims, Bystanders.* HarperCollins, 1992.

Orlev, Uri. *The Man from the Other Side*, trans. by Hillel Halkin. Houghton Mifflin, 1991. *A fictionalized account of a true incident in Nazi-occupied Warsaw.*

Rittner, Carol and Sondra Myers, ed. *The Courage to Care: Rescuers of Jews During the Holocaust.* New York University Press, 1986.

Tec, Nechama. *When Light Pierced the Darkness: Christian Rescue of Jews in Nazi-Occupied Poland.* Oxford University Press, 1986.

Key Concepts: memory, memorial, judgment, participation, courage

Chapter 7 correlates to Chapters 9, 10, and 11 of Holocaust and Human Behavior, *chapters that focus on issues of judgment, memory, and participation.*

☑ *Facing History and Ourselves: The Jews of Poland*, The Survivors of the Shoah Visual History Foundation. (video, color). Part 5, "Legacies" (approximately 5 min.) contains the reflections of Holocaust survivors.

☑ *Samuel Bak Poster Set*, Facing History and Ourselves. Reproductions of six paintings by Samuel Bak, whose work is featured on the cover of this book and other Facing History publications. A survivor of the Vilna Ghetto, Bak describes his work as speaking "of a world that was shattered, of the process of growing up and rebuilding, which when you think about it is everyone's experience." Bernard Pucker, whose Boston gallery features Bak's work and supported the creation of the posters, created a short guide to the paintings. (Use with **Readings 5, 6, and 7.**)

☑ *Witness to the Holocaust*, Cinema Guild. (Video, 7 parts, approximately 20 min. per segment b/w). The segments entitled "Freedom" and "Reflections" deepen understanding of themes developed in this chapter.

☑ *Witnesses to the Holocaust: The Trial of Adolf Eichmann*, Social Studies School Service (video, 90 min., black/white). A comprehensive look at Adolf Eichmann, including his capture and trial. The testimonies from the trial are particularly compelling. (Short clips from the film may be used with **Readings 4 and 5.**)

☑ *It Is Memory*, Nesson Media/Boston, (video, 13 min., color). This short video is a fascinating and moving look at both Natan Rapaport, the designer of the memorial to the Warsaw Ghetto uprising. (Use with **Reading 6.**)

☑ *Billings, MT: Not in Our Town*, We Do the Work (video, 25 min., color). In 1993, the people of Billings responded to antisemitic hate crimes by placing menorahs in their windows to show support for the targeted Jewish population. As other groups were also singled out, the community put together a broad coalition to show neo-Nazi groups that hate would not be tolerated in their town. (Use with **Reading 11.**)

Books for Further Reading: The following books may be helpful to students interested in the ideas developed in this chapter.

Anti-Defamation League, compil. *Spiritual Pilgrimage: Texts on Jews and Judaism, 1979-1995*, ed. by Eugene J. Fisher and Leon Klenicki. Crossroad, 1995.

Bar-On, Dan. *Fear & Hope: Three Generations of the Holocaust.* Harvard University Press, 1995.

Heschel, Susannah, ed. *Moral Grandeur and Spiritual Audacity.* Farrar, Straus, Giroux, 1996. *Essays by Rabbi Abraham Joshua Heschel.*

Kaufman, Jonathan. *A Hole in the Heart of the World: Being Jewish in Eastern Europe.* Viking, 1997.

1. In Search of Identity

To be a Jew does not mean "I believe this or that."
To be a Jew means "I am!". . .
To be a Jew means to open a book of Jewish history
and say, "This is my history, this is me."

Eliezer Berkovits

Who am I? is a question that almost everyone asks at one time or another. In answering, we define ourselves. No two people are exactly alike. Each of us is an individual with a unique combination of talents, interests, and values. At the same time, each of us is a member of many different groups. Everywhere to be human means to live with others. In groups, we meet our most basic needs. In groups, we learn a language, customs, and values. We also satisfy our yearning to belong, receive comfort in times of trouble, and find companions who share our hopes and dreams. Even as we struggle to define our particular identity, those groups may attach labels to us that may differ from those we would choose for ourselves.

This book explores the meanings people have attached to a Jewish identity in Poland and other parts of Eastern Europe at various periods in history. Many of those meanings still shape Jewish life today. They are complicated by the fact that Judaism is more than a religion. It also refers to a people, a culture, and a history. Jews everywhere are linked in what sociologist Daniel Bell once called "a community woven of memory."

In "Angels in America," Tony Kushner described those links through an eulogy a rabbi gives at the beginning of the play. He tells the children and grandchildren of an immigrant woman that they can never make the journey she made, "for such Great voyages in the world do not anymore exist." But he insists that every day of their lives, they travel between the place from which she came and the one in which they live. He tells them, "Every day. You understand me? In you that journey is." That journey is their cultural and spiritual heritage. In this chapter, you will consider a few of the ways North American Jews acknowledge, celebrate, or deny that heritage. In addition, Chapter 1 introduces questions that will be explored in greater depth in the chapters that follow. They include:

— How is our identity formed? To what extent do our actions define our own identity? To what extent is it defined by our parents; our membership in various groups; or our religion? How does our nation shape who we are?

— What does it mean to be a part of the majority in a society? What does it mean to be in the minority? How does the larger society shape the way members of a minority group see themselves and others?

— Are we limited by the groups to which we belong or can we expand our horizons? What opportunities do individuals have to expand their horizons? How does one make the most of those opportunities?

— How do our attitudes and beliefs influence our thinking? How does our thinking affect our actions?

— How can we keep our individuality and still be a part of a group?

Behind Closed Doors

Although we tend to see ourselves as unique individuals, we often view others as representatives of groups. The word prejudice *comes from the word pre-judge. We pre-judge when we have an opinion about a person because of his or her membership in a particular group. Sometimes a prejudice is based on real differences between "us" and "them." At other times, it is based on imagined differences. Both can have a very real impact not only on the way others view us but also on the way we see ourselves.*

Elsa Rosenberg grew up in Saskatoon, Saskatchewan, in the 1930s. It was a time when relations between Jews and non-Jews were shaped by prejudices. Rosenberg recalls:

> That I am Jewish, and, that we were terribly rich, have been the two most influencing factors in my life. The first I learned from my mother. Her "*ess paast nisht far a Yid*" ["It isn't becoming for a Jew"] cautioned me against the unseen enemies that were waiting for me to run when I should have been walking sedately, to laugh when a smile would have sufficed, so that they might use my lapses to further their quarrel with all of Jewry.
>
> The second I learned from my neighbors. I don't remember anyone actually taking me aside and saying, "Say, kid, your old man's loaded," but there are certain things that adults impart to a child, and without words a child knows that there are certain adults that one must not be found alone with—and why—that certain adults are held in contempt by others, that we were rich, or more precisely that we were "Rich Jews."
>
> If our clothes bragged patches in exactly the same spots as our neighbors' clothes, then it was only that there was something peculiarly Jewish in our wanting to hide from the world our enormous wealth. So never seeing any outward appearances of this wealth didn't bother me, because along with the many unbelievable things that the Gentile world accepts, was this vision of our Jewish wealth, and I very happily accepted it along with them. During the depression [of the 1930s] that we shared together, my neighbors lived in a world racked with fear, but I grew straight and strong, in the belief that the tomorrow would never come when there would not be enough for us to eat, because if this day threatened, my father who loved us would most surely divulge our hidden treasures, and the world would be set right. I am very grateful to our neighbors, for the serene and peaceful childhood they provided for me.
>
> With these neighbors we shared the same parched Saskatchewan soil that refused to grow grass, the same broken stoop, that defying all laws of gravity, remained upright, and led us to a dismal triplex. Then, three identical doors, and only to break the monotony of what would have been three identical windows, the middle house boasted a missing lower pane, someone with great ingenuity had used a pillow to defy the western winds and dust. The inside of the pillow was a bright red, but the elements had bleached it various shades of green on the outside; it was a most unusual feature.
>
> To further distinguish our home, my brother (the lawyer) who, at first gave promise of talent that ran in the literary field, had found in every bare space a challenge. When his masterpieces were discovered written on the wall behind the [sofa],

he was forced to take his creativity outside, since this moment coincided with the first of his *heder* lessons, his contribution to the decor of our home was an enormous message written in Hebraic script. . . . This writing on the wall. . . must have been regarded as an incantation by our neighbors, since soon the sidewalks and other suitable vehicles bore sizzling legends, but the wall and its message remained intact, unviolated. Together with the *mezuzah* that graced the parched doorway, it formed . . . an invisible shield. If outwardly there was nothing to distinguish our wretchedness from theirs, the moment we crossed our threshold, and penetrated the shield, we entered a world of such abundance and wealth, the likes of which our neighbors could never in their wildest fantasies have conjured up.

We lived in an era when every home came equipped with a [grandmother and grandfather]. To our already large family we added an assortment of uncles, aunts, and cousins, shy, bewildered creatures who had just stepped off the boat, and would stay with us until their first pay check. This motley crew was completed by our boarders. . . . . Adding the salt and pepper to our existence were the guests, for our home was a stopover for anyone who knew the secret passwords, *Ich bin a Yid* ["I am a Jew"]. . . .

At our dinner table we heard the mysteries of the Torah expounded, [psychiatrists Sigmund] Freud and [Erich] Fromm analyzed. At this table I learned to love words, and have since remained greedy for them. There was to our poverty such sweetness, how do you explain to a child—the stories I have enjoyed reading the most are the mysteries that came every Saturday night in the newspapers that wrapped our weekly groceries. Mysteries, yes, because the vital part of the paper was the one drenched in herring. You have never read a newspaper stained with herring—oh—it makes all other reading like wine without grapes. Your father has never been a peddler, and brought you home the things that people don't buy—a musty volume of Shakespeare, a cellar-soaked encyclopedia. People buy such strange things and leave such precious treasures to rot. Precious treasures, are there treasures more precious than memories? How does one pass them on?

"Are you crying, mummy, because you were so poor," asked my daughter, when I took her back to see the old stamping grounds. "No my dear, we were very, very rich, I'm crying because we had so much to share, so much we wanted to give, but all the doors were closed to us."[1]

CONNECTIONS

Elsa Rosenberg writes, "There are certain things that adults impart to a child, and without words a child knows." What kinds of things do children learn "without words"? How important are such lessons? What kinds of things have you or your friends learned "without words"? How did you learn them?

The word *define* means "to separate one from all of the others." Who is Elsa Rosenberg? What sets her apart? Create an identity chart for her. How does Rosenberg define herself? How would others define her? The diagram on the next page is an example of such an identity chart. Individuals fill it in with the words they call themselves and the labels society gives them.

Create an identity chart for yourself. Begin with the words or phrases that describe the way you see yourself. Add those words and phrases to the chart. Compare your chart

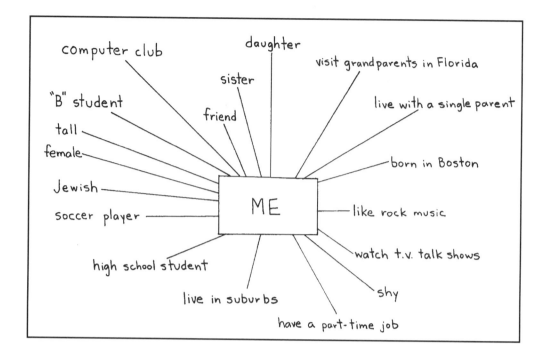

with those of your classmates. Which categories were on every chart? Which appeared on only a few? As you look at other charts, you may wish to add new categories to the one you created.

Creating an identity chart can help you see yourself through other perspectives. What labels would others attach to you? Do they see you as a leader or a follower? A conformist or a rebel? A person of action or a bystander? How do society's labels influence the way you see yourself? How do these labels affect kinds of choices you and others make each day?

In exploring these and other questions you will encounter in this book, it is useful to keep a journal. Unlike a finished work, a journal documents the process of thinking. Much like history itself, it always awaits further entries. A journal also allows a writer to witness his or her own history and consider the way ideas grow and change.

Why did non-Jews in Elsa Rosenberg's community regard her parents as "rich Jews"? Where did that idea come from? Why do you think people continued to believe it even though the Rosenbergs had very little money? How did the idea that "all Jews are rich" affect the way Elsa Rosenberg saw herself? How did it affect the way she viewed her family? How did her definition of "rich Jews" differ from that of her neighbors?

Elsa Rosenberg's neighbors saw her family as "the Jews." She and her parents saw them as "the Gentiles." (Jews use the word *Gentile* to refer to non-Jews; Mormons use it to refer to non-Mormons.) Psychologist Deborah Tannen writes, "We all know we are unique individuals but we tend to see others as representatives of groups. It's a natural tendency; since we must see the world in patterns in order to make sense of it; we wouldn't be able to deal with the daily onslaught of people and objects if we couldn't predict a lot about them and feel that we know who or what they are. But this natural and useful ability to see patterns of similarity has unfortunate consequences. It is offensive to reduce an individual to a category, and it is also misleading."[2] Give examples of the ways that generalizing can be useful. Give examples of its "unfortunate consequences." How do you think we can avoid those unfortunate consequences?

Elsa Rosenberg tells her daughter that "all the doors were closed to us." Were all the doors really closed or did she see them as closed? How did she and her family respond to those doors? How might they and others in the community have "opened" the doors? What laws or customs keep people apart in your life today? How can those doors be opened? Who is responsible for opening them?

Esther Hautzig also grew up in the 1930s but not in Canada. She was reared in Vilna, then a city in Poland. Like Rosenberg, she, too, grew up with a strong Jewish identity. In her memoirs, Hautzig recalls the way her mother taught her to write the alphabet in Yiddish, the everyday language of the Jews of Eastern Europe:

> She watched my hand and insisted that I copy every letter carefully and firmly. Then she made me erase each one. I had to repeat this on many lines, writing the entire Yiddish alphabet, then erasing each letter under her watchful gaze. Over and over I had to do it until the entire page was filled. When I stopped, Mama made me look carefully in the places I had written the letter *yud.*
>
> The *yud* looks like an exclamation point with the period under it. In Yiddish it is the middle of three letters that spell *Jew;* in Hebrew it's the first letter in the word *Israel.* While all the letters of the alphabet were erasable, the period in *yud* was still clearly visible on my notebook page.
>
> She pointed to it, "Remember my child, the pintelle yid, the dot that is part of the word that says who we are, cannot be erased. It will always be here if we write it firmly and strongly."[3]

What lesson did Hautzig's mother teach her daughter along with the ABCs? How was it like the one Elsa Rosenberg learned from her family?

Three Definitions of Jewishness

According to Jewish tradition, the answer to the question "Who are you?" is "I am the child of my parents" (literally "I am the son of my father, Isaac ben Abraham"). The three Jews quoted in this reading reflect that tradition, but each has been influenced by a different aspect of their heritage.

Avrohom Hecht grew up in Burlington, Vermont, in the 1960s. He told an interviewer:

> My father was the rabbi of the only Orthodox synagogue in the state: *Ahavath Gerim,* which means "a love for strangers." It was built by pack peddlers nearly a hundred years ago, and into my time remained a Shabbat destination for Orthodox travelers throughout New England. . . .
>
> We lived about a half mile from the synagogue, and of course we had to walk there and back every Shabbat regardless of the weather. I remember traipsing behind my father in the snow, putting my little feet in the big snowprints he made. I remember walking miles and miles with him on Rosh Hashanah so he could blow the *shofar* at the homes of people who were elderly or infirm and could not get to the synagogue.
>
> As there was no kosher butcher in Burlington, my father rented a huge freezer from some deer hunters. He used to go down to New York City and bring back a butchered cow cut up and packaged. He'd bring down bushels of produce that he got from local farmers—apples, tomatoes, corn, potatoes—and give them away to disadvantaged people in New York. That was one of the ways he practiced and taught us *tzedaka* [charity].
>
> There was always the awareness that we were Jewish in Vermont. My parents spoke Yiddish at home, not only so that we could converse with our immigrant grandparents but to reinforce our separateness. When we went to birthday parties, we brought along our own food. There were the temptations, wanting the ice cream and cake the other children were eating, wanting some of the foods I knew we could not have. But that was the challenge.[4]

Manny Azenberg grew up in New York City in the 1940s. His parents, particularly his father, believed strongly that Jews are a nation and that, like other nations, they ought to have their own homeland. Azenberg told an interviewer:

> My father was a Zionist, always a Zionist. A self-educated man who spoke five or six languages, he was born in Poland and lived in London before coming to America. In 1919 he worked directly with Chaim Weizmann [who would later become Israel's first president]. . . .
>
> Zionism was always around the house. We sent money to plant trees in Palestine; we dropped the coins in the Jewish National Fund box. My father worked for the Zionist Organization in New York. In the summer, he managed the Zionist Camp Kindleveilt. It was a joy. I was under pressure in school, at home, in Hebrew school, on the streets of the Bronx. At camp there was none of that. You played basketball, you swam, you necked, you had color wars with blue and white teams. You had social dancing and Israeli dancing, you sang Hebrew songs—dozens of them,

early 1940s Israeli songs about the Palmah [the elite soldiers in the army that fought for Israel's independence]. They sank into you.

Adults visited the camp, people like Golda Meir and Abba Eban and also people who painted houses, worked as butchers or in the garment center. Nobody rich, a very active group of working-class, lower-middle-class first-generation or immigrant Jews. They were not educated, but they knew the value of education. These were people who discussed and listened. These were people who read four newspapers: *The New York Times*, the *New York Post*, *PM*, the *Forward*. You saw the papers laying around the camp.

Famous Yiddish and Hebrew writers came up to talk. We kids weren't invited to the lectures. We wouldn't have gone anyway; we just wanted to play basketball. But we were surrounded by an atmosphere. It didn't hurt. We bumped into people who were committed. Coming back to the Bronx was culture shock. I started thinking about the next June.

We grew up in a traditional Jewish home. Friday nights, we waited for my father to come home, had challah from the G & R Bakery on 161st Street, said *Kiddush*, ate gefilte fish and chicken. We went to shul on the High Holy Days, and we had a seder. But as time went by, religion diminished in our lives. We moved from being pulled by religion to being pulled by Zionism.

When I was fourteen and my sister was ten, my father took us out of school and up to the Waldorf Astoria to meet Chaim Weizmann. This was the day before he went to Washington to persuade President Truman to recognize the State of Israel. Secret Servicemen escorted us into Weizmann's room. I had seen pictures of him in our house, and I expected him to be about seventeen feet tall. So I was surprised to meet this little man who had spots on his bald head and was going blind.

He asked me when I was going to Israel. "Next year if there's peace," I said because that's what I'd been told to say.

But he chastised me: "There will be peace."

And I, of course, agreed right away: "Don't worry, there will be peace."

As we were leaving, Weizmann said to my father, "*Tsvay feiner kinder*"—two fine children. It was like George Washington telling your father "nice kids."

Whatever my father was or wasn't, he was a Zionist. He had a passion about it. You were respectful of that passion no matter what.[5]

Arthur Weinberg's parents did not define their Jewish identity in terms of religion or a Jewish homeland. Yet Weinberg told an interviewer "I was always conscious and always aware that I was Jewish." He explained:

My experience as a Jewish boy in Chicago might be a little bit different from most. I was brought up in a non-religious home, but a very ethical and moral home. I was not bar mitzvahed. I went for many, many years—in fact, was graduated from the Arbeiter Ring [Workmen's Circle], and went to their high school for a while. The center of my Jewish activity was around the Arbeiter Ring, which was organized as a fraternal organization. It offered insurance and various medical care for the immigrant Jew who came into the United States. It also was founded as the "Red Cross" to the labor movement. In those days, the labor movement was poor and needed financial help, and the Arbeiter Ring was there always to help them. That was the adult organization. . . .

Then they had the Yiddish schools. In the Yiddish schools we learned how to read, write, talk Yiddish. We learned Jewish history. We met Yiddish poets. While they didn't call it Bible studies, we really learned the history of the Jews through the stories of the Bible. We learned about the Jews who were active in the revolutionary movement here in the United States and also in Europe.

The school was three times a week: twice during the week and once on the weekend, either a Saturday or Sunday. During the week, our class was reading and writing Yiddish, speaking Yiddish in class. We put out a little Yiddish magazine every so often. We put on plays. Saturday or Sunday was history day. It was then the teacher would give us the history of the Jews. We learned about the Maccabees, Haman—the whole history of the Jews. Socialism would be taught on Sundays. It would become part of the social philosophy of the school. There was a freedom there; there was a questioning that we always were permitted. We had some wonderful teachers . . . .

My family came from Poland. My father had to flee Poland on the day his father was on his deathbed because the police were looking for him. . . . He came here when he was about sixteen. My mother soon followed. They knew each other in the old country. My parents both became active in radical movements here, particularly the anarchist movement. . . .

Being active in the anarchist movement in those days—in the 1920s and 1930s—meant selling raffle tickets for helping the Spanish Civil War. It meant collecting money for the Kentucky miners on strike. I never heard either one of my parents or any of their friends who were anarchists ever speak in terms of violence. It was always a dream of how they could attain a society in which people lived together without the need of a state which told them, "You've got to do this."

We spoke Yiddish at home. We were identified as Jews. . . . We celebrated the culture. On Pesach, we'd have a dinner. We never went through the ceremony. . . . We celebrated Chanukah. We always took off from work on Rosh Hashonah and Yom Kippur because my father wanted people to know that he was Jewish. . . .

We discussed Palestine. You see, among socialists in those days prior to Israel, there was always this argument of is the answer to the Jewish question a homeland for the Jews? There was a lot of antagonism among socialists toward Zionism. The socialists felt the Jewish question was not a question unto itself. In other words, in order for the Jewish question to be solved, you've got to solve the working-class question, etcetera. With Hitler, a complete change came over the Jewish socialist movement. Many of them took on a Zionist tinge.[6]

CONNECTIONS

How did the parents described in this reading teach their children what it means to be a Jew? How did you learn about Judaism? What part did your parents play in that learning process? What other people have shaped your understanding of Judaism?

Compare and contrast the ways the three fathers described in this reading defined their Jewishness. How do you account for those differences?

Manny Azenberg uses words like *passion and committed* to describe his father and his father's friends. How did his father convey that passion and commitment to his children? How did the other two fathers covey theirs?

Reaching Back in Time

Our identity is shaped not only by the people we know but also by those we have never met, people who may have died long before we were born. These individuals are part of our heritage and they too can shape our identity. Their stories help us, as scientist Jacob Bronowski once wrote, "draw conclusions from what we see to what we do not see" and "recognize ourselves in the past, on the steps to the present."

Rachel Altman never knew either of her grandmothers but both have had a strong influence on the way she sees herself. She writes of them:

I was . . . named after my grandmothers: Ruchel, for my father's mother, who died in the gas chambers, and Miryam, for my mother's mother, who died before the war began. We lived the life of an extended family (my surviving aunts and uncles all settled, with my parents, in Kansas City and we saw a great deal of each other); even so, as a child I yearned to know my grandmothers. As an adult, I still yearn to know them, seeking connection in continuity and context. Like an archaeologist, I dig through the past, unearthing fragments, putting together the pieces in an attempt to envision what once was whole.

This is what I know about my grandmother Miryam: She bore thirteen children, four of whom died in an influenza epidemic during World War I. Her husband Avram—a pious man, busy with his religious studies—earned a meager living and the family was poor; it fell to Miryam to make ends meet. She was ill for most of her adult life—an illness about which little was known (I've been told at times that she had "heart trouble," at others that she had diabetes—and died in her early fifties, when my mother was nine.)

This is what I know about my grandmother Ruchel: She went against custom and married a man she loved, rather than having an arranged marriage. When her first husband died of pneumonia, leaving her with three children, she took over his shirt-making business, refusing many suitors, for fear that her new husband would not treat her children, his stepchildren, well. She ran the business with competence and acumen and expanded it, hiring three seamstresses who worked at the kitchen table of her small apartment. She eventually married again and bore another child with her second husband. Well-educated, unlike many women in the old country, and not religious, she was known as a rebel.

In Poland [on a trip] with my parents, I seek out these details and ask question after question, hungry for knowledge about them—these women from a shadowy past, always part of me, though absent. I try to picture my grandmother Miryam at the sanitarium in the forest, near Szewierz, where she was sent by her doctor for a rest cure; I try to imagine her feelings at this separation from her children. I try to put myself inside the mind of my grandmother Ruchel the day my father was taken to the [concentration] camps—a mother whose son went out on an errand and never returned. Is she frantic, does she search the streets, how long does she wait, what does she feel, when does she find out, and then what does she do?

I've been told that I bear an uncanny resemblance to my grandmother and namesake Ruchel who, like me, was small with dark eyes and dark curly hair. I spend hours gazing at a photograph of her daughter, the one that resembles her: We have the same nose and chin and though she wore her hair parted in the middle and pulled back in a severe bun, I can see that it is the same thick, wiry hair. But it wasn't until recently—in fact, during the trip to Poland—that my father told me how like her I am in other ways—her independent spirit, her rebellious nature, her "modern" ways and her insistence on standing alone—and when he told me, I felt a shiver of love and gratitude, then a deep sorrow at my not having known this woman. How is it possible to be so like someone you never knew?

In Jewish life women are the guardians of tradition—family, values, morals. In the old country, men sat for hours discoursing and arguing the Talmud, the book in which the law is encoded. But it fell to the women to insist that people behave as they should—as a *mensch,* a human being, should. The rituals of Jewish life and religious practice are not reserved for the synagogue; built into the liturgy are prayers to be spoken on awakening, prayers to be said when washing the hands, when seeing a rainbow, when eating a meal, prayers to be recited in the midst of life. In its purest form, Judaism brings us into an atmosphere of appreciation and awareness of every moment of life as sacred. At the center of Jewish life is the home, and at the center of the home is the woman.

At the same time, Judaism has discriminated against women: in Jewish mythology and tradition, women are given a clearly second-rate status and until recently, we have been excluded from the study of Talmud and the rabbinate.

In thinking about the women in my family—in allowing myself to feel a longing to be part of their world—I recognize a certain irony. I bemoan the loss of my family, of the Jewish world that existed in Eastern Europe before the war, with a grief that will never be assuaged. However, as a modern woman, I acknowledge that the Eastern European *shtetl* [village or small town] is not a world in which I would choose to live.

How different my grandmothers' lives were from mine! How can I—a woman who is educated and has explored options; a woman whose marriage was not arranged; a woman with rights, living in a time when a woman can choose to actively confront discrimination, can even become a rabbi—pretend to know them, these women who sat separate from men in the shul, who walked down narrow streets and bargained with shopkeepers, who raced home to complete the preparations for the Sabbath before the sun went down, who kept the children quiet so their husbands' studies would not be disturbed? How can I pretend to know my grandmother Miryam, who was pregnant for thirteen years of her life, who lived at the mercy of an illness that could not be named (though today it could probably easily be treated), whose life revolved around stretching a tiny piece of meat to provide food for fifteen people, while her husband sat at the kitchen table and prayed?. . .

Throughout my teenage years, my parents and I raged at each other. It was complicated: I came of age during the sixties, a time when we sought openness and freedom, a time of tearing down the old—and the old was all my parents knew. Picture where they had come from: the small Jewish community, with its boundaries and modes of behavior clear and fixed; a society in which sexuality was controlled through early, arranged marriages, through religious strictures and convention; a patriarchy in which the home was ruled by the iron hand of the father.

I was their eldest child, a product of America, and even the most innocent, widely accepted behavior of American adolescents came as a shock to them. At the same time, their restrictions, their unceasing questions and worry, their inability to trust, confused and alienated me.

The fact of my femaleness was a further complication. In the old country, my mother often told me, the bride and groom first met "under the *chuppa*," the bridal canopy, the daughter protected in innocence until that moment. My adolescence could not have been more different.

I remember sitting at the kitchen table and arguing with my father: I am appalled the year he decided to vote Republican. We argue about the Vietnam War, about how to deal with our nation's racism and poverty. In these arguments I cannot win: Who am I to tell my father—who survived Europe's great crime against humanity, whose life began anew when he was transplanted to the United States—that this government's policies and way of life are inhuman! My father tells me time and again, fist pounding the table: "America is the greatest country that ever was. God bless America." The history of their suffering, their enormous loss—the scale of it—rules these conversations, making my questions and problems look petty and, whether spoken of or not, brings many a conversation to a screeching halt.

Eventually we stop talking about politics. Like many of my generation, I grow alienated from my family, rejecting what I see as their outmoded values. I flee the confines of Midwestern Jewry and embark on a search for my identity.

As part of that search, Rachel Altman traveled to Israel. There she visited an uncle's wife, a Holocaust survivor whose husband and children perished during the war:

Chava invited me for Shabbat dinner. She made a point of telling me she was not an observant Jew, that the dinner would be a secular celebration. At sundown, as is traditional, she lit the candles, her head covered with a shawl, her hands covering her face as she recited the prayer. Afterward, she turned to me sheepishly and said, "Since the war, I no longer believe in God. Every Friday night I light the candles and say the blessing over them, but I do not do it for God. I do it for the memory of my mother."

Like Chava, I am not an observant Jew, but I light candles on Friday night to usher in the Sabbath. I enjoy the peace that the ritual brings to my household, and I appreciate this weekly reminder to be grateful for the beauty of the creation. Also, it is a way of knowing them—the women of my family, the mothers and grandmothers and daughters who, in the midst of hunger, illness, war, persecution, brought light to the darkness. I visualize a procession of them, a line reaching back in time and forward from this moment. Covering my head with a scarf, circling my hands over the flames three times and reciting the blessing, I join this procession of women, welcoming their spirit into my life, into my daughter's life.[7]

CONNECTIONS

There are many aspects to a person's identity. Rachel Altman is a child of her parents, a Jew, a modern woman, and an American citizen. What other labels might she attach to herself? How did she try to reconcile conflicts among these various parts of her identity? What does it mean to "embark on a search for one's identity?" What did Rachel Altman discover about herself on her journey?

The introduction to this chapter quoted a eulogy given in the play "Angels in America." A rabbi tells the children of an immigrant woman that they can never make the journey she made, "for such Great voyages in the world do not anymore exist." But he insists that every day of their lives, they travel between the place from which she came and the one in which they live. He tells them, "Every day. You understand me? In you that journey is." How does Rachel Altman journey between the place from which her parents came and the one in which she lives? How has that journey shaped her identity? How has that journey shaped your identity?

Daniel Bell, a sociologist, speaks of Judaism as "a community woven by memory." Would Rachel Altman agree with that view? Why do you think she sees her past as "a procession of women welcoming their spirit into my life"?

Writer Julius Lester stresses the importance of using one's imagination in studying the past:

> If I were no more than my experience, I could not communicate with anyone else, or they with me. Imagination is the wings of the soul, carrying me from the singularity of personal existence across the void of Time and Space to alight in that realm where each of us is the other and God is One. But we seldom give the imagination a place in our reflections on history and ourselves. We seldom include it as integral to history.[8]

How does Rachel Altman use the faculty of her imagination to confront her family's history?

Professor Martha Minow reminds us, "Memory is neither inevitable nor spontaneous, it is a moral choice." What does Rachel Altman choose to remember about her family's history? What moral choices do those decisions reflect?

Mistaken Identity

Rachel Altman embarked on a journey to better understand the way the past shaped her identity. Suppose she had discovered that her family history was not what she thought it was. That is what happened to Madeleine Albright, the first woman to be U.S. Secretary of State. Raised as a Catholic of Czech ancestry, she recently learned that her grandparents were Jews. Two of them and an aunt died in the Holocaust. What does it mean to discover that such an important part of your identity is not what you thought it was?

Kati Merton, a writer and a friend of Madeleine Albright, also discovered late in life that she was not who she thought she was. Merton explains:

> Fifteen years ago I made a discovery much like the one Albright is now confronting. On my first trip back to my native Hungary since our family fled after the 1956 revolution, I was interviewing a Holocaust survivor. As we talked she said—in a flat, matter-of-fact tone—"Of course, you know your grandparents were in one of the first transports to Auschwitz." As a matter of fact, I did not know. I had no idea. My parents—like Albright's—had not told me. . . .
>
> This is my story. I was raised as a devout Roman Catholic and was told that my grandparents had died during the siege of Budapest in 1945. Although religion was officially illegal in communist Hungary, my parents, who were Hungarian reporters for American wire services, kept me to a firm schedule: I never missed mass on Sundays. I was tutored in catechism by nuns who were no longer allowed to wear their habits. After my parents were arrested in early 1955 on (false) charges of spying for the United States, I prayed to the Virgin Mary six times a day for their release. When they were finally freed, I was certain it was due to my fervent prayers.
>
> When we reached the United States as political refugees in 1957, a new religion supplanted the old: Americanization. Learn the language. Adapt to the new culture. Work hard. We came here for you. These were the messages transmitted by my loving parents. Above all: Do Not Look Back. This was my new catechism. I learned to speak and act like an all-American girl, but the facade was shattered that day in Budapest in 1978. I was shocked, not because I minded being Jewish—I did not really know what that meant—but because I was stunned that something so essential had been kept from me.
>
> Refugees like Albright and me do not have normal relationships with our parents. We don't simply love them; we revere them. We know that they have been through great and terrible things, that they risked everything to bring us to this strange and wonderful country with its strange and wonderful ways. I had seen my parents' courage in the face of the communists. Now I learned that there were things about these heroic people—and about me—that I knew nothing about.
>
> Why? They had trouble explaining. We did this for you, so you would never have to live through the things we did. To protect you. I could understand the denial while in Hungary, where antisemitism was still a real problem in the communist era in which I grew up. But in America, I replied, you cannot seriously imagine we would be persecuted for our religion. I was young and perhaps a bit naive. There were things I simply did not understand about what life had been like under the Nazis—and how deeply that experience scarred those who survived.

When we came to America, they made the decision never to look back. Our family's history would begin here. As my parents saw it, there was danger in looking back. There were problems enough in being a refugee; why compound them by adding "Jewish" to the list of things we had to overcome? They had too much history. I did not have enough. They felt that to be American meant not having a past, or at least having the freedom to choose what to remember. I felt the opposite. To me, America means the freedom to unabashedly embrace your heritage, whatever it might be. People who survived the Holocaust and the cold war will never believe their heritage might not be dangerous again.

Even now the subject remains emotionally fraught within my family; it is very difficult for us to discuss it with one another. So I turned to writing. First, a biography of Raoul Wallenberg, which I dedicated "to those Hungarians for whom Wallenberg arrived too late," intending it as a small memorial to the grandparents I never knew. Then I wrote a novel about a Hungarian-American journalist who discovers she is Jewish. My history has become an obsession—in part because it was withheld for so long. My hope for all those who make similar discoveries is that they too can one day come to peace with their past.[9]

CONNECTIONS

Why did Kati Merton's parents choose "never to look back"? What fears may have prompted their decision? What beliefs may have shaped it? Why is their daughter uncomfortable with that decision? What does she suggest about the impact that our history has on the way we see ourselves?

Raoul Wallenberg was a Swedish diplomat who saved thousands of Hungarian Jews during the Holocaust. Although he was a Christian, he had some Jewish ancestors. Why do you think Merton chose to write about him in a book she saw as a memorial to her grandparents?

After Madeleine Albright's family history made the news, a reporter noted that "she remains a Christian who was born a Roman Catholic in 1937 and became an Episcopalian when she married in 1959. But, like it or not, the disclosure ties her in a personal and tragic way to one of the defining moments of modern Jewish history: the Holocaust." How is she tied to an identity that she knew nothing about for most of her life? Does having Jewish ancestors mean that Madeleine Albright looks at the world or herself differently? Does it mean that other people see her in a different way? Or is it, as someone in the State Department suggested, "a personal issue that is largely irrelevant to anyone outside her family"?

Some people condemned Albright's parents for lying about the family's ethnic and religious origins. Others argued that an individual has a right to make such a choice. Do people have the right to "never look back"? Do they have the right to make that choice not only for themselves but also for their children? In his book, *Thirteen Ways of Looking at a Black Man*, Henry Louis Gates, Jr. profiles Anatole Broyard, an African American who decided to live as a white man. Gates says that Broyard's life raises the question of "how much you can leave behind before the past rears up and strikes back." How might the parents of Kati Merton or Madeleine Albright answer that question? How might

Merton answer it? How would you answer it?

Writer James Carroll, a Catholic, reflected on the public discussion of Madeleine Albright's discovery of her Jewish roots. He asked, "It is possible that Josef and Mandula Korbel [Albright's parents] embraced the figure of Jesus Christ for reasons of politics or fear, but isn't it possible they did so . . . out of honest spiritual impulses? It is possible Madeleine Albright willfully turned her back on a painful family history out of shame or ambition, but isn't it possible she sought only to claim an unburdened, freely chosen identity of her own?"[10] How would you answer the questions he raises?

After hearing Albright's story, a number of Jews and non-Jews called in to radio talk shows to say, "Of course, Albright's Jewish, she smart; it's those Jewish genes." Scientists cringe at such comments. They point out that there no such thing as "Jewish genes" or even a "Jewish race." Indeed, the whole concept of "race" is scientifically invalid. Yet the idea persists not only in popular culture but also in such academic disciplines as history and literature. Anthony Appiah, a professor who teaches African American studies, maintains that the idea of a collective identity is not inherently wrong. He sees a problem only when we begin to assign moral or social value to the identity of a particular group. Then, he argues, we must rethink why we divide ourselves into "races." How do you explain the continuing acceptance of a meaningless idea?

Being Jewish

The Holocaust had a profound effect on the way Madeleine Albright and Kati Merton define their identity. It has also had an impact on the way many young Jews who were born and reared in the United States define theirs. The history of the Holocaust raises powerful questions about the distinctions societies make between "us" and "them."

Steve Blonder, a college student with a strong Jewish identity, writes:

> Most of my mother's family perished during World War II. My mother's father had a brother and a sister. The brother's name is Martin and he lives in Miami. The sister was Else. Martin is the only one of the three still alive. . . .
>
> A year ago December we were having dinner with Uncle Martin in Miami. His wife was making it clear that she wanted to go home, but he had some things he wanted to say.
>
> "Fifty years ago today, I escaped from the camp. . . ."
>
> None of us was aware of the date. We sat around the table, and tears formed in everyone's eyes, as we intently listened to his story. Uncle Martin told us of his experience, how he had been taken away and escaped, not once but twice. He told us of how he had snuck through a fence at night and remained in hiding during the day, about the underground network that had helped him. . . . Up until this point it had only been stories void of details. But now everything was coming together.
>
> We sat around discussing history for almost an hour, no one daring to move and nary a waiter coming near our table. Uncle Martin made sure that my sister and I understood everything he was telling us. I found myself in tears. I had just completed Professor Endelman's Holocaust class [at college]. My uncle's stories sounded like others I had heard, but something was different. This was my family he was talking about. Our family. The names of the places he mentioned were too painful for me to hear, let alone for him. I found myself crying on the inside at the horror before an angry feeling enveloped me. I don't know who I was angry at, other than the world as a whole. . . .
>
> I've been ingrained with stories about the Holocaust since I was a little kid. While I could never really comprehend the details or the atrocities that happened, nothing was ever hidden from my sister and me. If we wanted to know something, all we had to do was ask. For most of my life I never really understood. But that night with my uncle all of the pieces fell into place.
>
> Initially, my family's experiences in the Holocaust helped in distinguishing me from those living around me. I always knew I was different—Hitler saw to that. But I enjoyed being different. None of my Jewish friends could relate to my feelings about the Holocaust or my pride in living the life of a Jew. Being Jewish was never a burden or a chore, and performing things related to Judaism gave me a sense of inner pride, of joy. Skipping a basketball game or bowling league in seventh grade because I had to go to Hebrew school was no big deal to me. After all, I was doing something more important—being Jewish. I decided that being Jewish would never be a burden; it would be a privilege, an honor.
>
> No matter what anyone else says, I am different; I am Jewish, and no one can tell me otherwise. Hitler answered the question fifty years ago of who is a Jew, and

inside I feel a special bond to those people. From these initial experiences that bonded me, if you will, to Judaism, I have grown to try and understand everything about the ways Jews lived in the shtetlach (the small Jewish towns of Eastern Europe.) I wish I could go back and see the blooming Yiddish culture and distinctly Jewish way of life practiced by those Jews. . . . But we never can because, once a culture or way of life is destroyed, it cannot be resurrected. The best we can do is read and study how our ancestors lived and try to imagine what it would be like living in an all-Jewish world.[11]

CONNECTIONS

Make an identity chart for Steve Blonder. Compare and contrast it with others you have made. Whom is he most like? For what reasons?

Steve Blonder writes, "People used to tell me I was weird because I generally liked going to Hebrew School." He goes on to say: "I felt that they were making me out to be some kind of 'Super Jew.' These people were making me an example, setting me apart because of my strong faith. It really pissed me off. A Jew is a Jew! One group of Jews isn't better than another group of Jews because of the amount of devotion they have, or the number of mitzvot [commandments] they fulfill. Why couldn't other Jews accept me for my own choices about religion?" How would you answer the question he raises?

How does Blonder distinguish between the stories of Holocaust survivors he heard in a college classe and the one his uncle told him? How important is that difference?

In your journal, write a working definition of the phrase *Jewish identity*. A working definition is a definition that grows to include more information. Begin by explaining what the phrase means to you. You may want to include pictures with your working definition. Often they reveal more about a complex idea than a definition that relies solely on words. Then add meanings highlighted in this reading and others in the chapter. As you encounter new definitions, add them to your original definition.

"I'm Not Really Jewish"

The way we define our identity changes as we grow and change. At some times in life, one aspect of our identity may be more important than it is at another time.

In an essay he wrote for a college course, Joey Goldman defined his identity at three different periods in his life. He begins his essay just before his thirteenth birthday, a difficult time for him. His grandfather had recently died and his parents were planning a divorce. He was also attending a school where Jews were seen as outsiders. He recalls:

> I wanted my bar mitzvah to be over. I was tired of memorizing meaningless Hebrew words with no importance to me. At least the first Spanish dialogue I learned at [school] had made sense: it was a true daily conversation between people living somewhere. It wasn't a mess of archaic prayers. If only I were Mexican, I thought, I would be able to speak Spanish perfectly. Instead, I had to memorize useless Hebrew. Hebrew lessons bored me.
>
> I screamed when I arrived home from the Temple one Wednesday afternoon, "I'm *not* going to say the *haftorah* in Hebrew." (It was a decision left up to the boy or girl being bar or bat mitzvahed.)
>
> My mother looked blankly at me. "Fine. Do whatever you want."
>
> I don't think it was guilt that led me to do it in Hebrew. I decided that, for a reason I couldn't understand, I would feel better if I did. It certainly wasn't a matter of not wanting to let the congregation down. I was challenging myself to do it. With additional studying, I learned it. It became important to me.
>
> Other aspects of my bar mitzvah began to matter to me aside from the gifts and parties. One morning my mother led me to her bedroom. She handed a shimmering blue velour pouch to me. It was soft and brilliant, with a large embroidered Star of David on its face. Inside was the tallis (prayer shawl) that my great-grandfather, Papa Reuben, had worn to synagogue every Shabbat. I felt like my mother was presenting a gift to me in an important, formal ceremony. I believed something was very special about it; I could imagine my great-grandfather wearing it. I put it on and was excited that I possessed something so meaningful.

By the time he was in high school, Goldman was convinced that "being Jewish was nothing other than going to temple on Rosh Hashanah and Yom Kippur. It meant lighting the Chanukah candles and saying an occasional prayer on Friday night. The rest of my life had nothing to do with being Jewish, which didn't bother me at all. I was quite happy spending time with my non-Jewish friends, doing nonreligious things, and participating in numerous high school organizations, unrelated to any church or temple." He described himself during those years in this way:

> My identity wasn't at all an ethnic one but, rather, an activity-related one. I was the president of the Spanish Club for three years. I was in the Science Club to go on trips to the Okeefenokee, Savannah Beach, and the South Carolina mountains. I was on four Student Council committees. I was a member of the President's Council and the National Honor Society. I was active in the French Club, treasurer of the Beta Club, and a participant on the debate team.
>
> Human rights fascinated me. As president of the Human Relations Committee,

I accepted the School Service Award for everything the group had done. Odd as it was, I was responsible for several of the school's Black History Month events. I was active in feeding the hungry in Atlanta, raising money for people starving in Ethiopia, and promoting community volunteer projects.

This was my identity. I was a busy, school-oriented, creative Atlanta activist with divorced parents and a fascination with cities. Being Jewish was only a label, which I chose to set aside; it only complicated things. No longer required to attend religious school, I found Judaism was unimportant to me and I was happy with my freedom from it.

In college, Goldman gradually came to believe that he "needed to be Jewish for myself." As he explored his Jewish identity, he "started to tell other people I was Jewish without feeling the uneasiness I always had had because I had felt like there was something bad about being Jewish and because I never liked other Jews. But even though I accepted my religion and culture as my own, I refused to be only Jewish." In reflecting on the factors that influenced the way he now saw himself, he writes:

Religious school was one of the [influences]. My friends and experiences with them played key parts. But many of my values are those of my parents. Although they divorced, an event that had a powerful impact on my life when I was younger, I'm not hurt by what happened. It might not have been traditional at the time, but I was raised in a good Jewish family.

Sometimes I feel that I'm not really Jewish since I'm not a part of what Jewish-American society is (something that I still haven't defined for myself very clearly). I've had a lot of Jewish experiences, some positive and some negative. I can look back on my feelings about them and continue to explore in the directions I want to go.

Certainly not all of my experiences will revolve around being Jewish. It can give me an interesting perspective from which to look at our society, but I'm not going to be doing only Jewish things.

I'm an intelligent, creative, Southern, short, curly-haired, obnoxious, funny, quiet, active, confused, interested American who studied at the University of Michigan. And, yes, I'm definitely Jewish, too. Perhaps in the future I'll write autobiographies about each of my identities—My *Life as a Southerner, Living with Weird Hair, Being Creative: A Manual for the Unexciting*. While some of them may be longer than this [essay], I think the fact that I'm Jewish will come up in them often. Until that day arrives, I'll continue with my own agenda, spending each new year exploring different cultures as well as my own Jewish one. Maybe I'll go to Israel. Or perhaps I'll opt for India. Whatever I do, I'll probably be Jewish doing it.[12]

CONNECTIONS

Create three identity charts for Joey Goldman: one at the time of his bar mitzvah, the second when he was in high school, and the third at the time he wrote the essay quoted in this reading. In what ways are the three charts similar? How do you account for differences? Did Goldman change his identity or the way he viewed that identity? Why do you think he felt at one point that "there was something bad about being Jewish"? What caused him to change his mind? What led him to believe that "I needed to be Jewish for myself?"

A bar or bat mitzvah is an important event in the life of a Jew. Describe what it meant to Joey Goldman. Why do you think he included an account of his preparation for that event in an essay entitled "I Am Not Really Jewish"?

What does Joey Goldman mean when he writes, "I started to tell other people I was Jewish without feeling the uneasiness I always had had because I had felt like there was something bad about being Jewish and because I never liked other Jews." What is the uneasiness he describes? Where does it come from? Have you or anyone you know ever experienced it?

In an interview, a woman recalled that as a teenager she didn't want to be Jewish. "I didn't want to be set apart, to be different." Her attitude changed after she traveled to Israel with her synagogue youth group. She says of that journey:

> It's hard for me to articulate what happened, but I think I began to feel myself part of a five-thousand-year-old history, and a part of the Jewish people. I think there are chords within each of us that may remain unresponsive all our lives unless triggered by the right stimulus. I believe that my core was Jewish and that I had been absorbing Jewish feelings all my life through my parents, relatives, whatever, that I had suppressed them, and that being in Israel was just the right stimulus. Maybe it was being in a place where Jews were people like everyone else. I didn't have to hide my Judaism. I didn't have to be embarrassed about being a Jew. Not only were the people around me not embarrassed about it, they were proud of it. After I returned, I felt a difference in my being Jewish. I talked about Israel all the time. I did not have that sense of being apart anymore.[13]

How did the woman's need to belong affect the way she regarded her Jewish identity? What might have embarrassed her about being a Jew? How did her trip to Israel change the way she felt about herself and other Jews? What does she mean when she writes "there are chords within each of us that may remain unresponsive all our lives unless triggered by the right stimulus"? What are the chords within Joey Goldman? What triggered those chords for him?

Joey Goldman and Steve Blonder (Reading 5) wrote their essays for a sociology course they took in college. So did the young woman quoted in the next reading. As you reflect on their essays, review your own identity chart and your working definition of the term *Jewish identity*. Interview members of your family to find out how they would define the term. Add their ideas to your working definition. Use those ideas to write an essay describing how Judaism has shaped your identity. You may wish to revise, enrich, or expand it as you complete the chapter.

Belonging

Everywhere to be human means to live with others. We all have a need to belong. Perhaps that is why it can be so uncomfortable to be seen as an outsider.

Irving Greenberg is an Orthodox rabbi who grew up in New York City in the 1950s. He had few contacts with non-Jews until he attended graduate school at Harvard University. He told an interviewer that it took three years before he could bring himself to wear a headcovering to class. Only when he came to see Harvard as his school as well as theirs did he feel comfortable enough to wear his *kipah* wherever he went. Blu, the woman who later became his wife, recalls that when they were dating she experienced "an occasional sensation of discomfort at the fact that he never removed his *kipah*. Not to my credit, I even remember one evening at the opera, of which I didn't hear a word, while I sat thinking the whole time, 'Why can't he be more sensible, less conspicuous?'"[14]

Although Lauren Shapiro attended college over 30 years after the Greenbergs completed their education, she too longed to be "like everyone else." She wrote an essay about her identity in the form of letters addressed to a sister nicknamed "Bean." In one letter she notes:

Last night I was watching television, and they did this great show about the main character's best friend's bar mitzvah. I really loved seeing this awkward-looking thirteen-year-old get up and say his prayers over the Torah. I remember every one of his words as he sang the [blessing] before he began his Torah portion. . . .

While I watched that show . . . and got a little misty over the sappy ending, I tried to remember the time in my life when I really felt the most Jewish. Several things enter my mind immediately. Like Christmas, for instance, I really feel so alone and on the edge during this green-and-red holiday. It is the one time during the whole year when I really don't fit in with the majority at all. So, in a negative way, I feel really Jewish during Christmas, which I guess is really common for most Jews.

I never really understood all the traditions that went along with the Jewish funeral until Grandpa died. I do know that being with our whole family during that time, even at the graveyard, made me feel really warm and secure. I remember seeing the candlelight throughout Grandma's house for a week. With every drop of wax that hit my nightstand, a flicker of Grandpa would enter my heart. It was a sorrowful time, and I cried a lot, but I have also never felt so close to so many people in my life. I watched everyone in our family immediately adapt to take care of Grandma's needs. I think that I, of course, did the grocery shopping. Food always helps to calm my mind.

I'm not sure if the specialness of this sad time was related to the fact that Jews pull together very tightly when they experience grief or to the fact that we just have a very wonderful family. . . . I'm just glad that we were all there together to show our strength for one another.

I guess I feel this way a lot when I'm with a group of Jews and I feel comfortable. There's such strength in knowing that we share a kind of bond. Immediately, I feel like I could trust these people and even rely on them. Who knows? At least I feel my attitude toward our religious faith has been steadily improving. Well, Bean, I'll write again soon. I hope you're doing well and that you're on your toes.

Dear Bean,

I just finished writing this really interesting research paper for my English class. I wanted to write about an issue that has affected me deeply, so I chose JAP [Jewish American Princess] baiting. What I'm writing about are the consequences of all the jokes and harassment that the term JAP has been causing these days. I know that you and I used to sit around and ridicule women who we thought fit the JAP stereotype—the woman, for instance, with the oversized Benetton sweater, the skinny pants tucked into bulky socks, and high-top Reeboks, and she is wearing loads of jewelry and makeup, not to mention long red nails.

But now I'm really angry at us for acting this way and shunning people just because they choose to dress a certain way and wear their hair in a certain style. I guess we were just scared of being stereotyped ourselves, so we did the natural thing and created a division:

us and them,

JAP versus non-JAP. . . .

I know the whole issue of being a JAP has affected both of us a great deal. I remember when I came to college I chose to live in a certain dorm because I heard the other dorms on the hill were "too Jappy." I knew immediately that I didn't want to join a sorority, but I didn't want to join a Jewish one especially, because I thought all the women would be materialistic, whiny people. Looking back, my rationalizations seem obviously racist and even antisemitic. But at the time I really didn't want to hang out with what I considered a bunch of JAPs. This sounds so awful now, and I'm so humiliated that I actually felt this way about people of my own faith. You understand though, Bean. It's so hard to be from our area and surrounded by so much wealth and then have to hear all of these people complain . . . not even appreciating what they have. . . .

To be honest with you, until this semester I never considered the word *JAP* racist, although I knew it had derogatory undertones. I remember last year when the school board met and decided that the term was offensive and should not be used on campus, I was shocked. To me the word *JAP* was normal, everyday lingo that I heard from friends (Jews and non-Jews), family members (yourself included), and even people passing by on the streets. I realize only now that I actually liked using the term because, if I could call someone else a JAP and laugh at a JAP joke, then, obviously, I wasn't a JAP. Maintaining this image seemed very important to me until I started to really feel the scare of what could happen if the stereotype is perpetuated any further.

I've started to realize that, because I didn't understand my own Jewish identity, I resented other Jewish women. I didn't want to be affiliated with the negative stereotypes of Judaism. Now, though, with a lot of work (trust me) I'm learning to find a better balance for my Jewish identity, and I'm coming to grips with many of my own insecurities. I still feel uncomfortable with the materialism I see at home, but I'm learning not to judge other Jewish women by their clothing, their accents, or their seemingly cold exteriors; we all present fronts for our own self-protection. You better damn well believe, Bean, that I'm the first one to stop people when I hear them say "JAP" or make a JAP joke. I hope you're with me on this one. I feel pretty strongly that we have to stick together to beat JAP baiting down before it gets to us. Think about it.[15]

How would you answer the question Blu Greenberg asked about her husband-to-be? How might Lauren Shapiro answer it? What does the Greenbergs' story suggest about our need to be "like everyone else"? To "belong"? Is it necessary to be like everyone else to belong? If so, when does the price of belonging become too high?

Lauren Shapiro writes, "I really feel so alone and on the edge during this green-and-red holiday. It is the one time during the whole year when I really don't fit in with the majority at all. So, in a negative way, I feel really Jewish during Christmas, which I guess is really common for most Jews." Why do you think she feels "alone and on edge"? Is her feeling "common for most Jews"? Why does she label the feeling as "negative"? Do you agree?

A prejudice is based on real or imagined differences between groups and it attaches values to those differences in ways that benefit one group at the expense of the others. Not all prejudices result in discrimination. But they all have a similar effect—they reduce individuals to stereotypes. What stereotypes did Lauren Shapiro hold? How did she acquire them? Why did she come to see those stereotypes as dangerous? How did they shape her identity? Make an identity chart for Shapiro. How is it like the ones you made for Steve Blonder or Joey Goldman? What differences seem most striking?

What does Shapiro mean when she says that she and her sister were "scared of being stereotyped ourselves so we did the natural thing and created a division"? How "natural" is it to create divisions between "us" and "them"? What does Shapiro suggest about how we can break down such divisions?

Religious Stereotyping

Although it is "natural" to generalize about others, it is offensive to reduce individuals to categories. Stereotyping fosters prejudice and discrimination.

In reflecting on his experiences with stereotypes, Major General Robert Bailey Solomon recalled a Friday night in the 1950s. That evening when he returned to his barracks, he found a fellow soldier sitting on his bunk:

He says, "Hey Solomon, where were you?' I said, "I've been out." And he says, "Well, yeah, where were you?" I said, "Well, I went to religious services." He looked at me and said, "Well, what are you, a Seventh Day Adventist?" I said, "No." He said, "Well, what are you?" With a little trepidation, I said, "I'm Jewish." He said, "Are your parents Jewish?" And he is looking at me very intently. I said, "Yes, both my father and my mother and my grandparents are Jewish." And he said, "You don't look Jewish." And he is still looking at me. You remember the haircuts we had. Everybody looked alike. And so I finally said, "Well, why would you say I don't look Jewish?" because I always thought I did. He said, "Well," and he's looking at my head, he says, "You don't have horns." I said, "Pardon me!" You see I had led a very sheltered life, and I said, "Are you kidding me?" He said, "Well, Jews have horns." I said, "How many Jews do you know who have horns?" He said, "I never met a Jew before." So I found out that of the probably 220 people in that company, there weren't more than five of them that ever met a Jew. The only ones that had were a couple of kids who had lived in Chicago, a couple in Milwaukee.

Now, the interesting phenomenon is that I spent sixteen weeks in basic training and had probably somewhere between twenty and thirty prizefights. Usually it was some fellow who wanted to beat my brains out because I was Jewish. I didn't lose a fight. I got knocked on my keester a few times, but I think the fact that I was willing to fight sort of let them know that I was not a spindly little Jew that they could walk up to and push over.

As opposed to making me more Christianized, the military service, if anything, has made me more Jewish. I found nothing difficult about being in the army and I found nothing to compromise my faith in the army from the first day. I did find a lot of people who were antisemitic. And I also found out that many of those were antisemitic because they didn't have the foggiest notion of what Jews were, where they came from, what they might be, what they believed. They simply believed popular myths about Jews.[16]

Over 40 years later, Chana Schoenberger had an experience similar to Solomon's. Hers took place in Wisconsin the summer she, along with several other high school students, participated in the National Science Foundation Young Scholars program. She writes:

Represented among us were eight religions: Jewish, Roman Catholic, Muslim, Hindu, Methodist, Mormon, Jehovah's Witness and Lutheran. It was amazing, given the variety of backgrounds, to see the ignorance of some of the smartest young.

My friends, ever curious about Judaism, asked me about everything from our basic theology to food preferences. "How come, if Jesus was a Jew, Jews aren't

Christian?" my Catholic roommate asked me in all seriousness. Brought up in a small Wisconsin town, she had never met a Jew before, nor had she met people from most of the other "strange" religions (anything but Catholic or mainstream Protestant). Many of the other kids were the same way. . . .

Nobody was deliberately rude or antisemitic, but I got the feeling that I was representing the entire Jewish people through my actions. I realized that many of my friends would go back to their small towns thinking that all Jews liked Dairy Queen Blizzards and grilled cheese sandwiches. After all, that was true of all the Jews they knew (in most cases, me and the only other Jewish young scholar, period).

The most awful thing for me, however, was not the benign ignorance of my friends. Our biology professor had taken us on a field trip to the [Environmental Protection Agency] field site where he worked, and he was telling us about the project he was working on. He said that they had to make sure the EPA got its money's worth from the study—he "wouldn't wanted them to get jewed."

I was astounded. The professor had a doctorate, various other degrees and seemed to be a very intelligent man. He apparently had no idea that he had just made an antisemitic remark. . . .What scares me about the experience, in fact about my whole visit to Wisconsin, was that I never met a really vicious antisemite or a malignantly prejudiced person. Many of the people I met had been brought up to think that Jews (or Mormons or any other religion that's not mainstream Christian) were different and that difference was not good.[17]

CONNECTIONS

What stereotypes shaped the way Solomon's fellow soldiers regarded him? How did those stereotypes affect the way he saw himself? How did it shape the way he viewed other Jews?

Chana Shoenberger says of her experience with Jewish stereotypes, "Ignorance was the problem I faced this summer. By itself, ignorance is not always a problem, but it leads to misunderstandings, prejudice, and hatred." How are ignorance, misunderstanding, prejudice and hatred related? Have you ever had an experience like the one she describes? If so, how did you respond? How did it make you feel?

Chana Schoenberger writes, "Nobody was deliberately rude or antisemitic, but I got the feeling that I was representing the entire Jewish people through my actions." Henry Louis Gates, Jr. is an African American who has had similar experiences. In his book *Thirteen Ways of Looking at a Black Man*, each of the men he profiles rages at the notion "that you represent your race, thus that your actions can betray your race or honor it." Why do you think Gates and others view "representation" as a "burden"? Would Schoenberger and Solomon agree? Do you agree?

The Roots of Religious Stereotyping

Robert Solomon and Chana Schoenberger were surprised to learn that others saw them only as members of a group. They were even more surprised at the qualities attributed to them as a result of myths and misinformation. Where did those myths come from?

Historians have traced myths about Jews back to the time of the Roman Empire and the beginnings of Christianity. Historian Robert S. Wistrich writes. "Jesus was born, lived and died as a Jew in first-century Roman Palestine. He never conceived nor dreamed of a Christian Church. His father, mother, brothers and first disciples were all Jews, so that early Christianity can be said to have been essentially a rebellious Jewish sect that emerged out of . . . Judaism and had to define itself against the mother religion."[18]

Jesus lived at a time of crisis for Jews in Palestine. After the Romans conquered their country, they insisted that the Jews not only obey Roman laws but also worship Roman gods. Jews who refused to do so were labeled "stubborn" "clannish," and "hostile." As pressure to accept Roman culture mounted, they searched desperately for a way to maintain their religious identity. Some urged rebellion. Others, including Jesus, argued that Jews must reform their religious practices and atone for their sins.

As each side marshalled arguments in defense of its position, the debate increased in intensity. Still, all of the attacks and counterattacks took place within the context of Judaism. Only when Christians separated from Judaism, did those angry words take on new meaning. They became, in the words of Krister Stendhal, a professor of Christian Studies, missiles hurled from a "mainly gentile Church toward the Synagogue across the street, from which now those Jews who followed Jesus had been excommunicated. And by that shift Christian anti-Judaism was born." He goes on to say:

> Much has been written and more can be said about why and how that parting of the ways happened. No one factor was decisive. No one action or doctrine did it. As only a small number of Jews but an ever-increasing number of gentiles [or non-Jews] joined the Jesus movement, the outcome was Christian Churches, which, for all practical purposes, were gentile communities.

In time what began as a division within the Jewish community was transformed into two distinct communities, "the Synagogue and the Church." Stendhal notes that "once established, these two entities felt the necessity to define themselves by sharpening their differences."[19] By the fourth century, the word Jew had become an expression of contempt among Christians. Laws now protected Christians from "contamination" by not allowing them to eat or associate with Jews. By the eleventh century, Jews were a small vulnerable minority in Western Europe. How vulnerable they truly were became clear in 1096, when Church leaders launched a series of crusades against the Muslims to win control of Palestine. On their way to the Middle East, the crusaders attacked Jewish communities. Thousands of Jews were murdered.

As persecutions mounted, many survivors fled to Islamic countries in Southwest Asia and North Africa or to Eastern Europe, where they found more freedom for a time. But whether they stayed behind or ventured elsewhere, Jews could not escape violence based on myth and misinformation. Almost everywhere in Europe, they now faced a variety of restrictions.

Peter Abelard, a twelfth-century philosopher and priest, described some of them in his *Dialogue between a Philosopher, a Jew, and a Christian*: "Heaven is their only place of refuge. If they want to travel to the nearest town, they have to buy protection with the high sums of money from the Christian rulers who actually wish for their death so that they can confiscate their possessions. The Jews cannot own land or vineyards because there is nobody to vouch for their safekeeping. Thus, all that is left to them as a means of livelihood is the business of moneylending, and this in turn brings the hatred of Christians upon them."

Jews were allowed to become bankers, because the Church considered it a sin for a Christian to charge interest for a loan. Moneylending was also contrary to Jewish laws. But Jews had few other ways of earning a living, so many were forced to become bankers. That occupation led to a new stereotype: that of the Jew as a greedy moneylender. It was a stereotype that would linger long after the French and Italians forced the Jews from the banking industry.

Nowhere were Jews safe. In 1492, for example, Spain expelled any Jew who refused to convert to Christianity. Tens of thousands of Jews abandoned the country of their birth rather than give up their faith. Others pretended to be Christians but secretly practiced Judaism. The Spanish called these secret Jews *Marranos*, a word that means "pigs" according to some scholars. The Spanish Inquisition was an attempt to root out Marranos. Those accused of practicing Judaism were brought before the inquisition, a special court, and required to prove that they were good Christians. If they were unable do so, they could be burned at the stake. The evidence against them might include a reluctance to eat pork, the lighting of candles on Friday night, or even the absence of smoke from a chimney on Saturday. These were all said to be telltale signs of a "secret Jew."

Even in places where Jews were allowed to practice their faith, they were often isolated from their Christian neighbors except for a few business encounters. In many countries, people of the Jewish faith were confined to a ghetto, a section of a city or town that was enclosed by high walls and guarded by Christian gatekeepers. With more rigid separation came new myths and misinformation. Increasingly Jews were portrayed as agents of the devil responsible for every catastrophe from random crime to plague and drought. Artists now portrayed Jews with horns, tails, and evil faces. Priests and scholars elaborated on the idea that Jews were evil creatures who were less than human in sermons and lectures.

Beginning in 1517, a new division developed within Christian Europe. That year, in what is now Germany, Martin Luther protested corruption in the Catholic Church by calling on Church leaders to reform. Instead they branded him a heretic and excommunicated him. He started his own Protestant churches. As Luther's ideas became more popular, religious wars broke out in many parts of Europe.

Luther had assumed that Jews would want to become Protestants. But when they showed no interest in converting, an angry Luther wrote in part:

> First, their synagogues or churches should be set on fire, and whatever does not burn up should be covered or spread over with dirt so that no one may ever be able to see a cinder or stone of it. . . .Secondly, their homes should likewise be broken down and destroyed. For they perpetrate the same things there they do in their synagogues. For this reason they ought to be put under one roof or in a stable, like Gypsies, in order that they may realise that they are not masters in this land, as they boast, but miserable captives.[20]

Other Protestant leaders were more tolerant of Jews, in part because their quarrel was with Catholics. But even among those Protestants, old stereotypes lingered. Indeed they survived into modern times. As Malcolm Hay, a Catholic historian, explains: "Men are not born with hatred in their blood. The infection is usually acquired by contact; it may be injected deliberately or even unconsciously, by parents, or by teachers. . . .The disease may spread throughout the land like the plague, so that a class, a religion, a nation, will become the victim of popular hatred without anyone knowing exactly how it all began; and people will disagree, and even quarrel among themselves, about the real reason for its existence; and no one foresees the inevitable consequences."[21]

CONNECTIONS

Historian Robert S. Wistrich describes the stereotype of the Jews as being "divorced completely from the real, concrete Jews of everyday life." What allows stereotypes to flourish? What part do leaders play in keeping them alive? What part does segregation play? Why do people cling to stereotypes that have no basis in reality? How do such stereotypes affect "the real, concrete Jews of everyday life"? You may wish to test those ideas by researching another religion. Are your answers equally true of the group you researched?

How does a quarrel within a group differ from one between groups? Are there things you can say to a relative that you would not say to outsiders? What happens when words used in a "family quarrel" move outside the family?

Many scholars have reflected on the hatred directed at the Jews throughout history. Some have been struck by the way leaders have tried to set Jews apart, stir hatred, and teach contempt. What part does language play in the level of tolerance one group has for another? What can it play in dehumanizing a group of people?

In October, 1965, the Roman Catholic Church issued the now famous *Nostra Aetate*. In it, the Church deplores "the hatred, persecutions, and displays of antisemitism directed against the Jews at any time and from any source." The document also states that "liturgical passages that show the Jewish people will be carefully interpreted by the Church to avoid prejudice." In 1993, the Lutheran Church issued a similar statement. Why are such statements important? Why do you think neither statement has erased prejudice and discrimination against Jews?

In a novel set in what is now the Czech Republic, Sulamith Ish-Kishor describes the effects that the separation of Jews and Christians had on a young Christian boy. At the beginning of *A Boy of Old Prague,* Tomas hates and fears Jews. When his master sends him to work for a Jew, the frightened boy is convinced that the Jew will kill him and drink his blood. That notion resulted from stories that claimed Jews murdered for religious purposes. Tomas' terror shows the power of these stories. What do such stories suggest about the way fear blurs one's vision? What do they suggest about the way stereotypes distort the truth? In time, Tomas learned that Jews were not demons but people much like himself. Most people in his day did not have the opportunity he did to know Jews as individuals. How did the ghettos and other forms of separation encourage myths and misinformation?

Jewish by Choice

Not everyone who is Jewish was born a Jew. Some people have chosen to be Jewish. How do they define themselves? Do they regard Judaism as a religion or do they see themselves as part of "a community woven of memory"?

Carolyn Craven, a well-known journalist in the San Francisco area, is a Jew by choice. She described her search for identity to an interviewer:

I grew up in a nice, stable, black, upper-middle-class home in Chicago. My mother taught physics in the public schools, my father was a lawyer and a judge. My parents were basically unreligious, but my twin sister and I were sent to Sunday school in an interracial Baptist church around the corner. Our social peers, the other members of the black aristocracy, went to St. Edmund's Episcopal Church. My sister and I converted to Episcopalianism when we were twelve so we could get confirmed there. It was all black, upper-middle-class. The church was very beautiful, and we went with great regularity. I loved the service, like a Catholic mass in English, with religious fervor, in the quiet, sophisticated way that Episcopalians can have. It was a big part of our lives.

But most of our family's close friends were Jewish, and we went to seders every year, and to zillions of bar mitzvahs. I knew the *Shema Yisrael* [the prayer that affirms a Jew's belief in one God] as early as I knew the Lord's Prayer. A good number of these Jewish families were religious, some Reform, some Conservative, some were even Orthodox and kept kosher. . . .

By the time I went away to college at Goucher, I wasn't interested in religion anymore. I was involved in politics and civil rights. I worked in SNCC [the Student Nonviolent Coordinating Committee] and helped to start an SDS [Students for a Democratic Society] chapter. In 1965, I left Baltimore, moved to the West Coast, became a student at Berkeley, and worked as an SDS organizer. That's where I was when the Six-Day War broke out [in 1967]. It was incredible. In one day, the campus divided down the middle. But I didn't have any doubts in my mind. I remember shaking with rage at my leftist friends who were anti-Israel. I knew that I was in an untenable position with the Left. I was a national officer of SDS at the time. I resigned my job and resigned from the organization. And I was very aware of black antisemitism. . . . Some of it was just cynical. And some came from real problems. There was so much Jewish ownership in black neighborhoods. There were some black people whose only contact with Jews was with landlords and store owners.

I remember people talking about religion in the early seventies. My generation was having children, settling down. And the "movement" had fallen apart politically. Maybe this is oversimplistic, but I think politics served in the place of religion for some people. All of a sudden, some of my very good friends started seriously talking about being Jews again and what that meant. Now, I'm sure there were Christians who, doing the same thing, but I happened to be around people who were Jewish. And when I started to think about religion, it was Judaism I thought of. . . .

I remember being very embarrassed to say that what I was really thinking was that I wanted to learn more because I wanted to convert. I must have known people who converted for reasons of marriage, but not straight conversions. . . . Then I got sick and was in the hospital for a few months. A close friend brought me the Hertz edition of the Torah. I couldn't sleep in the hospital, and I used to stay up late at night and wake up early, and I read the Torah a lot. I was fascinated. I read the annotations and was maybe even more fascinated by these footnotes. Then, later, I started reading Jewish writers. I think I've read everything I. B. Singer [a noted Yiddish writer] ever wrote. And I read a lot of Holocaust stuff, especially Elie Wiesel. Then I got *Everyman's Talmud*, and I became more and more fascinated. I loved that convoluted kind of argumentation that's in the Talmud. My favorite stories in the whole world are in the Talmud. I use them when I speak in public. I love them.

Later I was talking to a friend from San Francisco, and I told her what I'd been studying and considering converting, but I didn't know what to do. Even though many of my friends were getting involved in Jewish things, none of them belonged to synagogues. She suggested Marty Weiner, a rabbi at Shearith Israel, in San Francisco.

So I called and made an appointment. I don't know if I told him I was black. And it was an advantage that he didn't know me from television. I wasn't "Carol Craven of Channel Nine News" to him. When I told him I'd decided to convert, he tried to discourage me, with all the kindness in the world, hinting, I think, Why would you want to be part of another minority? He talked for a long time about how hard the conversion process was, and how Judaism wasn't a proselytizing religion. And he asked, "Why take on the burden of becoming a Jew?" I explained that the burden for me now was not being a Jew. We agreed we would continue meeting and I would take the conversion class.

The class was given by an older woman, over seventy, taught on a one-to-one basis in her kitchen, at night. It went on for three or four months. There were books to read and papers to write, and work sheets. I just loved it. I started going to Saturday services at Shearith Israel. They were wonderful. . . . At the end of the class I went back to the rabbi to continue the conversations we had started about faith. . . .

In Shearith Israel, I met a lot of people like me who had converted because they wanted to convert. There are lots of us; we're not a rare breed. . . .

So the day came, and we went into the little chapel, with my teacher, and I answered the questions "yes," and then we said the *Shema* together, and a blessing, and it was over. The rabbi said that according to Jewish law this was the last time I would be referred to as a convert. But then he was really surprised. I told him this wasn't enough, that I wanted an Orthodox conversion. He finally arranged it, including the *mikvah* [a ritual bath]. The new assistant rabbi also wanted to come. It turned out that Marty Weiner had been to the *mikvah* only once, and the assistant rabbi never. The Orthodox rabbi was really nice, and very moved that the Reform rabbis wanted to come, so he said to Marty: "Such a day! I make you an Orthodox rabbi, and you make the ceremony," and he gave Marty the book. So we went in, and the ceremony itself was lovely; the blessings and the immersion are wonderful. We were all surprised at how touching the ceremony was. Then we went to the court, the *beth din.* There were two other women being converted for marriage purposes. Then we went to the chapel and the ceremony there was like the one I'd experienced already. The reason I had an Orthodox conversion was that I wanted to make it real, absolute, so there would be no questions asked anywhere in the world, not even in Israel. . . .

In the years since then, I've become less observant. But, as with every other Jew I know, becoming less observant in no way diminishes my feeling of Jewishness. I think of Jewish history as my history. The shtetl experience is my experience. Do I talk to my sister about this? Well, maybe other Jews aren't like this, but I don't really talk about this a lot with goyim. There is too much they don't understand. See, I have a four-thousand-year history that my sister doesn't share. We have separate histories now, we really do. I have this rich and wonderful four-thousand-year history.[22]

CONNECTIONS

Make an identity chart for Carol Craven. How is it similar to the other charts you made? What difference seems most striking?

In the chapter introduction, Eliezer Berkovits, a scholar and an Orthodox Jew, is quoted as saying, "To be a Jew does not mean 'I believe this or that.' To be a Jew means 'I am!'. . . . To be a Jew means to open a book of Jewish history and say, 'This is my history, this is me.'" Is she a Jew according to Jewish law? Would she be considered a Jew if she were to move to Israel? Is Craven a Jew in the sense that Berkovits defines the term in the chapter introduction?

What does Craven mean when she says, "I think of Jewish history as my history. The shtetl experience is my experience." The chapter opening quoted from the play "Angels in America." Tony Kushner, the playwright, described the legacy that Jews share in a speech a rabbi gave for a Jewish woman who had just died. He told her family they can never make the journey that she once made, "for such Great voyages in the world do not anymore exist." But he reminded them that every day of their lives, they journey between the place from which she came and the one in which they live. He tells them, "Every day. You understand me? In you that journey is." How is that journey a part of Carol Craven's daily life? How is she a part of that spiritual and cultural legacy?

Rabbi Abraham Joshua Heschel once wrote, "Being human is a surprise, not a foregone conclusion. A person has the capacity to create events. . . . Indeed the enigma of a human being is not in what he is but in what he is able to be." How does Craven's journey support that view of human-ness?

[1] Elsa Rosenberg, "Reminiscences of a Jewish Childhood" in *Growing Up Jewish in Europe, America and Israel,* ed. Jay David (Morrow, 1969), 305-309.

[2] Deborah Tannen, preface to *You Just Don't Understand* (Morrow, 1990).

[3] Esther Hautzig, *Remember Who You Are* (Crown, 1990), 220.

[4] Avrohom Hecht, Interview by Myrna K. Frommer and Harvey Frommer, in *Growing Up Jewish in America* (Harcourt, 1995), 31-32.

[5] Manny Azenberg, Interview. Ibid., 136-137.

[6] Arthur Weinberg, Interview by Howard Simons in *Jewish Times: Voices of the American Jewish Experience* (Houghton, 1988), 80-83.

[7] Rachel Altman, "Fragments of a Broken Past," in *Different Voices: Women and the Holocaust,* ed. Carol Rittner and John K. Roth (Paragon, 1993), 366-370.

[8] Julius Lester, *Falling Pieces of the Broken Sky* (Little, Brown, 1990) 263-264.

[9] Kati Marton, "Making Peace with the Past," *Newsweek,* February 17, 1997, 44.

[10] James Carroll, "Critics of Albright's Conversion Ignore the Essence of Judaism," *Boston Globe,* February 18, 1997, op. ed.

[11] Steve Blonder, "Jewish Identity: One Person's Experience." In *Inside Separate Worlds,* ed. David Schoem (University of Michigan Press, 1991), 203, 211-212.

[12] Joey M. Goldman, "I'm Not Really Jewish." In *Inside Separate Worlds,* 259-260, 263, 274-275.

[13] Interview in *Saving Remnants: Feeling Jewish in America* by Sara Bershtel and Allen Graubard (University of California Press, 1992), 125-127.

[14] Blu Greenberg, *On Women and Judaism: A View from Tradition* (Jewish Publication Society, 1981), 24.

[15] Lauren B. Shapiro, "Bean Soup: A Collection of Letters." In *Inside Separate Worlds,* 105-108.

[16] Robert Bailey Solomon, Interview by Howard Simons in *Jewish Times,* 239-240.

[17] Chana Schoenberger, "Getting to Know About You and Me," From *Newsweek,* September 20, 1993. All rights reserved. Reprinted by permission.

[18] Robert Wistrich, *Antisemitism: The Longest Hatred* (Pantheon, 1991), 7.

[19] Krister Stendahl, "Can Christianity Shed Its Anti-Judaism?" *Brandeis Review,* Spring, 1992, 27.

[20] Robert Wistrich, *Antisemitism,* 39-40.

[21] Malcom Hay, *Thy Brother's Blood: The Roots of Antisemitism* (Hart Publishing, 1975), 3.

[22] Interview in *Saving Remnants: Feeling Jewish in America* by Sara Bershtel and Allen Graubard, 293-298.

2. Outsiders in Eastern Europe

Whoever we are, we are,
But Jews we are.
Whatever we do, we do,
But on the Sabbath, we rest.
> Yiddish Folksong

Jews began arriving in Poland in the twelfth century. Many had been expelled from countries in Western Europe for refusing to convert to Christianity. Poland was one of the few places in Europe where they were free to enjoy the customs, traditions, and beliefs that set them apart from their neighbors. There, over many centuries, they built a civilization—a way of life that still shapes our ideas of what it means to be a Jew.

Chapter 1 considered some of the factors that shape our identity. This chapter explores questions of membership and belonging by focusing on the factors that define a group's identity. That definition has enormous significance. It indicates who holds power in a place and how individuals and groups within the larger society define their "universe of obligation"—the circle of individuals and groups toward whom it has responsibilities, to whom its rules apply, and whose injuries call for amends.

For much of history, birth determined a person's place in a community. In a traditional society, children inherit their status from their parents. Rights, privileges, even occupations are passed from mother to daughter, and father to son. Chapter 2 explores what happens to outsiders in such a society. How do newcomers make a place for themselves? How secure are those places? In reflecting on the ways his ancestors answered such questions, Arnold Zable came to realize that Jewish communities during the Middle Ages were never "entirely secure."

> Arbitrarily, a charter or privileges they had been granted could be repealed, and their function, place of residence, and status redefined. There was always the threat of a sudden whirlwind, a madman on the rampage full of drink and misdirected rage, inciting the mob to join in and take out its frenzy on these peculiar people who had settled among them with their private God and the countless prayer-houses in which they worshipped Him. So [Jews] maintained their talent for movement, traveling within the prescribed boundaries as itinerants, eking out a living from limited opportunities.[1]

By the 1700s and 1800s, ideas about membership and belonging were changing. Both centuries were a time of upheaval almost everywhere in the world. Nowhere were those changes more unsettling than in Poland. After a series of wars that tore the country apart, Poland's name disappeared from world maps. Its land and people were divided among the Austrian, Prussian, and Russian empires. Most Jews found themselves living under Russian rule. In the past, the Russians had not permitted Jews to settle anywhere in their empire. Now they gave Polish Jews the right to live in Russia but only in the far western section of the empire, in an area known as the Pale of Settlement.

Other changes were inspired by the ideas of the Enlightenment. In the 1700s, a group of thinkers in France began to emphasize reason over faith and the rights of the individual over the state. They believed that every person has a right to work out his or her own destiny. These ideas had enormous appeal for young Jews eager to escape the narrow confines of their village and explore the larger world. Suddenly birth no longer determined one's place in the world. Talent, skill, even perseverance seemed to matter more. Religious identity was also becoming a matter of choice. There were now many more ways to be a Jew.

By the early 1800s, Eastern Europeans were also feeling the impact of the Industrial Revolution. It began in England in the 1700s with the invention of machines powered by steam. That innovation quickly led to thousands of others. The Industrial Revolution changed not only the way goods were made but also where they were made. More and more people left the countryside for jobs in urban centers. For some, these changes were so unsettling that they looked for someone to blame for all that was new and disturbing. Increasingly in the 1800s, Eastern Europeans blamed the Jews. In doing so, they drew on a long history of violence against Jews.

This chapter and those that follow do not provide a complete history of Polish or Eastern European Jews. Rather they use autobiographies, official documents, literature, and other primary sources to explore the ways Jews and their non-Jewish neighbors responded to questions of difference at various times in their shared history. Those sources help us "draw conclusions from what we see to what we do not see" and "recognize ourselves in the past, on the steps to the present."

Strangers in a New Land

In 1492, Jews were expelled from Spain. According to one legend, as they journeyed eastward in search of a new home, a note miraculously dropped from the sky. It read, "Poh lin." In Hebrew, the words mean "Here, stay overnight." The exiles took those words as a sign and settled in the land they called "Polin" or "Poland." The legend suggests how important Poland was to the Jews of long ago. But it is just a story. Very few of the Jews who settled in Poland came from Spain.

Historians believe that Poland took its name from its founders— a group known as the Polanie or "people of the open fields." In the tenth century they built a kingdom between the Vistula and the Oder, two of the many rivers that wind their way across the plains of northern Europe. The first Jewish settlers probably arrived toward the end of the twelfth century or the beginning of the thirteenth. By the end of the 1200s, the country was home to several thousand Jews, mainly from neighboring lands like Germany, Bohemia, and Austria. Later they would be joined by Jews from places as far away as Spain, Greece, Italy, and Turkey. By the early 1400s, about 10,000 Jews made their home in Poland. Arnold Zable, an Australian Jew whose family came from Poland, says of these men and women:

> They lived on the edge of time and space, my ancestors, always on the verge of moving on, continually faced with the decision: do we stay, persist, take root within this kingdom, or do we take to the road again? Perhaps it is safer, greener, beyond the next river, over the next mountain-range, across yet another border. Often enough the choice was made for them, and they fled for their lives in the wake of expulsions, inquisitions, and massacres to seek a new place of refuge. At other times they were welcomed, initially, for the skills they had accumulated as wanderers; centuries on the move had made them masters of the ephemeral. They knew how to serve as middlemen, entrepreneurs, navigators and astronomers, court advisers and healers; even though their hearts longed for some soil to till.[2]

In those days, travelers did not need visas to enter a country. Permission was needed only if they wished to settle there. From the 1200s on, Polish rulers welcomed newcomers—especially artisans and merchants. At the time Poland was recovering from attacks by Mongol warriors. It needed settlers to rebuild the country and secure its borders.

As in neighboring kingdoms, an individual's place in Polish society was decided at birth. Who your parents were determined to a large extent not only who you were but also what you could become. At the top of Polish society were those who fought—the nobles and knights. Then came those who prayed—the priests and monks. At the bottom were those who toiled—the peasants or serfs who worked on the large estates of the upper classes. How did newcomers fit into such a society? Polish kings and princes, like rulers in other parts of Europe, created a place for new arrivals by issuing a charter. A charter was a contract that outlined the rights and responsibilities of both the ruler and the newcomers.

In 1264, Prince Boleslaw of Kalisz granted the first known charter to Jews in Poland. Like similar documents in Germany, Bohemia, and Hungary, it placed the newcomers under the prince's rule and specified the taxes they would have to pay. Like charters elsewhere, it was a source of revenue for the ruler. And like charters elsewhere, it dealt with Jews not as individuals but as members of a group. Many of the rights outlined in the charter were similar to those Jews had in other places. These included the following:

— Nobody may disturb or attack the Jews or take property they have inherited.
— Jews have the right to trade with anyone they choose to as long as the trade is legal.
— Jews have freedom of movement within the borders of the country to carry on theirbusinesses and trade without paying duties.
— No one may demand hospitality in a Jewish home without the family's consent.
— Jewish children may not be forcibly baptized. Jews who ask to be baptized must wait three days so that authorities may determine that they are doing so of their own free will. Those converts must give up any family property they have inherited.
— If a dispute between a Jew and Christian is taken to a court, each party may argue its case according to its own laws.
— Anyone who attacks or murders a Jew will not only receive the usual punishment for such crimes but also pay a fine to the royal treasury.

The charter issued by Boleslaw in 1264 also contained four privileges not found in charters issued by rulers of other countries.

1. In keeping with papal decrees, Jews are not to be accused of using Christian blood "because their law prohibits the use of any blood." A Christian who makes such a charge is to suffer the same punishment a Jew would receive if the accusation were true.
2. Jews can receive a horse as security for a loan only during the daylight hours. (This was to protect Jews against accusations that they had accepted stolen horses as pledges. Stolen horses were more likely to be transferred at night than during the day.)
3. A Jew may be accused of forfeiting money only if the accusation is authorized by the prince or his local representative.
4. A Christian who fails to help a Jew attacked at night is required to pay a fine.

Charters granted in Poland in the years that followed also safeguarded the right of Jews to practice their religion. They could not be forced to accept money on the Sabbath even in payment of a debt. They were also allowed to have their own slaughter houses so they could prepare kosher meat and protection for their funeral processions.

During the Middle Ages, kings and princes were not the only lawmakers in Poland. Nobles often proclaimed their own laws. So did the Church. Each tried to define the place of Jews and other minorities within its territory. Although these laws varied from place to place and time to time, Jews almost everywhere in Poland had more freedom than they did elsewhere. Jews in other parts of Europe were increasingly seen as the property of a ruler who could pawn, rob, or expel them whenever he or she chose. In Poland, however, Jews were treated as "freemen"—a rank similar to that of a knight.[3] Like knights, freemen were obligated to defend their king or lord in battle. So Jews formed their own battalions and even turned their synagogues into fortresses in times of war.

Polish Jews went to great lengths to guard their status as "freemen" against every challenge. In the 1500s, one group confronted a former Russian general who had been given control of a town in Volhynia, a Polish province. When a few Jews in the town refused to obey one of his orders, he confined them to a dungeon filled with water. He then demanded that other Jews in the town pay a ransom for their release. Outraged by such behavior, the Jews took their grievances to the king of Poland and the Sejm, a parliament of nobles. The Jews argued that the general had violated the terms of their charter. After hearing their story, the king and the nobles agreed. At their insistence, the general released his Jewish prisoners.

Not surprisingly, such stories attracted more and more Jews to Poland. Most towns and cities in the kingdom now had a "Jewish street." At first glance, it looked much like any other thoroughfare in the town. What set it apart were a handful of buildings important to Jewish life. Almost every town of any size had at least one synagogue, a ritual bath or mikvah, and a hospital. (In those days hospitals sheltered travelers as well as sick people.) The Jewish cemetery lay at the end of the street or just beyond the city gates. These institutions were organized and managed by a *kehilla*—an association that collected the taxes the Jewish community paid to its Polish ruler and provided a broad range of services.

At first, Polish kings or princes named the leaders of a town's *kehilla*. By the 1500s, however, Jews were choosing their own leaders and enforcing their own laws. They also decided who qualified for membership in their community. Those decisions were made by a small group of men chosen on the basis of their age, how long their family had lived in the community, their contribution to the community, and above all, their economic status and scholarship.

By the 1500s, many *kehillot* in Poland were confronting issues that involved Jews in more than one community. To address those concerns, they organized regional associations and later a national one. In those days, the Kingdom of Poland was divided into four provinces: Greater Poland with Poznan as its capital, Little Poland (Krakow), Red Russia (Lvov), and Volhynia (Ludmir). In 1569, a fifth province was added when the Principality of Lithuania with Vilna as its capital became part of Poland. All five regions had their own associations. And from time to time, the leaders of these groups would gather at the great trading fairs held in Lublin and Yaroslav to settle major disputes and discuss issues of common concern. The Vaad Arba Aratzot or Council of the Four Lands grew out of those meetings. Lithuania was initially part of the Council, but it separated from the group in 1623.

The leaders of the Vaad included noted rabbis and scholars. In deciding cases, they used a code of Jewish law known as Shulhan Arukh. It was compiled by Joseph Karo, an exile from Spain who settled in Palestine in the 1500s. In creating the code, he drew mainly on Sephardic (Spanish) and Middle Eastern traditions. Later Moses Isserles, a great Polish rabbi, added Ashkenazic (German-Polish) customs and practices to the code.

By the 1600s, there were Jewish settlements in every part of Poland "Yet," Zable warns, "at no time were these communities entirely secure. Arbitrarily, a charter or privileges they had been granted could be repealed, and their function, place of residence, and status redefined.[4]

CONNECTIONS

Arnold Zable describes his ancestors as continually faced with the decision: "Do we stay, persist, take root within this kingdom, or do we take to the road again?" These decisions were not made lightly. What were the possible consequences of each choice? What factors do you think influenced the way individuals and families answered the question?

The charter issued in 1264 states that "a Christian who fails to help a Jew attacked at night is required to pay a fine." What values are reflected in the statement? Why do you think this provision was included in a document that defined the rights of Jews in Poland? What does it suggest about the way many Christians defined their "universe of obligation"?

A contract is a written agreement between two or more parties that is enforceable by law. What are the advantages in having a piece of paper that spells out your rights and responsibilities? What are the disadvantages? What do the rights included in the charters suggest about relationships between Christians and Jews in other places and in other times? How do the charters hope to avoid the problems of the past? How do they try to anticipate the future? To what extent do your answers explain the four new rights included in the charter of 1264?

What is true in law is not always true in fact. What evidence can you find in the reading that suggest Jewish rights and privileges may not have been as secure as the charters would suggest?

Zable writes that his ancestors were "masters of the ephemeral." The word *ephemeral* refers to something that lasts for only a brief time. What are "masters of the ephemeral"? How secure are such people?

We and They

Everywhere in Poland, charters protected the right of Jews to worship together, teach their faith to their children, be tried according to their own laws, and be buried among their own people. The right to live apart was not only supported by rulers but also encouraged by religious leaders. That separation had a profound effect on the ways Christians and Jews viewed one another and the ways they saw themselves.

There were no ghettos in Poland. In almost every city and town, Jews and non-Jews lived side by side. As neighbors, the two groups shared many of the same problems and faced many of the same risks. Fires, floods, and a host of epidemics threatened Christian and Jewish homes alike. Rarely did thieves or invading armies take the time to distinguish between a Jewish household and a Christian one. Christians and Jews also experienced many of the same joys. A good harvest benefited everyone. So did times of peace and prosperity.

People shared in other ways too. As individuals from both groups gathered in the marketplace, they not only traded goods, swapped services, and lent one another money but also exchanged songs, stories, customs, and ideas. They came together in the workplace too. From the start, some Jews worked for Christians and some Christians were employed by Jews. And from time to time, individuals of both faiths entered into partnerships.

Travel also brought people together. During the Middle Ages, few individuals went any distance from home alone. Travelers almost always banded together for safety and companionship. Inns were few and far between. So strangers often found themselves camping side by side under the open sky. They also joined together to fight off the bandits who threatened even the briefest journey. Although such experiences did not always lead to friendships, they often built trust and mutual respect.

Despite such links, there were definite barriers between Christians and Jews. Poland did not become a Christian country until the tenth century. In the years that followed, Church leaders struggled to strengthen and reinforce Poland's Christian identity. As sociologist Kai Erikson points out, one of the surest ways to "confirm an identity, for communities as well as for individuals, is to find some way of measuring what one is not." Throughout the Middle Ages, church leaders in Poland tried to define what it meant to be a Christian by sharpening distinctions between Christianity and other faiths, particularly Judaism. As a result, the word Jew increasingly became an expression of contempt. Historian Bernard Weinryb writes, "For the Christian, the Jew was an infidel, a nonbeliever (this epithet is found in many medieval documents whenever a Jew is mentioned)."[5] These labels were meant to brand and humiliate.

At the same time they saw Jews as "infidels," Christians saw themselves as having been victimized "for the sake of the cross—recalling the scriptural teachings and the early struggles of Christianity."[6] It was an image that lingered on long after Christianity became the faith of the majority. And because every victim has an oppressor, Christians considered Jews their oppressors even though they were aware that Jews had little or no power. That image of the Jew as an oppressor contributed to new myths and more misinformation, including the false notion that Jews poisoned the water wells of Europe or killed Christian children for the purpose of taking their blood.

Such images also encouraged the belief that Jews oppressed Christians by "overcharging" for loans or driving an exceptionally "hard bargain" in the marketplace. The Church considered it a sin for a Christian to charge interest for a loan. Moneylending was also contrary to Jewish laws, but Jews had few other ways of making a living. So some were forced to become bankers. That occupation led to a new stereotype, the Jew as an unscrupulous moneylender. It was a stereotype that lived on long after Christians took over the banking industry.

Weinryb notes that Jews also had negative images of Christians. Those images were based on ideas "about the superiority of [their own] community, the chosenness of the Jews in comparison with the idolatry (paganism) of the others." In ancient times, Jews were required to keep their distance from idol-worshippers. During the Middle Ages, rabbis insisted that those laws be applied to Christian practices even though they recognized differences between the idol-worshippers of ancient Greece and Rome and the Christians of medieval Europe. The ways Jews viewed Christians were also shaped by the realities of life in the Middle Ages, a time when most Jews were oppressed by Christians. Weinryb writes:

> In such a social climate the Jew tended to look inward [toward other Jews] rather than outward, drawing strength from group solidarity. . . .This separateness molded most of the characteristics of the Jews. They lived apart, concentrated in the Jewish street; they wore somewhat distinctive clothing . . . ; they gathered around the same institutions: the synagogue, the cemetery, the ritual bath, and the hospital; they married within the group; they were engaged in similar occupations; and, at least theoretically, they identified themselves with the same ideals and values.[7]

CONNECTIONS

What factors encouraged links between Christians and Jews in Poland? What factors worked against them? Why do you think religious leaders of both faiths were fearful of the influence each group had on the other?

Yiddish, the everyday language of Eastern European Jews is a Germanic language that contains many Hebrew words. It also includes hundreds of Polish words. Many of those words can be traced to the marketplace. Others are words used at home or in the synagogue. The Yiddish word for the headcovering Jewish men wear when they pray is *yarmlke*, a Polish word. When Jews set aside money for charity, they often place coins in a *pushke*— the Polish word for box. In a kosher kitchen, foods that are neither meat nor dairy are *pareve*. It, too, is a Polish word. The words for grandmother and grandfather, *bobe* and *zeyde* are Polish words as well.

Polish has influenced Yiddish in other ways as well. The Yiddish word for boy is a *yung*. A little boy is called a *yungl* and his baby brother a *yungele*. The suffixes are Polish even though the root word is German. Polish and other Slavic languages sometimes turn verbs into nouns by adding the ending *-nik*. Yiddish does the same. The word *nudyen* means "tedious" or "boring." A *nudnik* is a world-class bore. What do these examples suggest about contacts between Jews and their non-Jewish neighbors? How do you explain such English expressions as *beatnik* or *peacenik*? What do your answers suggest about the way languages grow and change?

Kai Erikson believes that one of the surest ways to "confirm an identity, for communities as well as for individuals, is to find some way of measuring what one is not." What are the effects of a negative identity—of labeling someone by what he or she is not? What did it mean to Jews? To Christians? Have you ever been defined by what you are not? If so, how did it affect the way you viewed yourself? Why do you think that individuals often focus on differences rather than similarities when they meet someone? How may doing so encourage myths and misinformation?

For centuries rabbis and scholars have been interpreting Jewish law by answering questions brought to them by ordinary people. Many of the questions they answered in the 1500s and 1600s involved relationships with their non-Jewish neighbors. Some dealt with business arrangements: May a Jew accept a pig in payment of a debt? Are Christian workers allowed to use the tools of their Jewish employer on the Sabbath? Other questions dealt with social relationships: May Jews lend Christians clothing or jewelry to wear to church on one of their holidays? One noted rabbi allowed such loans because they were used to enhance "pleasure and prestige, not for dedication to idolatry or use in its service." In another case, that same rabbi criticized *hazanim*, or prayer leaders, for introducing Polish melodies and tunes into religious services. Yet another rabbi, Solomon Luria, spoke out against Jews who ate in non-Jewish restaurants.[8] What do the questions Jews brought to various rabbis suggest about relations between Jews and Christians? What concerns are reflected in the rabbis' responses?

How do you define the word *community*? Compare your definition with the one Suzanne Goldsmith provides in a recent book about communities in the United States.

> Communities are not built of friends, or of groups of people with similar styles and tastes, or even of people who like and understand each other. They are built of people who feel they are part of something that is bigger than themselves: a shared goal or enterprise, like righting a wrong, or building a road, or raising children, or living honorably, or worshipping a god. To build community requires only the ability to see value in others; to look at them and see a potential partner in one's enterprise.[9]

What are the strengths of a community like the one Goldsmith defines? How does her definition apply to Polish communities in the 1500s? To Jewish communities in Poland during those years?

Nations or groups, like individuals, have an identity. Make an identity chart for the Jews of Poland in the 1500s and early 1600s. What values were central to their identity? Make a similar chart for Jews in your community. How are the two charts similar? What differences seem most striking?

Why was the word *Pole* used only to describe Catholics in Poland, even though by the 1600s Jews had been living in the country for over 400 years?

On the Edge of Time and Space

In a society where membership is determined by birth, outsiders are always on the edge of time and space. As Arnold Zable reminds us, "Arbitrarily a charter or privileges they had been granted could be repealed, and their function, place of residence, and status redefined. There was always the threat of a sudden whirlwind, a madman on the rampage full of drink and misdirected rage, inciting the mob to join in and take out its frenzy on these peculiar people who had settled among them with their private God and the countless prayer-houses in which they worshipped Him."

In 1569, Poland and Lithuania were united into a single country, the second largest in Europe and one of the most diverse. Poles made up only about 40 percent of the total population. The country was also home to Ukrainians, White Russians, Lithuanians, Germans, Armenians, Tartars, and Jews. Some were conquered peoples. Others came to Poland as refugees from other parts of Europe or Asia. Although Poland was officially a Catholic country, it granted religious minorities more freedom than most countries did.

With Poland's growth came rivalries among the various groups who lived in the country. In the past, Jews were often the only artisans or merchants in a city or town. Now they had competition from German and Polish artisans and merchants who argued that Christians ought to be favored over Jews. They therefore demanded restrictions on their Jewish counterparts. In some cities, these Christian merchants and artisans won the right "not to tolerate Jews" and other outsiders.

By the 1600s, many Jews in Poland were seeking new opportunities in the recently conquered Ukraine where Polish nobles were building huge estates. The nobles needed help in managing those estates and supervising the work of the peasants, most of whom were Ukrainian or Russian. In 1569, there were about 4000 Jews in the Ukraine. By the 1640s, historians estimate that there were over 50,000 Jews in 115 separate communities. During those years, a new system developed in Poland known as the Arenda system. It was a complicated leasing arrangement in which Jews rented the right to manage an estate or group of estates at a fixed rate.

Those who held such a lease could in turn sub-lease parts of the estate or economic activities associated with it to friends and relatives. In theory, anyone could be a leaseholder. But in reality, almost all of the leaseholders were Jews. They paid for the right to work as tax collectors, artisans, administrators, and scribes. They also leased the right to run flour mills, breweries, and inns. Their rent had to be paid year in and year out, in good times and bad. And whenever the leases were renewed, nobles often increased the rent. Whenever a fee went up, that increase was usually passed on to the peasants in the form of higher taxes, fees, tolls, and prices.

The peasants deeply resented both the noble who ruled their land and the Jews who collected his taxes and carried out his orders. Differences in language and religion only increased tensions in the region. Not long after the massacres, Nathan Hanover, a Jewish scholar who lived in the Ukraine, explained why:

> [King Sigismund III] was a kind and upright man. He loved justice and loved Israel [the Jewish people]. In his days the religion of the Pope gained strength in the Kingdom of Poland. Formerly most of the dukes and the ruling nobility [in the Ukraine] adhered to the Greek Orthodox faith, thus the followers of both faiths were

treated with equal regard. King Sigismund, however, raised the status of the Catholic dukes and princes above those of the Ukrainians, so that most of the latter abandoned their Greek Orthodox faith and embraced Catholicism. And the masses that followed the Greek Orthodox Church became gradually impoverished. They were looked upon as lowly and inferior beings and became the slaves and handmaids of the Polish people and of the Jews.. . . . The nobles levied upon them heavy taxes, and some even resorted to cruelty and torture with the intent of persuading them to accept Catholicism. So wretched and lowly had they become that all classes of people, even the lowliest among them, became their overlords.[10]

In the spring of 1648, Bogdan Chmielnicki united the Ukrainian peasants against their Catholic Polish rulers and the "unbelieving" Jews with words such as these: "You know the wrongs done us by the Poles and Yids, their leaseholders and beloved factors, the oppressions, the evil deeds, and the impoverishment, you know and you remember."

From the start, much of the peasants' anger was directed at the Jews. Few ever saw the noble who owned their land. Most knew only the Jews who enforced the noble's laws in the Ukraine and collected his rents, taxes, and tolls. According to some sources, over one-fourth of all of the Jews in Poland were killed in the fighting and countless others left homeless. And the fighting did not end with the defeat of Chmielnicki and his men. Their attacks marked just the beginning of a series of bloody encounters in the Ukraine. They also marked the start of years of turmoil in Poland as one country after another took advantage of the nation's growing weakness. Little by little, Poland's land was divided among its neighbors.

Even those Jews who lived far from the battlefields were affected by the fighting. They were now required to pay more and more taxes. Some of the money was used for soldiers and weapons. The *Vaad* or Council of Four Lands used the rest to help Jewish victims of the fighting. So did *kehillot* throughout the country. Many of these groups went deeply into debt to meet their obligations. They borrowed not only from other Jews but also from Polish nobles and officials of the Catholic church.

CONNECTIONS

Arnold Zable (Reading 1) describes Jews as living "on the edge of time and space, . . . always on the verge of moving on, continually faced with the decision: do we stay, persist, take root within this kingdom, or do we take to the road again? How did Jews in the late 1500s and early 1600s answer the question? What were the consequences of their choices?

Why do you think Ukrainians directed much of their anger against the Jews rather than the Polish nobles? What does your answer suggest about the risks of being an outsider?

Write working definitions of the words *outsider*, *outlaw*, and *outcast*. How does an *outsider* become an *outcast*? How does an *outcast* become an *outlaw*? In the mid-1600s who were the *outsiders* in Poland? The *outlaws*? The *outcasts*?

The Pull of Hasidism

In the years after 1648, Poland seemed to be in almost constant turmoil as its neighbors took over more and more of its land. Some Jews responded to the upheavals by turning inward. Others waited anxiously for the coming of the Messiah only to be victimized by false prophets who betrayed their faith and trust. Then at a time when many had lost all hope, a new movement called Hasidism began in the Ukraine. Its leader was Israel Ben Eliezer known as the Baal Shem-Tov, the "master of the good name." He offered hope at a time when many had lost all hope.

As a child in what is now Hungary, Elie Wiesel learned about Israel Ben Eliezer from his grandfather. As an adult, he has continued to study the Baal Shem's life and legacy. To Wiesel, he was "a man of the people in the truest sense of the word."

[The Baal Shem-Tov] had no official titles, no influential friends, no powerful protectors. He had neither material possessions nor wealthy admirers. He could not even lay claim to vast Talmudic learning. . . .This partly explains his immediate success among the less fortunate—they identified with him. . . . His humble origins made it easier for the poor to approach him. . . . He told them what they wanted to hear: that every one of them existed in God's memory, that every one of them played a part in his people's destiny, each in his way and according to his means.

He assured them that a simple but sincere prayer has as much merit as a mystical incantation, that the fervor born in a pure heart is greater than the one born of a complex and unfathomable thought. He said: "The coachman who kisses the holy scrolls of the Torah pleases God more than the angels who praise Him and do nothing else." He wanted them to be suspicious of anyone claiming to have all the answers: "You want to know if a particular Rebbe is genuine? Go and ask his advice. Ask him if he knows a way to chase impure thoughts from your mind; if he says yes, you'll know he is a fake." He told them that pride derived from knowledge is worse than ignorance, that to seek is better than to find. The greatness of man, he taught them, lies in his capacity for humility. Let him start by submitting to God: he will grow and he will be free. . . .

. . . And since it is even to every man to acquire all the powers, why despair? Why give up the fight? One tear, one prayer can change the course of events; one fragment of melody can contain all the joy in the world, and by letting it go free, influence fate. And no elite has a monopoly on song or tears; God listens to the shepherd playing his flute as readily as He listens to the saint renouncing his earthly attachments. The prisoner's craving equals the wise man's: the one, like the other, has a bearing on the essence of man.

He taught them to fight sadness with joy. "The man who looks only at himself cannot but sink into despair, yet as soon as he opens his eyes to the creation around him, he will know joy." And this joy leads to the absolute, to redemption, to God; that was the new truth as defined by the Baal Shem. And Jews by the thousands let themselves be carried by this call, they needed to live and to survive. Thanks to it, there was joy—following pain—and it brought together the dispersed and exiled. . . . When he died in 1760, twenty-four years after his revelation, there remained in Central and Eastern Europe not a single Jewish town that was left unaffected. He had been the spark without which thousands of families would have succumbed to gloom and hopelessness—and the spark had fanned itself into a huge flame that tore into the darkness.[11]

After the Baal Shem's death, a number of his disciples became the leaders of groups of believers. Many of these groups saw their rebbe as a *zaddik*. A *zaddik* is a right-eous man—one who carries "God's light" in the world. To the *hasidim*, he was also a saint, an activist, and a wonder-worker. They believed that through his devotion and righteousness, their prayers would reach the heavens. They told and retold stories that celebrated the wisdom and power of both the Baal Shem and their own rebbe.

In one story, a group of *hasidim* gather at the Baal Shem's House of Prayer on Yom Kippur, the most solemn of the Jewish holidays. Among them is a villager whose 13-year-old son is unable to recognize the shapes of the letters let alone understand their meaning. Hour after hour, the boy sits silently as the men pray. Early in the afternoon, he asks his father if he can blow the whistle in his pocket. His father warns him not to disturb the service. But as the closing prayer begins, the boy takes out his whistle and blows it loudly. Although the congregation is startled, even frightened by the noise, the Baal Shem continues to pray but more quickly and easily than usual. Later he explains, "The boy made things easy for me."

In another story, a skeptical visitor is puzzled by the behavior of a *zaddik* who disappears for hours at a time during Elul, the month that comes just before the High Holy Days. It is a time for making peace with enemies, for resolutions, and for heroic efforts to correct personal flaws. Where does the *zaddik* go? What does he do? The visitor decides to find out. After secretly following the *zaddik*, he discovers that the rebbe dis-guises himself as a peasant so that he can help a poor woman without being recognized. When the visitor later hears the *hasidim* speak of how their *zaddik* ascends to heaven whenever he prays, he nods and quietly adds, "If not higher."

Such tales amused, delighted, and offered hope to hundreds of thousands of Jews throughout Eastern Europe. But not everyone accepted the teachings of the new movement. Opponents were know as *mitnagdim*. They were led by the most respected and learned rabbi of the day, Elijah ben Salomon Zalman— the Gaon of Vilna. To him, "the visions and miracles" of the rebbes were "so many illusions, dangerous lies, and idolatries." He and others were troubled by the fact that the title of *rebbe* was often inherited rather than earned. They were also concerned by the disdain many *hasidim* had for learning. The Gaon and others believed that an ignorant man cannot be truly pious.

The battles between *hasidim* and *mitnagdim* were so bitter that in some places hasidim were excommunicated, or excluded from membership in the Jewish community. In explaining why the movement flourished in spite of such antagonism, Wiesel writes:

> It is only natural that the Baal Shem was much talked about. People praised his pow-ers and quoted his maxims. The Jewish world was in an uproar; it followed his astounding ascent with fear or hope, or both. To remain indifferent was impossible; one took a stand for or against this extraordinary personality who seemed to be every-where at once, come and gone in a flash, leaving behind him a trail of wonder or anger. . . . The legend of the Baal Shem had fired the Jewish imagination with such violence and in so many places, nobody could stop or even brake his momentum. He answered a need.
>
> For the eighteenth century was not very kind toward these Jews who lived in the most ravaged parts of Central and Eastern Europe. . . . Their freedom, their life hinged on the good will of local squires who exploited their commercial talents. Let

the [Jewish] innkeeper or the superintendent present himself at week's end with a purse that was too light, and he would end up in jail savagely beaten. With no one to bail him out. The situation prevailed particularly in the small villages and isolated towns; none was to be pitied more than the Jew who lived in an out-of-the-way hamlet; he felt forgotten, forsaken by his brethren.

The larger communities had other kinds of problems; they were too divided. There were barriers between those with learning and those without, between the rich and the poor, the leaders and the craftsmen, the notables and the average citizens; the different classes watched each other with distrust, bitterness and rancor. At the top of the social ladder: the secular leaders (usually well-off if not rich), the rabbis named by them, the Talmudists, the devout, the teachers. Whoever possessed neither title nor fortune was ignored. Whoever showed neither knowledge nor piety belonged to the oppressed class. . . .

On a spiritual plane, Judaism went through a crisis that was no less serious . . . . Traumatized by the nightmare of false Messiahs of the seventeenth century, the rabbis looked askance at anything that seemed new, anything that was obscure. . . . And so, to protect tradition, they surrounded it with fences and obstacles; who tried to overturn them left himself open to fanatic, merciless repression. . . .

But man cannot live indefinitely without a dream and without a legend. Therefore, if someone appears who brings them both—it is enough. He will impose himself and reign.[12]

CONNECTIONS

Some scholars view *Hasidism* as revolutionary. In what sense was it a break with the past? In what respects was it in keeping with Jewish tradition?

What values do the stories retold in this reading teach? What is the moral, or lesson, of each? Y. L. Peretz, a Yiddish writer, retold many *hasidic* tales, including the one about the rebbe who went to heaven "if not higher." What was the appeal of such stories?

In the 1700s most women and many poor men knew only Yiddish. In 1622, a rabbi published a book for them called the *Tsena-Urena*. It contained prayers, summaries of the Torah readings, and stories from the Talmud. It also offered advice on how to be a good Jew. It quickly became a best-seller. Almost every family owned a copy even though scholars looked down on those who used it. The *hasidim* were the first to praise those who prayed in Yiddish. A descendent of the Baal Shem, Rabbi Nachman of Bratislav, told these women and men, "In Yiddish, it is possible to pour out your words, speaking everything that is in your heart before the Lord." How do such statements explain the appeal of *Hasidism*?

The *Tsene-Urena* enabled Jews who knew no Hebrew to pray and study the Bible.

Elie Wiesel writes that "man cannot live indefinitely without a dream and without a legend. Therefore, if someone appears who brings them both—it is enough. He will impose himself and reign." What does he mean? Are his words true for the world today or do they just apply to eighteenth-century Europe?

The Lure of the Modern World

In the late 1700s, as much of Poland came under Russian rule, Tadeusz Kosciuszko, a veteran of the American and French revolutions, urged Poles to fight for their country's independence. Among those who answered his call was a young Jew named Berek Yoselovich. He organized a military unit made up entirely of Jewish volunteers determined to "prove that we are worthy of freedom." Kosciuszko welcomed them: "Nothing can convince more the far away nations about the holiness of our cause and the justness of the present revolution than that, though separated from us by their religion and customs, [the Jews] sacrifice their own lives of their own free will in order to support the uprising." [13]

The uprising that Tadeusz Kosciuszko led in 1794 failed. In the years that followed, Poland was divided again and again by not only the Russians but also the Austrians and the Prussians. Yet the dream that inspired both Kosciuszko and Yoselovich did not die. It lived on in the hearts of a few Christians and Jews who were influenced by the ideas of the Enlightenment, which began in France and spread slowly eastward. It stressed reason over faith and the rights of the individual over the state. It was also based on a belief that people could work out their own destiny if they had sufficient courage.

The Jewish version of the Enlightenment was known as the *Haskalah*. In Poland, many of its followers, the *maskilim*, were convinced that it was possible to be both a Jew and a Pole. Although they were a small minority, the choices they made changed Judaism as surely as did those of the *hasidim*.

Among those attracted to the *Haskalah* was the son of a glazier and a trader in rabbit skins who lived in a shtetl called Hrubieszow. Biographer Betty Lifton describes Hirsh Goldszmit as "leaping over the fences" that surrounded the Jews of his day to attend medical school. No one knows what led him to break with tradition. We do know, however, that after receiving his degree, he returned to Hrubieszow where he became the town's first Jewish doctor. Lifton writes:

> In true Haskalah spirit, Hirsh gave his three sons and two daughters Christian as well as Hebrew names, and as a leader in the Jewish community—whose three thousand Jews made up half the town's population—he took advantage of any chance to praise ways in which Poles and Jews worked together. Soliciting funds for his small hospital in the regional Hebrew newspaper, Hirsh commended the two rabbis who had gone about like "beggars" collecting donations in spite of advanced age, poor health, and little means of their own, as well as the Gentile on the charity board who "spared no effort" in helping them.
>
> But Hirsh's claim that a secular education would not lead one's children away from their own faith and into the dreaded jaws of conversion was weakened in 1849 when his eldest son, eighteen-year-old Ludwik, converted. Although conversion was not an uncommon occurrence in that impassioned period of Polish uprisings against the Russians, Hirsh himself remained a Jew, continuing to exhaust himself with projects that would build bridges between his people and the Poles. [14]

Hirsh's two younger sons, Jozef and Jakub, followed in their father's footsteps. After leaving school, they settled in Warsaw where they wrote books and articles that aimed to uplift and educate Jews. Lifton writes of them.

Like so many of his generation who had become disillusioned with armed struggle after the failed insurrections against the Czar, Jozef believed that the only way to create a strong Polish nation was to build its economy from within. Wanting the Jewish people to be part of this vision, he took time from his law studies to raise money for Polish-language craft schools in both Lublin and Warsaw, where poor Jewish boys and girls could learn skills that would equip them to enter the Polish work force. Both he and his younger brother Jakub, who would follow him in law, wrote articles promoting those schools.

Jozef also collaborated with Jakub on a series of monographs called *Portraits of Famous Jews*, in which they hoped to enlighten the public about remarkable Jews of high moral character. (They later expanded this project to include famous Poles.) The first volume was on Moses Montefiore, the exuberant philanthropist and financial advisor to Queen Victoria, who traveled the globe with his carriage, wife, and doctor in tow, distributing large sums of money to poor Jews for hospitals and orphanages, never neglecting to slip something to the sultans and czars of those lands for their own poor.

"Sir Montefiore is a Jew and he never forgets it. But he is also an Englishman, and an exemplary citizen of his country who fights not with the sword but with the force of virtue," Jozef expounded in his flowery nineteenth-century Polish. This message was one that both he and his brother would stress in all their writings: it was possible to be both a loyal Jew and a loyal citizen of one's country. . . .[15]

Known as the "Brothers Goldszmit," Jozef and Jakub used their writing to not only educate Jews but also raise Polish consciousness. After Jozef died at the age of 52, his son Henryk continued the family tradition. Like his grandfather, he studied medicine. Like his father and uncle, he took an active interest in the social issues of his day. He focused, in particular, on the children of the peasants and poor Jews who were beginning to flock to Warsaw in search of jobs.

Goldszmit was also involved in efforts to keep alive Polish culture at a time when the Russians had outlawed the study of Polish literature and history. Like other young Polish patriots, he took courses at the "Flying University." Its name came from the way its students and professors fled from the Russian police at a moment's notice.

The founder of the Flying University was a Polish Catholic named Jadwiga Szezawinska. She started the school in her apartment to educate young Polish women. As word of the school spread, a number of men asked if they could take courses. By the middle of the 1880s over a thousand women and men were taking classes at dozens of secret locations. In these hidden classrooms, young Goldszmit discovered that he could also show his patriotism by secretly teaching children to read Polish at Warsaw's Free Lending Library. This too was illegal. Indeed classes often ended with the arrest of teachers and students alike.

Despite the risks, Goldszmit took part in these activities because he saw himself as a Polish patriot. In an article he wrote for a Polish journal, he responded to Poles who believed that there was room in Poland only for "true Poles." There are, he wrote, "three distinct currents in Polish society. The first is made up of aristocratic Poles whose names end in '-ski and -icz.' The second is made up of those whose names end in '-berg, -sohn, and -stein.' Both groups have long preferred to live separately. But there is also, he argued, a third current in Poland. Its members have always declared, 'We are sons of the same clay. Ages of mutual suffering and success link us on the same chain. The same sun shines upon us, the same hail destroys our fields, the same earth hides the bones of our

PARTITIONED POLAND, 1815–1918

*Former Polish provinces only

The map shows how Poland's neighbors divided up the nation's land and people.

ancestors. There have been more tears than smiles in our history, but that was neither of our faults. Let us light a common fire together.' . . ." Goldszmit ended the article by proudly stating: "I am in the third current."[16]

Historian Lucy Dawidowicz has written that "likenesses between *Hasidisn* and *Haskalah* were as striking as their differences." List ways the two differed. Then list the ways they were alike. Use your two lists to decide whether you agree with her assessment.

In 1866, Judah Leib Gordon wrote a Hebrew poem that expressed the views of many followers of the *Haskalah*. Its most quoted line urges readers to "be a man abroad and a Jew in your tent." What the statement mean? What does it suggest about the goals of the *Haskalah*? To what extent did the Goldszmit family achieve those goals? To what extent have Jews today achieved them? (You may wish to review your journal and the readings in Chapter 1 before answering.) Do African Americans, Hispanic Americans, Chinese Americans, and other "hyphenated Americans" have similar goals? To what extent have they achieved their goals?

By the 1870s, Gordon was disillusioned with the Enlightenment. He was particularly disappointed that many young *maskilim* were abandoning their Jewish faith. He feared for the future of the Jewish people He now wrote:,

> And our sons? The generation to follow us?
> From their youth on they will be strangers to us.
> —My heart bleeds for them—
> They make progress, year by year they forge ahead:
> Who knows where they will reach, how far they will go?
> Perhaps that place from which they shall never return. . . .[17]

What connection does Gordon suggest between assimilating, or becoming part of the majority, and conversion to Christianity? How do you think Hirsh Goldszmit would have responded to his poem? How might his sons have responded? His grandson?

What group or groups does Henryk Goldszmit leave out of his essay about Polish society? How important are those omissions? What do the omissions suggest about his views of Polish life?

Choices in a Modern World

Jewish men, like the Goldszmits, searched for ways to live in two civilizations at the same time. They wanted to be both Jews and Poles. What choices did the women in their family have? What did the Enlightenment mean for them?

The autobiography of Pauline Wengeroff offers some clues to the ways the Enlightenment affected Jewish women. It is the first memoir to look at the *Haskalah* through a woman's eyes. In it, she reflects on the choices that she and her husband Hanan made.

Born at the beginning of the 1830s in Bobruysk and brought up by strictly observant parents, I was in a position to see the transformation which European education wrought on Jewish family life. . . .

My parents were God-fearing, deeply pious, and respectable people. This was the prevalent type among the Jews then, whose aim in life was above all the love of God and of family. Most of the day was spent in the study of the Talmud, and only appointed hours were set aside for business. Nevertheless, my father's business affairs often involved hundreds of thousands of rubles. Like my grandfather, my father was a contractor, an occupation which, in the first half of the nineteenth century played a great economic role, enabling the Russian government to erect fortifications, build roads and canals, and thus supply the army.

A marriage was arranged between me and Hanan Wengeroff, and at eighteen I became the bride of a man I loved deeply but knew not at all. Konotop, where my husband's parents lived, was to be my new home. . . . Most Konotop Jews, including the Wegeroffs, were *hasidim*. A daughter of *mitnagdim*, I saw and heard much that was new.

I read a lot in Konotop, especially Russian. First I read the German books I had brought from home. . . . Then I started on the Russian books which stood on the shelves of the Wengeroff library. I read. . . and taught my husband, eager to learn, German. But his chief study was Talmud. . . .

Since our betrothal, my husband experienced mystical religious moods and devoted himself to the sacred mysteries of the Kabbala [Jewish mysticism]. Then, this fervent young man yearned to make a pilgrimage to Lubavich, the seat of the head of the Lithuanian *hasidim*. The rabbi would surely have the complete answers to all disturbing questions and enigmas. . . . One morning while I was busy at household tasks, my husband came into the kitchen and told me, elatedly, excitedly, that his father had permitted him and his elder brother to go to Lubavich in the company of their rabbi.

What happened there I do not know, for my husband never spoke of the tragic experience. All I know was that this young man, hopeful and inspired, made a pilgrimage to the rabbi, hoping he would unveil the great mystery, but returned sobered. He continued his religious observances and studied with the rabbi, but the magic and ecstasy had gone. Thereafter, little by little, he began to neglect his religious observances. Then he decided to cut his beard. We had our first quarrel. . . . He reminded me that he was the man of the house and demanded my obedience and submission....

In 1859, my husband's father, grandfather, and another partner obtained the leasehold on liquor for the province of Kovno. My husband was put at the head of the office. We liquidated our business, packed our possessions, and moved.

But before I go on about myself, I want to say something about 1855, which marked a new era in Russia, especially for Jews. It was the year Alexander II ascended the throne. He liberated sixty million peasants from bondage and the Jews from their chains. He opened the gates of his main cities into which swarms of Jewish youth thronged to quench their thirst of European education in the universities.

In this brilliant period of intellectual flowering, the Jews took part in the ferment in the whole country, the rise of the fine arts, the development of the sciences. The effects of the reforms in the forties were apparent now: a succession of Jewish professors, doctors, engineers, writers, musicians, and sculptors had won recognition abroad and brought fame to their country. . . .

[In the 1860s] we moved to St. Petersburg. . . . The St. Petersburg Jewish community had a magnificent synagogue and even two rabbis—one modern and seminary-trained, the other Orthodox. But the Jewish community had abandoned many Jewish customs and traditions. The more fashionable even celebrated Christmas. . . . Passover . . . remained a festival of remembrance, joyful because it recalled not the Exodus from Egypt, but one's own childhood in the *shtetl*. The *seder* was observed, in a highly abbreviated form. Even baptized Jews kept the *seder*. Though they did not themselves make the holiday feast, they welcomed invitations from their not-yet-baptized friends.

These were the customs of the upper stratum of Jewish Petersburg. . . . Yet here. . . I often witnessed the strong feeling of solidarity among these Jews who had given up traditional Judaism. Jews in trouble with the authorities anywhere in Russia used to turn to the Petersburg Jewish community for help. Petersburg Jews spared neither money nor time. They appealed to the highest authorities on behalf of oppressed Jews. . . .

In our family, the struggle to keep the Jewish tradition went on in much the same way as in many other families. First my husband requested, and then demanded, that his wishes be fulfilled. It was not enough for him to have complete freedom over all matters outside our home: I had to "reform" myself and my home. It began with small things, intimate things, dear to me.

As soon as we settled in Petersburg, I had to discard the wig which pious Jewish women wore. It was here in Petersburg, after a violent struggle, that I ceased to keep a kosher home. Little by little, I had to drive each cherished custom from our home. "Drive" is not the right word, for I accompanied each to the door with tears and sobs. I loved my husband intensely and as faithfully as in the first days of our marriage, yet I could not submit without resistance. . . .

In the sixties the government had begun its policy of Russifying the Jews. After the Polish uprising of 1863, Russian was made compulsory in the Jewish schools in Poland and Lithuania. Then the subject matter began to be regulated. Gradually, Jewish studies were shortened to make time for the general curriculum. . . .

Then came March 1, 1881, and the sun which had risen on Jewish life in the fifties suddenly set. Alexander II was killed by a bomb on the bank of the Catherine Canal in St. Petersburg. . . .

Now different times came. The reptiles that had shunned the light emerged. Antisemitism erupted; the Jews were forced back into the ghetto. Without ceremony, the gateways to education were closed. The jubilation of the fifties and sixties turned into lamentation.

The few rights Jews had enjoyed were withdrawn. Disabilities began to pile up. Rights of residence for Jews in the cities became ever more restricted. An academic education became more and more difficult for Jews to attain, for only a very small Jewish quota was admitted to the gymnasium and even fewer were admitted to the universities.

Pogrom was a new word, coined in the eighties. The Jews of Kiev, Romny, Donotop were among the first to experience the savage assault of the local mobs.

That was the beginning.

In the eighties, with antisemitism raging all over Russia, a Jew had two choices. He could, in the name of Judaism, renounce everything that had become indispensable to him, or he could choose freedom with its offers of education and career—through baptism. Hundreds of enlightened Jews chose the latter. These apostates were not converts out of conviction, nor were they like the Marranos of an earlier age. These apostates disbelieved in all religions. . . .

My children went the way of so many others. The first to leave us was Simon. Upon learning this, my husband wrote him: "It is not becoming to abandon the camp of the besieged."

Volodya, my favorite child, no longer among the living, followed Simon's example. After completing the gymnasium in Minsk with a brilliant record, he applied to the university at St. Petersburg. He submitted his papers. The admissions clerk rejected them. "These are not your papers. You must have stolen them. You are a Jew, but these papers refer to someone with a Russian name—Vladimir." Several times more he applied to the university, with the same results. Then he took the fateful step, and was immediately accepted.[18]

CONNECTIONS

Pauline Wengeroff and her husband saw themselves as "modern." Do you agree? What does the word mean to you? What did it mean to them?

Pauline Wengeroff writes of the way many men interpreted the Enlightenment: "Preaching modern ideas like equality and fraternity in society, these young men were at home the greatest despots toward their wives, demanding ruthlessly the fulfillment of their wishes. Quite a few wives did not want to give way, but the spirit of the age won in this struggle and the weaker yielded, with bleeding hearts. This is what happened to others, and to me." What is the "spirit of the age" and why did she find it so difficult to fight it? Why do you think Pauline Wengeroff and other Jewish women tried to preserve tradition, while their husbands championed progress and sought acceptance in the outside world? Why did she think men were more attracted to the outside word than their mothers, wives, sisters, or daughters?

Pogrom is a Russian word that literally means "riot" or "destruction." It has come to mean a government-organized or inspired massacre of a minority group, particularly of Jews. Over one hundred years ago, the nobles of St. Petersburg demanded that the "people's wrath" be vented against the Jews. The peasants in the nearby town of Elizanetgrad responded with the first pogrom in modern times. A Russian writer has described the subsequent murders, rapes, and looting as the "unending torture" of a religious and ethnic minority. How did *pogroms* shape the way Jews like the Wengeroffs viewed themselves and others?

Many "enlightened" Poles favored equal rights for Jews because they believed that once Jews had those rights they would abandon their faith and end the "Jewish problem." Instead many Jews responded to freedom not by converting but by assimilating—by becoming more like the majority. They were confident that once they were "more German," "more Russian," or "more Polish," the discrimination would end. How did the events that Pauline Wengeroff details alter such beliefs?

Pauline Wengeroff believed that a Jew had only two choices: "He could, in the name of Judaism, renounce everything that had become indispensable to him, or he could choose freedom with its offers of education and career—through baptism." Were these the only choices? How do you think Hirsh Goldszmit, his sons, and grandson would have responded to her statement?

Lucy Dawidowicz writes that converts like Wengeroffs' children lived in a "shadowy land on the margins of both Gentile and Jewish society." What might be the benefits of living on the margins of society and walking in more than one world? What are the dangers of living on "the margins of society"? Why is it often an uncomfortable place to be?

Separated

Most Eastern European Jews in the late 1800s did not make their home in large cities like St. Petersberg or Warsaw. They lived in shtetlach much the way their parents and grandparents had. Yet even in the smallest towns, life was beginning to change. And like their counterparts in large cities, these Jews were also faced with important questions about membership and belonging. They too were seen as "the other."

Chaim Weizmann, who would later become Israel's first president, was born and reared in Motol, one of the many villages that dotted Russian-occupied Poland. In his day, Jews were allowed to live only in one small part of the Russian Empire, the area known as the Pale of Settlement. (See map on page 50.) In his autobiography, Weizmann writes that his *shtetl* was located in "one of the darkest and most forlorn corners of the Pale of Settlement." "Here," he writes, "in this half-townlet, half-village, I lived from the time of my birth, in 1874, till the age of eleven; and here I wove my first pictures of the Jewish and Gentile worlds."

Motol stood—and perhaps still stands—on the banks of a little river in the great marsh area which occupies much of the province of Minsk and adjacent provinces in White Russia; flat, open country, mournful and monotonous but, with its rivers, forests and lakes, not wholly unpicturesque. . . . In the spring and autumn the area was a sea of mud, in the winter a world of snow and ice; in the summer it was covered with a haze of dust. All about, in hundreds of towns and villages, Jews live, as they had lived for many generations, scattered islands in a gentile ocean; and among them my own people, on my father's and mother's side, made up a not inconsiderable proportion.

Just outside Motol, the river flowed into a large lake and emerged again at the other end on its way to join the Pina; that in turn was a tributary of the Pripet, itself a tributary of the Dnieper, which fell into the Black Sea many hundreds of miles away. On the further banks of the lake were some villages, mysterious to my childhood by virtue of their general name— "the Beyond-the-River." For them Motol (or Motelle, as we affectionately Yiddishized the name) was a sort of metropolis.

A very tiny and isolated metropolis it was, with some four or five hundred families of White Russians and less than two hundred Jewish families. Communication with the outside world was precarious and intermittent. No railway, no metaled road, passed within twenty miles of us. There was no post office. Mail was brought in by anyone from the townlet who happened to pass by the nearest railway station on his own business. Sometimes these chance messengers would hold on to the mail for days, or for weeks, distributing it when the spirit moved them. But letters played no very important part in our lives; there were few in the outside world who had reason to communicate with us.

There were streets of a kind in Motol—unpaved, of course—and two or three of them were Jewish, for even in the open spaces we drew together, for comfort, for safety, and for companionship. All the buildings were of wood, with two exceptions: the brick house of the "richest Jew in town", and the church. . . . Our synagogues, too, were of wood, both of them, the "Old Synagogue" and the "New Synagogue." How old the first was, and how new the second, I cannot tell; but this I do remember: the Old Synagogue was for the "better" class, the New for the poor. Members of the Old Synagogue seldom went to the New Synagogue; it was beneath their dignity. But occasionally my father (we belonged to the Old Synagogue) went there by special request. For among other gifts my father had that of a fine voice, and was an amateur hazan, or prayer leader, much esteemed and sought after in Motol. On the Day of Atonement he would conduct perhaps half of the services—to the edification of his townsmen and the awe and delight of his children—and sometimes he was invited to perform this office in the New Synagogue and would graciously accept.[19]

A shtetl much like the one Chaim Weizmann describes in his autobiography.

Weizmann recollects the many quarrels and intrigues that were part of shtetl life. "There were," he recalls, "occasional scandals and on one or two occasions near-riots in the synagogue." But he is also reminded of the fact that even though his father was often away on business and his mother busy with the babies in the family, he and the other older children (there were twelve in his family) were never without supervision. The rabbi kept an eye on them. So did "uncles and aunts without number in Motol, in Pinsk, and in nearby villages. They took an active, loving, and contentious interest in our welfare and our education, more especially in our religious education." The children's teachers watched out for them as well. Like other Jewish boys in the village, Weizmann started *heder* at the age of four.

Weizmann's father was seldom home because of his job. He worked as a "transportier" in the timber industry. That is, he arranged to have logs cut and then hauled to the port of Danzig where they were sold. Although his father rarely earned more than three hundred dollars a year, the family was considered fairly well-to-do by Motol's standards. After all, the Weizmanns had their own house, "some acres of land, chickens, two cows, a vegetable garden, a few fruit trees." As a result, he recalls, "we had a supply of milk, and sometimes butter; we had fruit and vegetables in season; we had enough bread—which my mother baked herself; we had fish, and we had meat once a week—on the Sabbath. And there was always plenty of fresh air."

Although no one in Motol could afford to buy a newspaper regularly, people knew what was happening in other parts of Russia. Even as a small child, Weizmann writes, he was always aware of violence against Jews in other places:

> I was a child, and I had lived in the separateness of Jewish life of our townlet. Non-Jews were for me something peripheral. But even I did not escape a consciousness of the general gloom. Almost as far as my memory goes back, I can remember the stampede—the frantic rush from the Russian prison house, the tremendous tide of migration which carried hundreds of thousands of Jews from their ancient homes to far-off lands across the seas. I was a witnesss in boyhood and early manhood to the emptying of whole villages and towns. . . . In a sense, my childhood was passed in a world which was breaking up under the impact of renewed persecution. We did not have to live in the midst of pogroms to experience their social effects, or to know that the gentile world was poisoned. I knew little of gentiles, but they became to me, from early on, the symbols of the menacing forces against which I should have to butt with all my young strength in order to make my way in life. The acquisition of knowledge was not for us so much a normal means of education as the storing up of weapons in an arsenal by means of which we hoped later to hold our own in a hostile world.[20]

Weizmann reflected on why there were no pogroms in Motol:

> In our particular corner of the world we lived on tolerable terms with our neighbors. They were a mild, kindly, hard-working lot. They had a fair quantity of land, they were not starved; some of them were even prosperous. They had—like the Jews—large families, and were always on the lookout for auxiliary occupations, one of which was the timber trade. From each peasant hut one of the men would hire himself out in the winter for the felling, and in the summer for the logging. . . .
>
> Though personal contacts might generally be friendly, the economic structure of this part of the country, and the history of its growth did not encourage good relations between Jews and peasants. There were many great estates, usually owned by Poles. The Polish landowners had about them numbers of Jews who acted as their factors, bought their timber, rented some of the land or leased the lakes for fishing. The Poles constituted a [gentry] class, though in my time their wings were already being clipped by the Russians. Inherently they were hostile to the Jews, but under the common czarist oppression they assumed a kindlier attitude. The peasants, however, had no point of direct contact with the landed gentry; the Jews stood between the two classes. The Jews were therefore the only visible instrument of the exploiting nobility. Still, the exploitation did not produce the same disastrous effects as elsewhere, for this was a landed peasantry. . . . With a piece of land, a few pigs, chickens, and cows, and employment on the side, the peasants could manage well enough. . . . Except during the Christmas and Easter festivals, when they were roused to a high pitch of religious excitement by their priests, they were quite friendly toward us. At worst they never got wholly out of hand, and there were never any pogroms in Motol or the neighboring villages.

The differences between the peasants and the Jews must not be minimized, for even in that townlet we lived mainly apart. And much more striking than the physical separation was the spiritual. We were strangers to each other's ways of thought, to each other's dreams, religions, festivals, and even languages.

We were separated from the peasants by a whole inner universe of memories and experiences. In my early childhood Zionist ideas and aspirations were already awake in Russian Jewry. My father was not yet a Zionist, but the house was steeped in rich Jewish tradition, and Palestine was at the center of the ritual, a longing for it implicit in our life.[21]

CONNECTIONS

The word *pale* means to enclose or "fence in." The expression "beyond the pale" refers to something that is totally unacceptable or unreasonable. How do both terms apply to the Pale of Settlement? Why does Weizmann call it a prison house? What does his definition suggest about what it means to live "beyond the pale."

How did Christians and Jews in Motol learn to fear one another? To what extent were fears and suspicions passed from one generation to the next? What were the consequences of the way both Jewish and non-Jewish parents taught their children to regard one another?

Why didn't religious excitement during Christmas and Easter get out of hand in Motol? Why were there no pogroms there?

How did the pogroms of the 1880s shape the way Weizmann viewed himself and others? The way he and his family prepared for the future? What social, economic, religious, and political conditions seem to encourage violence against Jews? Which does Weizmann consider the most significant? Which factor or combination of factors do you think is most significant? Which factor or combination of factors seems most likely to turn hate into acts of violence?

David Schoem, a sociology professor, wrote about ethnic divisions in the United States:

The effort it takes for us to know so little about one another across racial and ethnic groups is truly remarkable. That we can live so closely together, that our lives can be so intertwined socially, economically, and politically, and that we can spend so many years of study in grade school and even in higher education and yet still manage to be ignorant of one another is clear testimony to the deep-seated roots of this human and national tragedy. What we do learn along the way is to place heavy reliance on stereotypes, gossip, rumor, and fear to shape our lack of knowledge.[22]

How does the isolation Schoem describes apply to *shtetlach* like the one Weizmann describes? How does isolation shape values and beliefs? Opportunities to know others?

Find out more about the life of Chaim Weizmann. How did he come to leave Russia? What part did he play in making Israel a reality? How did his early years in Motol shape not only his work as a Zionist but also the way he viewed the world?

Jewish Pride

The Russian government made no secret of its antisemitism. Jews were discriminated against in every part of the Russian Empire. And from time to time, those expressions of hatred led to violence in the form of pogroms. That violence shaped the way Jews throughout Russia viewed the world around them as well as the ways they defined their identity.

Golda Mabovitch was born in Kiev, Russia, in 1898. She is better know today as Golda Meir, a founder of the State of Israel and the first woman to serve as its prime minister. When she was in her late seventies, she described her earliest memories of life in Russia.

> I must have been very young, maybe only three and a half or four. We lived then on the first floor of a house in Kiev, and I can still recall distinctly hearing about a pogrom that was to descend on us. I didn't know then, of course, what a pogrom was, but I knew it had something to do with being Jewish and with the rabble that used to surge through town, brandishing knives and huge sticks, screaming "Christ killers" as they looked for the Jews, and who were now going to do terrible things to me and to my family.
>
> I can remember how I stood on the stairs that led to the second floor, where another Jewish family lived, holding hands with their little daughter and watching our fathers trying to barricade the entrance with boards of wood. That pogrom never materialized, but to this day I remember how scared I was and how angry that all my father could do to protect me was to nail a few planks together while we waited for the hooligans to come. And, above all, I remember being aware that this was happening to me because I was Jewish, which made me different from most of the other children in the yard. It was a feeling that I was to know again many times during my life—the fear, the frustration, the consciousness of being different and the profound instinctive belief that if one wanted to survive, one had to take effective action about it personally.[23]

Those feelings remained with her long after Golda, her mother, and fourteen-year-old sister moved to Pinsk in 1903. They stayed with relatives there, while her father went to the United States to make his fortune. In Pinsk, her older sister Sheyna became involved in revolutionary causes. According to Meir, Sheyna was "an earnest, dedicated member of the Socialist-Zionist movement, as such doubly dangerous in the eyes of police and liable to punishment. Not only were she and her friends 'conspiring' to overthrow the all-powerful tsar, but they also proclaimed their dream of bringing into existence a Jewish socialist state in Palestine. In the Russia of the early twentieth century, even a fourteen- or fifteen-year-old schoolgirl who held such views would be arrested for subversive activity, and I still remember hearing the screams of young men and women being brutally beaten in the police station around the corner from where we lived."[24]

The girls' mother also heard those screams and begged Sheyna to leave the movement. The teenager stubbornly refused. Five-year-old Golda loved to curl up in a corner and listen to her sister's friends whenever they gathered at her house. She learned that they were involved in a "special kind of struggle that concerned not only the Russian people, but also, and more especially, the Jews." Of that struggle, Meir wrote:

A great deal has already been written . . . about the Zionist movement, and most people by now have at least some notion of what the word "Zionism" means and that it has to do with the return of the Jewish people to the land of their forefathers—the Land of Israel, as it is called in Hebrew. But perhaps even today not everyone realizes that this remarkable movement sprang up spontaneously, and more or less simultaneously, in various parts of Europe toward the end of the nineteenth century. It was like a drama that was being enacted in different ways on different stages in different languages but that dealt with the same theme everywhere: that the so-called Jewish problem (of course, it was really a Christian problem) was basically the result of Jewish homelessness and that it could not, and would not, be solved unless the Jews had a land of their own again. . . .

Although the yearning of the Jews for their own land was not the direct result of the pogroms (the idea of the Jewish resettlement of Palestine had been urged by Jews and even some non-Jews long before the word "pogrom" became part of the vocabulary of European Jewry), the Russian pogroms of my childhood gave the idea immediacy, especially when it became clear that the Russian government itself was using them as scapegoats of the regime's struggle to put down the revolutionary movement.

Most of the young Jewish revolutionaries in Pinsk, although united in their determination to press for an end to the tsarist regime and in their immense enthusiasm with which to liberate Russia's exploited and oppressed masses, were divided at that point into two main groups. There were the members of the Bund [the General Union of Jewish Workers in Lithuania, Poland and Russia], who believed that the solution to the plight of the Jews in Russia and elsewhere would be found when socialism prevailed. Once the economic and social structure of the Jews was changed, said the Bundists, antisemitism would totally disappear. In that better, brighter, socialist world, the Jews could still, if they so desired, retain their cultural identity, go on speaking Yiddish, maintain whatever customs and traditions they chose, eat whatever foods they wanted to eat. But there would be no reason at all for clinging to the obsolete idea of Jewish nationhood.

The Paolei Zion (Labor Zionists), like Sheyna, saw it all differently. They believed that the so-called Jewish problem had other roots, and its solution therefore had to be more far-reaching and radical than merely the righting of economic wrongs or social inequalities. In addition to the shared social idea, they clung to a national ideal based on the concept of Jewish peoplehood and the re-establishment of Jewish independence. At the time, although both these movements were secret and illegal, ironically enough the bitterest enemies of Zionism were the Bundists, and most of the debates that whirled about my head whenever Sheyna and her friends got together in our house had to do with the conflict between the two groups.[25]

In April of 1903, during Easter, the first pogrom of the twentieth century took place in Kishinev, then the capital of Bessarabia, a province in the southwestern part of the Russian Empire. At the time about 50,000 Jews lived in the city; they made up about 45 percent of its population. Members of the Bund explained the causes and the effects of the pogrom in a proclamation addressed to "all Jewish workers, male and female."

What do we see in the Kishinev pogrom?

A month earlier a Christian boy was killed in Dubosar, not far from Kishinev. The murderers were not found and the antisemitic paper *Bessarabets* disseminated the rumor that Jews had murdered the boy to use his blood for religious purposes. The antisemitic press did not cease from inciting Christians against the Jews, to awaken all

Members of a Labor Zionist youth group.

those base feelings and instincts among the folk, and the utterly debased mob began to attack Jews with a frenzy. The huge mass of police and Cossacks who descend like locusts on workers at every demonstration, at every battle with capitalists and the government, who rout the demonstrators in an instant, couldn't restrain a few hundred angry rioters (there are more than three hundred policemen, three army regiments, three brigades and a battalion of reserves stationed in Kishinev). The government did not step in because it didn't want to, because it has a vested interest in such things as pogroms.

How can we overcome the causes that bring about national hated, antisemitism and pogroms, and what can we do when pogroms break out?

The so-called "Friends of the Jewish People" spill rivers of tears over the new Jewish calamity; the [St. Petersburg daily] *Fraynd* [Friend] wrings its hands in despair; the [Warsaw weekly] *Yiddishe Folkstaytung* [Jewish People's Paper] instructs us to be as still as the waters, as low as the grass, while the Zionist poet [S. Frug] laments, "How weak is our hand to do battle, how great and heavy is our woe."

Only slaves can talk this way, people who are accustomed to enduring all acts of violence submissively, who don't believe in their own powers and who always await salvation from other quarters—from God, from friends, from the government.

This is not the way we, Jewish workers, think. The struggle that we've been waging for so many years has convinced us that help lies in us alone. Our unity has increased our power; our solidarity and readiness to protect our interests at all times have instilled fear in our enemies.

Ignorant, debased and enraged masses took part in the Kishinev pogrom. The intelligent, class-conscious Christian worker is our comrade; he fights together with us under a single flag, under the flag of international socialism. Spreading class consciousness, aiding the growth of the socialist movement that will destroy the whole capitalist order—this is the best and only way to bring an end to antisemitism and pogroms.

What, then, should we do during the pogroms themselves?

We must answer violence with violence, no matter where it comes from. Not with sweet words but with arms in our hands can we prevail upon the frenzied pogromists. We mustn't hide in attics but must go out face to face, "with a mighty arm" to fight these beasts.

Let not the Kishinev pogrom weaken our faith in our sacred ideal. With hatred and with a threefold curse on our lips let us sew the shrouds for the Russian autocratic regime, for the antisemitic band of swindlers, for the whole capitalist system. May the number of conscious and active fighters for socialism keep growing; may the solidarity with our fellow workers of other nations keep on growing!

Down with antisemitism!

Down with Tsardom!

Long live international proletarian solidarity!

Long live socialism![26]

At the end of two days of rioting in Kishinev, 47 Jews were dead, 424 wounded, 700 houses burned, and 600 shops looted.[27] The pogrom shocked not only Jews around the world but also many Christians. In cities and towns throughout the Russian Empire, young Jews gathered weapons and formed dozens of self-defense groups. Many of them did not belong to any political party. Others were Bundists or Zionists like Chaim Weizmann, who was then studying chemistry in Switzerland. In his autobiography, he recalls his own reaction to the massacre at Kishinev:

The Kishinev pogrom was the reply of czarist Russia to the cry of freedom of its Jewish subjects. We knew intuitively that it was not to be the last, but was rather the signal for a whole series. The massacres were deliberately organized, carefully planned, and everywhere carried out under the eyes of the civil and military authorities, which stepped in only when they judged that the slaughter and pillaging had gone far enough. The general Russian press was forbidden to tell the true story. . . . For the general Russian public it was reported that there had been "incidents," drunken brawls of no particular importance.

Perhaps the most tormenting feature of the Kishinev pogrom was the fact that the Jews had allowed themselves to be slaughtered like sheep, without offering general resistance. . . . [Only] here and there younger people, who happened to be in possession of firearms, put up a fight; they were at once disarmed by the military.

I had intended to proceed from Warsaw to Geneva. I abandoned my classes, such as they were, and returned to the [the Jewish Pale of Settlement]. Together with friends and acquaintances I proceeded to organize self-defense groups in all the larger Jewish centers. Not long afterward, when a pogrom broke out in Homel, not far from

A student and a member of the Bund.

Pinsk, the hooligans were suddenly confronted by a strongly organized Jewish self-defense corps. Again the military interfered, and did its best to disarm the Jews; but at least the self-defense had broken the first wave of the attack, which was not able to gather again its original momentum. Thus, throughout the Pale, an inverted guerrilla warfare spread, between the Jews and the Russian authorities, the former trying to maintain order, the latter encouraging disorder. The Jews grew more and more exasperated and our life therefore more and more intolerable.[28]

CONNECTIONS

In listening to her sister and her sister's friends, Golda Meir wrote that she learned "at least one important nonpolitical lesson": "that nothing in life just happens. It isn't enough to believe in something; you have to have the stamina to meet obstacles and overcome them, to struggle." How important is that lesson? What other lessons might she have learned?

Chaim Weizmann wrote that "perhaps the most tormenting feature of the Kishinev pogrom was the fact that the Jews had allowed themselves to be slaughtered like sheep, without offering general resistance." The phrase "like a sheep to slaughter" appears in the Bible. In Isaiah, it is written: "He was oppressed and he was afflicted, yet he opened not his mouth; he is brought as a lamb to the slaughter, and as a sheep before her shearer is dumb, so he openeth not his mouth." What does that passage mean to you? Why did it take on special meaning to Weizmann and other Jews in the Russian Empire in 1903? Why did he personally find the lack of resistance so disturbing?

There were 45 pogroms, including the one in Kishinev, between April of 1903 and the end of 1904. As a result of the efforts of both Zionists and Bundists, Jews actively defended themselves in over a third of these pogroms. A man who participated in the defense of one town claimed that "despite the suffering it was good for the soul. There are no longer the former downtrodden, timid Jews. A new-born unprecedented type appeared on the scene—a man who defends his dignity."[29] How was his response to self-defense similar to Weizmann's? Why did both believe that Jews had to fight back to maintain their self-respect? What non-violent choices were available to Jews? What were the advantages and disadvantages of those choices? Why do you think many regarded self-defense as the only choice that preserved "Jewish dignity"? What is "Jewish dignity"? Was violence the only way to preserve it?

Leo Tolstoy, the great Russian writer, was silent during the pogroms of the 1880s. But after the massacre at Kishinev, he spoke out. He argued that the "chief culprit" was "our government and its clergy which rouse in the people animal emotions and fanaticism, and with its gang of officials and brigands."[30] He saw the pogrom itself as "a direct result of that propaganda of falsehood and violence which our government carried on with such energy." How can words be weapons? How do they turn neighbor against neighbor? Should people be held responsible for their words? Are people also responsible for the words they fail to say?

Maxim Gorky, yet another noted Russian writer, stated, "Cultivated society is not less guilty of the disgraceful and horrible deeds committed at Kishinev than the actual murderers and ravishers. Its members' guilt consists in the fact that, not merely did they not protect the victim, but that they rejoiced over the murders; it consists chiefly in committing themselves for long years to be corrupted by man-haters and persons who have long enjoyed the disgusting glory of being the lackeys of power and the glorifiers of lies." According to Gorky, what are the responsibilities of bystanders? How does Gorky define a society's "universe of obligation"? Do you agree? How does his definition apply to today's world?

Chaim Weizmann joined a group called Hovevei Zion (Lovers of Zion) while attending a Russian high school in Pinsk in the 1880s. Compare his memories of the early days of the movement with those of Golda Meir. What similarities do you notice? How do you account for differences?

> Looking back from the vantage point of present-day Zionism, I can see that we had not the slightest idea of how the practical ends of the movement were to be realized. We knew that the doors of Palestine were closed to us. We knew that every Jew who entered Palestine was given "the red ticket," which he had to produce on demand, and by virtue of which he could be expelled at once by the Turkish authorities. We knew that the Turkish law forbade the acquisition of land by Jews. Perhaps if we had considered the matter too closely, or tried to be too systematic, we would have been frightened off. We merely went ahead in a small, blind, persistent way. Jews settled in Palestine, and they were not expelled. . . . Things got done, somehow; not big things, but enough to whet the appetite and keep us going.
>
> The obstinacy and persistence of the movement cannot be understood except in terms of faith. This faith was part of our make-up; our Jewishness and our Zionism were interchangeable; you could not destroy the second without destroying the first. We did not need propagandizing.[31]

Weizmann did not view Zionism as a rejection of Russian, Polish, or any other culture. He later wrote, "I think I may say that we spoke and wrote the [Russian] language better, were more intimately acquainted with its literature, than most Russians. But we were rooted heart and soul in our own culture, and it did not occur to us to give it up in deference to another." Does taking pride in one's own culture mean rejection of other cultures? Is it possible to take pride in who you are without putting someone else down? Why is it often hard to do so? Why might it have been particularly difficult in tsarist Russia?

In 1917, one of the bloodiest race riots in American history took place in East St. Louis, Illinois. It was started by white workers who were protesting the hiring of African Americans. By the time the violence ended, 39 blacks had been murdered and nearly 6,000 others had been driven from their homes. The editors of the *Forward,* a Yiddish newspaper founded by Eastern European Jews, wrote, "Kishinev and St. Louis—the same soil, the same people. It is a distance of four and half thousand miles between these two cities and yet they are so close and so similar to each other. . . . Actually twin sisters, which could easily be mistaken for each other."[32] What is the similarity the editors of the *Forward* saw? How important was that likeness to the violence that shook both cities?

In *Thirteen Ways of Looking at a Black Man,* Henry Louis Gates, Jr. recalls the impact that rioting in Watts, a poor neighborhood in Los Angeles that was home mainly to African Americans, had on him. He was 14 years old at the time and attending an integrated summer camp. As he watched himself being watched by the white campers, he says, he "experienced that strange combination of power and powerlessness that you feel when the actions of another black person affect your own life simply because you both are black." How did that same "combination of power and powerlessness" affect Jews in Russia in the early 1900s?

Golda Meir's family settled in Milwaukee, Wisconsin, not long after the pogrom in Kishinev. Find out how she became a Zionist. How did the attitudes and values she learned as a child in Russia shape her work as a Zionist? How did those attitudes and values shape her view of the world?

Hatred

Wislawa Szymborska, a Pole who won the Nobel Prize for Literature in 1996, describes
"hatred" in a poem.

See how efficient it still is,
how it keeps itself in shape—
our century's hatred.
How easily it vaults the tallest obstacles.
How rapidly it pounces, tracks us down.

It is not like other feelings.
At once both older and younger.
It gives birth itself to the reasons that give it life.
When it sleeps, it's never eternal rest.
And sleeplessness won't sap its strength; it feeds it.

One religion or another—
whatever gets it ready, in position.
One fatherland or another—
whatever helps it get a running start.
Just also works well at the outset
until hate gets its own momentum going.
Hatred. Hatred.
Its face twisted in a grimace
of erotic ecstasy.

Oh these other feelings, listless weaklings.
Since when does brotherhood draw crowds?
Has compassion ever finished first?
Does doubt ever really rouse the rabble?
Only hatred has just what it takes.

Gifted, diligent, hard-working.
Need we mention all the songs it has composed?
All the pages it has added to our history books?
All the human carpets it has spread
over countless city squares and football fields?

Let's face it:
it knows how to make beauty.
The splendid fire-glow in midnight skies.
Magnificent bursting bombs in rosy dawns.
You can't deny the inspiring pathos of ruins
and a certain bawdy humor to be found
in the sturdy column jutting from their midst.

Hatred is a master of contrast—between explosions and dead quiet,
red blood and white snow.
Above all, it never tires
of its leitmotif—the impeccable executioner
towering over its soiled victim.

It's always ready for new challenges.
If it has to wait awhile, it will.
They say it's blind. Blind?
It has a sniper's keen sight
and gazes unflinchingly at the future
as only it can.[33]

CONNECTIONS

What words does Wislawa Szymborska use to describe hatred? What factors does she consider most important in keeping hate alive? How are her views similar to those expressed in Readings 7 and 8? How do you account for differences?

People often speak of hatred as "blind"? Why does Szymborska describe it as having "a sniper's keen sight"? Do you agree?

If you were to write a poem about hatred, what words would you use to describe it? How is it like other emotions? How is it different? Why does Szymborska see it as more powerful than other emotions? How does hatred get its power?

In the introduction to the guide that Facing History and Ourselves created for his film *Schindler's List,* Steven Spielberg wrote of the Holocaust, "Even today the world has not yet learned the lesson of those terrible years. There are far too many places where hate, intolerance, and genocide still exist. Thus *Schindler's List* is no less a "Jewish story" or a "German story" than it is a human story. And its subject matter applies to every generation." To what extent do his comments apply to the hatred that inspired the Kishinev Massacre? To what extent is he describing "our century's hatred"?

Traveling Third Class

As one crisis after another rocked Eastern Europe, Jews responded in a variety of ways. This reading, taken from a story by Sholem Aleichem, considers not only why many of them left home but also what they found in the outside world.

By the late 1800s, dozens of small towns in both Poland and the Pale of Settlement were linked to the outside world by newly built railroads. They allowed many people to journey from home for the first time. Sholem Rabinovich, the great Yiddish writer better known as Sholem Aleichem, urged them to travel third class so they could "feel right at home."

In fact, if you happen to be in a car whose passengers are exclusively Jews, you may feel a bit too much at home. Granted, third class is not the height of luxury; if you don't use your elbows, you'll never find a seat; the noise level, the sheer hubbub is ear-splitting; you can never be sure where you end and where your neighbors begin . . . and yet there's no denying that's an excellent way to meet them. Everyone knows who you are, where you're bound for, and what you do, and you know the same about everyone. At night you can save yourself the bother of having to fall asleep, because there's always someone to talk to—and if you're not in the mood to talk, someone else will be glad to do it for you. Who expects to sleep on a train ride anyway? Talking is far better, because you never know what may come of it. I should only live another year of my life for each time I've seen perfect strangers on the train end up by making a business deal, arranging a match for their children, or learning something worth knowing from each other. . . .

When you go third class and wake up in the morning to discover that you've left your *tefillin* and your prayer shawl at home, there isn't any cause for alarm—you only need to ask and you'll be given someone else's, along with whatever else you require. All that's expected of you in return, once you're done praying, is to open your suitcase and display your own wares. Vodka, cake, a hard-boiled egg, a drumstick, a piece of fish—it's all grist for the mill. Perhaps you have an apple, an orange, a piece of strudel? Out with it, no need to be ashamed! Everyone will be glad to share it with you, no one stands on ceremony here. A train ride and good company, you understand, are two things that create an appetite. . . . . . And of course, if you happen to have a wee bit of wine with you, there's no lack of volunteer tasters, each with his own verdict and name for it. . . .

Before long each of us not only knows all about the others' troubles, he knows about every trial and tribulation that ever befell a Jew anywhere. It's enough to warm the cockles of your heart!

When you travel third class and arrive in some town and don't know where to stay, you have a car full of Jews to help you out. In fact, the number of different places recommended will tally exactly with the number of Jews in the car. "The Hotel Frankfurt," says one of them, singing the praises of his choice. "It's bright and it's cheery, it's clean and it's breezy, it's the biggest bargain in town." "The Hotel Frankfurt?" exclaims someone else. "God forbid! It's dark and it's dreary, it's sordid and it's sleazy, it's the biggest gyp joint around. If you really want to enjoy yourself, I suggest you try the Hotel New York." "The only reason I can think of for staying in the

New York," puts in another traveler, "is that you're homesick for bedbugs. Here, hand me your bag and come with me to my favorite, the Hotel Russia. It's the only place for a Jew."

Of course, having given him your bag you had better keep an eye on him to make sure he doesn't make off with it. . . . but I ask you, where in this wonderful world of ours aren't there thieves nowadays? Either you're fated to meet up with one or you're not. If it's in your crystal ball to be robbed, you can be cleaned out in broad daylight, and no amount of prayers or policemen will make the slightest difference. If anything, you'll thank your lucky stars that you got away with your life. . . .

In a word, go third class.[34]

Like Arnold Zable's ancestors (Reading 1), Sholem Aleichem's readers were people "on the verge of moving on." They had to decide: "Do we stay, persist, take root within this kingdom, or do we take to the road again? Perhaps it is safer, greener, beyond the next river, over the next mountain-range, across yet another border." In the late 1800s and early 1900s, thousands took to the road again. Some headed for Warsaw and other large cities in Europe, while others set sail for Palestine or the United States.

CONNECTIONS

Where is home for the people in the third-class car? How have they turned the car into a "home away from home"? What symbols in the story bind Jew to Jew? Do those symbols still link Jews today?

Bella Chagall was the youngest child and the only girl in a Hasidic family that made its home in the town of Vitebsk. Her future husband, the artist Marc Chagall, also grew up there. At a time when few Jewish girls received even an elementary school education, Bella Chagall was admitted to the University of Moscow. Her academic work was so outstanding that not even the Russians could deny her a place. In 1939, long after Bella and her husband had settled in Paris, she wrote her autobiography. In the foreword, she noted she and her brothers carried "our lost heritage, like a piece of our father's shroud, the breath of home." How is her view of her heritage similar to Sholem Aleichem's? What differences seem most striking? Like Sholem Aleichem, Bella Chagall wrote in Yiddish. Why do you think they did so even though they were both fluent in Russian?

In the 1960s, one of Sholem Aleichem's most popular stories was turned into a musical called *Fiddler on the Roof* even though none of his stories refer to a fiddler on a roof. That image comes from the work of Marc Chagall. In his autobiography, he wrote of a time when a family search for his grandfather led to the discovery that, "because of the fine weather, Grandfather had climbed up on the roof, had sat down on one of the chimney-pipes and was regaling himself with carrots. Not a bad picture." Later Chagall would combine that image of his grandfather with one of a favorite uncle who played the violin "like a shoemaker."

How does a "fiddler on a roof" keep from falling off? What does the image of the fiddler suggest about Jewish life in the late 1800s and early 1900s? What does it suggest about their future? In the 1980s, an African American poet described herself as an acrobat walking a tightrope. What does she mean? In what ways might her feelings resemble those of a fiddler on a roof? How might they differ?

1 Arnold Zable, *Jewels and Ashes,* (Harcourt Brace, 1991), 12.

2 Ibid., 11.

3 Bernard Weinryb, *The Jews of Poland: A Social and Economic History of the Jewish Community in Poland from 1100 to 1800* (Jewish Publication Society, 1972), 38-39.

4 Arnold Zable, *Jewels and Ashes*, 12.

5 Bernard Weinryb, *The Jews of Poland,* 95

6 Ibid., 96.

7 Ibid.

8 Quoted in *The Jews of Poland* by Myer S. Lew (Goldston, 1944), 125-127.

9 Suzanne Goldsmith, *A City Year* (New Press, 1993), 275.

10 Nathan Hanover, *Abyss of Despair*, trans. by Abraham J. Mesch. (Transaction Books, 1983), 27-28.

11 Elie Wiesel, *Souls on Fire: Portraits and Legends of Hasidic Masters* (Random House, 1972), 25-27.

12 Ibid., 20-22.

13 Quoted in Isaac Lewin, *The Jewish Community in Poland* (Philosophical Library, 1985), 22-23.

14 Betty Lifton, *The King of Children: A Biography of Janusz Korczak* (Farrar, Straus and Giroux, 1988), 20-21.

15 Ibid., 22-23.

16 Ibid., 75.

17 Judah Leib Gordon, "For Whom Do I Toil?" Trans. by D. Goldman in *The Jew in the Modern World*, eds. Paul Mendes-Flohr & Yehuda Reinharz (Oxford University Press, 1995), 386.

18 From *The Golden Tradition: Jewish Life and Thought in Eastern Europe,* edited and translated by Lucy S. Dawidowicz, c 1967 by Lucy S. Dawidowicz. Reprinted by permission of Henry Holt and Company, Inc.

19 Chaim Weizmann, *Trial and Error* (Harper, 1949), 3-4

20 Ibid., 17-18.

21 Ibid., 9-10.

22 David Schoem, *Inside Separate Worlds* (University of Michigan Press, 1991), 3.

23 Golda Meir, *My Life* (Putnam, 1975), 13-14.

24 Ibid., 22.

25 Ibid., 23-25.

26 "Proclamation of the Jewish Labor Bund" in *The Literature of Destruction: Jewish Responses to Catastrophe,* ed. David G. Roskies (Jewish Publication Society, 1989), 154-156.

27 Quoted by Slomo Lambroza "The Pogroms of 1903-1906," in *Pogroms: Anti-Jewish Violence in Modern Russian History,* eds. John D. Klier and Shlomo Lambroza (Cambridge University Press, 1992), 200.

28 Chaim Weizmann, *Trial and Error,* 79-80.

29 Quoted by Slomo Lambroza "The Pogroms of 1903-1906," in *Pogroms: Anti-Jewish Violence in Modern Russian History*, eds. John D. Klier and Shlomo Lambroza, 209.

30 Quoted in Cyrus Adler, ed., *The Voice of America on Kishineff* (Philadelphia, 1904), 241.

31 Chaim Weizmann, *Trial and Error.*

32 Quoted in Jonathan Kaufman, *Broken Alliance* (Simon & Schuster, 1988), 29-30.

33 Wislawa Szymborska, *View with a Grain of Sand: Selected Poems,* trans. by Stanislaw Baranczak and Clare Cavanagh (Harcourt Brace, 1995), 181-183.

34 Sholem Aleichem, "Third Class" in *Tevye the Dairyman and the Railroad Stories,* trans. Hillel Halkin (Shocken, 1987), 281-284.

3. At the Crossroads

White and brown, black and yellow,
Mix the colors with one another.
We are all sisters and brothers
Of one father and one mother,
And God created us all.

From "Brothers" by Y. L. Peretz

In this popular Yiddish poem, Y.L. Peretz expresses a longing for a world that values what we have in common rather than the things that set *us* apart from *them*. In his own world—Russian-occupied Poland—differences were viewed with suspicion and fear. Chapter 2 revealed how those suspicions and fears often led to discrimination and even violence in times of crisis. In Peretz's day, the late 1800s, a new idea—nationalism— was inspiring new divisions in Europe. In the past, people used the word nation to refer to an ethnic group, a people who share a language and a culture. Now, the word was increasingly used to describe those who share not only a language and a culture but also a homeland.

For groups that did not have a land of their own, nationalism became a crusade. Sociologist Theodore Abel defined it as a feeling "more positive than patriotism" and one that often involved "a certain amount of ethnocentrism, a feeling of superiority of one's nation over other nations." It was that kind of passionate nationalism that led a young Serbian to assassinate the Austrian Archduke Ferdinand and his wife on June 28, 1914, in the small town of Sarajevo.

Within a month, one European nation after another had chosen sides in what quickly became "the first world war." On one side was the Austro-Hungarian Empire, Germany, and their allies. On the other was Serbia, Russia, France, Britain, and their allies. By the time the war officially ended on November 11, 1918, 30 countries had been involved in the fighting and over 10 million soldiers had been killed. What did not die was the extreme nationalism that sparked the conflict and fed its growth. It influenced the treaty that ended that war and shaped the choices governments and individuals made in the years that followed.

During the war, the three empires that had long dominated Eastern Europe disappeared. In 1917, the Russian Empire collapsed and a new Communist government took charge of the nation. By 1918, the Austrian and German empires had also fallen apart. As a result, Poland and many of the other countries that had been part of those empires won their freedom. In each, leaders had to decide what kind of nation they wanted to build: Would it be a Poland only for Poles? Or would membership be open to everyone in the country? How would minorities be treated? Could they become citizens? If so, would they have to give up their identity to belong or would their right to be different from the majority be protected?

This chapter focuses on the ways people in Poland answered such questions in the years before and after World War I and the consequences of their responses. The chapter begins with readings that consider how people have defined the term nation at various times in history. The readings that follow describe the impact of those definitions on Jews in Poland before and after independence. The chapter also explores the ways Jews and other groups responded to the opportunities and the challenges of those years.

Nationalism and "Race"

In the late 1800s, a growing number of ethnic groups within the great empires of Eastern Europe longed for freedom. Each dreamed, schemed, plotted, and planned for the day when its people would be united in a single nation. Each also struggled with the question of who would be included in that nation. Would everyone who lived in a country be a citizen? Or would Poland be only for Poles?

In the late 1700s, the leaders of the American and French revolutions declared that anyone who shared their nation's ideals and was committed to its goals could become a citizen. Britain's leaders held similar views. Yet few leaders in any of the three nations practiced what they preached. For example, in the late 1700s each of the three limited participation in government to white men who owned property. Still the idea of equal rights for all profoundly influenced the way each came to view the individuals and groups that either had lived within its borders for generations or recently arrived as immigrants.

By the early 1800s, a new idea was shaping the way many people—including some in the United States, France, and Britain—were defining the word *nation*. They saw a nation as a "race," a group of people who are somehow related to one another and share characteristics passed from one generation to the next. Among the leaders in this movement were a number of Germans who viewed people of other "races" as a threat to the unity of their own nation.

By the late 1800s, this new understanding of the word *nation* had the support of a number of scientists who claimed that "racial differences" explained many aspects of human behavior. They then ranked the "races" in ways that strengthened old prejudices, gave new life to long-held myths, and fostered misinformation. Few people who belonged to the so-called "superior race" questioned the work of these "scientists." Instead many Germans and other Europeans took pride in tracing their ancestry to the "Aryans," a mythical people that left India in the distant past and carried its language and culture westward. Increasingly, these Europeans believed that as the descendants of the "Aryans," they were superior to other "races," including the Jewish or "Semitic race." In the past, Jews were targeted for discrimination because of their religious beliefs. Now they were hated because of their "race." The word antisemitism, which literally means "against Semites," was coined to describe this new hatred of Jews.

Scientists who showed the flaws in racist thinking were ignored. In the late 1800s, the German Anthropological Society tried to determine whether there really were racial differences between Jewish and "Aryan" children. After studying nearly seven million students in Germany, the society concluded that that the two groups were more alike than different. Historian George Mosse writes:

> This survey should have ended controversies about the existence of pure Aryans and Jews. However, it seems to have had surprisingly little impact. The idea of race had been infused with myths, stereotypes, and subjectivities long ago, and a scientific survey could change little. The idea of pure, superior races and the concept of a racial enemy solved too many pressing problems to be easily discarded.[1]

Nationalism developed in Poland as these ideas about "race" were being discussed in newspapers, taught in schools, and preached from pulpits. They affected the way many Polish nationalists viewed the question of membership. The ideas of two men,

The Jews of Poland 73

political rivals, dominated that discussion: Jozef Pilsudski, the hero of Poland's fight for independence, and Roman Dmowski, the "father" of Polish nationalism.

"In Pilsudski's view," writes historian Norman Davies, "the nation was a product of history, a community sharing the same values and loyalties, though not necessarily the same ethnicity or origins."[2] Within such a Poland, there was room for a wide variety of ethnic groups as long as each was loyal to the nation as a whole. Pilsudski's idea of a multi-ethnic state was drawn from the old Commonwealth of Poland-Lithuania. It also had much in common with the way the French, the British, and the Americans had long defined a nation.

Dmowski had a very different view. He saw nations as "the result of the God-given division of mankind into distinct entities each possessing its own exclusive language, territory, and history." According to Davies, "he came extremely close to thinking of the nation as a race, a biological kinship group possessing its own 'blood' and its own genetic 'stock'."[3] Dmowski blamed most of the evils of modern Europe on the "indiscriminate mixing of the peoples." He wanted to create a Poland that would be only for Poles. He and his followers regarded Jews and other minorities in Poland as "problems."

CONNECTIONS

Most scientists today believe that there is no such thing as a "race." They point out that there are more genetic variations among those within a single "racial" group than among the world's population as a whole. Why do you think we have no difficulty in telling individuals apart in our own group, but some say that *they* all look alike—even though there are more differences among us than there are between *us* and *them*? What is the relationship between seeing *them* as looking alike and perceiving "the other" as "less than human"?

How do you decide who belongs and who does not? What effect do your decisions have on the way you view others? What effect do those decisions have on the way you see yourself? How do they influence the way you define your universe of obligation—the circle of individuals and groups toward whom they have responsibilities, to whom societies rules apply, and whose injuries call for amends? How do nations decide who belongs and who does not? What effect do their decisions have on the way individuals and groups view themselves and others? What effect do such decisions have on the ways they define their universe of obligation?

To what extent do you practice what you preach? How important is it that you try to do so? To what extent do nations practice what they preach? How important is it that they try to do so? How important is it they be perceived as doing so?

Sociologists say that what people perceive as true is sometimes more important than the truth. How do Mosse's comments about the flawed science of "race" support that view? Give an example from your own experiences that supports the idea that what things really *are* is often less significant than what those things mean in everyday life. Write a working definition of the word *perception*. Use your journal to express your ideas about the relationship between our perception of the world and reality. As you continue reading, you may wish to refer back to your ideas to revise or expand your thinking.

Write a working definition of the word *nation*. Use your definition to explain the meaning of the word *nationalism*. Keep in mind that the ending *ism* refers to a doctrine or principle. Expand your definitions as you continue reading.

The fighting in the Balkans in the early 1990s prompted columnist A. M. Rosenthal to write, "Bosnians, Serbs, Croats, Albanians, Macedonians, Muslim or Christian, come out of a world where for centuries loyalties were built on the importance of separateness. The separate clan, tribe, family and village gave protection. The histories and fantasies of the individual group gave meaning and texture to life. The separateness created fear of others, which was intensified when the outsider was too close, a neighbor. Leaders used the fears to build their own power—feudal dukes once, now onetime Communist bosses like President Slobodan Milosevic of Serbia are building new power on old separations."[4] To what extent are his remarks true of nationalism in the late 1800s? To what extent are they true of the world today? How did scientists who used "racial differences" to explain human behavior intensify "fear of others"? How did leaders take advantage of those fears?

In *The Three Arched Bridge*, Ismail Kadare, an Albanian writer, noted, "The maps and flags of the world bear witness to dozens of states, kingdoms, languages, and peoples, but in fact there are only two peoples who live in two kingdoms: this world, and the next." The novel goes on to describe a world where legends, lies, and rumors make it impossible to separate myth from reality. What does Kadare suggest is at the heart of every "state," "kingdom," and "nation"? What does he think the maps and flags obscure?

Nationalism and European Jews

No idea in the 1800s had more appeal than nationalism. It inspired people the world over, including many Jews in Poland.

The Jews of Poland were by no means united. They did not respond to questions of membership and belonging in the same ways. Some saw themselves as Polish patriots. As one Jew declared in the early 1900s, "We do not ask anyone for certification of our Polishness, because it is already proven by the beating of our hearts and the rhythm of our feelings; nor do we ask from anyone for proof of our Jewishness, since we are rooted in it by the strength of our blood, by the faith of our forefathers, and by the love of our brothers."[5] Jews who shared these feelings wholeheartedly supported Poland's struggle for independence.

Other Jews became convinced that nationalism was a source of many of the injustices they saw in the world. They joined groups that wanted to overthrow the old multi-national empires as well as the newer nation-states and replace them with a world in which there were no borders, one in which everyone was equal. A number of these Jews joined the anarchists, socialists, communists, and other groups committed to a utopian or ideal society.

Still another group of Jews in the late 1800s and early 1900s became convinced that antisemitism would never disappear and Jews would never be secure until they had their own country. Nothing else had worked. Reason, silence, assimilation, and conversion had all failed to end antisemitism. Yiddish writer Sholom Aleichem traced the history of Zionism, in an article written in 1897:

> Only sixteen years ago a great man, Dr. [Leon] Pinsker, published a little pamphlet [that] caused a stir in the Jewish world. "To end our troubles," Dr. Pinsker said, "we must have a land. But not to wait for someone to give us the land. We must find a land ourselves, a piece of earth, a corner that is our own, no matter where it is, so long as it is ours."
>
> Does a Jew realize what lies in these few simple words— "a piece of earth, a corner that is our own"? Does a Jew feel how necessary and how advantageous it is for each and every one of us, and for the whole community, for us all? Does a Jew ever think what we would have looked like among the nations of the world if we had a piece of land somewhere, our own small corner— that we would be no longer paupers, wandering Gypsies, outcast and unwanted! . . .
>
> [Dr. Pinsker] started a search over the world for a land where we could settle Jews who had got stuck like a bone in the throat in the countries where they lived. One said Palestine. Another Argentina. A third Brazil. Some thought Africa would be the place. Others plumped for Cyprus. Back of beyond! God knows where!. . . [6]

After much discussion, some decided that "if Jews want to live as a nation, there is no other way but to go there, to the ancient Holy Land of our forefathers, the land of the patriarchs." Therefore in 1881, a group of Russian Jews formed "Hovevei Zion" [Lovers of Zion]. Members prepared to emigrate to Palestine, which was then a part of the Ottoman Empire and encouraged their friends and relatives to do the same. However, wrote Sholem Aleichem:

Time has shown that the colonizing of Palestine is proceeding too slowly. The number of Jewish people grows and their poverty grows more. Jews need, most of all, a land of their own, where they can go and settle openly, not having to sneak in as in the past. These are the words of [Theodore] Herzl, who convened the first Jewish Congress held in Basel [in 1897].

Indeed, Dr. Herzl . . . said almost the same thing that Dr. Pinsker had said sixteen or seventeen years before. The difference was that Pinsker spoke in general terms, that Jews must have a country, and Herzl came out openly before the whole world with the demand that Jews must have a country, their own land, and pointed straight at Palestine. . . . I refer to Herzl's *Judenstadt,* which made a stir not only among Jews but also among other people.

Herzl went on to present his plan—how Jews should make their land purchases in Eretz Israel, and how in time a Jewish state would develop there, of course, with the consent of the sultan [of the Ottoman Empire which then controlled Palestine] and of all the European powers.

It would take a whole book to reproduce the plan in its entirety. Yet everybody will understand that building a grand structure like that is no easy matter. It is a work not for a year or even ten years. As the saying goes, "Things don't work as fast as we talk." Jews must first of all understand the idea properly, grow accustomed to it, get done with the question posed before, "Why do Jews need a land of their own?"

That means we must see to it that all Jews should feel and understand how necessary and useful it is. We must see to it that this idea should be the ideal of the entire People. We must see to it that our wives and sisters should understand it, so that our children will be brought up under our national flag, so that our children should be Jewish children, who will not be ashamed of their People. . . Jews must return to the Jewish People before they return to the Jewish land.[7]

CONNECTIONS

In Facing History and Ourselves publications, the word *antisemitism* is spelled without a hyphen. A person can be anti-Catholic, anti-Protestant, anti-Jewish, because each refers to a group label. But since there is no such group as *semites,* there should be no hyphen. The first people to use the term hyphenated it, because they assumed that the Jews belonged to the "Semitic race." No matter how Jews responded to acts of antisemitism in the late 1800s and early 1900s, they were criticized. Have you or anyone you know been stereotyped? What is the most effective way to fight a stereotype? What is the least effective way?

What did Sholom Aleichem mean when he said that before Jews could return to the Jewish land, they had to "return to the Jewish People"? How does one return "to the Jewish People"? What role does education play in the process? What kind of education would it be?

How did Zionists define the Jewish nation? Whom did they include in that nation? How did they define the Jewish homeland? Compare and contrast their definition with definitions of the word *nation.* How are they similar? What differences do you see?

A Matter of Loyalty

When World War I began in August of 1914, about half of the 15 million Jews in the world lived on or near the battlefields of Eastern Europe. Two million made their homes in Russian Poland; about one million lived in Galicia, a province in the southeastern corner of Austria-Hungary; and another four million were confined by the Russians to the Pale of Jewish Settlement—Lithuania, Bessarabia, Volhynia, and the other western provinces. Throughout the war, Jews in all three areas faced difficult and sometimes impossible choices as their loyalty was challenged by the competing armies that fought for control of the region.

Despite prejudice and discrimination, many Jews shared in the patriotic enthusiasm that swept Europe in 1914. N. M. Friedman, a Jewish deputy in the Russian Duma (parliament), was among those who insisted that Jews were eager to defend their country "not only from a sense of duty but also out of deep affection." Thousands enlisted not only in the Russian army but also in the Austrian, and German armies.

The war did not go well for Russia. In many ways, it was an old-fashioned country fighting a modern war. In battle after battle, its soldiers faced their German counterparts with little more than courage. They lacked guns, ammunition, warm clothes, and food. As their losses mounted, Russian generals began to accuse "the Jews" of aiding the enemy. Historian Norman Davies explains:

> In those parts of Austrian Galicia that Russian troops occupied, the Jews of course were enemies in fact. . . . And it is here that the Russian policy of treating all Jews as potential spies was begun. In the eyes of the Russian authorities, disloyalty was seen to spill over among the Jews on their own side of the border as language and customs did. The accusation first became vehement in Lemberg (Lwow) in January, 1915, when the Russian occupiers posted a proclamation all over the city saying that "the progress of the war has disclosed an open hostility on the part of the Jewish population of Poland, Galicia and Bukovina."

Only Galicia and Bukovina were enemy territories. Poland was then part of Russia. The generals were accusing Polish Jews of treason. They forcibly removed thousands of Jews from parts of Lithuania, Russian Poland, and the Ukraine. After witnessing their evacuation, the French ambassador to Russia wrote in his diary, "Hundreds of thousands of unfortunates have been seen wandering across the snow, driven like cattle by squads of Cossacks, abandoned in distress in railway stations, parked in the open on the outskirts of cities, dying of hunger, of exhaustion, of cold." Vladimir Grossman, a reporter for a Yiddish newspaper during World War I, described the effect those refugees had on one city:

> When I came to Warsaw two months after the outbreak of the war there were over 80,000 Jewish refugees in Warsaw. Children were dying like flies. The streets were full of Russian soldiers. There were military patrols everywhere. Armed columns, guns and munitions, and food were being moved to the front. At the same time carts rolled in from all the outlying places loaded with beds and bedding and whatever else the refugees could save from their abandoned homes, and carrying their old folk who could not walk. . . . All the homeless Jews found their way to the Jewish community building in the Grzybowska Street. The big courtyard was packed with carts heaped

high with their belongings. All the roads to Warsaw were thronged with Jews on their way there; whole communities were on the march, long processions, long caravans, fleeing from their own armies.[8]

With the encouragement of Russian military commanders, many Christians in Warsaw and other cities came to see those refugees as a threat. Grossman observed:

From the Russian Army Headquarters came one persistent cry of "Jewish treason," and with it went the death cries of masses of Jews who were hanged because of it. Jews were hanged for supposedly cutting telephone and telegraph wires, for "signaling to the enemy," for "spying."

The Jewish Committee in St. Petersburg collected material, and briefed lawyers to defend Jews who were put on trial. But it was useless trying to fight against it. One day a communiqué was issued by the Russian General Staff about a German attack on the village of Guzi in Lithuania. The Russian regiments, it said, had been forced to retreat, and when the Germans occupied the place the Jews gave them information about the Russian positions, resulting in heavy Russian losses. Later the Germans withdrew, and the Russians reoccupied the village and of course made the "traitors" pay for it.[9] Investigations by the Jewish Committee established that it was all pure invention; there had been no battle in or near the village; no one had retreated and no one had attacked.

Among those who protested these and other charges was a Russian Jew who had emigrated to the United States. When the war began, he returned to Russia to fight for his homeland. After losing a hand in combat, he asked Friedman to read his letter aloud on the floor of the Duma:

Scarcely had I reached Riga when I met at the station my mother and my relatives, who had just arrived there and who on that same day were compelled to leave their hearth and home at the order of the military authorities. Tell the gentlemen who sit on the benches of the Right that I do not mourn my lost hand, but that I mourn deeply the lost human dignity.[10]

CONNECTIONS

Grossman writes that not long after the war began, Russian Headquarters "issued an order to stop giving distinctions for bravery to Jewish soldiers. Too many Jewish soldiers had won the George Cross, the highest Russian award for valor." Jews also fought in the German army. They too found that no matter how many medals they won or acts of courage they performed, they were regarded as "shirkers" and "traitors." Why do you think Russian and German leaders promoted the image of the "Jewish traitor"? Why do you think that myth was stronger than the truth?

During World War I, former President Theodore Roosevelt told Americans, "There can be no fifty-fifty Americanism in this country. There is room here for only 100 percent Americanism, only for those who are Americans and nothing else." To whom do you think he was referring? What is he suggesting about their loyalty? How are his comments similar to Russian accusations of "divided loyalties?" What differences are most striking?

Jews were not the only people accused of "divided loyalties" during World War I. The Turks leveled the same charge against the Armenians, a Christian ethnic group that had lived for generations within the mostly Muslim Ottoman Empire. The charge was based on the fact that there were Armenians in Russia as well in the Ottoman Empire, and Russia was now the enemy. Those accusations led to the murder of thousands of children, women, and men. The Armenians were victims of the century's first genocide.

U.S. President Woodrow Wilson told a friend a few weeks before the United States entered World War I, "Once you lead this people into war and they'll forget there ever was such a thing as tolerance. To fight you must be brutal and ruthless, and the spirit of ruthless brutality will enter into every fibre of our national life. . . . A nation cannot put its strength into a war and keep its head level; it never has been done." What is Wilson suggesting happens to minorities in times of war? How do the wartime experiences of the Armenians and other minorities support his thinking? To what extent do those experiences call his views into question?

Historian George Mosse writes that war is "a powerful engine for the enforcement of conformity." How does war promote conformity? How does it strengthen stereotypes?

During the war, the military stopped publication of all Jewish newspapers in the Russian Empire. Others newspapers continued to publish but most stories were subject to censorship. What is the role of the press in peacetime? What role do newspapers play in wartime? Why is it a time when even democratic governments often choose to censor the news?

The young Jewish soldier told members of the Russian parliament that he mourned "deeply the lost human dignity." What is "human dignity"? How were Jews stripped of it during World War I? How might such a loss affect their perceptions, feelings, and actions? How might it affect the way others perceived, felt, and acted toward Jews? To what extent is the loss of dignity a step toward dehumanization?

"Only So Many Jews"

Philosopher Hannah Arendt described the years before and after World War I as "separated not like the end of an old and the beginning of a new period, but like the day before and the day after an explosion. "Yet" she writes, "this figure of speech is as inaccurate as are all others, because the quiet of sorrow which settles down after a catastrophe has never come to pass. The first explosion seems to have touched off a chain reaction in which we have been caught ever since and which nobody seems able to stop."

In 1917, the Russian Empire collapsed and a new Communist government took charge of the nation. By 1918, the Austrian, German, and Ottoman empires had also fallen apart. In the months that followed, Poles and other ethnic groups within those empires struggled to establish independent nations. Those struggles sometimes led to civil war.

Joseph Tenenbaum was one of many Jewish soldiers who fought for the Austro-Hungarian Empire during World War I. When the fighting ended, he returned to his hometown of Lemberg, or Lwow, in Galicia. There Tenenbaum quickly discovered that "peoples and nationalities held together in a makeshift empire for centuries" had become free, "free to hate and to make war on each other." Tenenbaum described the fighting in eastern Galicia as a "bloody conflict" between "3,293,023 Ukrainians who hated the Poles, a minority of 1,349,626 Poles who in turn despised the Ukrainians, and 658,722 Jews thrust between them."[11]

Some Jews in Galicia chose sides in that conflict, but according to Tenenbaum, most were convinced "there was but one choice; the strictest neutrality in this gory business of neighbor fighting neighbor, with all the bitterness and brutality of long suppressed enmities. This was the dictate of common sense, of fairness as well as of statesmanship."[12] The Jewish community sent delegates to explain its stand to both the Polish and the Ukrainian authorities. At the same time, members organized a militia to guard Jewish neighborhoods.

Among the 200 volunteers in the Jewish militia were recent veterans like Tenenbaum, secular businessmen, and *hasidim*. Although Tenenbaum describes the militia as the "most popular" group in Lemberg, many Poles had a different view. Rosa Bailly also lived in Lemberg. She and her friends believed that the Jewish militia was "supplied with arms by the Ukrainians." But even if they were not, she writes, "the mere existence of this militia was a help to the enemy, as it transformed the important and sizable Jewish quarter into a form of buffer state behind which the Ukrainians were free to concentrate their forces."[13]

Although Polish leaders in the city had agreed to the formation of a Jewish militia, rumors of Jewish betrayal persisted. A Polish newspaper reported, "In our military circles, there are complaints that the Jewish population is shooting at our patrols from their windows, and civilians who go into the quarter tell of things done by the Jews against the Polish population that are absolutely irreconcilable with their proclaimed neutrality."[14] As proof, the reporter cited an "anonymous" source.

Such reports encouraged talk of a "Day of Reckoning" for the Jews of Lemberg. It came on November 22, 1918. The day before, with the help of reinforcements, the Poles had pushed the Ukrainians out of the city. Although fighting continued on the outskirts of Lemberg, Rosa Bailly describes the morning of the 22nd as one of celebration with red-and-white Polish flags "fluttering from every window." In the early hours of

THE SECOND POLISH REPUBLIC 1921–1939

The new Polish Republic was home to many ethnic groups including Germans, Russians, Ukrainians, and Jews.

the day, she recalls "a bewildering succession of scenes that were as touching as they were comical. People ran to and fro to pass the glad tidings on to their friends and relatives without even pausing to dress, still in slippers and dressing gowns." As Polish soldiers paraded through the streets, the crowds rushed forward to greet them with "tears of joy and gratitude, and longing to embrace those youngsters who had brought them deliverance."[15]

Tenenbaum remembers that morning very differently. Well before dawn, he writes, "the frightened population of the Jewish quarter heard the whistling and hooting of Polish soldiers coming in, accompanied by shooting and harmonica-playing, as well as by curses and foul names called out to the Jews." On some streets, the soldiers began plundering as early as four in the morning, but most of the looting did not begin until dawn. The soldiers moved through the community as if following "a plan worked out with military precision."

> Machine guns and armored cars were stationed on the thoroughfares of the Jewish quarter and the streets were raked with fire, so that no one dared step out of his house. . . . At the same time, patrols were organized and every larger one was assigned to an area in which it could "work" without restriction or curtailment. A headquarters for the plundering legionaries was set up in the State Theater, where orders were issued and reports received. A large reserve squad—of robbers and murderers—also was posted there. . . . The Jewish quarter was cut off from the rest of the city by a powerful military cordon, through which no unauthorized person could enter or leave.[16]

For the next three days and three nights, the Jewish quarter was a "blazing inferno." When the fires finally went out, according to a British investigator, 72 Jews lay dead, over 400 were wounded, and 25,000 people were left homeless. Tenenbaum described the community itself as in a state of "utter, mute terror."

The violence against Jews in Lemberg was not an isolated incident. Between 1917 and 1921, there were over 2000 anti-Jewish riots in Eastern Europe. Many of them occurred in areas where newly independent nations were vying for control. In 1919, US President Woodrow Wilson sent Henry Morgenthau to investigate the violence.

Henry Morgenthau in Poland with a group of American officers.

Morgenthau was an American Jew who had served as the United States ambassador to the Ottoman Empire during the war. He was among the first to alert the world to the Armenian Genocide. Now he traveled through Poland gathering information and opinions. In Pinsk, he discovered that a few months before he arrived, a Polish officer had entered a hall and arrested the 70 Jews who had gathered there to distribute flour to poor families. After accusing them of being "Bolshevists" [Russian Communists], his men lined up half of the group against a wall and shot them "in cold blood."

Angry Jews in Poland called the incident a "pogrom." Jozef Pilsudski, who was now Poland's chief of state, disagreed, "There have been no pogroms in Poland!—nothing but unavoidable accidents." He told Morgenthau, "A pogrom is a massacre ordered by the government, or not prevented by it when prevention is possible. Among us no wholesale killings of Jews have been permitted." At another meeting, he told Morgenthau, "The exaggerations of the foreign press concerning what had happened to a relatively small number of Jews has been monstrous—one would think the country drenched with blood, whereas the occurrences have been mere trifles inevitably incident to any conquest."[17] As he listened to Pilsudski and others, Morgenthau was struck by the fact that the Poles never spoke of the victims. In his autobiography, he writes:

> Who were these thirty-five victims? They were the leaders of the local Jewish community, the spiritual and moral leaders of the 5,000 Jews in a city, . . the organizers of the charities, the directors of the hospitals, the friends of the poor. And yet, to that incredibly brutal, and even more incredibly stupid, officer who ordered their execution, they were only so many Jews.[18]

CONNECTIONS

People often say that the things they learned as children have stayed with them all of their lives. How might negative feelings about "the other" turn into acts of hatred and violence in times of crisis? What is the relationship between tolerance and fear?

How did Joseph Tenenbaum and his neighbors define their universe of obligation? How did Rosa Bailly and her neighbors define theirs? What do those definitions have in common? To what extent is each unique?

According to Martha Minow, a legal scholar, "Human beings use labels to describe and sort their perceptions of the world." She notes that the labels often lead to conclusions about an individual or group without any discussion of what that label means. How did the label of "Jew" allow the Polish officer to view his victims as "only so many Jews"?

In the 1990s, Joseph Brodsky, a Nobel-Prize-winning Russian poet, wrote about the conflict in what was once Yugoslavia:

> What's happening now in the Balkans is very simple: It is a bloodbath. Terms such as "Serbs," "Croats," "Bosnians" mean absolutely nothing. Any other combination of vowels and consonants will amount to the same thing: killing people. Neither religious distinctions—Orthodox, Catholic, Muslim—nor ethnic ones are of consequence. . . .
> Evocations of history here are bare nonsense. Whenever one pulls the trigger in order to rectify history's mistake, one lies. For history makes no mistakes, since it has

no purpose. One always pulls the trigger out of self-interest and quotes history to avoid responsibility or pangs of conscience.[19]

How do Brodsky's comments apply to events in Eastern Europe during World War I? Immediately after the war? To violence in other parts of the world today?

Protecting Minorities

The violence in Eastern Europe troubled many people, including some world leaders. They feared it might lead to yet another world war.

When the United States declared war on Germany and its allies in April 1917, President Woodrow Wilson vowed that this would be "the war to end all wars." In an address to Congress in January of 1918, the President listed "fourteen points" he considered essential to a lasting peace. Many of them dealt with what Wilson called "frustrated nationalism," which he believed was responsible for the war. Therefore he favored a division of the old Eastern European empires into independent nations. Wilson's fourteenth point, and in his mind, the most important, called for a "general association" or league of nations to keep peace and guarantee the political independence of "great and small States alike."

Wilson's Fourteen Points drew almost every minority group in Eastern Europe to the peace conference. Many of them wanted a nation of their own, including a number of Jewish groups. During the war, British Foreign Secretary Arthur James Balfour had issued a declaration stating that the British Government "views with favor the establishment of Palestine as a national home of the Jewish people and would use its best endeavors to facilitate the achievement of this object." Now with the collapse of the Ottoman Empire, Zionists came to argue for a Jewish homeland in Palestine

Many American and Western European Jews were deeply concerned about the anti-Jewish violence in Eastern Europe. They wanted to ensure the safety of Jews throughout the region. Many believed that the best way to accomplish that goal was by making sure that Eastern European Jews had the same rights Jews enjoyed in New York, London, and Paris. Eastern European Jews at the peace conference, including Joseph Tenenbaum, saw the problem differently. Tenenbaum wrote:

> One of the great surprises to the Western Great Powers was the emergence of a new political entity: a living, aspiring and irrepressible Jewish nationality. . . . To them the Jews were a sect, a religion, a race, but not a nationality. "Why does not America grant the Jews minority rights?" was the common question raised by most of the peace envoys. The answer was: Because America, the great melting pot, does not preach nationalism. There is no such thing as group rights in America, because fundamentally there is no such thing as group domination.[20]

Such arguments convinced Louis Marshall, president of the American Jewish Committee, that "we must be careful not to permit ourselves to judge what is most desirable for the people who live in Eastern Europe by the standards which prevail on Fifth Avenue or in the States of Maine or Ohio, where a different horizon from that which prevails in Poland, Galicia, Ukrainia, or Lithuania bounds one's vision." He and other Jewish leaders were also swayed by what Henry Morgenthau called a "real fear" that the anti-Jewish violence in the region might develop into pogroms like those in Russia at the turn of the century. "There was the feeling that Poland, who had just emerged from her yoke of tyranny, should be reminded of the world's expectation that she should grant to her minorities the same privileges which her centuries of oppression had taught her to value for herself."[21]

Morgenthau did not believe that granting "national rights" to Eastern European Jews was the right solution. He later wrote:

> Every man has his master-passion: mine is for democracy. I believe that history's best effort in democracy is the United States, which has rooted in its Constitution all that any group of its citizens can legitimately desire. Yet here were Americans willing to cooperate with central Europeans who wanted to establish in their own countries a "nation within a nation"—a proposition fundamentally opposed to our American principles.
>
> I pointed this out. I said that, under this plan, a Jew in Poland or Romania, for example, would soon face conflicting duties, and that any American who advocated such a conflict of allegiance for the Jews of central Europe would perhaps expose the Jews in America to the suspicion of harboring a similar desire. Minorities everywhere, I maintained, would fare better if they protected their religious rights in the countries where they resided, and then joined their fellow countrymen in bettering for all its inhabitants the land of their common citizenship.[22]

A number of Jews in the West agreed with Morgenthau. Their views also affected the recommendations made by the Jewish delegations in Paris. The compromises both groups made and the concerns of the "Great Powers" can be seen in the Minorities Treaty, a document that many new nations in Eastern Europe were required to accept. Polish leaders were among the first to do so. They reluctantly signed the treaty on June 28, 1919, the same day they signed the one that guaranteed their nation's independence.

The Minorities Treaty to which Poland agreed contained twelve articles. Six of the articles were to become part of the nation's constitution. These articles guaranteed the right to life, liberty, and freedom of religion to all minorities in the country. They guaranteed that differences of religion, creed, or confession would "not prejudice any Polish national in matters relating to the enjoyment of civil or political rights, as for instance the admission to public employment, functions and honors, or the exercise of professions and industries."

The other six articles focused on specific minorities. Two of them dealt with Jews. The first required that the Polish government support Jewish schools much as it did Catholic schools. The other article stated that the government could not force Jews to violate their Sabbath. That meant that the government could not hold elections or require Jews to work on Saturday. In his autobiography, Morgenthau recalled Pilsudski's response to the treaty:

> "Why not trust to Poland's honor?" he shouted. "Don't plead that the articles' concessions are few in number or negative in character! Let them be as small or as negative as you please, that article creates an authority—a power to which to appeal—outside the laws of this country! Every faction within Poland was agreed on doing justice to the Jew and yet the Peace Conference, at the insistence of America, insults us by telling us that we *must* do justice. That was a public insult to my country just as she was assuming her rightful place among the sovereign nations of the world!"[23]

CONNECTIONS

Henry Morgenthau feared that if Jews in Eastern Europe were regarded as a "national minority," "a Jew in Poland or Romania, for example, would soon face conflicting duties, and that any American who advocated such a conflict of allegiance for the Jews of Central Europe would perhaps expose the Jews in America to the suspicion of harbouring a similar desire." Louis Brandeis, a justice on the United States Supreme Court, was also a Jew. But he responded to such concerns by insisting that just as Irish Americans who supported freedom for their country were better people and better Americans for their sacrifice, Jews who helped advance Jewish settlements in Palestine were better people and better Americans for their sacrifice. How did each man seem to define the word *loyalty?* Which definition is closest to your own?

Compare and contrast the Minorities Treaty to the charters Jews received from Polish rulers in the 1500s and 1600s. (See Chapter 2.) What similarities do you notice? How do you account for those similarities? What differences seem most striking?

Woodrow Wilson was the world leader who argued most strongly in favor of the Minorities Treaty. Yet as president of the United States, he was responsible for the segregation of African Americans in the offices of the federal government and in the nation's capital. Why would he support equal rights for minorities in Eastern Europe but not in the United States? What do his actions suggest about his "universe of obligation"?

Like the Poles, Czechs also had to sign the Minorities Treaty. And like the Poles, many Czechs resented doing so. But unlike Polish leaders, President Thomas Masaryk of Czechoslovakia defended the agreement. When asked why, he replied, "How can the suppressed nations deny the Jews that which they demand for themselves"? How was he defining his nation's universe of obligation? How did Poland's leaders answer Masaryk's question? In doing so, how did they define their universe of obligation?

Pilsudski, like many Eastern European leaders, saw the Minorities Treaty as an example of outsiders "meddling" in their affairs. How would you answer the questions he raises in his meeting with Morgenthau? When, if ever, does one nation or a group of nations have the right to intervene in another nation's affairs?

Henry Morgenthau wrote, "Every man has his master-passion: mine is for democracy." Pilsudski's "master-passion" was nationalism. How does our "master-passion" shape the way we see ourselves and others? How does it affect the way we define our universe of obligation? How does it influence our ideas about what is just or fair? What is your "master-passion"? How does it shape your perceptions, your feelings, and your actions?

Uniting a Nation

The new Republic of Poland was a multi-national state. Poles made up about 70 percent of the population; Ukrainians, 15 percent, Jews, 9; Belorussians, 5; and Germans, 2. But those numbers do not reveal the full extent of Poland's diversity. For example, the nine percent of the population that was Jewish included families that had lived in Poland for generations as well as people who thought of themselves as Lithuanian, Russian, or Austrian Jews. Leaders had to find ways to unite those diverse groups into a nation.

In 1918, few deputies in Poland's Sejm or parliament had much experience with democracy. Many of them were Polish nationalists who had spent years in opposition to the Russian, Austrian, or German governments. They were experts at protest and rebellion but had little experience with negotiation. Yitzhak Gruenbaum, a Jewish deputy who had served in Russia's parliament, described the Sejm as a place where "the Russian spirit still lingered, the Russian ways of dispute, the political style to which one was accustomed in Russia—clear and unambiguous words, stinging and caustic expressions and slogans, no subtleties."

The 17 political parties in that first Sejm included three Jewish groups. Two deputies belonged to Agudat Israel. Its members were Orthodox Jews who wanted to preserve traditional Jewish life. They were also opposed to Zionism. Two other deputies represented the Folkist party; they too were anti-Zionist. The remaining seven deputies were Zionists. Among them was Roza Pomerantz-Meltzer, the first woman to serve in the Sejm. The eleven deputies from the Jewish parties were united only in their concern for the growing violence against Jews in Poland and their committment to the right of Jews to participate fully in Polish life. But they did not agree on how to achieve those goals.

Eight of the thirteen Jewish representatives in the first Polish Parliament in 1919. Among them are members of Orthodox, Folkist, and Zionist parties.

And they quickly discovered that eleven votes were not enough to make a difference. They needed allies.

Some Jewish deputies wanted to work with liberal parties in the Sejm. After all, these deputies were also committed to a democracy based on equality. But when it came to specific issues, the two groups disagreed. For example, most Polish liberals wanted a Sunday Rest Law. They saw a six-day work week as an important social and economic goal. Jewish deputies opposed it because it discriminated against those who observed the Sabbath on Saturday. Jews who closed their businesses on Saturday would no longer be allowed to open on Sunday. Few people in Poland—Christians or Jews— could afford to work only five days a week. So Jews would either have to violate their own Sabbath or suffer economic hardship. The conservatives also had some interests in common with Jewish groups. But as long as the National Democrats, the largest party in the Sejm, wanted Poland to be an exclusively Polish state, cooperation between the two groups was unlikely.

In 1922, Gruenbaum came up with the idea of joining with other minority groups in electing members of the next Sejm. Many Jews questioned whether it was possible to unite with Ukrainians, Belorussians, and Germans. Others questioned whether it was wise to do so. At a time when the loyalty of Jews was being questioned, did they really want to unite with groups that were demanding their own country? Despite these and other concerns, the National Minorities bloc elected 80 deputies and 26 senators to the first Sejm to meet under the new constitution. They held the balance of power in a parliament where neither conservatives nor liberals had a clear majority.

The first test of the bloc came just a month after the election. Under the nation's new constitution, the Sejm was to choose Poland's president. Members were about to elect Pilsudski, when he surprised everyone by announcing his retirement. The election was now up for grabs and members of the Minorities bloc cast the deciding votes. Their support of Grabriel Narutowicz, a liberal friend of Pilsudski, ensured his election. The outraged National Democrats announced that they would not support any government that was "created by a President imposed by foreign nationalities: Jews, Germans, and Ukrainians."

Wherever Narutowicz went, gangs of extreme nationalists threw stones at his car and taunted him as "the Jews' president." Nationalist newspapers encouraged such attacks by expressing outrage at the new president's promise to follow a policy of peace, justice and impartiality toward all Polish citizens.

Five days after Narutowicz's inauguration, he was killed by a Polish nationalist. Every political party denounced the murder, as the nation's leaders moved quickly to restore order. Just four days after the assassination, the deputies gathered once again to elect a new president. This time, their choice was sworn in without incident even though he also had the support of the Minorities bloc. Still the old antagonisms between *us* and *them* that caused the crisis remained. In January of 1923, one month after the assassination, the new president named a prime minister who sent the following message to lawmakers:

> The Jewish minority undoubtedly believes that the rights which Poland has voluntarily granted it will be safeguarded by the government. But a note of warning is necessary here, because too often the defense of its justified interests has been turned by the Jewish side into a struggle for a privilege. Many organs of the international press, which are so eager to attack us, label the equality which prevails in Poland "oppression." There are no rights without responsibilities.[24]

Osias Thon, a Zionist from Galicia, responded with a reminder that there are no "givers" or "takers" when it comes to rights; everyone is equal. He asked: When Jews seek protection of life and property, "is this our 'right' or are we here demanding a 'privilege'?" The prime minister agreed that protection is a right. But, he added, "it is your privilege to make of every tiny adventure an anti-Jewish pogrom."[25]

In the years that followed, the wrangling continued. Even as old alliances broke apart, including the National Minorities bloc, new ones were established. In just eight years, Poland had thirteen governments. Each tried and failed to solve the nation's economic and social problems. By 1926, unemployment had reached staggering levels in Poland's cities and towns and its farmers were among the poorest in Europe. That May, with a call for Sanacja or moral cleansing, Jozef Pilsudski came out of retirement and took control of the country.

Pilsudski ruled Poland until his death in 1935. Although the Sejm continued to meet, there was no doubt as to who ran the country. Agudat Israel was the only major Jewish party that supported Pilsudski's new Non-Party Bloc for Cooperation with the Government. The others continued to operate independently in elections that mattered less and less. Yet whether they supported Pilsudski or mourned the loss of democracy, *Sanacja* did mark a new beginning. For the first time, the government acknowledged the concerns of its Jewish citizens. A government official told the Sejm "that economic antisemitism is harmful to the country" and vowed to safeguard the principle of impartiality and justice." Yet discriminatory laws established by the Russians remained on the books.

CONNECTIONS

Soon after independence, Jozef Pilsudski asked various Jewish groups three questions.

— What form of government did they wish for Poland?
— What method should be used to create that government?
— What special requests did the Jewish people have?

Both Jewish religious and secular groups expressed loyalty to the nation and a desire for full equality. What do Pilsudski's questions suggest about the way he defined his universe of obligation? What do the answers suggest about the way Jewish groups defined theirs?

Few people in Eastern Europe had much experience with democracy in the 1920s. How does one learn democratic principles and values? Is it possible to practice democracy without an education in democracy or a history of democracy?

What do the experiences of Polish political parties in the 1920s suggest about the importance of compromise to democracy? Are there times when compromise is wrong?

Chapter 2 explored some of the social, economic, political, and religious factors that turn neighbor against neighbor. What does this reading suggest about the consequences of uniting a nation by creating enemies? What does it suggest about the effects of political instability on the ways people view one another?

Jozef Pilsudski came out of retirement with a call for Sanacja or "moral cleansing." What does the term mean? What does his call suggest about the way he and others in Poland viewed democracy?

In the United States, Jews belong to every political party. They have never tried to create one just for Jews. Why do you think that many Polish Jews felt the need to create not just one such party but several, each with its own agenda?

In the 1600s, a noted rabbi or a wealthy Jewish businessman would go to a noble for help in resolving a problem or righting a wrong. He acted as the *shadlan*, or intermediary, between the Jewish people and a noble, prince, or other ruler. That was the role Agudat Israel hoped to play in Poland. The Zionists saw the role of *shadlan* as a "shameful relic" of a bygone era. In Yitzhak Gruenbaum's words, Jews in the modern world must stand up for their rights, rather than "look with begging eyes at the Polish lord." What role should leaders of minority groups play in a democracy? Is there a place for a *shadlan* in a democracy?

Winds of Change

Poland's independence came at a time of change everywhere in the world. Many of those changes began much earlier and were speeded up by the war. Others were linked to innovations in science that altered the way people saw the world. As young women and men explored new ideas, they began to break with tradition and see themselves and others in new ways.

Isaac Bashevis Singer, the famous Yiddish novelist and Nobel Prize winner, was a teenager when World War I ended. At the time, he and his family were living in a town called Bilgoray. Singer recalled the way life there changed after the war.

> A few months after we arrived, a Zionist society was established by the young people of the town. Certain young men indicated Bolshevik [Communist] sympathies. Youthful worshippers at the house of prayer separated into two factions: The Mizrachi [Orthodox Jews who favored Zionism] and the Traditionalists. My friend Notte Shverdsharf formed a pioneer division, *Hachalutz* [which means "pioneer" in Hebrew] or *Hashomer* [the Guardian], and was trailed by hordes of children who called themselves *Zebim*, wolves. Whether larger cities showed the same tendencies as Bilgoray, I did not know. In the streets, boys passing each other would straighten up, click their heels in the Austrian manner, and shout, "*Chazak!*—Be strong!"
>
> All kinds of evening discussions and parties were now being held in this town, which a year before had been a sleepy Jewish community. A Warsaw dramatic company performed *Shulamit* in the firehouse. The Austrians, who had started a school in Bilgoray, erected a theater in the marketplace.

For young Singer, the greatest change was the opening of a library that contained worldly books.

> Now, under the apple tree in the garden, I would start a book one day and finish it the next. Often, sitting on an overturned bookcase in the attic, I would read among old pots, broken barrels, and stacks of pages torn from sacred books. Omnivorously, I read stories, novels, plays, essays, works written in Yiddish, and translations. As I read, I decided which was good, which mediocre, and where truth and falsity lay. At that time America was sending us sacks of white flour and Yiddish translations of European writers, and these books fascinated me. I read Reisen, Strindberg, Don Kaplanovitch, Turgenev, Tolstoy, Maupassant, and Chekhov. One day I devoured *The Problem of Good and Evil* by Hillel Zeitlin. In this book Zeitlin gives the history and summation of world philosophy and the philosophy of the Jews. Sometime later I discovered Stupnicki's book on Spinoza.

The Spinoza book intoxicated Singer. He later recalled:

> I was exalted; everything seemed good. There was no difference between heaven and earth, the most distant star and my red hair. My tangled thoughts were divine. The fly alighting on my page had to be there, just as an ocean wave or a planet had to be where it was at a specific time. The most foolish fantasy in my mind had been

thought for me by God . . . Heaven and earth became the same thing. The laws of nature were divine; the true sciences of God were mathematics, physics, and chemistry. My desire to learn intensified.

Other boys, Notte Shverdsharf and Meir Hadas, were not, to my astonishment, at all interested in my discoveries. My absorption amazed them, just as their indifference shocked me.

One day Notte approached me and asked if I would be willing to teach Hebrew. "To whom?"

"Beginners. Boys and girls."

"But what about Mottel Shur?" I asked. "He is the Hebrew teacher."

"They don't want him."

I still don't know why they didn't want Mottel Shur, unless it was because he had quarreled with the founders of the night school that now sought to employ me. Mottel had a weakness for telling people what he thought of them; also, he boasted too much—and perhaps he asked too high a fee. I hardly dared accept the position, knowing it would embarrass my mother and cause consternation in the town. But something made me accept.

In the private home where the first class was held, I discovered that my pupils were not, as I had assumed, children, but young men and women, and somewhat more of the latter. The girls, my age and even older, came dressed in their best clothes. I faced them in a long gabardine, a velvet hat, and with dangling sidelocks. How, since I am naturally shy, I had the nerve to accept this assignment I do not know, but it has been my experience that shy persons are sometimes unusually bold. I told them everything I knew about Hebrew. The class created a furor in Bilgoray—to think that the rabbi's grandson had lectured worldly boys and girls on the Hebrew language!

After the lesson, the girls surrounded me, asking questions, smiling. Suddenly I was dazzled by a particular narrow face, a dark girl with coal-black eyes and an indescribable smile. 1 became confused, and when she asked me a question I did not know what she was saying. Many novels and a lot of poetry had filled my mind by then; I was prepared for the turmoil that writers call "love."[26]

CONNECTIONS

Create two identity charts for Singer, one before the changes in Bilgoray and the other after. How are the two charts alike? What differences are most striking?

Why do you think young men and women were so eager to learn the Hebrew language? Why did their decision to study "create a furor" in Bilgoray

Why did Singer think teaching in a night school might "embarrass" his mother and cause trouble in the town? To what extent was teaching in the school a break with tradition? What other revolutionary acts does he describe?

Journalist I.F. Stone once wrote, " The only absolute value which I would affirm is freedom of the mind. Without it there cannot be social justice, which is our duty toward others." Would Singer agree? Do you agree?

Tradition and Change

An American who visited Poland shortly after independence was startled to discover that hasidic rabbis served in the Sejm. He might have been even more startled if he had realized that those rabbis were elected by observant Jewish women as well as men. In the Republic of Poland, women had the right to vote and some Orthodox women went to the polls along with their husbands, fathers, and sons. Orthodox rabbis not only ran for political office but also published newspapers, founded girls' schools, and operated summer camps.

What prompted men and women committed to preserving traditional ways to take on untraditional roles? An appeal for newspaper subscribers written in 1916 by Abraham Mordecai Alter, known as the *Gerer Rebbe,* offers some clues:

> For a long time now I have striven for the establishment of a newspaper which should walk in the path of Judaism and be managed in a way that is free from irreligious and immoral ideas. A great many of you have shed tears because you saw your sons and daughters being alienated from Judaism by the influence of the newspapers. Now, under the masthead of *Dos Yiddishe Vort,* a newspaper is being published by people who belong to a circle devoted to God and the Torah. I urge you therefore to support this newspaper in every possible way. . . . Let this not be taken lightly by you. . . . I especially request all my friends who deem it important to carry out my wishes to let me know that you have subscribed to the paper or that you buy it at the newsstands. Send me your name and address. Although other newspapers may contain more news than this one, it is better, because of its religious character, to be content with a little less.[27]

Despite some initial success, the rebbe's paper failed, but he did not give up. In 1919, he helped found yet another newspaper. When it closed in 1929, it was replaced with still another. This time, the rebbe's efforts were more successful in part because this paper was a cooperative venture with the socialist Bund. Printing both newspapers in the same plant saved the two groups money, even though occasionally the slogan "down with religion" would appear in the rebbe's paper and the expression "God be praised" would find its way into a report of a Bundist meeting.

That publishing enterprise was not the rebbe's first joint venture. In 1916, with the encouragement and support of two rabbis from Germany, he and a number of other rabbis founded a new organization aimed at bringing together all religious Jews in Poland. As one rabbi explained, "We must unite under one flag—the flag of Torah—all sections of our people, high and low, rich and poor, *hasidim* and *mitnagdim.*"

The new group, which became known as the Agudat Israel, took an interest in every aspect of life in modern Poland not just politics. In 1917, a young Orthodox woman named Sarah Schenirer started a school for girls with the permission of the Belzer *rebbe.* It was called *Beit Yakov,* literally the "House of Jacob." The name is used traditionally to refer to the "women of Israel." In 1919, Agudat Israel decided not only to support the school but also expand its operations. One rabbi defended the decision by arguing that in "these times of assimilation," it is a *mitzvah* to teach Jewish girls the fundamentals of their faith. (A *mitzvah* is the fulfillment of a commandment.) By 1937, 38,000 Jewish girls were attending over 250 Beit Yaakov schools throughout Eastern

Europe. They received vocational training as well as a religious education. Many girls also attended Beit Yaakov summer camps and took part in Beit Yaakov youth groups, one for students and the other for graduates of the schools.

As Agudat Israel became more and more involved in education, members established a teacher's college in Krakow and later in Vienna and Chernovitz. The group also became a publisher of textbooks, magazines, and other educational materials. Little by little, Agudat Israel was expanding the choices open to young Jewish women. In much the same way and for much the same reasons, it also expanded the options for young Jewish men.

Heders for girls are one of many changes that took place in the years after the war.

CONNECTIONS

It has been said that change rarely occurs overnight. Most changes take place little by little, step by step. How does the work of the Agudat Israel support that view of change?

Sarah Schenirer started her school to preserve Jewish tradition. Yet in doing so, she broke with tradition. What tradition did she break? Why did some rabbis defend and even actively support her action?

In 1939, Raymond Buell, the president of the Foreign Policy Association, visited Poland. He said of the Orthodox Jews he observed there: "The American visitor unaccustomed to the Polish tradition wonders why more interracial disputes have not occurred when, on visiting a typical village, he sees the Orthodox Jew, wearing his skullcap, black boots, long double-breasted coat, curls and beard, mingling with the Poles proper."[28] What relationship does Buell see between differences in dress and conflict, even violence? Do you agree?

The Agudat Israel did not include all observant Jews in Poland. It deliberately excluded members of the Mizrachi, a group of Orthodox Jews who were also Zionists. As one supporter explained, "It might lead to conflicts of conscience if the Agudat were to take positions contrary to the Zionist viewpoint." Some *hasidim* and *mitnagim* refused to join because they did not want to work together. Others feared the group was too revolutionary. How revolutionary was it? What criteria did you use to decide?

A Yearning to Belong

Sholom Aleichem believed that before Jews could return to the Jewish land, they had to "return to the Jewish People." It was an idea that struck a chord with Jews throughout Eastern Europe—including many with little or no interest in Zionism.

Throughout the 1920s and 1930s, thousands of young people, Jews and Christians alike, joined youth groups, clubs, unions and other organizations that sprang up throughout Poland. These groups gave members a sense of purpose and satisfied their yearning to belong.

One of the earliest of these groups in Poland was the General Union of Jewish Workers, a socialist party known as the Bund. It attracted thousands of young Jewish workingwomen and men. Members had their own schools, holidays, literature, and meeting places. A member described the group's headquarters in Warsaw as a "beehive" with "meetings going on in all the rooms, the choir was rehearsing, the reading room was filled with people; one could hardly pass through the hallways."

There were similar clubs in almost every village, town, and city. Borukh Yismakh grew up in Vishkov, a small community near Warsaw where politics often went hand-in-hand with sports. Every Jewish political party had not only its own schools and libraries but also its own soccer team. Players put aside their differences only when they played against a Polish team. "Then Maccabi and Gwiazda were in complete solidarity," writes Yismakh. He looked back with particular pride at a trip his club took in the late 1920s:

> Gwiazda (nearly the entire group), consisting of the men's section, the women's sec-
> tion, and the youth section, all in their own uniforms and bearing their sports equip-
> ment, marched from the center of town to the railroad station, from where they trav-
> eled to Poplava Station, and finally, in full uniform, into the town of Rozhan. Our
> arrival in Rozhan set off a virtual revolution. It was a pious town, which wasn't used
> to seeing gangs of young men, young women, and children, who were dressed like
> soldiers but weren't soldiers. The Jews ran to their rabbi to ask what was to be done
> about us. The rabbi decided that since it was just before the Sabbath, we were to be
> given a warm reception. We enjoyed ourselves that Saturday and Sunday. Monday
> evening, when we returned, a large crowd awaited us, and our march into town was a
> magnificent demonstration of Jewish strength and organization.[29]

Yismakh also recalled a time when the Jewish clubs banded together against a gang of Poles who disrupted quiet evening strolls with shouts of "Jews to Palestine." Jews who went out for a walk, Yismakh writes, "knew there were strong hands among them, ready to ward off any attack. There were times when we had to use our fists against hooligans who refused to calm down and go home. Our procedure was to first take them in hand and suggest that they stop, since they were bound to be unsuccessful this time anyway. Sometimes we managed to avoid further struggle; other times we had to punish them, and give them a taste of the water in the gutter, where we left them to sober up." The strategy worked until the "hooligans" turned to the police for help. As tensions mounted, the self-defense group had to disband. As Yismakh put it, "We were capable of defending ourselves against hooligans, but we were no match for the police."[30]

The Jewish Sports Club of Bialystok was one of many Jewish clubs in the 1920s.

CONNECTIONS

How important is it to you to "look right"? To "act right"? Fit in? How do you feel when you don't belong? How does it affect the way you think of yourself? The way others think of you? Who is most vulnerable to issues related to "in" and "out" group behavior: adolescents or young children?

What role did sports play in Poland during the 1920s? What role do sports play in the United States today? Why do you think rivalries disappear when there is a "common enemy"?

One young Jew recalls that he joined a Zionist youth group without giving much thought to the decision, but the group soon played a "dominant role" in his life:

> Akiva tried to instill in us an altruistic philosophy, an altruistic outlook that we were asked to apply to both Jews and non-Jews. . . . My home life, my parents, served as models for behavior, as examples for me to imitate. They were not offering me any education in a formal way. This I received from Akiva, and a large part of it had to do with a special philosophy of life. I had a home but I also had a second home. . . .Every day I would go out, every evening I would come back late. But I was not unique in this respect. Others lived like this too.[31]

What did his group provide that neither family nor teachers could offer?

After visiting the many "national" schools in Poland in the 1920s, Alfred Doeblin, a

German writer of Jewish descent, expressed disappointment and sorrow:

> They sit here in the schools, Ukrainians, Jews, White Russians, and whoever else.
> Their nations are torn apart. They are not permitted to develop as they wish. And
> now everything is twisted and wrong. They close themselves off, are spiritually over-
> heated. And obsessed, obsessed. . . . Oh, all the hundred little languages! And history.
> I know how "history" is taught: megalomania is coupled with ignorance. I know how
> "freedom" is taught: with hatred toward the neighbor. National consciousness, nation-
> al unconsciousness. . . . [32]

Education can help individuals learn to see the world from someone else's perspective.
To what extent did schools Doeblin describes break isolation? To what extent did they
increase isolation? How did the youth groups help young people get to know one another? To what extent did they reinforce separation?

In reflecting on the effects of the nationalism he observed in Poland and in Germany,
Alfred Doeblin wrote, "Who will gush over a nation—one is forced to say it—and not
prefer turning his back on it today rather than tomorrow, if it practices slavery, if it does
not do justice, if the people there know each other only in order to climb over each
other? One loves a nation and a country for the sake of their values". What does it
mean to love a nation for the sake of its values? How is that different from those who
believe "my country, right or wrong"? How is it different from those who believe "my
country may it always be in the right, and if in the wrong, may I help to set it right"?
Where do you stand on the issue?

Two Separate Groups

Arthur L. Goodhart traveled to Poland as part of the commission Henry Morgenthau headed. When Goodhart's work was done, both Jewish and Polish leaders came to the railroad station to say good-bye. As the train pulled away, Goodhart noticed that the two groups stood apart from one another. He wrote in his diary, "All that evening I kept wondering whether it was possible that these two groups would ever join into one."

The divisions that troubled Goodhart were particularly evident in Polish cities and towns. Everywhere, Jews and Poles lived near one another. Yet they often knew very little about one another. To young Poles like Helena Wasiutynska, the Jews were an "alien" people. As an adult, she could still recall her daily walk through a Jewish neighborhood in Warsaw:

> To get to our school we crossed Nowe Miasto and turned left to Freta Street. The middle section of this street was very narrow, on either side were neglected houses in which Jews lived. But only the very poor ones. They looked strange to me, especially the boys with their long black coats, yarmulkes, and side curls. There were a lot of them and they played in the narrow, foul-smelling hallways. On the doorsteps very old Jewesses wearing wigs and dark and untidy dresses sat selling broad beans. I tried not to look at them, not to look into the hallways, to pass this part of the street as quickly as possible. but never in all the years I lived in this part of the city did I ever witness any act of aggression or animosity from either side. We did not mix, we belonged to different circles, but in my home and in my school there was not a trace of antisemitism.[33]

Just as Wasiutynska felt uncomfortable among Jews, many Jews felt uncomfortable among Poles. Helene Deutsch recalled how she felt when she saw the neighborhood priest walking down the street followed by an altar boy who shook a bell "to remind the faithful to kneel down. All the passersby would sink to their knees like wheat stalks in the wind. I alone, the Jew, would remain standing in solemn silence. I felt marked by a stigma and full of shame."[34]

Many Jewish children had similar feelings. A young Jew recalled that when he was in first grade, he saw a group of Polish children beat up a Jewish classmate. "Why," he asked, "didn't the teacher punish the guilty?" After the incident, he found that "school took on a different aspect; the enemy was everywhere." When Henryk Goldszmit (see Chapter 2) started a Polish-language newspaper for Jewish children, many of the letters he received dealt with antisemitism. A boy wrote, "I am the only Jewish child in my class, and I feel like a stranger, an outsider." Even young people who lived in predominately Jewish neighborhoods and attended Jewish schools experienced negative stereotypes. Hanna Hirshaut who grew up in Warsaw defended her neighborhood:

> We were right across from Nalewki Street, an extremely busy section always teeming with people. This was actually the commercial center. The buildings there were like huge compounds of houses with two or three courtyards. On the ground level were countless businesses and small shops. Many wholesale representatives had their showrooms there. I remember my father's friend had the exclusive representation of BATA [a chain of women's clothing stores]. Another one had exclusive representation for

A street in a Jewish neighborhood in Warsaw.

Trader Horn. There were wholesale businesses selling French perfumes and cosmetics. Contrary to [popular] opinion Nalewki Street was not some backward market place.

Gensia Street was mainly crowded with wholesale textile businesses, Franciszkanska Street with shops selling leather skins and goods. . . . On the Sabbath the stores were closed and there was serene peace; people attended services. In the afternoon families would stroll toward the Saxon Gardens dressed in their best. . . . We skated in Krasinski Park and Saxon Gardens or in Dolina Szwajcarskiej during the winter months, which were bitter cold.

Hirshaut emphasizes that even though a "significant segment of the Jewish population" was very poor, "there was a large middle class—businessmen, manufacturers, teachers, artisans. Some of those who were more affluent, like industrialists, professionals, people in the arts, were living in the more elegant sections of Warsaw." She describes her Warsaw as "vibrant, creative and deeply involved in new political ideas and cultural progress."[35]

CONNECTIONS

Sociologist David Schoem has written, "The effort it takes for us to know so little about one another across racial and ethnic groups is truly remarkable. That we can live so closely together, that our lives can be so intertwined socially, economically and politically, and . . . yet still manage to be ignorant of one another is clear testimony to the deep-seated roots of this human and national tragedy. What we do learn along the way is to place heavy reliance on stereotypes, gossip, rumor, and fear to shape our lack of knowledge." To what extent does his statement describe Warsaw in the 1920s and 1930s? The United States today? How can people break the isolation he describes?

Helene Deutch writes that as a Jew in Warsaw, she felt "marked by a stigma and full of shame." A stigma is a mark of reproach or disgrace. What attitudes and values might encourage such strong feelings? What does your answer suggest about the way *their* stereotypes of *us* affect the way we perceive ourselves?

Many Poles described Jewish neighborhoods much the way Helena Wasiutynska did. Jews who lived there had a different view. One man wrote, "Jews wearing the long, traditional black caftans, others wearing small, black caps with visors and clean-shaven heads, elegantly dressed women or some in the simplest garments. Filthy children and clean ones, some well-nourished and others thin as a rail—one could find everything here." How do our prejudices shape our perceptions of both *us* and *them?*

In the introduction to this reading, Arthur Goodhart asked whether it was possible for Jews and Poles to "ever join into one." How would you answer his question? What do you think it would have taken to bring Poles and Jews together in Poland?

Economic Competition

A worldwide depression began in the 1920s and continued through much of the 1930s. A depression is a time when economic activity slows; more and more businesses decrease production and lay off workers. In a poor country like Poland, the effects were devastating for everyone, Christian and Jew alike.

As Poland's economy worsened, many people turned to leaders who saw the crisis as an economic war between *us* and *them*. Wanda Wasilewska, a Polish writer, described the effects of such attitudes:

> The slogan of economic struggle is raised against the paupers of the Jewish street. Why look for those responsible [for Poland's economic problems elsewhere] when it is so easy to find them nearby, in a street in the Jewish quarter? Why suppress when it is so easy and so safe to vent one's anger in a fight with a bowed porter [one who earns a living carrying heavy loads on his back], with a Jewish boy selling watches, with an old Jewish woman [selling bagels]?[36]

In big cities and small towns alike, it became harder and harder for Jews to find work. Belkhatov, located just south of Lodz, was typical of many places during those years. Although the town had a number of modern textile factories, they employed only Poles and ethnic Germans to run the huge mechanical looms. Jewish weavers in the town worked at home on hand looms. Unlike their counterparts in the factories, they received no benefits and earned no regular salary. A young Jewish worker recalls:

> The Jewish youth, who were already in the habit of frequenting the locals of the various left-wing political parties and the textile workers' union, began to envy the legal benefits that the Polish workers enjoyed: eight-hour workdays, health and unemployment insurance, annual vacations, and so forth. The Jewish workers, who had to work halfway through the night, had no legal protection whatsoever, since they worked at home. Furthermore, it grew harder and harder to protest for better pay, because a new type of competition had arisen. These were the peasants of the surrounding villages, who installed looms in their homes and did the work much more cheaply. For them it was an extra source of income, which they did when they weren't busy in the fields; for the Jews it was the only source of income.[37]

Some Jewish weavers decided to learn how to use the mechanical looms. Once they mastered the craft, they faced a new stumbling block: the textile workers' union to which many of them belonged. The union claimed that if Jews took factory jobs, Polish unemployment would rise.

Many Jewish workers left town in disgust. Others saw a new opportunity when a factory opened in Belkhatov in 1930. The owner, an Orthodox Jew, said he would hire Jewish weavers, but they could not work on the Sabbath or on Jewish holidays even if they wanted to do so. On Fridays, they could work only the morning shift. Clearly, to take advantage of the owner's offer, Jewish workers needed the cooperation of Christian employees. After much negotiating, they persuaded their Polish co-workers to take the Friday afternoon shifts and work all day on Saturday for extra pay. Although the Jewish workers lost a day's pay each week, they at least had jobs with benefits.

For a time, the two groups worked side by side without conflict. Then little by little, Polish workers began to complain about the agreement. They were stirred by anti-semitic newspapers, radio broadcasts, and speakers eager to arouse old prejudices and give new life to ancient myths. Before long, those workers were demanding that everyone work a standard eight-hour day, six days a week. Many Jewish workers were willing to do so but the owner refused to let them.

The Jewish workers decided to fight for their jobs. They began by withholding their union dues. If the union would not support them, they would not support it. A worker recalled the suspenseful weeks that followed.

> The antisemitic agitators spread propaganda saying that Jews wanted to destroy the eight-hour day; meanwhile, we began an educational campaign among the more class-conscious workers. With great effort we succeeded, and the factories remained open. On the one hand, we warned the Polish workers that under no circumstances would we allow ourselves to be pushed out of the factories; on the other hand, we argued that the maintenance of the previously established conditions was in the common interest of all the workers. The conflict continued for quite some time, but seeing our determination to defend our right to work, the Polish delegates eventually announced that they would accept our demands.[38]

CONNECTIONS

Historians note an increase in the number of hate groups during periods of economic crisis like a depression. How do you account for their findings? How are those findings similar to what happens during periods of political or social instability? What other factors encourage a rise in the number of hate groups?

Create identity charts for both a Jewish and a Christian factory worker in Belkhatov. What did they have in common? What divided them? What special problems did Jewish workers face that their Christian counterparts did not encounter? How did they try to overcome those problems? To what extent did the Depression complicate their efforts?

How did Jewish workers in Belkhatov fight for their jobs? How were their methods similar to those of the Jewish deputies in the Sejm? What differences seem most striking?

What does this reading suggest about the ways individuals and groups can end isolation and about the time it would take to do so? In your experience, what kinds of interaction break down barriers? What kinds enhance existing barriers or raise new ones?

Building Bridges in Changing Times

Like his father and grandfather before him, Henryk Goldszmit spent much of his life trying to bring together Poles and Jews. But in the 1930s, he was finding it harder to do.

By 1930, Henryk Goldszmit was a respected physician and a noted author of adventure stories for children and scholarly works for parents, psychologists, and educators. He also headed two of the most progressive orphanages in Poland, one for Jewish children and the other for Catholics. In addition, he published the first national newspaper written for and by children and served as the defender of their rights in the nation's juvenile courts. Yet few people in Poland knew his real name.

Goldszmit wrote under the pseudonym *Janusz Korczak*—the name of a patriotic hero in a popular novel. Biographer Betty Lifton believes the pen name was not chosen by chance. "In a country where one's last name reveals one's religious affiliation, Goldszmit was unmistakably a Jew, the outsider. With an old gentry name such as Janusz Korczak, Henryk could re-create himself as an insider, linked to an heroic Polish past. People who were unwilling to buy their child a book by someone named Goldszmit were more than willing to read a story by someone with a name as respectable as Korczak. Still, by 1933, it was common knowledge that Janusz Korczak was really Henryk Goldszmit."[39]

That year, Goldszmit was offered his own radio show on the condition that he use another pseudonym. Executives at the radio station were fearful that they would be accused of letting a Jewish educator shape the minds of Polish children. Korczak reluctantly agreed. He saw it as the opportunity of a lifetime. What other medium, he wondered, can bring the world "into the home, into the intimate areas of life, and into the human heart"? Korczak decided to call himself the "Old Doctor," the name he had used when he worked for Polish independence.

The program was a huge success. Children and adults alike rushed home on Thursday afternoons to listen to the Old Doctor on the radio. They never knew what to expect when they tuned in. One week, he might interview young patients in a hospital and the next, chat with listeners about everything from a child's relationships with adults to current events. Other weeks, he acted out stories with the help of children in his orphanage.

Then on May 12, 1935, Goldszmit and his listeners alike were stunned by a news bulletin: Jozef Pilsudski had died of cancer at the age of 67. As the entire nation mourned the loss of a beloved leader, Goldszmit wrote a tribute to Pilsudski entitled "A Pole Does Not Cry." Contrary to an old saying that Poland's heroes never cry, Goldszmit planned to tell his listeners that Pilsudski had cried at least twice in his life—once when his soldiers were surrounded by the Russians and again when his favorite horse died. It was the Old Doctor's way of telling his audience that it was OK to feel sad and even to cry. It was also a way of reminding listeners that, like all leaders, Pilsudski was human.

The government now controlled the nation's radio stations and reviewed programs before they were allowed to air. When the censors read Goldszmit's script, they ordered him to replace it with one that was less controversial. Although influential friends appealed the decision, the Old Doctor was forced to abandon his tribute. Only after Pilsudski's widow intervened was he allowed to read his tribute over the airwaves.

The show was broadcast on December 5. By then, nationalist newspapers had identified the Old Doctor as Janusz Korczak, the "so-called Pole" who was really Henryk Goldszmit the Jew. A few months later, his show was canceled.

CONNECTIONS

William Shakespeare once wrote that a rose by any other name would smell as sweet. How do Henryk Goldszmit's experiences challenge that idea? Would he have been as popular a writer if he had used his given name?

Make two identity charts, one for Henryk Goldszmit at the turn of the century and the other in 1936. How do you account for changes between the two charts?

After visiting Poland in 1938, Raymond Buell, the president of the Foreign Policy Association, called the government radio "an antisemitic weapon." How can the radio serve as a "weapon"? How dangerous a weapon is it?

By 1936, Korczak was seriously considering moving to Palestine. Why would a man who saw himself as a Polish patriot even think about moving to another country?

Abraham Lewin, a teacher in Warsaw, was deeply committed to Zionism and encouraged many of his students to settle in Palestine. He traveled there twice but returned to Poland after each visit, in part due to the poor health of his wife and child. In January, 1933 he wrote to a former student now living in Palestine:

> I often ask myself if I could put the Diaspora life, with all the doubts and soul-searching that characterize those around me, behind me and start an entirely new life there, of the sort that you live? The question arises of its own accord and cuts deeply, but I admit without shame that I find it difficult to give a positive answer. It seems that within me there is a terrible fear of "there," a fear that cannot be quieted solely by logic and reason. Yes, I think that this is a weakness that has its origins in man's too great love for himself . . . . I do not have the internal resources to throw off the chains of the past and to involve myself in the new life I have dreamt about, even if the fetters constraining me to my present circumstances were to be removed."[40]

The "Diaspora life" to which Lewin refers is life outside Palestine. How does he regard that life? Why is he reluctant to leave it? What would it take for you to leave all that's familiar for life somewhere else? What does it take to overcome the kinds of fears Lewin discusses in his letter?

In the fall of 1936, Goldszmit was asked to resign as a director of the Polish orphanage. Soon after, he also lost his job as a consultant in juvenile court. One of the lawyers who witnessed his dismissal later wrote, "I still cannot forgive myself for my silence at that time. Those officials who represented Polish law and justice informed Korczak: 'No Jew can be in charge of our juvenile offenders.'" Why is the lawyer unable to forgive his own silence? Suppose he and others had protested the dismissal. Would it have made a difference in overturning Korczak's dismissal? Would it have made him feel less alone? How might such a protest have affected the way they felt about themselves? How might it have affected actions they might take in the future?

Explosions of Violence

In the years after Pilsudski's death, extreme nationalists in Poland were encouraged by events in Germany. In 1933, Adolf Hitler became chancellor of Germany. By 1935, he and his Nazi followers had stripped Jews of their citizenship. Few people in Poland were prepared to go as far as Hitler had by 1935. Still, as the talk became more and more inflammatory, violence against Jews increased sharply. In the year after Pilsudski's death, nearly 1400 Jews were wounded and several hundred killed in antisemitic attacks.

The explosion of violence against Jews between 1935 and 1936 alarmed many people in Poland, including the nation's prime minister. In 1936, he assured members of the Sejm that "my government considers that nobody in Poland should be injured. An honest host does not allow anybody to be harmed in his house." But he insisted on the right to continue to exclude Jews economically. The Catholic church took a similar stand. In an open letter, Cardinal August Hlond advised Polish Catholics that "one does well to prefer his own kind in commercial dealings. . .but it is not permissible to demolish Jewish businesses, destroy their merchandise, break windows, torpedo their houses. One ought to fence oneself off against [the Jews'] anti-Christian culture but it is not permissible to assault Jews, to hit, maim or blacken them."

Such statements encouraged troublemakers who distributed leaflets calling for more violence. On March 9, 1936, in the town of Przytyk, a gang of extreme Polish nationalists put those words into action. By the time the dust had settled, two Jews and one of their attackers lay dead. When the news reached Warsaw, the Bund called for a general strike to protest the violence. To the surprise of many people, on March 17, thousands of workers, Poles and Jews alike, turned out for the demonstration. Many of the Polish workers belonged to the Socialist party. They regarded antisemitism as a "smoke screen" that diverted attention from the real causes of the nation's economic problems.

Although the Bundists and the Socialists continued to work together, their efforts did not stop antisemitism. In August of 1937 alone, there were 400 attacks on Jews in 79 cities and towns throughout Poland. In addition to the physical attacks, the nationalists intensified their campaign to isolate the Jews and force them out of Poland. In November of 1937, the Ministry of Education called upon the universities to set up "ghetto benches," segregated seating for Jewish students. Many Jews who chose to stand rather than sit on the ghetto benches were beaten by antisemitic students and then expelled from school.

Once again, the Bund took the protest to the streets by calling a two-day general strike. A Jewish high school student who participated wrote:

> The whole Jewish community chose to protest against this injustice. . . . We know well that after the university ghetto will come ghettos in other aspects of life. . . . I got up early. Despite the warning of the school director, I found many schoolmates in front of the school ready to join the march. . . . The streets were filled with Jews. Jewish stores were closed. The whole community showed its solidarity. . . nobody forgot this day. It stayed in our minds as one of the important Jewish days.[42]

A number of Polish scholars also protested the separation. A professor at the University of Warsaw announced that he would continue to abide by the nation's consti-

Members of the Jewish self-defense group in Przytyk stand guard as bread is distributed to poor Jewish families.

tution which prohibited discrimination based on religion or ethnicity. The rector of the University of Lvov resigned rather than allow "ghetto benches." He explained:

> Science cannot develop under conditions of constraint—not because of the professors' fancy, but because science signifies free thinking. Thought that is not free is not scientific. Without science it will be difficult to live, not only for the professors but also for those who are today destroying the Polish scientific institutions.[41]

By 1938, public opinion was beginning to change. When extreme nationalists tried to keep Poles from shopping in Jewish-owned businesses, they were stopped in some places by socialist workers and peasants. In city elections held in December 1938 and January of 1939, the socialists and the Bund worked together to win a majority in the town councils of Warsaw, Lodz, Lvov, Piotrkow, Krakow, Bialystok, Vilna, and other cities.

CONNECTIONS

Often it is a minority who favors violence, while the majority want peace. Why then is it the majority that is often silenced rather than the violent minority?

Why do many people view the late 1930s as a time of fear and despair in Poland? Why do others find hope in those years? Which view is closest to your own? Find out what was happening in the United States during those years. Were they a time of fear or hope?

What does this reading suggest about the ways individuals and groups can end isolation? How are the efforts described in this reading similar to those described in Reading 11? How do you explain differences in outcome? What other ways of protesting an injustice are described in this reading? Which do you consider most effective?

Write a working definition of the word *ghetto*. How is it like a neighborhood? How does a *ghetto* differ from other neighborhoods, including an ethnic neighborhood? What is a "ghetto bench"?

An English visitor to Poland in 1938 wrote of the controversy over education:

To even a reasonable Pole, it appeared intolerable that 30 to 40 percent of the places of influence in the life of the nation should be in the hands of Jews. That was the Polish side of the picture. To the Jew it appeared fantastic that a young and poor community, such as Poland desperately in need of expert services of all kinds, . . . should prefer vacancies and incompetence to the employment of qualified Jewish men and women anxious to take part in the building of the common life. But the picture had yet a third side. The output of graduates was far larger than the economic capacity of the country to absorb them. This was no peculiar Polish feature; the unemployment of graduates was almost a major world problem . . . , since in every country they provided the seedbeds of violence and extremism."[43]

The Englishman regarded the anti-Jewish riots and the "ghetto benches" as "safety valves"—ways of safely letting off steam. Were the riots and the benches "safe" ways of reducing tension? If so, for whom were they "safe"? How did the rector of the University of Lvov view such "safety valves"?

The Doors Close

Close to 400,000 Jews chose to leave Poland between 1919 and 1939. Many people wonder why more Jews didn't leave as antisemitism increased.

Polish Jews were not the only people unwelcome in their own country in the years between 1918 and 1939. American columnist Dorothy Thompson wrote in 1938:

> Since the end of [the war] some four million people have been compelled by political pressure to leave their homes. A whole nation of people, although they come from many nations, wanders the world, homeless except for refuges which may at any moment prove to be temporary. They are men and women who often have no passports; who, if they have money, cannot command it; who, though they have skills, are not allowed to use them. This migration—unprecedented in modern times, set loose by the World War and the revolutions in its wake—includes people of every race and every social class, every trade and every profession.[44]

Thompson feared for these refugees in a world in which "many countries have serious unemployment problems" and "strong barriers against immigration." She also noted an increase in anti-immigrant feelings and antisemitism in "countries which never before were conscious of having a 'Jewish problem' or an 'alien problem' where, prior to the past five years, the Jews were satisfactorily assimilated to the whole society, and where there is actual under-population."

Many of these refugees lacked "papers" in a world where "the right papers" could save one's life. Before World War I, it was possible to travel anywhere in the world without a passport or visa. Wartime fears of spies and anxieties over open borders changed the way nations regarded not only refugees but also ordinary travelers. Long after the war ended, the border guards and immigration agents continued to stop anyone who did not have the right papers.

Increasingly, government officials and police officers in many countries were prepared to turn citizens into "outlaws" at a moment's notice. Two years after Adolf Hitler came to power, Germans of Jewish descent were stripped of all political rights. Hitler's policies were based on a belief that "race" not only furnished "the key to world history but also to world culture." As he began to conquer neighboring countries, he put those theories into practice. After taking over Austria in 1938, he encouraged Austrian Jews to emigrate as long as they left their money behind. Other nations, however, did not want penniless Jewish refugees.

In July, 1938, delegates from 32 nations met in Evian, France. Each representative expressed sorrow over the growing number of "refugees" and "deportees", boasted of his nation's traditional hospitality and lamented its inability to do more in the "present situation." The Americans explained that laws they passed in the 1920s set "quotas" on the number of immigrants who could enter the nation from a particular country in any single year. And sadly, the quotas were filled. The British were aware that many refugees wanted to go to Palestine, then under British rule. Britain would like to admit them, but in view of the ongoing conflict between Arabs and Jews, it was not a practical solution. And so it went, with each nation speaking not about people but about "numbers" and "quotas."

Golda Meir, who would later become prime minister of Israel, attended the conference as the Jewish observer from Palestine. To her sorrow, she was not allowed to speak. She later wrote, "I wanted to get up and scream at them, 'Don't you know these so-called numbers are human beings, people who may spend the rest of their lives in concentration camps, or wandering around the world like lepers if you don't let them in?' Of course, I didn't know then that not concentration camps but death camps awaited the refugees whom no one wanted."[45] Hitler agreed with her assessment. After the conference, he concluded, "Nobody wants these criminals."

A number of Polish representatives attended the conference. Although they did not speak, they did listen. In the fall of 1938, soon after Hitler expelled Jews with Russian passports, the Poles took action. Fearing that Polish Jews would be the next to be expelled, Polish officials announced that the nation's passports would be considered invalid unless they had a special stamp. Although few Polish Jews in Germany wanted to return to Poland, they needed their passports to emigrate elsewhere. Yet when they tried to get the stamp, they were turned away. The crisis came to a head when the government announced that it would not issue stamps after October 31, 1938.

On the night of October 27, Zindel Grynszpan, a tailor born in Poland but then living in Hanover, Germany, heard a knock on the door.

> A policeman came and told us to come to Region II [police headquarters]. He said, "You are going to come back immediately; you shouldn't take anything with you. Take your passports.
>
> When I reached the Region, I saw a large number of people; . . . The police were shouting, "Sign, sign, sign." I had to sign, as everyone else did. . . . They took us to the concert hall on the bank of the Leine. . . . There we stayed until Friday night, about twenty-four hours; then they took us in police trucks, in prisoners' vans, about twenty in each truck, to the railroad station. The streets were filled with people shouting, "The Jews to Palestine!"
>
> After that, they took us by train to Neubenschen on the German-Polish border. . . . When we reached the border, we were searched to see if anybody had money, and if anybody had more than ten marks, the rest was taken from him. . . . The SS were giving us, as it were, protective custody, and we walked two kilometers on foot to the Polish border. . . . The SS men whipped us and hit those who fell behind, and blood was flowing on the road. . . . Then a Polish general and some officers arrived. They examined our papers and saw that we were Polish citizens, and they decided to let us enter the country. They took us to a village of about six thousand people, even though we were twelve thousand. The rain was driving hard, people were fainting. . . . There was no food.[46]

In Paris, Grynszpan's 17-year-old son Herschel learned about the deportation in a letter. Furious at the news, he marched into the German Embassy on November 7 and shot a Nazi official. The man died two days later. The Nazis used the incident to unleash a night of violence on the Jews of Germany and Austria. The night of November 9-10 came to be known as *Kristallnacht* (the "Night of Broken Glass"). That evening, the Nazis destroyed hundreds of Jewish businesses, synagogues, and private homes. About 20,000 Jews were arrested, dozens of others were wounded or killed. Although leaders around the world expressed their outrage at the violence, none of them offered to take in Jewish refugees.

Dorothy Thompson believed that a democratic nation cannot "wash its hands of [the problems of the refugees] if it wishes to retain its own soul." She insisted that "democracy cannot survive" if people deny minorities "the right to existence." How does she define the word *democracy?* Why does she believe that a democracy must protect the rights of minorities? Do you agree?

Take a careful look at a passport. What information does it provide? How does it define its owner? How important is that definition?

As a result of the events of *Kristallnacht,* President Franklin D. Roosevelt withdrew the American ambassador to Germany. Diplomats regard the removal of an ambassador as a serious move. The next step is to break off all relations—a move that usually precedes a declaration of war. According to a poll, 57 percent of all Americans approved the recall. But 72 percent were unwilling to allow more Jewish refugees into the nation and over half opposed aid to refugees who wished to settle elsewhere. What does the poll suggest about the limits of people's sense of outrage? What does it suggest about the way Americans viewed refugees in the 1930s?

[1] George Mosse, *Toward the Final Solution:* A History of European Racism (Fertig, 1978)

[2] Norman Davies, *Heart of Europe: A Short History of Poland* (Oxford University Press, 1984), 138.

[3] Ibid.

[4] A. M. Rosenthal, Copyright 1992 by The New York Times Company.

[5] Quoted in Joseph Lichten, "Notes on the Assimilation and Acculturation of Jews in Poland, 1863-1943" in The Jews in Poland, ed. Chimen Abramsky, et. al. (Basil Blackwell, 1986), 108.

[6] Sholom Aleichem, *Why Do the Jews Need a Land of Their Own?* trans. by Joseph Leftwich and Mordecai S. Chertoff (Cornwall Books, 1984), 54-55

[7] Ibid., 55-56.

[8] Vladimir Grossman, "The Jewish Expulsion in Russia 1914," in *Great Yiddish Writers of the Twentieth Century*, trans. Joseph Leftwich (Jason Aronson Inc., 1987), 497.

[9] Ibid., 496-497.

[10] The National Workingmen's Committee on Jewish Rights, The War and the Jews in Russia (New York, 1916), 77. Quoted in Ronald Sanders, *Shores of Refuge: A Hundred Years of Jewish Immigration* (Henry Holt, 1988), 228.

[11] Joseph Tenenbaum, *In Search of a Lost People: The Old and the New Poland* (Beechhurst Press, 1948), 11.

[12] Ibid., 11-12.

[13] Quoted in Ronald Sanders, *Shores of Refuge*, 315.

[14] Ibid., 316-317.

[15] Ibid., 317-318.

[16] Ibid., 318

[17] Henry Morgenthau, *All in a Life-Time* (Doubleday, 1922), 371.

[18] Ibid., 370.

[19] Joseph Brodsky, "Blood, Lies and the Trigger of History," *New York Times,* August 4, 1993, Op-Ed page. Copyright 1993 by The New York Times Company. Reprinted by Permission.

[20] Joseph Tenenbaum, *In Search of a Lost People,* 176-177.

[21] Henry Morgenthau, *All in a Life-Time,* 352.

[22] Ibid., 351.

[23] Ibid., 373-374.

[24] Quoted in Isaac Lewin, *The Jewish Community in Poland* (Philosophical Society, 1985), 221.

[25] Ibid., 222-223.

[26] Isaac Bashevis Singer, *A Day of Pleasure: Stories of a Boy Growing Up in Warsaw* (Farrar, Straus and Giroux, 1969), 211-216.

[27] Quoted in Isaac Lewin, *The Jewish Community in Poland,* 193-194.

[28] Raymond Buell, *Poland: Key to Europe* (Knopf, 1939), 308-309.

[29] Borukh Yismakh, "Sports Clubs and Self-Defense" in *From a Ruined Garden: The Memorial Books of Polish Jewry,* ed. and trans. Jack Kugelmass and Jonathan Boyrain (Schocken Books, 1983), 62

[30] Ibid., 63.

[31] Quoted in Nechama Tec, *In the Lion's Den: The Life of Oswald Rufeisen* (Oxford University Press, 1990), 14.

[32] Alfred Doeblin, *Journey to Poland,* trans. Joachim Neugroschel (Paragon House, 1991)

[33] Quoted in Ron Nowicki, *Warsaw: The Cabaret Years* (Mercury House, 1972), 170.

[34] Quoted in Celia S. Heller, *On the Edge of Destruction: Jews of Poland between the Two World Wars* (Wayne State University Press, 1977), 70-71.

[35] Quoted in Ron Nowicki, *Warsaw: The Cabaret Years,* 169.

[36] Quoted in Celia S. Heller, *On the Edge of Destruction,* 117.

[37] Hersh Goldmints, "The Struggle for the Right to Work," in *From a Ruined Garden,* 48-49.

[38] Ibid., 51.

[39] Betty Jean Lifton, *The King of Children,* (Farrar, Straus and Giroux, 1988), 207.

[40] Abraham Lewin, *A Cup of Tears: A Diary of the Warsaw Ghetto,* (Basil Blackwell, 1988), 9.

[41] Quoted in Raymond Buell, *Poland: Key to Europe,* 302.

[42] Quoted in Celia S. Heller, *On the Edge of Destruction,* 286.

[43] Quoted in Raymond Buell, *Poland: Key to Europe,* 302

[44] Dorothy Thompson, *Refugees: Anarchy or Organization?* (Random House, 1938)

[45] Golda Meir, *My Life* (Putnam, 1975), 158.

[46] From testimony at the 14th session of the trial in Jerusalem of Adolf Eichmann, April 25, 1961 and quoted in Ronald Sanders, *Shores of Refuge,* 446-447.

4. In Time of War

I want to talk about a certain time. . . .
This time was measured not in months but in a word
—we no longer said "in the beautiful month of May,"
but "after the first 'aktion,' or the second, or right before the third."

Ida Fink

On September 1, 1939, time took on new meaning for every Jew in Poland. On that day the German army invaded the nation. Three days later, France and Britain declared war on Germany. World War II had begun in Europe.

Immediately after the invasion, Germany's Quartermaster General, Colonel Eduard Wagner noted in his diary that it was Adolf Hitler's "intention to destroy and exterminate the Polish nation." Almost from the start, the Nazis waged two wars. One was fought openly on the battlefields of Europe. The other took place less publicly and its victims were not soldiers but children, women, and men whose only "crime" was their "race." This war within a war was not defined by battles but by "aktions"— German-led pogroms against civilians.

Hitler had long insisted that another world war would mean "the annihilation of the Jewish race in Europe." Now his soldiers seemed determined to carry out that threat. As the Germans marched triumphantly through town after town in Poland, they singled out Jews for "special treatment."

Some Polish Jews quickly fled the country. More would have left if they had had somewhere to go. Few nations in 1939 were willing to open their doors to large numbers of immigrants, particularly those with little or no money. Other Jews were determined to stay in Poland. It was their home. Their families had lived in the country for generations and they had survived other wars, other invasions, other pogroms. They had no reason to believe that this campaign against the Jews would be different from those in the past. This time antisemitism would lead to genocide.

This chapter describes Jewish life during the first year of World War II. Like the chapters that follow, it focuses on Warsaw, Poland's capital. Because it was home to more Jews than any city in Europe, its people came to symbolize the plight of all of Europe's Jews. This chapter also explores the choices Jews made there, as week by week, month by month, their options narrowed and often disappeared entirely.

On the Eve of War

When German troops marched into Austria in March of 1938, the world's leaders were silent. A few months later, Adolf Hitler threatened Czechoslovakia. This time, a few leaders protested. Still, in the end, they chose to appease Hitler rather than challenge him. By March of 1939, he controlled all of Czechoslovakia. Hitler then turned his attention to Poland. Throughout the spring and summer of 1939, he waged a war of nerves against the nation. Although many were alarmed by his threats, few believed that he would risk another world war by actually invading the country.

In 1939, Janina Bauman lived with her parents and sister in a prosperous suburb of Warsaw. She writes of her family, "We were all Polish, born on Polish soil, brought up in the Polish tradition, permeated with the spirit of Polish history and literature. Yet— Jewish at the same time, conscious of being Jewish every minute of our lives." That awareness was heightened in the spring of 1939. It was a time, Bauman recalls, when "the swelling menace of war hung over the country and aroused strong nationalist feelings. These often degenerated into chauvinism. Antisemitic slogans, speeches, articles became a staple diet. The common unrest could easily result in anti-Jewish riots. Jews were expecting them, fearing them. The ominous word 'pogrom' entered my vocabulary."[1]

Despite the unease, life for the Baumans and other Jewish families in Poland went on much as usual. In August, Janina celebrated her thirteenth birthday. She and her parents marked the event with a month-long vacation at a resort in Galicia near Lwow. Their holiday was cut short, when the world learned that Germany and the Soviet Union had signed a treaty promising that they would not go to war with one another. That news worried Poland's military leaders so much that they called all reserve officers to active duty. Among them was Janina's father. Janina recalls the family's hasty trip back to Warsaw:

We all travelled one whole day and night, stopping only to have a hasty meal wherever we could get it. There were [lines] of cars, wagons, and bicycles on the roads; people hurried in all directions driven by the same fears. We drove by quiet fields and woods, passed small villages already stirred by anxiety. Once we stopped in Rawa Ruska, a sordid little town near the Russian border. It was dark, but the narrow streets of the town were swarming with panic-stricken Jews packing their shabby bundles into their shabby carts, wailing in Yiddish. I picked up one word I could understand: "*Krieg*"— war. They were obviously trying to run away—but from whom and where to?

When, in the small hours of that same night, we approached Warsaw, we were stopped for a while by passing troops. Young, perhaps just called up, the soldiers looked sleepy and frightened. There were singing an enthusiastic military song with so little enthusiasm that it sounded sad.

Back in my peaceful [home], among loving people and reassuringly familiar objects, I can't help thinking about all this, I can't stop going through the horrors of the journey again and again. I don't know what to do with myself, the time drags by. . . . A nauseating anxiety fills my soul. Where is Father, what will happen to him, what will happen to all those other people, those poor panicking Jews, those dismayed young soldiers?

. . . . About nine o'clock on Friday morning we heard from a radio announcement that war had begun. High in the clear sky we could see planes flying from the west and back. Polish planes, we presumed, but could not be sure. The tense atmosphere brought about by waiting for the unknown was now suddenly broken. The villa was full of people again, as some relatives came and stayed with us. . . .

By Saturday, we had learned these were German, not Polish planes, speeding above us towards Warsaw. The radio now announced, now called off an air raid. Warsaw was being bombarded. We could hear the hollow sounds of distant explosions as well as the spanking noise of the anti-aircraft defense. We could see heavy clouds of smoke darkening the bright September sky.

Towards evening, Mother arrived from Warsaw, pale and distressed. She had been in a raid with Father, whom she had managed to meet for a while. A bomb had gone off quite near. They saw people wounded by the blast. An elderly man was killed. Father insisted she travel back to the villa and stay with us.[2]

A week later, Janina's father arrived at the villa. He came to bring the family back to Warsaw. The suburbs were no longer safe.

CONNECTIONS

What does Janina Bauman mean when she describes herself and her family as "all Polish" but "conscious of being Jewish every minute of our lives"?

What does *chauvinism* mean? At what point does nationalism become chauvinism?

Janina Bauman had a great-aunt who lived in Berlin. She visited Janina's family in the summer of 1937. Janina writes of her:

She was very distressed and sad and always sighed heavily when she spoke about what was going on in Germany. She would lower her voice and give frightened, furtive glances around every time she was about to say "Hitler". I developed a sense that "Hitler" was a rude, shameful word and I never used it. Whenever conversation in the sitting room touched upon the future—the next holidays, for example, or plans for another family get-together—Aunt Eugenia would sigh, "First let's survive." I sensed that nobody really believed what she was telling us. Her frightened glances and whispers they would explain away as an obsession of old age or the first symptoms of paranoia. I think we all felt relieved when she went home to Berlin. None of us ever saw her again. She died in a German concentration camp before the war even began.[3]

Why do you think Janina's family refused to believe Aunt Eugenia? What are the main differences between stories you believe without question and those you doubt?

In September of 1939, Chaim Kaplan, a Hebrew teacher in Warsaw, wrote in his diary, "War was expected, and had been expected for a long time, but when it actually broke out, it surprised everyone." How does Bauman's account support Kaplan's statement?

The Siege of Warsaw

As German fighter planes and dive bombers bombarded Polish cities and towns, German tanks and trucks roared across the frontier to occupy those communities. People called this new kind of warfare a blitzkrieg—*"lightning war."*

Martin Gray was fourteen years old when the Germans bombed Warsaw. He later wrote:

Suddenly, the war. My father is in officer's uniform, he clasps me by the shoulders, and I realize that I'm almost as tall as he is. We leave my mother and my brothers at home and set off together for the [train] station. In the streets, everything has already changed: groups of soldiers, trucks, the first lines outside the shops. We walk side by side in the road, shoulder to shoulder. He's stopped holding my hand: I'm a man. He shouts something to me from the window of the train which I can't hear, then I am alone in the street. I think this was the day we had the first raid: I watched the bombers, silver with black crosses, flying low in groups of three. . . .

A Polish policeman yells in my direction from a porch where some terrified passersby are huddling. I begin to run down the empty street: I must get home, I don't have to obey anyone. I saw my father shouting something from the train. I've got to be as strong as he is. My mother pushes me down to the cellar: the plaster falls, we're suffocating, women are sobbing and wailing. After the alert, we see from the window the first fires, in the working-class areas, in the direction of the Praga market-place. I begin to read the papers: France, England, America, everyone's sure to help us. We're going to fight to the end, the Germans will never enter Warsaw. I listen to the mayor's proclamations on the radio: Warsaw will never surrender. My mother's crying, my two brothers playing together. She and I are sitting in front of the radio. Often I put my arm around her shoulder as we wait for the news. There's fighting all along the frontier and everything's going badly. We listen to German broadcasts: they're announcing thousands of prisoners, tomorrow Hitler will be in Warsaw. "Poles," says the cheerful voice, "it's the Jews who are the cause of your troubles, the Jews who wanted the war, the Jews who are going to pay." Then the choirs, the songs. I turn the knob: Radio Warsaw is playing long pieces of mournful piano music. Then the bombers come back, at regular intervals; the cellar shakes. Incendiary bombs fall on the Jewish quarter, near us, and when we go upstairs again, the air is filled with dense smoke. "They're after the Jews," someone keeps saying.

My uncle comes to see us. He speaks to me. "If the Germans enter Warsaw, it's the Jews they'll go for first. You know what they did in Germany. Your father doesn't trust them." I nod as if I know. My mother is sitting near us and doesn't say a word. I nod uncomprehendingly: who are these German people whose language I know, why are they demolishing our lives, why do they hate the Jews? . . . . I'm now constantly out in the streets: I want to see, know, understand, fight, defend. The streets are full of ragged soldiers without rifles. . . . They talk about thousands of tanks, dead horses rotting on the roads, raids on Grudziadz—where the entire Polish Army is, including my father. My mother has stopped even trying to make me stay in. . . .

All along Nowy Swiat Street, the shops are closed. I run along behind the red and yellow buses full of soldiers en route for Zoliborz. There, for several days, I and some others dig holes and trenches. Because we are going to fight to the end and the

French and English will soon be on their way. When I return, covered with dust and mud, my mother doesn't say a word. One evening when I go to wash, I notice there isn't any water.

"Ever since this morning," my mother says.

Then we run out of food. I stop going to the suburbs to dig trenches. We have to live, we have to struggle like beasts to eat and drink. And the streets are full of beasts. I know men. But the species seems to have vanished. I fight to keep my place in a long line outside the local baker's. I push and shove women, like the others. I'm strong: I watch, I want my share for myself and my family, but I'm trying to understand. Maybe this struggle for yourself, for your people, is natural. Everyone seems to have stopped recognizing each other. Sometimes the soldiers hand out their rations. In one of the Warsaw parks, near where we live, are two of them with large greenish hats, who have opened their haversacks. Around them are women, children, and one of those old, bearded Jews, in a black skullcap. The women begin to shout, "Not the Jew, Poles first! Don't give the Jew anything!"

The soldiers shrug and hand the Jew a chunk of gray bread, but a woman rushes up, gives the Jew a shove and takes his bread. She's screaming like a lunatic, "Not the Jew! Poles first!"

The Jew doesn't answer, but moves off. The soldiers go on handing out food. I grit my teeth, don't say a word. I take a chunk of bread. I don't look Jewish. The streets are full of hate, now I know. You have to be on the alert, ready to spring, to run away. I fight to keep my place by the well and bring home water. . . .

I carry on, day after day. Then suddenly, one afternoon, the streets empty out. Smoke from the fires still hangs over the city, I'm on the far side of the Vistula. I feel alone, I run. From time to time, I pass others who are running too. I call out to one of them:

"What is it?"

"The Germans, the German! We've surrendered!"

They'd won. They were coming.[4]

CONNECTIONS

Why was Martin Gray drawn to the streets in the first days of the war? What did he know about the Germans in September of 1939? What did he fear? Why does he describe the streets as "full of hate"?

Martin Gray begins his memoirs with these words: "I was born with the war. The sirens wailed, the bombers skimmed the rooftops, their shadows glided across the road, and in the streets people were running, clutching their heads." Why do you think he sees the war as the beginning of a new existence?

Gray writes, "Everyone has stopped recognizing each other." What does he mean? Compare the way people responded to their neighbors in the early days of this war with the way they responded during World War I. (See Chapter 3.) How does the stress of war affect the ways people regard minorities? What other factors influence how we tend to see *them*?

How did Janina Bauman (Reading 1) define the word *Pole*? How is the word defined in this reading? What does your answer suggest about the ways many Poles and Jews defined "their universe of obligation"— the circle of individuals and groups toward whom it has responsibilities, to whom its rules apply, and whose injuries call for amends— in the first days of occupation?

Flight

Many people fled Warsaw even before the Germans entered the city. Among them were some Polish and Jewish leaders. For ordinary people, the options were more limited until September 17—the day the world learned that Germany and the Soviet Union, long-time enemies, had secretly agreed to divide up Poland. Now, as much of the eastern part of the nation fell under Russian rule, thousands headed east to Soviet territory.

Leaving home, even in time of war, is never a simple decision. It depends on many factors, some external and others internal. Chaim Kaplan, the principal of a Hebrew high school in Warsaw before the war, described a few of those factors in his diary:

> Jewish youth has no present and no future, and it is fleeing for its very life. . . .There is no obstacle from the Soviet side, and the Nazi conqueror has no established policy. One never knows what is prohibited and what is permitted . . . .
>
> Right after the conquest, the border was open. You could cross it without a permit, and whoever wanted to queue up for three days could even receive a permit explicitly stating that the bearer was entitled to cross the border into Russia, with his baggage and possessions, using any means of transportation. But in reality the route is full of dangers. According to the law, those crossing the border are permitted to take only 20 zloty with them. Since this is a regulation which cannot possibly be obeyed, people connive to smuggle out larger sums, and here many fail. On the way they are assaulted and robbed. The border guards know that Jewish lives and money are public property and they deal with those who cross in whatever fashion strikes their fancy.
>
> People therefore prefer to cross without permission: they do not trust the legalities of the conqueror. When they cross secretly they feel more secure, for there is no refugee that does not take with him a larger sum of money than the law permits. And so the "green border" has been publicized among the refugees, and experts in border crossings earn tremendous sums at their "profession."
>
> Those in the know estimate that over a million refugees have fled to Russia. And no matter how the numbers swell, they are welcomed. But where will this large mass of people settle? Some particularly skilled workers have already been transferred to the interior of Russia, but the majority either have some cash and are managing, or have nothing and are hungry and thirsty.[5]

Many of the refugees in Russian-occupied territory were young men mobilized after the invasion. On September 6, the Polish government had ordered all able-bodied men to assemble east of the Bug River to form an army in defense of Warsaw. Among those who left was Alexander Donat, the publisher of a Warsaw newspaper. When Poland surrendered on September 27, he was stationed in Lutsk, a town now under Russian control. He recalled:

> Jews had to face the decision: to return to Nazi-occupied Warsaw to join their families, or remain under Soviet rule. The new Nazi-Soviet border was not too difficult or too dangerous to cross. Wave after wave of refugees from Nazi-held Poland brought terrifying reports of what was happening there. From that side thousands fled Nazi persecution; from the other thousands returned, overwhelmed by family attachments.

Donat wanted to stay in Russia, but his wife refused to leave Warsaw. He recalled:

> She took me on a tour of our beautiful seven-room apartment and talked about how miserable life was in Russia. It was November, already turning cold, and how could we expect to sneak across the frontier with a baby not yet two years old? And what about the seventy-two-year-old aunt who lived with us? And the rest of our family? Lena was sure the Germans would be vicious, but what could happen to women and children? She was a licensed pharmacist, and war or no war they would need her. She could support herself and our son. But I was in danger. Hadn't I published . . . exposes of the Nazis? The sensible thing was for me to return to the Soviet-held sector of Poland. The war wouldn't last long and we'd be reunited then. In the meantime, they'd make out somehow.[6]

Not long after Donat returned to Russian-occupied territory, he heard that the borders were about to be closed. He decided that if he did not act quickly, he might be separated from his family forever. So at the end of December, he rejoined his wife and son in Warsaw.

Before the war, Adina Blady Szwajger was a medical student. Her husband Stefan, a law student, was among the thousands of men mobilized soon after the war began. After Poland surrendered, he too found himself in Russian territory. Adina Szwajger decided to join him there and complete her education. She later wrote:

> There were rumors that "there" (in Bialystok, Vilna, and Lvov), life was practically normal and that the border was open, so we would be able to go there and back. I didn't take long to think it over. . . . On 11 October, with my friend Ewa Pat, her mother and my cousin Boris Szwajger, I left Warsaw in a cart. There were a few others with us on that cart who also wanted to cross the border.
>
> On 13 October, I was in Bialystok. I met Stefan almost immediately. It wasn't difficult. There were so many people we knew. Almost all from Warsaw. On 15 October, we filled in a questionnaire. One of the questions was: "Do you intend to go back to Poland after the war or to stay in the Soviet Union?" Obviously, the majority answered that they were going back to Poland. In that way they sealed their fate.
>
> The fate of deportees. All those who answered like that were sent, several months later, to [Siberia]. My answer was the same. But I didn't go to the depths of Russia. I managed to escape even though I didn't quite realize the danger of deportation. . . .
>
> The fact that I managed to leave in time I owe—something never explained—to a colleague, a Ukrainian from Lvov. I don't know why but that day he approached me at the university and whispered: "Go—I've seen your name on the list of deportees." I didn't go back to where I was staying with my cousin and her son and, just as I stood, without anything and in my worst clothes, I went to the station and left for Bialystok. I urged my cousin to go with me. She didn't want to. She didn't believe it. I went alone. The next day, they took her and her one-and-a-half-year-old child. Miraculously, they survived the far north.
>
> The border was closed. You had to "smuggle" yourself out of the country. No, I didn't realize the danger I was in. I remember only a feeling of boundless horror at not returning to Poland, at staying in Russia away from Mamma and my country. I was— we were—even so naive as to think that, after waiting out the period of "deporations", we'd be able to go back and finish our studies. That's why Stefan stayed on in Bialystok for a while. He was to get the feel of the situation and follow me or wait for my return. We thought that the journey would be safer for a woman. Of course,

returning to Lvov proved to be impossible. Stefan came back to Warsaw a few days after me. We were happy to be together again.

My colleagues were deported. Many never returned.[7]

Szwajger trekked across the icy countryside, "hungry, dirty, short of sleep and frozen." For a time, she traveled with a band of smugglers who regularly crossed the border. But in the darkness, she was unable to keep up with them. So she stubbornly trudged on alone until she finally reached the "right" side of the border.

After taking a train to Warsaw, Szwajger walked to her mother's apartment from the station. Her mother stared at her in horror. "Why did you come back?" she asked.

CONNECTIONS

This reading describes a number of decisions made in the fall and early winter of 1939. Those decisions were based at least in part on information. What did Jews know in the fall of 1939? Decisions are also based on assumptions about "human nature" and the way the world functions. People sometimes call these assumptions "common sense." What did common sense suggest was the "right thing" for a Jew to do in the fall of 1939? Decisions also reflect people's values. On what values were these decisions based?

In retrospect, fleeing east was the right decision. Despite the possibility of labor camps and great suffering, most of the Jews from Poland who survived the war were those who chose to go east. At the time, however, it was virtually impossible to know it was the right choice. Alexander Donat says of the decision he made in December of 1939, "We knew we faced dreadful anguish, but never in our wildest dreams did we anticipate the ultimate holocaust." What did he mean? Is his evaluation also true of Szwajger's decision? How would you answer the question Adina Szwajger's mother raised? What does your answer suggest about why more Jews did not flee in 1939?

For over twenty years, Germans were taught to regard Russian communists as their enemies. Now they were told otherwise. How do enemy nations become allies? How does the average citizen come to view a former enemy as a friend? What part does propaganda play in the creation of enemies? What part does it play in turning those same enemies into allies?

On April 13, 1943, the Germans announced that they had discovered the mass graves of Polish officers in the Katyn forest near Smolensk in western Russia. The International Red Cross later confirmed that the Russians had executed about 14,500 prisoners of war—mainly officers — in Katyn in the spring of 1940. Among them were Janina Bauman's father and uncle. They died not because they were Jews but because they were Poles. How does the Katyn Massacre explain why many Jews and Poles came to believe that they had no meaningful options during the war?

The Star

Soon after the invasion, the Germans incorporated western Poland into Hitler's Third Reich. The rest of German-occupied Poland, including Warsaw, was organized into the General Government with Krakow as its capital. In both sections, the Nazis issued orders that set Jews apart from their neighbors. One such order required that every Jew in Warsaw over the age of ten wear "a white armband at least 10 centimeters wide with a Star of David on it."

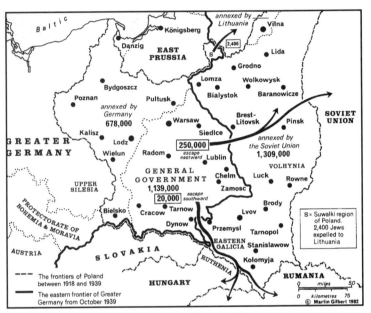

The German-Soviet Partition of Poland, September 28, 1939.

In late 1939, a Jewish leader wrote, "Until the entry of the Germans into Warsaw the Jews suffered equally with the Poles. There were dead and injured from among both peoples." But almost immediately, the Germans made it clear that they intended to deal very differently with the Jews than with the rest of the population. Halina Birenbaum, who was just ten years old at the time, recognized the difference almost immediately.

> Columns of German troops marched into the burning, ruined city. . . . Here and there the Nazis distributed bread and soup from kettles. The famished people of Warsaw stood in lines from which the Nazis at once dragged out any Jews and beat them mercilessly.
>
> For right at the beginning, they began to separate their victims into "better" and "worse" categories, Aryans and Semites, Poles and Jews—so as then to ill-treat, loot and murder all alike. They set up districts for Germans only, with separate districts for Poles and yet others for Jews. To simplify the differentiation of Jews from other nationalities, they forced Jews to wear a special armband bearing the Star of David; this made it easier to ill-treat them, for the armband served as an identification mark.[8]

Alexander Donat recalls that "quite an industry sprang up to produce these armbands; some were made of finest linen, with or without embroidery, but there were paper and celluloid ones too. For the first few weeks armband peddlers loudly hawked their wares and except for a few rare rebels, Jews accepted the armbands and wore them with dignity, feeling that to do so disgraced not us but those who imposed them on us."9 Chaim Kaplan had a similar view of the decree. He noted in his diary:

> [The] conqueror is turning us into Jews whether we like it or not. Nobody is being discriminated against. The Nazis have marked us with the Jewish national colors, which are our pride. In this sense we have been set apart from the Jews of Lodz, the city which has been annexed to the Third Reich. The "yellow badge" of medieval days has been stuck to them, but I shall wear my badge with personal satisfaction.
>
> I shall, however, have revenge on our "converts." I will laugh aloud at the sight of their tragedy. These poor creatures, whose number has increased radically in recent times, should have known that the "racial" laws do not differentiate between Jews who become Christians and those who retain their faith. Conversion brought them but small deliverance. The conqueror was accustomed to ask the Jews seized for forced labor, "*Jude?*" The convert could of course "tell the truth" and say no. But now the conqueror will not ask, and the convert will not "tell the truth." This is the first time in my life that a feeling of vengeance has given me pleasure.10

Young Martin Gray found no "personal satisfaction" in wearing an armband. To him, it meant one thing: "This is a man you can rob, beat, or kill." As someone who now helped support his family by trading in the local market, he decided it was safer to pretend to be a Pole. He kept his armband in his pocket.

Janusz Korczak, the noted educator (Chapter 3), was one of the "few rare rebels" who dared to protest the decree. Instead of wearing the band, he took to appearing in public in his old Polish army uniform. When a colleague expressed surprise, Korczak told him that he was protesting German attempts to brand him "only a Jew." He was not willing to give up his Polish identity. The Nazis responded to his silent protest by sending him to prison. He was released only with the help of influential friends who bribed Nazi officials.

Yitzhak Zuckerman, a young Zionist leader, also objected to the regulations. Rather than take off his hat to the Germans, he chose to go bare-headed even when winter temperatures in Warsaw fell below zero. Many of his friends did the same, but they all wore their armbands. As Zuckerman later explained, if you did not wear it you could be jailed but "you could also be murdered on the spot, without a trial." He decided that the protest was not worth the risk.

A few weeks after the decree requiring armbands, Jews were forbidden to move from one house or apartment to another without permission. Then came a decree requiring that Jews register their property and possessions. By January, Jews were no longer allowed to use trains without special permission. They were barred from restaurants, bars, even public parks. Next Jews were required to sit in special sections on public street cars. Little by little, step by step, Jews were increasingly identified, stigmatized, and segregated.

Apolinary Hartglas, a Zionist leader and a former member of the Polish Parliament, described the way the Poles initially responded to the armbands:

> Occasionally, [Poles] attack Jewish passers-by, but such attacks are not common. There is also another side to the picture. Poles often rise and offer their seats when women wearing the Jewish badge enter street cars. Once a German soldier came into a train shouting "*Juden raus*!" [Jews out!] Thereupon a dignified elderly Pole rose and said: "If the Jews go, we go too." He left the car and was followed by all the other Poles present.[11]

The incidents Hartglas describes took place in the winter of 1939-1940. In Reading 2, Martin Gray offers an account of the relationship between Poles and Jews in September of 1939. What are the differences? How do you account for those differences?

By the spring of 1940, Polish attitudes toward Jews seemed to be shifting again. One man wrote: "At first the Poles tended to express support for the Jews forced to wear armbands, but in time this feeling cooled, and Poles apparently avoided encounters in the streets with their branded Jewish friends." How do you account for this change?

Soon after the occupation of Poland, a Nazi official urged that Germans in Poland make the most of the traditional distrust that existed between Jews and Poles. How did the requirement that Jews wear armbands further that objective?

On February 23, 1940, Emmanuel Ringelblum, an historian who lived in Warsaw, wrote that Nalewki Street [in the heart of the Jewish section of the city] "looks like Hollywood nowadays—wherever you go, you see a star."[12] Being a Jew in Warsaw was no longer a matter of self-definition or self-identification. What does it mean to lose the right to define yourself? How important is that right?

Chaim Kaplan called Jewish converts to Christianity "poor creatures." Another Jew in Warsaw said of those converts: "Their suffering took on a different quality. For us it was an inevitable adjunct of our heritage; for them it was an additional burden, an unrelieved trauma." What was that "additional burden"? Why was it seen as traumatic?

After the war, Yitzhak Zuckerman reflected on his decision to wear an armband:

> Who could have understood in that first moment that from the white and blue armband with the Shield of David—that from the Band of Shame—a straight line that would extend direct to Treblinka [a Nazi death camp]? The incidents began and we grew accustomed to them. We were humiliated when we were forced to remove our caps in the presence of the German commanders . . . and we grew accustomed to that. We wrestled with ourselves when the Germans seized us for the slave labor battalions. . . and we grew accustomed to that. We became used to not eating, to dying of the typhus, to starving. We grew accustomed to all of this. There was a certain force that prevented us from seeing reality as it actually was.[13]

How does each incident Zuckerman describes prepare for the next? What danger does Zuckerman see in becoming "accustomed" to one humiliating incident after another?

Collective Responsibility

The Germans used terror to control the peoples they conquered. They also relied on a doctrine they called "collective responsibility." In the first months of the occupation, Jewish leaders discovered how effective that doctrine was in stifling resistance.

During the siege of Warsaw, many Jewish leaders, including members of the Warsaw *kehillah,* had left the country. Among the few who remained in the city was Adam Czerniakow, an engineer. When the Germans took over the city, they brought him to Gestapo [German secret police] headquarters and ordered him to form a Judenrat or Jewish Council and serve as its leader. Shmuel Ziegelboim, a Bundist who reluctantly served on the Jewish Council, described its first meeting:

> A Gestapo officer by the name of Mende came to the meeting and delivered a speech as if he were speaking to criminals. He ordered the Judenrat to stand while listening. He said that the fate of the Jews and of the Judenrat was in the hands of the Gestapo. The Judenrat is not to approach any other Nazi officer. No discussions. . . . What the Gestapo orders has to be executed promptly and meticulously. . . .
>
> Three weeks after the appointment of the Judenrat in Warsaw, its members were suddenly called to an urgent meeting. It was on a Sabbath. At 12 o'clock, Gestapo men came to the chairman and ordered him to call a meeting for 4 o'clock the same day. Out of the 24 members of the Judenrat, only 16 could be located. . . . At a quarter past four the doors were abruptly forced open. Gestapo men entered, rifles, pistols, and whips in their hands. They took up places in a half-circle around us and looked at us with angry, evil eyes without saying a word. They appeared so unexpectedly, with such force and in such a terrifying manner that all sixteen people seated around the table jumped up. For a long time, there was an agonizing, stifling stillness in the room. The Gestapo men, standing around, saying nothing, looked at each one of us, some artfully smiling, until one of them barked out in barracks-like tone: "All present?

When the Nazis discovered that only 16 people were present, they gave the group thirty minutes to locate the missing members and 24 alternates. Members frantically pulled in people from the street. The Germans ordered the Jews to form two lines—one for members and the other for alternates. Ziegelboim described what happened next:

> [About] 50 Gestapo men under the command of an officer entered the hall. All carried pistols or whips. . . . Finally, in a threatening, harsh voice the officer uttered: "Jews you listen to me, and listen carefully! The commandant has ordered that all Jews of Warsaw must leave their present homes and move to the streets that have been designated for the ghetto, not later than Tuesday. To assure that the order is strictly carried out, all 24 alternates will be taken hostages. With their heads they are responsible for the exact execution of the order. You, the members of the Judenrat, are also responsible with your heads. We are not taking you away now simply because somebody must remain here to take care of the execution of the order." The 24 Jews, present only by accident, were then surrounded by the Gestapo men. Orders were shouted.
>
> "About face, forward march" and they marched out. Outside in the street, trucks were waiting and the Jews were carried away.[14]

The shaken members of the Judenrat were faced with a virtually impossible task: They had to move over 100,000 Jews into a small section of the city in just three days. Ziegelboim argued strongly against even trying to do so. Bernard Goldstein, a Bundist leader, described what happened next.

> After some further discussion, the Judenrat agreed on a compromise: It would take no responsibility for setting up the ghetto, but would inform the Jews of what was being planned so they could prepare to move out of the proscribed sections of the city.
>
> That night the rumor that there was to be a Warsaw ghetto spread through the Jewish neighborhoods. The following morning thousands of Jews appeared in a panic before the Community Building . . . clamoring for information. Before a crowd of more than ten thousand people, [Ziegelboim] was lifted to the shoulders of two comrades. In the name of the Jewish trade unions and the Bund, he told the people to keep up their courage, to refuse to go into a ghetto, and to resist if they were forced to do so. The substance of his defiant speech spread quickly through the city by word of mouth. Such boldness in the face of the Germans was unheard of; it acted as a tonic, strengthening the spirit of resistance among the Jews.
>
> The obvious approval with which the Jews greeted [Ziegelboim's] audacity had its effect upon the Judenrat. A delegation was sent to the Warsaw commandant of the Wehrmacht [German army] to appeal for a reversal of the Gestapo's orders. The Army was still supreme in Warsaw, and the commandant, who professed never to have heard of the Gestapo plan, issued the necessary instructions to nullify it. For a time the threat of a ghetto receded.[15]

Because Ziegelboim's speech was "the equivalent of his death warrant," his fellow Bundists smuggled him out of the country. With their help, he eventually reached London, where he represented the Bund in the Polish parliament-in-exile. Within weeks of the incident, the Nazis had resolved the power struggle between the army and the Gestapo. And both groups continued to use "collective responsibility" as a way of maintaining order.

For example, on November 13, a Jew shot and killed a Polish policeman during a fight at 9 Nalewki Street. The Nazis promptly arrested every man in the building that evening—53 men in all. Their wives turned to the Judenrat for help. The Gestapo said it would release the men in return for a ransom of 300,000 zlotys (about 60,000 dollars). Members frantically tried to raise the money. By Friday, November 25, they had all but 38,000 zlotys. The Gestapo agreed to wait until Monday for the balance. As soon as they had all of the money, the Nazis announced that the 53 men were dead. The Judenrat later learned that they had been executed even before the Nazis demanded the ransom.

In his diary Czerniakow wrote of meeting with the families of the murdered men: "A scene very difficult to describe. The wretched people in confusion. Then bitter recriminations against me. I left the Community at 1:30. The poor creatures were clinging to the carriage. What could I have done for them?"[16]

That question haunted Czerniakow and other members of the Judenrat. Less then two months later, it would be raised yet again. This time, the Nazis were trying to locate a young man named Andrzej Kot, the founder of a Polish underground group and the son of Jewish converts to Christianity. Although Kot had no ties to the Jewish community, the Germans demanded that the Judenrat find him and turn him over to authorities. When members were unable to do so, hundreds of Jewish and Polish doctors, lawyers, engineers, teachers, and rabbis were arrested and promptly executed. Each of these incidents left Czerniakow and other members of the Jewish council less and less willing to challenge the Nazis' authority and more and more likely to "cooperate" with the regime.

CONNECTIONS

What does the term *collective responsibility* mean to you? How did the Nazis use the term? What is the relationship between "collective responsibility" and terror? How is "collective responsibility" related to reprisals? What assumptions about human nature inspired the strategy? On what values was it based? Why did the Germans see it as a valuable tool for preventing resistance? Based on this reading, how effective do you think it was?

Czerniakow was a secular Jew who spoke Polish and German fluently but knew little or no Yiddish. What does this reading suggest about the way he saw himself? What does it suggest about the way he viewed the people of the community he now served? At one point in the reading, Czerniakow asks himself, "What could I have done for them?" Why was he haunted by that question?

David Wdowinski, a psychiatrist active in Warsaw's Jewish community, believed that members of the Judenrat failed to understand that in "the tragic burlesque that the Germans created for them," "they were merely miserable puppets on a string." How do you think Czerniakow and his associates would have responded to that assessment?

Judenrat leaders in every Polish city faced similar moral dilemmas but came up with very different solutions. You may want to research other Jewish councils so that you can compare and contrast their decisions with those of Warsaw's Judenrat.

Terror and Humiliation

Throughout the fall of 1939 and the winter of 1939-1940, the Germans singled out Jews for special treatment. They snatched Jewish men off the streets of Warsaw and forced them to engage in menial and often humiliating tasks.

The Nazis take a group of Jews from Warsaw for forced labor.

Two entries from a diary left by an unknown Jew describe the way the Nazis terrorized Jews in Warsaw and other cities:

> I was captured for forced-labor on Nowogrodzka Str. I was beaten and dragged into a post-office, where I was forced to carry very heavy buckets with bricks, cement, garbage, until I collapsed, my nose bleeding hard.
>
> After 7 hours of hard labor, I was released.
>
> I had to stay 5 days in bed, very sick. I remained 14 days at home, suffering physically and mentally. Then only was I able to go out.[17]

Just one month later, the same man wrote:

> I was among the 330 Jews whom they captured at noon. We were led outside the city to a square and ordered to sing and dance for a while. Then we were told to dig the humid clay with our hands. We were forced to dig till our hands swelled. Late in the evening, we were beaten; many of us were robbed of our coats. Then we were driven at a run back to town. We had to run as fast as we could continuing to sing. Those who stopped singing, were beaten murderously. Many of us came home crippled.[18]

The Judenrat offered to provide the Nazis with a daily quota of workers on the condition that the roundups stop. Bernard Goldstein described what happened next:

> The Germans agreed to this plan. Although the Judenrat set it up in what appeared to be a fair way, serving subpoenas on the list of registered Jewish citizens in rotation, the operation very quickly became corrupt. . . .
>
> From the outset the Nazi racial policy was a hardship for all Jews, but the wealthy found they could soften its effects. They were able not only to buy themselves out of forced labor but to get black-market food and to buy other favors, while the poor in some cases could not even afford to pay the few zlotys required to register for a ration card. Some families even found it necessary to sell the ration cards of some members in advance so that they might have money to buy cards and food for the others. . . .
>
> In spite of the wishes of its members, the *Judenrat* was forced to become an instrument of the anti-Jewish policy of the authorities. The blows of the Nazis were struck at the Jews through the *Judenrat*, which acted as the involuntary agent of the occupation in the Jewish community[19]

CONNECTIONS

At first, the Nazis rounded up only Jewish men. In time, however, writes David Wdowinski, they hunted women: "Jews were caught and forced to work without food or water all day long whenever the Germans wanted them to perform menial tasks. Women, especially the most elegant, were captured and ordered to clean private apartments and offices. They were given no rags or cleaning implements and were compelled to take off their undergarments and use them as rags.[20] Why do you think the Nazis targeted "the most elegant" Jewish women? What effect do you think acts of humiliation like those described in this reading had on Jews? On German soldiers who participated in these roundups? On both Jewish and Polish bystanders?

Historian Israel Gutman assessed the efforts of the Judenrat to end the kidnappings by providing the Germans with work crews:

> While the snatching did not cease, it was reduced. Systematic exploitation of Jewish labor in organized work details had replaced a chaotic and disruptive process. The Germans had their laborers whom the Judenrat would provide in an orderly process without requiring the expenditure of German personnel.[21]

What did the Judenrat know about the Germans when they made the offer to provide labor battalions? What assumptions about human behavior guided their offer? On what values was it based? Why do you think it failed to stop the kidnappings or end the humiliation and terror? What do your answers suggest about why many consider it difficult if not impossible to judge the choices people made during those years?

Jewish Self-Help

Little by little, many Jews in Warsaw came to distrust the leaders of the Judenrat. They wanted an organization that served them <u>not</u> the Nazis. And so they created new democratically elected organizations dedicated to helping one another.

For many Jews in Warsaw, soup kitchens provide the only meal of the day.

For centuries Jews in Poland had reached out to one another and to their non-Jewish neighbors in times of trouble. That tradition continued during World War II. For example, soon after the war began, Adina Blady Szwajger and a neighbor who was a nurse organized a first aid station on their block. After the city surrendered to the Nazis, there was no longer a need for emergency nursing on every block, but there was a need for other kinds of help.

Szwajger went to work in a children's hospital where the number of patients suffering from typhus and tuberculosis increased dramatically during the first year of the war. The hospital was supported by not only the Jews of Warsaw but also the American Joint Distribution Committee (the "Joint"). It had been helping the Jews of Poland since World War I. The hospital also received aid from a new organization in the Jewish community—tenants' committees. Alexander Donat, a leader of one of those committees, explains their work:

> Where the Judenrat was an institution created by the Nazi occupiers to transmit their decrees to the Jewish population, the Tenants' Committees were created by the Jews themselves to defend their own interests. The man who promoted them in Warsaw was generally believed to be the eminent historian Emmanuel Ringelblum. Eventually

the individual house committees were grouped into a federation, the Z.T.O.S., [in English] the Jewish Society of Social Welfare, and what remained of active social and intellectual leadership in Warsaw gravitated toward this organization. As the Judenrat became increasingly remote from the people, the Z.T.O.S. became more closely identified with them. These committees resisted all efforts by the Judenrat to make them its tools and they also served as the core of opposition to it. Small wonder, then, that the Z.T.O.S. was unpopular with the Judenrat . . . .

The Tenants' Committees were democratically elected and served as the real authority in each apartment house. At first they confined themselves to helping poor tenants, especially poor children. Gradually their activities were extended to health and hygiene, education and entertainment. In some buildings they organized communal kitchens and coordinated fuel and food purchases. At one stage a certificate issued by any Tenants' Committee was a document respected and honored by all Jewish authorities. The first big campaign the Committees organized was a clothing collection for Jewish prisoners of war who came back to Warsaw in large numbers in March, 1940. Forbidden to wear their uniforms and without any civilian clothes, these men were helped by the Tenants' Committees.[22]

The leaders of Z.T.O.S., also known as the Jewish Welfare Society, published annual reports that documented their work. These reports reveal not only the extent of their efforts but also the enormity of the need:

Every one of the Jewish [apartment] houses—some 1500 in Warsaw nowadays—and all residents are organized, with the House Committee at their head. Some eight or ten thousand people are thus involved.

The residents of each house must remember at all times that they are a cell, *a member of a great Jewish Family*, one part of a whole.

This is no doubt that direct aid to poor neighbors is vitally important. The initiative for neighborly assistance had its origin in this circumstance. But it is a grave, harmful thing when residents of a house believe they are doing all their duty when they only assist their immediate neighbors.

1. There are houses all of whose residents are utterly poor, and in some houses the majority are poor. Who shall assist them?

2. And there are orphanages, boarding-schools, refugee-points, public kitchens, clinics, laundries, and bath houses. All these have no House Committees of their own, nor good, helpful residents. . . .

Receiving the assistance from a central social institution enables the destitute to preserve his dignity, not to feel humiliated. . . .[23]

The publication goes on to itemize income and expenses between September, 1939 and August, 1940. Most of the money the committees raised went for food served at public kitchens. The report ends by urging every Jew to "contribute his share to the Jewish Social Mutual Aid. The Monthly Rate should be a sacred untouchable duty. This is the foundation upon which the moderate, little support we are able to provide is erected. Whoever does not regard the Monthly Rate as sacred undermines our very foundation, and defeats every effort to achieve anything."[24]

Michel Mazor, who worked for the Tenants' Committees, describes how the group came into being:

> Through the long winter evenings, the Jews could communicate only with residents of their own buildings, for the curfew started earlier for them than for the rest of the population generally at 9:00 P.M., but in certain periods even at 7:00 P.M. In addition, the impending danger facing all Jews, the violence and looting to which they were subjected, the sinister rumors of the fate that awaited them—all this bred the need to exchange ideas and to establish closer ties. In my own case, for example, I knew almost none of the neighbors in our building before the war; but with the onset of the hostilities, all the Jews left in our apartment building struck up acquaintances and were in constant contact with one another. Through this entirely natural need to unite and the necessity to remedy the plight of those Jews who had lost their incomes and means or had been ruined by lootings—and their numbers were always increasing—the general outlines of what would become the . . . [Tenants'] Committees began to take shape.[25]

Poles had their own organizations in Warsaw. Why do you think these groups did not band together with Jewish groups?

What did the Jews of Warsaw mean when they used the term "collective responsibility"? How did their understanding of it differ from the way the Nazis used the term?

What does the Jewish Welfare Society mean when it argues that each Tenants' Committee is a part of "a great Jewish Family"? In what sense are the committees part of a whole? How do they define their universe of obligation?

Religious Jews often quote Rabbi Hillel who taught, "If I am not for myself, who is for me? If I care only for myself, what am I? If not now, when?" What does the saying mean? How does it apply to Jews in Warsaw in the first year of the war?

At a time when the Germans were attacking Jews on the streets of Warsaw, why were Jewish groups so concerned with preserving the dignity of the poor?

Shortly after Z.T.O.S. was established, the Germans included it in a central organization along with Polish and Ukrainian social-welfare institutions in the General Government. Michael Weichert, the Jewish representative to the group, later wrote in his memoirs:

> It simply wasn't logical. On the one hand they persecute Jews to the utmost, and on the other they discuss a central organization for social aid with them. We didn't know that they were under pressure from the American Red Cross and the Commission for Polish Relief in the America, which sent a few boatloads of food, medicine, and clothing for the civilian population of the [General Government] and emphatically demanded that the distribution be handled by representatives of the population itself.[26]

Many Jews in Poland wondered why the rest of the world remained silent about the Nazis' treatment of the Jews. What do Wiechert's comments suggest about what "the world" might have done in 1939 and 1940?

Self-Defense

Historian Richard Rubenstein has written that people without political rights are "superfluous. They have lost all right to life and human dignity. Political rights are neither God-given, autonomous nor self-validating. The Germans understood that no person has any rights unless they are guaranteed by an organized community with the power to defend such rights." Jews had no one to defend them. They now lay outside the world's universe of obligation.

By the spring of 1940, Jews in Warsaw had become a hunted people. They were the target of not only the Nazis but also gangs of young Poles. Bernard Goldstein wrote of that time:

> Without let-up the Germans maintained a barrage of propaganda to stir up hatred against the Jews. In this they received the wholehearted cooperation of those groups of Poles for whom antisemtism had always been a political stock in trade. The Jews were depicted as filthy, lousy, diseased, scabrous, as bearers of sickness and epidemics. Again and again the propagandists demanded that they be isolated because they represented a danger to the health of the entire Polish population. . . .
>
> This propaganda had its effects, and incidents began to multiply.
>
> Early in April 1940, just before the Easter holiday, a Polish hooligan attacked an old religious Jew on a Praga street and began to tear out his beard and sideburns. Comrade Friedman, a husky, well-built slaughterhouse worker, happened by. He came to the defense of the helpless old man and gave the Pole a thorough beating.
>
> A crowd gathered quickly and a street battle broke out between Jews and Poles. German police arrested Friedman and shot him the following day. The Jews of Praga waited in terror for the consequences of Friedman's boldness.
>
> But the pogrom that followed had obviously been organized long before this incident. Groups of hooligans, mostly youths, stormed through the Jewish sections of Warsaw. They charged down the streets shouting, "Beat the Jews! Kill the Jews!" They broke into Jewish homes and stores, smashed furniture, seized valuables, and beat the occupants. In the district near the Polish Handicraft High School at 72 Lesno Street the older students joined the pogrom as soon as school was out.
>
> All over the city Jews barricaded their doors and hid in cellars and attics. Panic spread through the Jewish community.
>
> The Germans did not intervene. They neither helped nor hindered the pogromists. We saw many smiling German cameramen recording the scenes with relish. We later learned that the pictures appeared in German magazines. They were also shown in movie theaters as graphic evidence that the Poles were winning their freedom from Jewish domination.
>
> We were immediately besieged by requests from comrades that something be done. An emergency meeting of the Bund collective was held in my apartment at 12 Novolipya and we discussed the possibility of active resistance. Over us hung the danger of the German doctrine of collective responsibility. Whatever we might do to hinder the pogromists could bring terrible German vengeance on all the Jews of the city. Despite that danger, we concluded that we had no choice—we must strike back.
>
> We decided to fight back with "cold weapons"—iron pipes and brass knuckles, but not with knives or firearms. We wanted to reduce the danger that a pogromist

might be killed accidentally. We hoped in this way to teach the hooligans a lesson and to minimize the possibility that the Germans would inflict some terrible punishment on the entire Jewish community.

Every fighting contingent was mobilized—slaughterhouse workers, transport workers, party members. We organized them into three groups: one near the Mirovsky Market, another in the Fraciskanska-Nalefky-Zamenof district, and the third in the Leshno-Karmelitzka-Smotcha district.

When the pogromists appeared in these sections on the following morning they were surprised to find our comrades waiting for them. A bloody battle broke out immediately. Ambulances rushed to carry off wounded pogromists. Our own wounded were hidden and cared for in private homes to avoid their arrest by Polish or German police. The fight lasted for several houses against many waves of hooligans and raged throughout a large portion of the Jewish quarter.

The battle kept shifting to various parts of the city. Our organized groups were joined spontaneously by other workers. In the Wola district, our comrades received help from non-Jewish Socialist workers to whom we had appealed for aid. Many Christians tried to persuade the pogromists to stop. Many Jews, afraid of the dangers of "collective responsibility," tried to keep us from hitting back.

The fight lasted almost until the eight o'clock curfew. The following morning it was resumed. At about one o'clock in the afternoon the Polish police finally intervened and dispersed the combatants.

The expected retaliation against the entire community did not come. The Jews of Warsaw breathed easier. This dramatic demonstration that the Jews need not accept every blow helplessly gave them renewed courage. On all sides the Bund received expressions of thanks.[27]

CONNECTIONS

Adolf Hitler insisted that propaganda "must be limited to a very few points and must harp on these in slogans until the last member of the public understands what you want him to understand by your slogan. As soon as you sacrifice this slogan and try to be many-sided, the effect will be piddled away." What was the slogan Hitler wanted the Poles to understand? How did his commanders in Poland reinforce that message? How successful were they?

Why do you think Friedman attacked the Poles rather than the Germans? Why do you think the Germans chose not to intervene in the fight between Jews and Poles?

How did the doctrine of "collective responsibility" affect the decision-making described in this reading?

Many Jews believed that they had lost control of their lives. They could not make a difference no matter what they did or failed to do. What evidence can you find in this reading to support that view? How does the reading call that idea into question?

Violence is one form of resistance. What is its aim? What risks are associated with it? What other kinds of resistance are there? What are goals and the risks associated with each form of resistance?

Resistance

Almost immediately after the Germans occupied Warsaw, they outlawed all political and social groups in the city. They also made it a crime for Jews to attend school or gather for prayer. From the start, thousands of Jews organized secretly to defy these bans. We know about only a small portion of those resistance efforts.

In a diary entry dated October 2, 1940, the eve of the Jewish New Year, Chaim Kaplan described an act of defiance punishable by death:

> We have no public worship, even on the high holy days. There is darkness in our synagogues, for there are no worshipers—silence and desolation within, and sorrow looking on from without. Even for the high holy days, there was no permission for communal worship. . . .
>
> Everything is forbidden to us. The wonder is that we are still alive, and that we do everything. And this is true of public prayer, too. Secret *minyanim* by the hundreds throughout Warsaw organize services, and do not skip over even the most difficult hymns in the liturgy. There is not even a shortage of sermons. Everything is in accordance with the ancient customs of Israel. . . .
>
> They pick some inside room whose windows look out onto the courtyard, and pour out their supplications before the God of Israel "who kept us alive and supported us and brought us unto this season."[28]

Emmanuel Ringelblum reported in his diary that Warsaw alone had over 600 prayer groups. Each *minyan* consisted of at least ten men, the number needed for communal prayer.

The Nazis also outlawed education, banned newspapers, and closed libraries. Once again, thousands of Jews defied those decrees. Many parents banded together secretly to arrange schooling for small groups of four to eight children. They paid the teachers in loaves of bread. Others sent their children to secret schools run by the Bund or the various Zionist groups. One Zionist youth group, Dror, even organized a high school. When it opened in 1940, it had three students and seven teachers. By the spring of 1942, thirteen teachers were secretly teaching 120 students.

Dror and other youth groups ran soup kitchens and offered medical help to members and non-members alike, but they considered education their most important task. Many also tried to inform the public by publishing "newspapers." Bernard Goldstein's description of the one published by the Bund was true of others as well:

> Every Jewish printing plant of any description . . . had been confiscated by the Germans. One small press was allotted to the Judenrat. Our underground press therefore consisted of two mimeograph machines which far-sighted comrades had removed from institutional offices and hidden. After the small initial supplies of ink, paper, and stencils had been used, we acquired new supplies with difficulty. We worked in constant fear that if copies of our newspaper fell into the hands of the Gestapo they would be able to track us down through discovering our sources of paper or ink.[29]

The Bund, like other political groups, used messengers to distribute its publications to people in other towns and cities in Poland. By the end of the first year of occupation, members in Warsaw were in touch with groups in 60 Polish cities and towns through a network of couriers. Those couriers also secretly set up and then maintained connections with the Polish underground. Goldstein says of the links established by the Bund, "At first our contact was limited to the trade unions and the two wings of the Polish socialist movement, but later we were in close touch with other political groups, as well as with the underground Polish government."

CONNECTIONS

What forms of resistance did Jews engage in? What was the aim of their resistance? Is prayer a form of resistance?

Religious Jews, secular Jews, Zionists, and Bundists disagreed among themselves and with one another on many issues, but they were in complete agreement in 1940 on the importance of educating young Jews. They were even willing to risk their lives to do so. Why do you think they felt so strongly? What does their decision to educate young people suggest about their values and beliefs? Their assumptions about the future?

Why do you think many young people were attracted to youth groups in 1940? What did they offer that no other group in Warsaw could provide?

Historian Yisrael Gutman reports that underground newspapers began to appear in early 1940. With one exception, they were all printed on duplicating machines. Few groups printed more than 300 to 500 copies but each copy was passed from person to person. Even those who never saw a paper heard much of its contents through word of mouth. What role do you think a group's newspapers played in uniting members? In uniting the entire Jewish community? Why do you think members of each group organized couriers to distribute their papers to communities throughout Poland?

Most of the couriers who carried newspapers, letters, and information from town to town were young women. Ringelblum called them "heroic girls" He wrote of them:

> They are in mortal danger every day. They rely entirely on their "Aryan" faces and on the peasant kerchiefs that cover their heads. Without a murmur, without a second's hesitation, they accept and carry out the most dangerous missions. Is someone needed to travel to Vilna, Bialystok, Lemberg, Kowel, Lublin, Czestochowa, or Random to smuggle in contraband such as illegal publications, goods, money? The girls volunteer as though it were the most natural thing in the world.[30]

Why is information so critical to any act of resistance? What knowledge and skills would these young messengers need? Why do you think they took on such dangerous work?

The Germans also required that the Poles "leave the pavement free" for their conquerors, serve Germans first in every shop, and tip their hats to "important personalities of State, Party, and armed forces." Educated Poles were subject to arbitrary arrest. One of the questions historians have long debated is why the Germans ignored the Jewish underground movement, even though they were quick to suppress any hint of independent political thought among the Poles. How would you answer the question?

Adjustments

By the fall of 1940, Jews were finding it harder and harder to make a living. Many men were reluctant to leave home for fear that German soldiers would round them up for weeks, even months, of forced labor. Yet despite these and other obstacles, the Jews of Warsaw were, in the words of historian Israel Gutman, showing "an astonishing ability to adjust to the circumstances as well as a surprising imagination."

In a diary entry dated August 1, 1940, Chaim Kaplan noted:

> In these days of our misfortune, we live the life of Marranos [Spanish Jews who practiced their faith secretly in the 1500s]. Everything is forbidden to us, and yet we do everything. Every Jewish occupation is under a ban, yet nevertheless we somehow support ourselves; true, we do it with grief, but we do survive.[31]

Bernard Goldstein, a leader of the Bund, described the plight of Jewish workers during the first year of occupation:

> In the first weeks of the war the ruined city of Warsaw was the goal of tens of thousands of Jewish refugees who streamed in from all over the country. They swelled the normal Jewish population of 350,000 to more than half a million. Terrorized, bewildered, and helpless, they rushed to their brethren in the capital city, hoping that among the great numbers of Jews there they would find anonymity and peace. Many came in caravans from villages destroyed by the war or from sections from which the entire Jewish population had been expelled by the Germans.
>
> The refugee problem was a severe burden for the Jews of Warsaw. The food shortage was so severe that it was difficult to maintain life. There were no apartments for the great influx of new people. The refugees filled every vacant building, moving into the synagogues and schools and into every office belonging to the Judenrat. A few wealthy refugees paid fancy prices for apartments; others were fortunate enough to settle with relatives. But the overwhelming majority were poor and hungry and wandered from place to place seeking help. Many died daily of hunger and disease.
>
> The Jews of Warsaw, particularly those of the working class and lower middle class, who had no money or negotiable valuables, were themselves hard hit. The first to suffer were the white-collar workers—clerks in banks, offices, and government bureaus. They were fired immediately after the occupation. Every Jew connected in any way with the printing, paper, or publishing business was also discharged. The Germans prohibited the production of shoes, clothing, metal goods, or textiles for the Jewish market. The workers whose industries had formerly supplied Jewish consumers were left jobless. The Jewish food industry was hard hit due to the extremely low ration allotted to Jewish citizens.[32]

How did Jews survive under these circumstances? Simha Rotem, a teenager in Warsaw in 1939, offers one answer:

> To escape from hunger, my family started doing what others did: selling everything we had on the flourishing black market. Gangs of smugglers, especially youths, went into that business, although it entailed mortal danger. . . .
>
> I tried my hand at smuggling a few times. My parents opposed it for fear I

would get hurt, but when hunger intensified at home, no one could stop me. Apparently I was rather successful. Friends and relatives used to come to us for a bowl of soup, a sign that there was at least some food in our house.[33]

Some families had nothing to sell. Others quickly ran out of items people were willing to buy. So a number of Jews in Warsaw looked for other ways of making a living—some legal, some illegal. Bernard Goldstein describes a few of those efforts:

In place of leather shoes, the shoemakers, with the permission of the German authorities, created an entirely new industry. They manufactured shoes with uppers of fabric and soles of wood. Since the Germans had cut off the clothing supply completely and had excluded Jews from the textile and clothing industries, Jewish tailors developed methods of extracting, and even resewing the suit inside out to make it less shabby.

The city slaughterhouse was closed to Jewish workers, who had been a large part of its personnel. Many of them established small illegal slaughterhouses which depended upon the cooperation of peasant smugglers. Although Jews were not permitted to have either soap or candles, illegal factories were soon making them out of fat procured from the clandestine slaughterhouses. The shortage of sugar created an illegal saccharin industry. . . .

Salvage reached new levels of importance. Many Jews earned their livelihood by collecting rags, paper, bones, tin, and other metals from garbage cans or burned-out buildings to sell to the Germans.

To meet the need to repair the broken windows of the city's buildings thousands of Jews became glaziers. Since there was no glass, windows were repaired either by boarding them up with wood which kept out the cold but made the house dark and unpleasant, or by piecing together small bits of glass with putty to make larger panes. In a short time there were experts whose trade was making big panes of glass out of thousands of little ones in a mosaic pattern.

The lack of electricity, gas, and kerosene brought forth a lighting substitute—calcium carbide lamps. These were made by mounting two small metal pots one above the other. The lower one contained lumps of calcium carbide. The upper contained water, which was allowed to drip on the calcium carbide drop by drop, releasing acetylene gas which was the fuel for the flame. The use of these lamps spread quickly, and they became a commonplace in every Jewish home.[34]

CONNECTIONS

Why do you think Israel Gutman calls the kind of adjustments Bernard Goldstein describes in this reading both astonishing and imaginative? What do they suggest about the human capacity to adapt to adversity? What do they suggest about the ways Jews resisted the Nazis?

To whom do you think Jews sold the goods they produced? What do you think they purchased with the money they earned? What does your answer suggest about the links between Jews and Poles during the first year of the occupation?

The Walls Rise

Throughout the spring and summer of 1940, the Jews of Warsaw were increasingly isolated from others in the city. The Germans claimed this new segregation was a "health measure" to stop the spread of typhus. But by late fall, the real reasons for the separation were becoming apparent.

In March of 1940, the Germans began referring to the Jewish residential areas of the city as "plague-infected." On March 27th, they ordered the Judenrat to build a wall around the area. In June, they posted signs outside the Jewish area warning, "Danger. Epidemic."

The Jews of Warsaw found themselves trapped in the ghetto.

In August, the Nazis announced that the city would be officially divided into three quarters: German, Polish, and Jewish. In the weeks that followed, the Germans extended the curfew for Jews living outside the Jewish quarter, established special trolleys "for Jews only," and quietly began evicting Jews from certain apartment houses and streets in the German and later the Polish quarter. In September, they announced that Poles who still lived in the "infected" Jewish quarter would have to leave.

October 12, 1940 was Yom Kippur, the holiest day in the Jewish year. That morning the Germans set up loudspeakers to inform Jews that they would have to move to the "Jewish quarter" by October 30. One-third of Warsaw's population was to be crammed into just 2.4 percent of the city's land. Over 250,000 people were to be relocated: 113,000 Poles and 138,000 Jews. Tosha Bialer, described the days before the deadline:

> Try to picture one-third of a large city's population moving through the streets in an endless stream, pushing, wheeling, dragging all their belongings from every part of the city to one small section, crowding one another more and more as they converged. No cars, no horses, no help of any sort was available to us by order of the occupying authorities. Pushcarts were about the only method of conveyance we had, and these were piled high with household goods, furnishing much amusement to the German onlookers who delighted in overturning the carts and seeing us scrambling for our effects. Many of the goods were confiscated arbitrarily without explanation. . .
>
> In the ghetto, as some of us had begun to call it half ironically and in jest, there was appalling chaos. Thousands of people were rushing around at the last minute trying to find a place to stay. Everything was already filled up but still they kept coming

and somehow more room was found. The narrow, crooked streets of the most dilapidated section of Warsaw were crowded with pushcarts, their owners going from house to house asking the inevitable question: Have you room? The sidewalks were covered with their belongings. Children wandered, lost and crying, parents ran hither and yon seeking them, their cries drowned in the tremendous hubbub of half a million uprooted people.[35]

The Germans never used the term *ghetto*. They spoke only of a "Jewish quarter," thus giving the impression that it would be similar to the German and the Polish quarters. Therefore many Jews assumed that they would be able to leave their quarter to work or shop much as they always had. On November 16, 1940, they discovered those assumptions were incorrect. Bialer writes:

> In the morning, as on every other, men and women go out on their way to work. . . . As they came to the various points where thoroughfares and streets crossed from the Jewish section into the non-Jewish districts, they ran against barbed wire strung across and guarded by German police who were stopping all traffic out of the Jewish section. Hastily they tried other streets, avenues, alleys, only to find in every case barbed wire or a solid brick wall spread through the section. Other people came out of their houses and stared at the barricades, pathetically silent, stunned by the frightful suspicion that was creeping into their minds. Then, suddenly, the realization struck us. What had been, up till now, seemingly unrelated parts—a piece of wall here, a blocked-up house there, another piece of wall somewhere else—had overnight been joined to form an enclosure from which there was no escape. The barbed wire was the missing piece in the puzzle. Like cattle we had been herded into the corral, and the gate had been barred behind us.[36]

CONNECTIONS

On October 17, 1940, Chaim Kaplan wrote in his diary:

> Instead of a ghetto, which is a medieval concept, they call it a "Jewish quarter." And the fact that the same order refers also to a Polish quarter and a German quarter is supposed to be a sign that the enemy treats them all alike. He even gives a "humane" reason for the creation of the Jewish quarter—because there are so many victims of the epidemics, especially in the Jewish streets, these areas must be quarantined. We know very well that what they are saying is a lie, but we have no way of testifying to the contrary before them. They have doomed us to silence, and we are still.[37]

Hitler believed that if you tell a lie big enough and often enough, people will come to believe it is true. How did the claim that a ghetto was needed for "humanitarian reasons" reflect that idea?

Tosha Bialer writes, "Like cattle we had been herded into the corral, and the gate had been barred behind us." Why does she see the closing of the ghetto as ominous?
The Germans used euphemisms to mask their plans for the Jews. Euphemisms are used to distance oneself from an event, deny it, camouflage it, or trivialize it. Find examples of euphemisms in this reading. How does each reflect these aims? How did they differ from others you have encountered?

The Germans insisted that they moved the Jews into the ghetto to stop the spread of typhus and other diseases. Yet in May of 1941, a Polish underground newspaper claimed the move had the opposite effect. "Forcing the Jews together in what was already the worst section of the city had dire consequences for their health." The paper went on to describe how the crowding "resulted in unspeakable hygienic and sanitary conditions" and warned that "contagious diseases, above all tuberculosis, are spreading." How do you think Germans might have responded to the article?

[1] Janina Bauman, *Winter in the Morning: A Young Girl's Life in the Warsaw Ghetto and Beyond, 1939-1945* (Free Press, 1986), 14-15.

[2] Ibid.. 18-19.

[3] Ibid., 7.

[4] Martin Gray, *For Those I Loved* (Little Brown, 1971) 10-12, 14.

[5] Excerpted with the permission of Simon & Schuster from *The Scroll of Agony*, Revised edition and translated by Abraham I. Katsh. Copyright 1965, 1973 by Abraham I. Katsh.

[6] Alexander Donat, *The Holocaust Kingdom* (Holt, 1965), 4.

[7] Adina Blady Szwajger, *I Remember Nothing More,* trans. Tasja Darowska and Danusia Stok (Pantheon, 1990), 8-10.

[8] Halina Birenbaum, *Hope Is the Last to Die,* trans. David Welsh (Twayne Publishers, 1971), 3.

[9] Alexander Donat, *The Holocaust Kingdom,* 6-7.

[10] Excerpted from *The Scroll of Agony*, 78-79.

[11] Quoted in *The Black Book of Polish Jewry* ed. Jacob Apenszlak, et al. (American Federation for Polish Jews, 1943), 32

[12] *Notes from the Warsaw Ghetto: The Journal of Emmanuel Ringelblum*, ed. and trans. Jacob Sloan (Schocken, 1974), 22.

[13] Yitzhak Zuckerman, "The Jewish Revolt," in *The Fighting Ghettos: Firsthand Accounts of Jewish Resistance to the Germans*, trans. and ed. by Meyer Barkai (Lippincott, 1962), 3-4.

[14] Quoted in Nora Levin *The Holocaust Years* (Krieger Publishers, 1990), 203.

[15] Bernard Goldstein, *The Stars Bear Witness*, trans. and ed. Leonard Shatzkin (Viking Press, 1949), 37-38.

[16] *The Warsaw Diary of Adam Czerniakow,* ed. Raul Hilberg, et. al. Trans. Stanislaw Staron et al. (Stein and Day, 1979), 93.

[17] Quoted in *To Live with Honor and Die with Honor: Selected Documents from the Warsaw Ghetto Underground Archives*, ed. and annotated by Joseph Kermish (Yad Vashem, 1986), 71.

[18] Ibid., 71.

[19] Bernard Goldstein, *The Stars Bear Witness*, 35-36.

[20] David Wdowinski, *And We Are Not Saved* (Philosophical Library, 1985), 25.

[21] Yisrael Gutman, *The Jews of Warsaw 1939-1943: Ghetto, Underground, Revolt* (Indiana University Press, 1982), 22.

[22] Alexander Donat, *The Holocaust Kingdom,* 8-9.

[23] Quoted in *To Live with Honor and Die with Honor,* 346-349

[24] Ibid.

[25] Michel Mazor, *The Vanished City: Everyday Life in the Warsaw Ghetto,* trans. by David Jacobson (Marsilio Publishers, 1993), 67.

[26] Quoted in Yisrael Gutman, *The Jews of Warsaw,* 41.

[27] Bernard Goldstein, *The Stars Bear Witness,* 51-53.

[28] Excerpted from *The Scroll of Agony*, 202-203.

[29] Bernard Goldstein, *The Stars Bear Witness,* 44-45.

[30] *Notes from the Warsaw Ghetto: The Journal of Emmanuel Ringelblum,* 273.

[31] Excerpted from *The Scroll of Agony,* 174.

[32] Bernard Goldstein, *The Stars Bear Witness,* 38-39.

[33] Simha Rotem, *Memoirs of a Warsaw Ghetto Fighter: The Past Within Me,* trans. and ed. Barbara Harshav (Yale University Press, 1994), 12-13.

[34] Bernard Goldstein, *The Stars Bear Witness,* 39-41.

[35] Quoted in *Martyrs and Fighters*, ed. Philip Friedman (Praeger, 1954), 36-37.

[36] Ibid.

[37] Excerpted from *The Scroll of Agony,* 210.

5. The Warsaw Ghetto

We have entered into a new life. . . .
Suddenly we see ourselves penned in on all sides.
We are segregated and separated from the world and the fullness thereof,
driven out of the society of the human race.

Chaim Kaplan

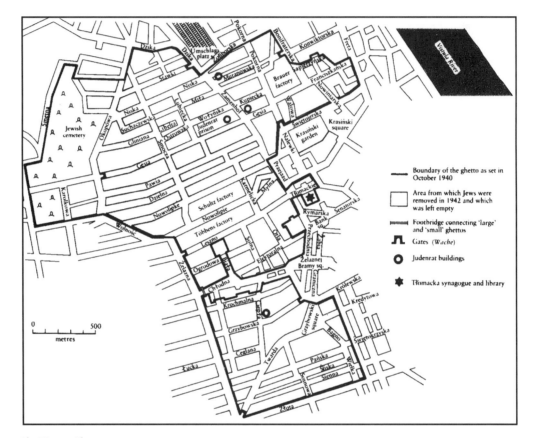

The Warsaw Ghetto

Chaim Kaplan, like many Jews in Warsaw, saw the ghetto as the beginning of a new phase in Hitler's war against the Jews. To many outsiders, however, the ghetto seemed to mark a return to an earlier time in history, a time when many European Jews were confined to separate sections of a city or town. Michel Mazor, who lived in the Warsaw Ghetto, disagreed:

> It takes no great knowledge of Jewish history to note the essential difference between the ghettos of the Middle Ages and those created by the Master Race. . . . The former were not completely cut off from the world: Jews could leave them by day; ordinary life took on forms that allowed generations of Jews to live and to succeed one another upholding their distinctive traditions, even creating a civilization. The medieval ghettos still represented a form of life. . . . In the twentieth century, especially in Warsaw, the ghetto was no longer anything but an organized form of death.[1]

Less than a year after the Nazis created the Warsaw Ghetto, they escalated their war against the Jewish people. A new policy went into effect on June 22, 1941, the day Germany invaded Russia. As the German army advanced eastward, SS units known as the Einsatzgruppen followed close behind with orders to murder anyone the Nazis considered an "enemy of the state." In town after town, those orders resulted in the massacre of every Jew. The Germans were killing Jews long before the invasion, but now the number of murders increased sharply and the killings became more systematic, more deliberate, more routine.

The new policy was part of a "master plan" to annihilate the Jews of Europe. On July 31, 1941, Reinhard Heydrich, the chief of the German Security Police, was instructed to make "all necessary preparations" "for bringing about a complete solution of the Jewish question in the German sphere of influence in Europe." As part of those preparations, Jews were killed outright or concentrated in ghettos like the one in Warsaw. At the same time, the Nazis began to build mechanized "death camps." The first was at Chelmno outside Lodz. By the summer of 1942, four more of these camps were operational: Auschwitz, Belzec, Sobibor, and Treblinka, which was just 40 miles from Warsaw.

Few people knew the purpose of these camps until later that summer. Even then, many did not believe that the Germans really intended to murder every Jew in Europe. After all, most Jewish communities were still intact— despite hunger, violence, and the effects of over two years of war. Yet by the year's end, only a handful survived. In city after city, thousands of children, women, and men were herded onto cattle cars and transported to the "killing centers." These murders are collectively known as the Holocaust, a word that literally means "complete destruction by fire." Historian Paul Bookbinder writes that "the crematoria [in the death camps] brought the word *holocaust* to mind and in its sound the enormity of the horror of those days was confirmed."

This chapter focuses on the way this new phase in Hitler's war against the Jews affected Warsaw from November 16, 1940, the day the ghetto was sealed, through the summer of 1942. The readings are drawn mainly from eyewitness accounts. As the leader of Oneg Shabbat, a group dedicated to preserving such accounts, Emmanuel Ringelblum declared that the aim of these ghetto writers was "to convey the whole truth, no matter how bitter, and we presented faithful unadorned pictures."

This chapter focuses on a few of those "faithful unadorned pictures." Each offers a glimpse of life in Warsaw during the Holocaust. Neither our vocabulary nor our standards of behavior can adequately imagine what people actually experienced. After the war, Abba Kovner, a poet who lived in the Vilna Ghetto, recalled being "shown a model of the Treblinka death camp, and told that it was an 'accurate and authentic picture' of Treblinka. But it was not; it was the buildings without the anguish and the horror. Treblinka was not the buildings and the fence; without the horror, it was just another youth camp. What is the ghetto in socio-historical accounts without the horror?"2 Perhaps that is why Elie Wiesel believes that "he who has not lived the event will never know it. And he who went through it will not reveal it, not really, not entirely. Between his memory and his reflection there is a wall—and it cannot be pierced."

Confronting this history is extraordinariy difficult. The choices Jews made during the Holocaust are unlike any other. It was a time, as Professor Lawrence Langer reminds us, "when moral choices as we know them did not exist" and Jews were "left with the task of redefining decency in an atmosphere that could not support it."

No Exit

"When the Ghetto was officially sealed off, a sociological 'experiment' without parallel began," Alexander Donat wrote. "Half a million people, locked behind walls in the heart of a great city, were increasingly isolated from that city and the rest of the world."

The main bridge linking the "big" and "little" ghettos.

Those who entered the ghetto found themselves in a world unlike any they had ever known. To orient outsiders to that world, Michel Mazor described a "tourist guide" that mysteriously appeared in the Warsaw Ghetto. At first glance, he recalls, it read much like any other travel brochure. Readers were urged to "visit the ghetto, its gates and its bridges, sample its delicious *cholent* [stew], marvel at its 'musical cupboards,' its lively streets." But unlike most brochures, every word and phrase in this one required explanation "since the content in no way corresponds to what foreign tourists are normally led to expect."

> The gates of the ghetto . . . bore no stamp of hallowed ages, but were, on the contrary, the work of the most advanced totalitarian technology: each was guarded outside by German sentinels and inside by the Jewish police, effectively sealing a half-million condemned people into a virtual death-site. Only rarely did these gates open to allow some German or Pole to enter on official business and to let out gangs of Jewish workers. . . .
>
> The bridges of the ghetto had an even more remarkable and ultramodern character, for they were not built for crossing water, but passed over streets that did not belong to the ghetto and were off-limits to Jews. The main bridge was erected above Chlodna Street; it linked the two parts of Zelazna Street that intersected it and served as the only passage between the "big" and the "little" ghettos.
>
> On this bridge crowds of people would circulate in both directions with the greatest difficulty, in an indescribable crush. . . . Still, this bridge did not exist from the outset. Earlier, the two perpendicular streets—the Aryan Chlodna Street and the Jewish Zelazna Street—were separated by heavy iron gates, guarded by the Germans and opening alternately for the passage of Aryans and Jews. In its Aryan part, Chlodna Street had little commotion on it, the gates stayed open most of the time and the traffic flowed without congestion. But on Zelazna Street, which served as the only link between two parts of the ghetto, and where the Jews were in constant circulation, the gates opened only rarely, and very briefly. Once they opened them, the German policemen kept the crowd moving to the beat of their riding crops, which created an atmosphere of panic. On approaching this intersection, the Jews could not

help but feel feverish agitation. The crowd would pack in, and everyone would try to squeeze inside in order not to be exposed to the blows of the Germans. For this reason, movement slowed, and the riding crops came down all the more furiously on the hapless outsiders. What is more, it was routine for these defenseless people to be humiliated. The policemen would pick some poor wretch from the crowd at random and force him to do calisthenics while beating him mercilessly, or in winter make him kneel in the puddles of melting snow.

The construction of the bridge improved this situation. Crossing it, we could get a glimpse of the Aryan street, spacious and clean, where traffic was normal, where cars wheeled by and trolley cars passed . . . .

Moving on to the next sections of our "Tourist Guide," I shall mention that the *cholent* was a very rich item of Jewish ritual food, eaten on Saturdays. In the ghetto, given the scarcity of fat in the diet, this dish was considered a national delicacy.

The "musical cupboards" had a highly specific meaning. The expression "the cupboard is playing" meant that someone had bribed the police. . . . In the past, shady deals had been worked out with officials in the cabarets, which had mechanical music boxes in the shape of cupboards [juke boxes]. When a coin was put into the slot, the music box would start playing a song. The connection is very clear: you pay, and we'll do what's necessary. . . .

At its conclusion the "Tourist Guide" mentions the ghetto's bustling streets: yes, these streets were much-traveled, but they were also like nothing else found in any other city in the world.

For the streets of any other city in the world lead somewhere. They form part of the vast world to which they connect their cities. They open the way to freedom. By walking along them, one can come out at the broad avenues at the center of town or, on the contrary, emerge into the fields, the forests, onto the banks of rivers. . . . The streets of the ghetto led nowhere. They came up against an insurmountable wall, or a German sentinel. All the streets of the ghetto were dead ends, and the people thronging them amid the tumult and the stench found themselves facing that impasse: they had nowhere to go, could find no exit.[3]

CONNECTIONS

In the introduction, Abba Kovner is quoted as saying that a model of Treblinka can never be an "accurate and authentic picture" because it shows "the buildings without the anguish and the horror." And he asks, "What is the ghetto in socio-historical accounts without the horror?" How do Kovner's comments explain why the guide requires interpretation? How does Mazor help us glimpse "the anguish and the horror" that lay within the ghetto walls? Why did many in the ghetto risk their lives so that we and others might learn the truth?

In reading or hearing stories about the death camps, writes Professor Lawrence Langer, "one is plunged into a world of moral turmoil that may silence judgment. . . . As one wavers between the 'dreadful' and the 'impossible,' one begins to glimpse a deeper level of reality in the death camps, where moral choice as we know it was superfluous and inmates were left with the futile task of redefining decency in an atmosphere that could not support it."[4] How do Langer's comments apply to Michel Mazor's description of the Warsaw Ghetto as a place where the streets led "nowhere" and humiliation was "routine"?

The Germans who beat and humiliated the Jews on Zelazna Street were following orders. A number of historians, psychologists, and sociologists have tried to explain why so many Germans not only willingly obeyed but did so with great enthusiasm. They often treated the Jews far worse than their superiors demanded. Some scholars trace their behavior to antisemitism. They argue that most Germans saw Jews not only as "different" but as "less than human." Other scholars have focused on opportunism, terror, peer pressure, a strong desire to please authority figures, or the need to conform. Based on what you know about human behavior and what you have read so far, what factor or combination of factors encourages such obedience?

Philip Zimbardo, a psychologist at Stanford University, chose 24 young men— "mature, emotionally stable, normal, intelligent college students"— for an experiment. He arbitrarily assigned them to be "guards" or "prisoners" in a simulated prison. He reported:

> At the end of only six days we had to close down our mock prison because what we saw was frightening. It was no longer apparent to most of the subjects (or to us) where reality ended and their roles began. The majority had indeed become prisoners or guards, no longer able to clearly differentiate between role playing and self. There were dramatic changes in virtually every aspect of their behavior, thinking and feeling. In less than a week the experience of imprisonment undid (temporarily) a lifetime of learning; human values were suspended, self-concepts were challenged and the ugliest, most base, pathological side of human nature surfaced. We were horrified because we saw some boys (guards) treat others as if they were dispicable animals, taking pleasure in cruelty, while other boys (prisoners) became servile, dehumanized robots who thought only of escape, of their own individual survival and their mounting hatred for the guards.[5]

Zimbardo said that he "called off the experiment not because of the horror I saw out there in the prison yard, but because of the horror of realizing that I could have easily traded places with the most brutal guard or become the weakest prisoner full of hatred at being so powerless I could not eat, sleep or go to the toilet without permission of the authorities." What does his statement suggest about the dangers of power and of powerlessness? What other explanations for the behavior might you suggest?

Hunger

In the ghetto, parents, teachers and other adults no longer knew how to prepare their children for the future or even keep them safe in the present. The enormity of their failure was evident in the thousands of "orphaned or abandoned half-starved waifs who roamed barefoot through the ghetto streets." Bernard Goldstein said of them, "These had once been our future, these broken little bodies, these cracked voices begging for bread."

Halina Birenbaum was eleven years old when the ghetto was established. She was among the "lucky" ones. Her family had enough to eat, thanks in part to Christian Poles who had worked with her father before the war. They sent food and other help to the family even after the ghetto was closed. Birenbaum recalls those who were not as fortunate:

> The streets of the Warsaw ghetto swarmed with beggars in lice-infested, dirty rags. Whole families, swollen with famine, camped in hallways, gates and streets; dead bodies lay there, covered by newspapers or by snow in winter.
>
> An epidemic of typhus broke out, accompanied by indescribable famine. The death rate was so high that it was impossible to keep up with taking the dead bodies away, and carting them to common graves in a cemetery.
>
> Such were the conditions under which I grew up and learned to understand the world. I eyed the beggars, the starving urchins, the dead bodies in the streets, the carts moving through the ghetto carrying boxes in which they piled ten or more dead bodies at a time, so that the lids would not shut. . . .
>
> Although I myself had not yet starved, my heart bled at the sight of the hunger of others, my girl-friend Elusia and her family, the children of the dentist we lived with. . . . Day and night, for many months and despite the curfew, groans and cries resounded in the yards and streets under our windows "*A shtykele broit, a shtykele broit!*" [A little piece of bread, a little piece of bread!]. I often stole bread or potatoes from home and took them out into the street, but there were so many starving people, so very many—how could I help them all? I reproached my mother for not letting me give food to the beggars or to Elusia. . . . I did not understand that we ourselves did not have too much food, that my mother was sick with apprehension at the thought that tomorrow or the next day we too should want for bread.
>
> There were many things I did not understand. For instance, I could not understand why the misfortune that was Hitler had come upon us, and what it was he wanted from the Jews. I did not understand why the rest of the world watched but said nothing. I wanted to live, and hoped none of my family or friends would perish. . . . The eyes of the starving reduced me to despair. I recall how I first learned to read them.
>
> One of my younger brother's friends, a very handsome 18-year-old boy, tall and fair-haired, with blue eyes and an intelligent, noble expression, used to sell bread from door to door. He could not buy the bread for himself. . . . He appeared at our house, and when he was taking money from my mother, he glanced at the bread with so much tragic yearning in his eyes that they appeared ready to jump out; his protruding Adam's apple moved rapidly, uneasily . . .
>
> At the time I was eleven years old. I suddenly realized the inhuman anguish of hunger, its humiliation, its helplessness. I felt as though something had burst within

me. Yet it was not pity! . . .The boy's glance penetrated the depths of my being, it fastened on to me like a leech, and for some time I could not eat the bread he had sold us. I also lost the desire to play, to do anything at all. For long afterwards I could not regain my mental balance, or shake off my depression.[6]

CONNECTIONS

What does Halina Birenbaum fails to understand? What does she understand all too well? How did she learn to "read" "the eyes of the starving." To understand her account and others like it, Abba Kovner once urged that we "read between the lines." In each word, he insisted, there is "an anguish so deep" that the more you read it, "the less you understand." How does Birenbaum help us imagine the unimaginable?

Alexander Donat (Chapter 4) recalled a conversation with Israel Milejkowski, a physician and the Judenrat member in charge of public heath:

One day Dr. Milejkowski came home visibly shaken. His face was ashen and he seemed to have aged immeasurably. At one of the refugee centers an eight-year-old child had gone out of his mind with hunger, and begun to scream, "I want to rob and steal. I want to eat. I want to be a German!" Milejkowski also told us that at the funeral of some children who had died of hunger, the children in the orphans' home in Wolska Street had sent a wreath inscribed, "From children who are starving to children who have died of starvation." Milejkowski wept as he told me this, and we cried with him. We felt powerless. The same thing would be happening tomorrow and the day after that and the day after that.[8]

Lawrence Langer writes that during the Holocaust Jews faced what he calls "choice-less choices," decisions made in the "absense of humanly significant alternatives." To what extent were the options the two men faced "choice-less choices"? What distinguishes a "choice-less choice" from other decisions?

The Germans kept records of the number of deaths. How do those numbers support the belief that the Nazis were trying to wipe out the ghetto by starving people to death?

Death Rates in the Warsaw Ghetto[9]		
No. of Deaths in 1941		*1942*
Jan.	898	5,123
Feb.	1,023	4,618
March	1,608	4,951
April	2,061	4,432
May	3,821	4,636
June	4,290	
July	5,550	
Aug.	5,560	
Sept.	4,545	
Oct.	4,716	

Germans and Germans

From the beginning, German policies sharply limited the food supply in the ghetto. The only way Jews in the Warsaw Ghetto could survive was by defying the Nazis.

Day in and day out, smugglers brought in about 80 percent of the food in the ghetto. To stop them, the Germans built walls around the Jewish quarter. They also declared that anyone caught sneaking food into the ghetto would be killed on the spot. "And yet," writes Emmanuel Ringelblum, "smuggling did not stop for a moment."

Why weren't the Germans able to stop smuggling? Some believe that it was because the need was too great. Abraham Lewin, a Hebrew teacher, suggests other reasons in a diary entry in which he recorded three stories he heard from a friend:

As is known, there is as yet no wall at Krochmalna Street, only a wire fence. Consequently the location serves as the main center for smuggling in the ghetto. While my friend was standing at a window that looks out over the fence she saw that the wire was being raised and from the Aryan side a sack of rye or something or other rolled into the ghetto. This was happening in full view of the Polish policeman standing on guard. So far there is nothing remarkable in all this, for this is a regular occurrence. Except that the policeman failed to see that a German gendarme was slowly approaching. . . .

The gendarme arrived, but in the meantime the sack had disappeared. The Polish policeman stood there completely terrified and distraught. The gendarme had spotted the sack "vanishing." The gendarme said to the policeman: "I will come back in 20 minutes and by then the sack must be back where it was." The gendarme went off, and the policeman was left standing completely helpless. His position really was a difficult one. There was no way of getting the same sack back, as it was far out of his sight. The minutes were ticking away fast. What could he do? Just at that moment he saw a Jew passing by on the "Semitic" side carrying a sack at his side. The policeman shouted out "Halt! Bring that sack here!" The Jew protested: he had a permit and the goods were perfectly legal. But the policeman didn't give up: "I put myself in danger for your sakes and turn a blind eye to your smuggling and you're giving me trouble over some sack. There is nothing to discuss: the sack stays here!"

Other smugglers came up and tried to calm the Jew down. They promised to collect money and to compensate him for the sack and its contents. The Jew stood there confused, uncertain what to do. The 20 minutes passed and the gendarme returned exactly as the time was up. He asked the policeman whether the sack had been returned. The policeman pointed to the sack and said: "There it is, in front of you!" The gendarme asked: "Is this the same sack?" accompanying the question with a wink. The policeman replied that, yes, it really was the same sack.

The Jew, who the whole time had been standing to one side listening intently to the exchanges, did not stand idly by, but went up to the gendarme and returned to his refrain, that he had a permit, that the sack was his and the goods were perfectly legal. Hearing this, the gendarme ordered the Jew to take the sack and rebuked the policeman severely. "What is the meaning of all this?" The policeman stood deathly pale, not knowing what to do or to answer. Finally he explained, stammering, that the sack in question had disappeared and he didn't know where. He had been unable to get it back. "In that case," said the gendarme, "this will cost you 500 zloty."

Without much hesitation the policeman took out his wallet and paid the gendarme 500 zloty in cash. The gendarme took the money, stood looking round him, then, catching sight of an old Jew crossing the street, he called out to him: "Come here!" the Jew, trembling with fear, came up to the gendarme. "How old are you?" asked the gendarme. "Seventy-two," the old man managed to splutter. "There you go," said the gendarme, "here's 72 zloty for you," and handed him the sum. Then he called over a girl from among those begging for a handout and put the same question to her. The Jews whispered in her ear that she should say "15." The gendarme gave her 8 zloty. The gendarme went on like this until he had distributed all of the 500 zloty.

The Jews began to crowd around the strange gendarme. He smiled at them and said "*Ja, ein guter Deutcher, nicht war?*" [Yes, a good German, aren't I?]

The same woman told me about two other events that happened in the last few weeks on this well-known street.

In the first, a German gendarme chanced upon a Jewish girl, about ten years old, on the Aryan side. He ordered her to move about some linens from one place to another. The girl refused to carry out the order and replied stubbornly: "What will you do to me? Shoot me? Go ahead, shoot! I've got nothing to lose and I couldn't care less." . . . When the girl tried to get back into the ghetto through a hole in the wall the gendarme fired and killed her on the spot.

In the second incident, a gendarme came across a group of Jewish children, nearly 20 in number, in the corner of one of the courtyards on the Aryan side. Of course they were terrified. The German smiled at them from a distance and ordered them to come up to him. The children approached him and the gendarme called over a Jewish policeman and ordered him to lead the children back to the ghetto.

One girl was sobbing bitterly. The gendarme asked why she was crying, and was told that she had left behind a few potatoes collected from the Christians. She had left them in the corner of the courtyard when they were discovered. The gendarme went with the girl, took her back to the corner of the courtyard and helped her to gather up the potatoes. He then accompanied her until she reached the Jewish side of the wall safely.

Yes, it seems there are Germans and Germans.[10]

CONNECTIONS

What choices were open to the Germans described in this reading? What factors may have influenced their behavior? What part did antisemitism play in their behavior? What part did peer pressure play? How did opportunism affect the choices they made?

What similarities do you notice in the behavior of the German officers described in this reading? What differences seem most striking? How do those differences explain what Lewin means when he says, "It seems there are Germans and Germans."

One of the soldiers claims to be "a good German." What did it mean to be a "good German" in the Warsaw Ghetto?

For Those I Loved

Like many people in the Warsaw Ghetto, Rachel Auerbach believed that smugglers ought to be included in the "list of saints and heroes of our dark age. The smugglers do what they do in order to eat themselves, it is true; but in spite of this—and perhaps just because of this—they are among the most important and determined combatants in the unequal fight waged by our city, bound hand and foot, against a cruel and criminal power."

Martin Gray (Chapter 4) was among the many young Jews who smuggled to help support a family. Gray's father, who was involved in the resistance movement, was in hiding from the Nazis. So at fifteen, Martin became the "man in the family." He later wrote:

> Hopping on and off streetcars, hiding my armband in my shirt, sometimes slipping it onto my arm, knowing the police who would "cooperate"—the ones you could take a chance on because they could be bribed—discovering goods, selling them, working out profits and expenses: that was now my life.
>
> I used to leave as curfew ended, in the still icy night. I'd check on the streetcars: which Blue [Polish police officer] was on duty that morning. Sometimes I'd have to wait, sometimes I'd take a chance, sometimes I'd back a certainty. But I gambled. I'd cross the wall and back several times a day: I'd gamble on my life several times a day. But I was alive, free. With each journey, my system grew more perfect, new plans emerged. When you're in danger of your life, your brain moves fast. I now had contacts, business connections, regulars, official suppliers in Aryan Warsaw. False papers, too: a travel-pass which had already saved me a couple of times. It certified that I was living on the Aryan side and that I was a young Pole of pure race. Though it was cold, I wore an open-necked shirt: this revealed a thin gold chain and a small medallion of the Virgin Mary. In the evenings I learned the Mass in Latin and the main prayers: my life could hang on a few words.
>
> My profits were huge because the ghetto was hungry, the ghetto was cold. A few days before Christmas, the temperature went down to zero. In Karmelicka Street, I saw groups of ragged children huddled together, holding out their hands; the whole ghetto was swarming with famished orphans, begging. They used to hang about the soup kitchens. I gave what I could. . . .
>
> At the gate in Leszno Street, a street I didn't like, a dangerous street when there were raids, I'd seen a group of Jewish laborers on their way home. They were employed on the Aryan side. German guards sprang at them like wolves, setting to with rifle butts, hurling insults, forcing the weary, hollow-cheeked men to their knees. Then they searched them, and hunks of bread, potatoes, and a small sack of flour were piled up on the road. The guards forced the workers to throw their goods over the other side of the wall. Some tried to tear off a mouthful of bread: they were beaten.
>
> They wanted us dead. Sometimes I felt ashamed of filling my belly, ashamed of selling, ashamed of watching corpselike children clutching at passersby, dying beggars, a heavily made-up women extending her hand and trying to smile. Ashamed at not being able to stop it. Sometimes, I felt that I too ought to lie on the pavement, dying of cold and hunger.
>
> But my shame didn't last. They wanted us all dead: but they wouldn't have me

and a few more with me. Father told me about Dr. Janusz Korczak's orphanage: thanks to him, hundreds of children were avoiding starvation. When I could, I brought money and grain. . . . But what I gave amounted to almost nothing. Our ghetto was an inferno of misery, a sick creature with half a million wounds, each one crying out in hunger, cold and desperation.. . .

They wanted us dead. I was, in my own way, struggling to prevent their succeeding. If the ghetto kept going, day after day, it was because I wasn't the only one to cross the wall: there were smugglers everywhere. Aryans were entering the ghetto, selling their goods and leaving, after being paid in "hard money (gold) or "soft" money (paper). In Kozla Street, contact with the Aryan side could be made through an attic. It was not easy, even for the butchers, to keep track of half a million people, to kill them off at one stroke. Yet the butchers were zealous: they'd open shops and factories, and were making us work like slaves; we were turning out uniforms, helmets, and belts for the great army of butchers.

They were shrewd. As they couldn't slaughter us all in one day, they let a few of us organize our lives. At 13 Leszno Street, with the approval of the Gestapo, Ganzweich and Sternfeld established an economic police force, a looting and smuggling firm, a mafia which *they* supervised. But "the Thirteen," as they were known, also helped us to live: they gave to the poor. They stole and gave alms. It was the same with Kohn and Heller, two shopkeepers, officially tolerated ghetto smugglers; their horse-drawn rattletraps were our "streetcars," filthy and smelly but useful; cars drove slowly through the rickshaws, bicycle-taxis which plowed into the throng: fat, well-dressed men drawn by starving men through a sad and hungry crowd.

[Everything] in the ghetto was extreme, both wealth and poverty. I know: there were nightclubs and yet children died of hunger at their doors. Yes, corruption and devotion went hand in hand. I sold my goods at exorbitant prices. . . and dispensed charity. Was it unfair? I lived as best I could in the hell which *they* had created. I was holding my own, all of us were trying to hold our own.

It was true that I'd grown selfish, it was true that I could see a dying man and pass him by without stopping. Because I'd realized that in order to have my revenge I had to live, at all costs. And to live I had to be able not to stop, to be able to watch him dying.

Selfishness was the weapon they'd given me, and I had seized it to use on them. For those I loved. . . .[11]

CONNECTIONS

Review the identity chart you created for Martin Gray in Chapter 4. How has he changed since the war began? To what extent was smuggling an act of resistance for Gray? To what extent was it a way of maintaining his identity in a world that increasingly saw him only as a Jew?

Was smuggling an example of corruption? What do people mean when they say that power corrupts? Does powerlessness also corrupt?

Martin Gray was troubled by the extremes he saw in the Ghetto. Those extremes also worried Michel Mazor. But he noted that food was so scarce in the ghetto that even if someone had emptied the storerooms in every restaurant and nightclub, there would still not have been enough to give everyone who was hungry a single meal. Mazor believes that the restaurants and clubs served an important function: "They gave the illusion of the normal life from which the Jews had been severed. And their continued existence in a city which the Germans regarded as a cemetery—was it not, in a certain sense, the ghetto's protest, its affirmation of the right to life?"[12] How would you answer his question? How might Gray answer it?

Henryka Lazowert, a young woman in the ghetto, wrote a poem entitled "Little Smuggler." How does she portray the "unknown smuggler"? Why do you think she sees the smuggler as a very young child rather than as a teenager or an adult? Why do you think the poem was so popular with the Jews of Warsaw?

> Over the wall, through holes, and past the guard,
> Through the wires, ruins, and fences,
> Plucky, hungry, and determined
> I sneak through, dart like a cat.
>
> At noon, at night, at dawn,
> In snowstorm, cold or heat,
> A hundred times I risk my life
> And put my head on the line.
>
> Under my arm a gunny sack,
> Tatters on my back,
> On nimble young feet,
> With endless fear in my heart. . . .
>
> And if the hand of destiny
> Should seize me in the game,
> That's a common trick of life.
> You, mother, do not wait up for me.
>
> I will return no more to you,
> My voice will not be heard from afar.
> The dust of the street will bury
> The lost fate of a child.
>
> And only one request
> Will stiffen on my lips:
> Who, mother mine, who
> Will bring your bread tomorrow?[13]

The Jewish Police

On September 20, 1940, even as the walls of the ghetto were rising, the Gestapo ordered the establishment of a Jewish police force. Members were to take over the duties of the Polish police in the "Jewish living quarters." Two weeks after the ghetto was sealed, the first Jewish police officers appeared on the streets. Although they quickly became objects of both hatred and fear in the ghetto, everyone knew that they only followed orders. It was the Germans who controlled the ghetto. And it was they who decided its fate.

The Jewish police consisted mainly of young men with some military training. Initially they directed traffic and maintained order. Before long, however, directors of traffic became guards at the gates of the ghetto. In time, those gatekeepers found themselves rounding up Jews for forced labor, seizing smugglers, and tracking down reluctant taxpayers. The better these new policemen were at their jobs, the less popular they were in their own community.

In December of 1940, historian Emmanuel Ringelblum wrote, "The Jewish Police is composed of experienced and sympathetic men." In February, he added, "The public stands behind the Jewish policeman: 'Would you obey a Pole and not a Jew?' There are intelligent men among the police who prefer persuasion to giving orders."[14] By December of 1942, his attitude had changed considerably. "Unlike the Polish Police, which did not take part in the abductions for the labor camps, the Jewish Police did engage in this dirty work. The police were also notorious for their shocking corruption and demoralization."[15]

Who joined the police? Some were outsiders—mainly Jews the Nazis had relocated from smaller cities and towns in Poland. A number of the men, including the chief, were Christians. Warsaw's first Jewish police chief was Jozef Szerynski, formerly a colonel in the Polish police and a convert to Catholicism. He recruited about 100 other converts and assigned them to prominent positions. The vast majority of the recruits, however, were neither outsiders nor converts. They were young Jews from Warsaw.

No one was forced to become a policeman. Indeed, there were often many more applicants than there were jobs. Why did so many apply? Paul (Pawel) Trepman recalled the reply he received when he asked that question of a boyhood friend:

> "I know that people are saying all sorts of bad things about the ghetto police force," he told me, "and I am afraid a lot of the talk is founded on fact—at least in my opinion. But on the whole, the ghetto police is not the unmitigated disaster that some make it out to be. If we Jews here in the ghetto had not organized our own police force, the Germans would have done it for us, and it isn't hard to imagine what kind of character they would have recruited. And as for the idea of having the Germans do the policing themselves—just picture what that would be like. We wouldn't be able to exist. You can always, somehow, cope with even the lowest type of Jewish official, but never with a German.
>
> "Sure, we have some shady characters who used all kinds of tricks to get into the police force; they are the ones to blame for our bad reputation. But then, tell me Pawel, what organization does not have its share of shady characters nowadays? You will find them everywhere, also in our ghetto institutions. The damned Germans have a way of cultivating the worst types, especially among us Jews.

"But on the whole, we aren't nearly as bad as we look. Much of the talk against the ghetto police force is simple envy. People envy us because we can walk about freely even during the raids, when other Jews are rounded up to be sent to labor camps. They envy us because the wives and children of our policemen are not forced to do hard labor and because, as policemen, we get supplementary rations of food and other essentials."[16]

Janina Bauman's Uncle Julian also joined the Jewish police (Chapter 4). She later recalled how another uncle, Stefan, responded to the news:

Once, at the beginning of the ghetto, Stefan had been offered a job with them too, but he flatly refused and went to work as a volunteer in the hospital, slaving away at the most appalling jobs there, just to be useful. For him the Jewish police meant Nazi lackeys and collaborators. True enough, joining the police was for some young men their only way of earning money and supporting their families. But Julian was a doctor, he could easily have managed otherwise. On the other hand, he did work as a police doctor. "Don't you think that working as a doctor is all right whatever the circumstances?" I said to Stefan, trying to defend my paternal uncle against my maternal uncle's scorn. But Stefan said that in the war and the ghetto we were all so much exposed to evil, so vulnerable to being infected by it, that we should take the utmost care not to become involved in any morally ambiguous situations; just keep away from such things as long as we could.[17]

CONNECTIONS

In his journal, Emmanuel Ringelblum tells of a Jewish woman who smuggled a sack of potatoes into the ghetto. When a German guard confiscated the sack, a Jewish policeman asked that it be returned to the woman. The guard responded by knocking the policeman down, bayoneting him, and then shooting him. What does the incident suggest about the relationship between the Jewish police and the Germans? What does it suggest about the source of a Jewish policeman's power and the limits of that power?

Janina Bauman's Uncle Stefan told her "that in the war and the ghetto we were all so much exposed to evil, so vulnerable to being infected by it, that we should take the utmost care not to become involved in any morally ambiguous situations." What is a "morally ambiguous situation"? Why did Stefan fear such situations? Why did he believe that the Jewish police were bound to become involved in them?

Elie Wiesel writes of those who cooperated with the Nazis:

How is one to judge them? I do not. I cannot condemn anyone who failed to withstand trials and temptations. Guilty or not, the ghetto police, the *kapos* [prisoners in the camps who were forced to oversee other prisoners], may plead extenuating circumstances. They arouse pity more than contempt. The weak, the cowardly, all those who sold their soul to live another day, another anxious night, I prefer to include them in the category of victims. More than the others, they need forgiveness. More and in other ways than their companions, they deserve compassion and charity.[18]

Why does Wiesel find it so difficult to condemn those who cooperated with the Nazis? What does he suggest about the complexity of human behavior?

The Limits of Healing

David Wdowinski, a physician in the Warsaw Ghetto, wrote in his autobiography, "The realities of Ghetto life became the normal existence for children who did not know any other way of living, and so they made up songs and games where 'aktion,' blockade, sorrow, tears, hunger became the ordinary vocabulary of their make-believe. And although they lived in close proximity with death, they talked of the sun that would shine tomorrow, and wanted so much to live to see it."

Adina Blady Szwajger (Chapter 4) worked in the Warsaw Children's Hospital. There she and her co-workers watched helplessly as many of their young patients died of hunger, typhus, and tuberculosis. They looked for ways to bring even briefly some joy into the lives of children "deprived of everything." She writes:

> The Head Doctor's daughter-in-law . . . came and in the afternoons the two of us tried to set up a "play room." Well, at the beginning, we just didn't know how to go about it. It was easier with the toddlers. When we'd gather them all in one ward or in the hall, they gladly listened to stories, even those about fairies, or they played. . . house. In the house, there'd be Mamma and Papa, and there'd be a table and candles would be burning because it was Friday and on the table there'd be bread and "sprats" [herring]. I never heard them make up anything about white rolls or Sabbath fish. And one Friday they cooked soup for the children and there were "real" potatoes in it.
>
> But we had absolutely no idea where to start with the older children because they were, after all, older and wiser than we by a whole century of suffering and by the deaths of those nearest to them. So, at the beginning, we told them to help us a bit with the little ones, those who wanted to, of course. Two or three of them came and the rest laughed at us—although we didn't see this. But one day, or rather one night, I was sitting in the hall on duty, filling out case histories by the light of a lamp, when I heard a conversation:
>
> "They're playing with the children . . . They think that. . ."
>
> "What?"
>
> "Well, that this is ordinary life and that they're real children."
>
> "Probably because they're still ignorant."
>
> "Maybe they've never been hungry?"
>
> "Or maybe they're scared and would rather be with us than by themselves?"
>
> "You know what? I'd actually like to be able to play and walk around normally and sing. I liked singing."
>
> "Sing something, Fajgele."
>
> "What, in the middle of the night?"
>
> "Tomorrow, then?"
>
> "Maybe."
>
> "Let's tell stories."
>
> "Well, when my sister died and Mamma carried her out, she didn't have any strength left to go and beg, so she just lay there and cried a bit. But I didn't have any strength to go out either, so Mamma died too, and I wanted to live so terribly much and I prayed like Papa did before, before they killed him that is. He said: '*Shema Yisrael*' and I started to say that too and they came to get the corpses and saw that I

was alive and they brought me here and I'm going to live."

"Maybe we should say '*Shema Yisrael*' too?"

I didn't hear any more because I dropped a file and the children fell silent.

So the following day, when the older children came to watch the little ones play house, I suddenly said: "Fajgele, sing us something." "Why me?" "Because you look as if you can sing." And Fajgele sang a lullaby. And then we started to talk. Somehow it turned out that we were talking like equals. That we were all equally afraid and that we, too, didn't have much to eat but if we wanted to survive, we had to try to live like human beings, we had to remain human because they wanted to turn us into animals. . . . Then, finally, it somehow came naturally to tell them that they were young and ought to survive, that they mustn't forget that there used to be a time when they could smile.[19]

The children decided to organize a concert. Szwajger described the night it was held:

The children laughed and played, but I already knew that pretty Fajgele, Fajgele with her nightingale's voice, had a positive result for [tuberculosis], so it was only a matter of weeks. But I laughed so "merrily" that tears streamed down my face and the children shouted: "You're laughing so much you're crying."[20]

CONNECTIONS

What did Fajgele mean when she said that the hospital staff seemed to think "this is ordinary life"? Why didn't she and her friend see themselves and the other patients as "real children"? What did these children know that the adults did not yet accept?

"*Shema Yisrael*" are the opening words of a prayer that religious Jews recite three times a day. It says: "Hear O' Israel. The Lord is our God. The Lord is One." The prayer reaffirms one's faith in God. It also reminds Jews to keep God in their hearts and pass their faith on to their children. When Jews die, the prayer is traditionally the last words they utter. Why do you think the girls recited the prayer? What did it mean to them?

Adina Szwajger insisted that we have "to remain human because they want to turn us into animals." What distinguishes a human from an animal? Why did Szwajger believe it was critical to preserve that distinction? Elie Wiesel writes that the Nazis tried to reduce a person to a prisoner, a prisoner to a number; and a number to an ash, which is then dispersed. How did Szwajger struggle against that policy of dehumanization?

How do you explain Szwajger's laughter? Why did her laughter turn into tears? What do your answers suggest about the way laughter and sorrow were blended in the Ghetto?

Typhus threatened adults as well as children. Michel Mazor recalls a social worker who did not hesitate to reach out to the "desperate crowd of refugees" who besieged her office. "She would mix with this louse-ridden multitude, taking children in her arms and finding a word of consolation for everyone. Our warnings had no effect upon her. She saw things more clearly than others and would answer: 'In present conditions dying from typhus transmitted by a louse is not the worst of deaths.'" Why does Mazor believe that the woman saw "more clearly than others"? What did she see?

In the Heart of Europe

In time, the Jews of Warsaw began to adjust to ghetto life. As Halina Birenbaum explains, "We found that people can live under even the most inhuman conditions. People adapt, cope and fight as best they can for existence, trusting that the morrow will be better. We were helped by our belief that the final defeat of Fascism was close at hand."

No matter what happened, many people in Warsaw and other ghettos found reason to be optimistic. David Wdowinski recalled:

> There were days when suddenly there was hope, when a ray of hope came to us from the outer world. Such a day was one in June 1941 when Germany attacked Russia. The population of the Ghetto assembled in masses to hear the news blaring through the two megaphones installed by the Germans in the ghetto. One had waited for this news so eagerly, so greedily . . . . Perhaps this would bring an end to our martyrdom.
>
> But this was not our fate. Even this hope was shattered in the ensuing weeks and months when the Germans made steady advances. Vilna, Bialystok, Grodno, Brest, Lvov were taken. The Germans advanced further, ever further.
>
> In the winter of 1941-1942, four young men came from Vilna to Warsaw. Two of them belonged to our youth movement, Betar. They made their way disguised as Aryans. Through them we received the first authentic reports from the Polish eastern districts. They told us of mass deportations, executions, annihilation. In the course of a few weeks, of the 70,000 Jews in Vilna only 13,000 remained alive. Still worse were the reports from other cities. Complete liquidation. Part of the youth fled to the forests and organized into partisan groups. But this was only a small part. Eighty percent or more of the Jewry in the eastern districts was already exterminated.[21]

News also came from other sources. In September, Heniek Grabowski, a Polish Boy Scout, visited Vilna at the request of young Zionists in Warsaw. Before the war, he and other Polish Scouts had made friends with their counterparts in Jewish scouting groups like Akiva and Hashomer Hatzair. Now Grabowski gathered information for them about the mass murders. More news reached Warsaw in October, when young Jews from Vilna arrived in the city. They reported that in many towns near Vilna, "every last Jew was murdered." Most were slaughtered in Ponar, a forested resort area only a few miles from Vilna.

In late December, youth groups in Warsaw sent more couriers to Vilna. At a meeting on New Year's Day, they and about 150 other young people heard Abba Kovner declare that "Hitler is plotting to annihilate all the Jews of Europe. It is the fate of the Jews of Lithuania to be the first in line. . . . It is true that we are weak and defenseless, but the only answer to the murder is self-defense." After the meeting, Kovner published an appeal to young Jews in which he urged, "Let us not be led like sheep to the slaughter." It is better, he wrote, "to fall with honor than to be led like sheep to Ponar."

After their initial shock at the news, many people in Warsaw seemed to believe that Vilna was a special case. Wdowinski writes:

> People [in Warsaw] consoled themselves with the thought that the Eastern districts were recognized as Russian territory, but other laws prevailed in the General Government and that the Jews in this part of Poland would therefore be saved. Many

believed that it would be impossible to exterminate the half a million people of the Warsaw Ghetto. Basically, man is an optimist after all. One drove away sad thoughts. Life is sad enough, why add misgivings as to what was yet to happen? It was self-deceit, to be sure, but how could it have been otherwise?[22]

Later that month, Yakov Grojanowski escaped from Chelmno, the first mechanized death camp. His detailed testimony was not as easy to dismiss. Chelmno was in one of the provinces annexed to the Third Reich. Its very location suggested that the murders were part of a systematic plan of enormous scope. Time and time again, leaders of the various youth movements tried to pass on such information to public figures and even arrange for them to meet with witnesses. Zivia Lubetkin, a leader of a Zionist youth group known as Dror, was struck by their refusal to believe what they heard:

One of the important leaders said: "It isn't possible, that such a thing could happen in the heart of Europe, here in the city of Warsaw. The world will learn of it and not remain silent. We shouldn't speak of extermination, the word should never even pass our lips."

The Jewish masses didn't believe it either. They couldn't believe it. Every man was so involved with the daily problem of finding a piece of bread for his children, that he couldn't see the truth. No one wanted to hear, and it was a very difficult thing to believe in such an atmosphere of total helplessness.

There were a few, however, who said from the first: "*This is wholesale planned murder.*" I cannot describe this terrible feeling. We walked along the overcrowded streets of Warsaw, hundreds of thousands of people pushing and rushing about in fright, antagonistic and tense, living the illusion that they were fighting for their lives, their meager livelihood, but, in reality, when you closed your eyes you could see that they were all dead. . . .

When we realized clearly that the final destiny of the Jews had been irrevocably decided, the first question that came to our minds was, did the Jews simply surrender? Did they just go off to the slaughter without any resistance? The man who brought the news explained almost apologetically: "But the Jews didn't believe that they were going to their deaths. In any case they had nothing to defend themselves with . . . ." It was then that we made our decision. We must resist! The question that we immediately asked ourselves was: "How, and with what?"

We knew that we lacked sufficient strength to carry out the task of self-defense. We would have to persuade the Jewish masses to join our cause. This could only be accomplished by making them realize and believe the brutal fate awaiting us. They would have to recognize the fact that we were all destined for a rapidly approaching death. Today Vilna-Ponar and Chelmno, tomorrow Warsaw and the rest of Poland.[23]

CONNECTIONS

Zivia Lubetkin called it "very difficult" to believe that something is true when others deny that truth. Why is it difficult? How does one make people believe something they do not wish to believe? Lubetkin writes that some people in the youth movement "questioned our right to tell the Jews the whole truth. Were we justified in destroying this last sheltering illusion of the doomed and telling them outright: 'Tomorrow you shall die'?" How would you answer those questions? How do you think she answered them?

What did Jewish leaders in Warsaw know about Nazi plans in the winter of 1941-1942? How did they respond to what they knew? What did they know by the spring of 1942? How did they respond to what they knew then? How did Wdowinski account for their responses? How do you account for them?

Lawrence Langer believes that an underlying reason for people's failure to respond to the news of the Holocaust was the "passive notion of what we might call the imagination of disaster, even with the evidence before our eyes, we hesitate to accept the worst. When the evidence is founded on unconfirmed rumor, we hesitate even more." From what you have learned so far, how do you account for the widespread failure to believe reports of mass murders? Why were those who reported the murders often thought of as "mad"?

Yitzhak Zuckerman, also a leader of the youth group Dror, was stunned by Grabowski's report: "I didn't know what to do with myself." He later explained, "I am from Vilna myself. I was born in Vilna. In Vilna I left behind my parents and my relatives. And here he brought this tragic news from Vilna. While still a child, I had played among the trees in Ponar, and here he spoke about Ponar. My Vilna, the Jews of Vilna, were being killed in Ponar, my playground." Zuckerman's meeting with Grabowski marked a turning point in his thinking. He left convinced that "this wasn't a pogrom anymore! For the first time, the news that 'Ponar was death' sliced through me like a razor. The thought had often been on the tip of my tongue but, for the first time that night, I realized that this was total death."[24]

Why did the news from Vilna have such an effect on Zuckerman and other young Jewish activists? Why do you think older people responded differently? Why might they be more willing to accept the assurances of German leaders than information smuggled into the ghetto by young Poles? Why might they be more willing to accept those assurances than eyewitness accounts by members of Betar, Dror, and other youth groups? What kinds of stories do you find it easiest to believe? What kinds of stories do you find it hardest to accept as true?

In *Night*, Elie Wiesel tells of how the people of Sighet, his hometown in Hungary, viewed messengers like Grojanowski as "madmen." How was their response similar to the response in Warsaw? To what extent are "madmen" people who speak openly of the things we fear? To what extent are they prophets?

The Rush for Papers

It took the Germans months to prepare for the deportation of the Jews of Warsaw. They began by turning the labor camp at Treblinka into a mechanized death camp. Only then did they set up a deportation center (the Umschlagplatz) within the walls of the ghetto and gather the hundreds of boxcars necessary to transport the Jews to Treblinka and their death. By July 22, 1942, the Germans were ready.

On the morning of July 22, brick-red posters were glued to walls throughout the Warsaw Ghetto. They announced that "all Jews residing in Warsaw, regardless of age and sex, will be deported to the East." The only exceptions were:

— Jews employed by the German authorities or by German employers and able to produce sufficient proof of this fact;
— members or employees of the Judenrat;
— the Jewish police;
— the staffs of Jewish hospitals or Jewish disinfection teams;
— wives and children of Jews exempt from the order;
— Jews who, on the day of deportation, were being cared for in Jewish hospitals, with the exception of those able to be moved.

The next day, Adam Czerniakow, the head of the Judenrat, committed suicide. For weeks he had been hearing rumors of a deportation. But Nazi officials assured him that only those unable to work would be affected. When the rumors persisted, he asked again and was again told that workers would be safe. Then, just two days later, the Nazis came to him with a demand that 6,000 Jews be deported each day. Czerniakow wrote in his diary, "When I asked for the number of days per week in which the operation would be carried out, the number was seven days a week." He concluded, "there is nothing left for me but to die." He killed himself that same day.

Czerniakow's death changed nothing. The deportations took place as planned. Even as the police cordoned off one section of the Ghetto after another, Jews were frantically looking for ways to secure the "right" papers—papers that proved they were exceptions to the order. Vladka Meed, a young member of the Bund, recalled:

Though I read and re-read the new posters, I still could not believe that the deportation had really started. People exchanged reassuring words, perhaps seeking to delude themselves as much as to console one another. The clouds would yet disperse. At most, some sixty thousand would be deported. Certainly no more than that. This was the accepted opinion among the community leaders.

Everyone was anxious not to be one of "them." It was necessary to find work, to obtain an employment card; then, according to the German edict, one could be sure of being permitted to stay in the ghetto. The ghetto put its trust in the printed word; workers would not be deported. Life might be hard, but still bearable. However, it was as good as impossible to find a position in a German factory. Such jobs were extremely scarce. A certain amount of money had to be paid to the employer, or else you needed to have pull with the Jewish owners of a shop. Another possibility was to make friends with someone who had already been working in a German factory for some time, and could put in a good word. Barring any of these prospects, the final alternative was to own a sewing machine. If you did, you might be able to exchange it for a job.

The section around Leszno, Prosta, and Nowolipki streets, where the German shops were concentrated, was besieged daily by Jews. Each morning after the curfew had ended, lines formed at the closed factory gates. The earlier you go there, the closer you were to the door, the better your chance of being admitted. Those not waiting in line scurried about in search of a job—any job—the key to survival. Every day new workshops were opened—sometimes without a permit.

As soon as anyone put a few sewing machines into a couple of vacant rooms and began issuing employment cards, Jews stormed the doors. We snatched at straws. Scalpers forged employment cards and sold them at exorbitant prices. A job was a precious commodity, to be sold to the highest bidder.[25]

CONNECTIONS

Thirty years after the war was over, Abba Kovner said in a speech, "It is not a question of when [people] knew or what they knew; it was a question of what they should have done when they knew. What were the alternatives? What conclusions can be drawn when there was no choice?" How did Adam Czerniakow answer those questions? How did Vladka Meed answer them? Were the choices they made real or were they "choiceless choices"?

The Jews of Warsaw were deeply divided about the significance of Czerniakow's death. Yitzhak Zuckerman later wrote, "He could have called out, sounded the alarm, warned us." And he wondered, "Why couldn't he have issued a proclamation: 'Jews, don't go!' signed 'Czerniakow,' and committed suicide before the Germans came to arrest him? We would have gone out and plastered those big posters all over Warsaw."

Historian Yisrael Gutman, who was also a survivor of the Warsaw Ghetto, takes a different view. "Czerniakow put an end to his life rather than collaborate in handing over Jews. He would not be an accessory to the crime. This was his humanitarian and personal reaction, and it is possible that he did not grasp the full significance of what was occurring and, from his own point of view, could not decide how and what the ghetto community as a whole should do."

Which view is closest to your own? Use your answer to define the word resistance. What is the difference between an act of protest and one of resistance?

After the occupation, the Germans tried to turn neighbor against neighbor by dividing Polish Christians from Polish Jews. How did this new set of orders continue that process? Who were "they" in Vladka Meed's account? Why were people anxious "not to be one of 'them'"? What separated "us" from "them"?

How do you account for people's willingness to put their "trust in the printed word"? Was that faith justified?

The Great Aktion

On July 28, 1942, not long after the Aktion began, Heinrich Himmler sent a memo to Gottlob Berger, the Chief of the SS Main Office: "The occupied Eastern territories will be made free of Jews. The Fuehrer has placed the implementation of this very difficult order on my shoulders. Therefore, I forbid all discussion." Orders were orders and they were to be carried out even if they interfered with war production.

In less than two months, the Nazis transported about 300,000 Jews from Warsaw to Treblinka. Countless others were murdered on the streets as they tried to protect themselves or their families. In October, 1942, Antoni Dzymanowski, an officer in the *Armja Krajowa* (AK)—the main Polish underground army—prepared a report based on the eyewitness accounts of Poles allowed to live or work in the ghetto. The day-by-day chronicle was published by an underground group under the title "The Liquidation of the Warsaw Ghetto." On Wednesday, July 22, 1942—the first day of the Aktion—Dzymanowski noted:

> So this is the end of the ghetto that has been fighting desperately to stay alive for two years. This afternoon it was announced that everyone, regardless of sex or age, will be resettled "to the East." There is no need to fool ourselves; the announcement is a death sentence. The Germans will not settle, feed, and clothe thousands of people in any "East" after consistently exterminating them in Warsaw. Death—whether sudden or gradual—is waiting for them. Perhaps those exempted from resettlement have a chance to survive since they are useful to the Germans: the ones working for them in factories and in the trades, the police, the city employees, etc. They are even permitted to protect their wives and children from being deported. But the rest? Do we need any more indication than that amazingly cynical sentence: each person being resettled is permitted to take along fifteen kilograms of his personal belongings. All valuables such as money, jewelry, gold can be taken along. Gold, which Jews have been forbidden to own for months now! Line up in rows so that we can kill you, but have your jewelry ready to save us trouble.
>
> . . . The Jewish Police have been hunting for humans since noon. The Germans are staying out of it. There are two kinds of them: black and red, according to their uniforms. Machine guns have been posted at all city [exits], and bursts of fire can be heard almost continuously, but they seem to be more of a deterrent. But the wild, even frenzied shooting has been going on all night. They are shooting into windows with carbines, at passersby with revolvers. Today a doctor from the hospital on Sienna Street told me that there is not a room in her building that has not been shot into from the street. . . .
>
> Larger groups are led to the connection track in the square on Stawki Street. Our messenger ran over there and caught a glimpse of how they were hastily loaded into open railway cars; when a car was full, it was wired shut with bared wire, worse than with animals! It is raining, and the sight of this agony is—he says— unbearable. . . .The atmosphere of panic and terror, intensified by the continuous reverberations of erratic shooting, is so terrible that I breathed a sigh of relief when I left the ghetto in the evening. At the same time, though, it was difficult for me, after watching the more or less normal life on the streets of Warsaw, really to believe that this "resettlement" of hundreds of people into the beyond is taking place right beside it.[26]

Jews being deported.

In her autobiography, Janina Bauman recalls the routine she and her family followed as the Aktion continued:

Day after day, including Saturday and Sunday, [the roundups] started at 8 a.m. and ended at 4 p.m. We soon learned to live according to this timetable, going out early in the morning to be back home before eight, then in the evening again, until curfew time. The streets, deserted during the long hours of daily horror, came to life again during those short spells. People hurried to see whether their relatives and friends had survived the day's Aktion, to make another attempt to get into the factories, to telephone friends on the "Aryan" side, to find some food. All shops, cafes and restaurants had been closed since the beginning of deportation, all entrances to the ghetto thoroughly blocked by the Nazis. Food was getting scarce. Yet, in the evenings the streets swarmed with resourceful vendors selling bread, potatoes, or sweets at sky-high prices.

There were no more beggars lying on the pavements and no calls for help were heard. The "human refuse" had been swept away and put on the trains during the very first days of the *Aktion*. The ghetto orphanages, old people's homes and refugee shelters had been gradually cleared away as well. Now the Nazis, keenly helped by the Ukrainian and Latvian troops as well as by the Jewish police, launched a systematic house-to-house hunt. Houses were surrounded by the troops, all gates and exits blocked, residents summoned to the back yards. Their documents checked. Only those with an *Aussweis* [an employment card] that proved their usefulness to the Germans were exempted from deportation. All the others were forced to form ranks and march to the *Umschlagplatz*. Meanwhile the flats were searched; anybody found hiding was, as a rule, killed on the spot.

At the beginning of August we learned that the "little ghetto" had ceased to exist, the inhabitants deported or forced to move farther north. . . . We expected our turn to come any time now, without much hope of getting an *Aussweis* before then.

And when it really came, on 13 August, we were still without the coveted documents, all six of us.

The house at 15 Leszno Street was surrounded and closed off first thing in the morning. From our fifth-floor flat we heard the uproar of troops bursting into the courtyard, the ear-splitting whistle, then the loud cry: "*Alle Juden raus, schnell, schell, alle Juden herunter.*" (All Jews out, quick, quick, all Jews down here) repeated in Polish. Then the sound of dozens of feet running down, down to disaster. Then shouts, screaming, whistles, lamenting in the courtyard. . . . Two single shots. . . A turmoil of violence and misery.

We stayed in our flat, waiting, listening. We had decided long before not to obey, not to go down. To be shot dead instantly seemed far better than to endure the long, slow process of dying in pain and humiliation. Besides, there was no chance of survival if we obeyed the order; there might be some if we disobeyed. So we sat still, listening.

Soon we heard a rumble of heavy boots climbing up the stairs, of smashed locks and doors flung open by force: the hunters were searching through the flats. We could hear them coming up and up, approaching the third floor, then the fourth. We could already hear their voices, make out Polish and Latvian words. The fourth floor was taking them a long time: they were obviously busy plundering. Now we had only minutes left. We waited.

Then suddenly a long, sharp whistle and a German command from the court-yard announced the end of the round-up, summoning back the hunters.

We had survived.[27]

After a sleepless night, the family decided to go to a cousin who lived on a street not yet targeted for a roundup. A few days later, they were on the move yet another time. No place was safe for long as the hunt for Jews continued—not even an orphanage. Early on the morning of August 4, 1942, as Janusz Korczak looked out of a window in his orphanage, he wondered about the men who "hunted" Jews. He focused on one man in particular. He wrote in his diary that day:

I watered the flowers, the poor plants of the orphanage. The burned earth breathed a sigh of relief.

The [German] sentry watched me work. Did my peaceful work of 6 a.m. antag-onize him or touch him?

He stands there and watches, his legs far apart

. . . . I water flowers. My bald head in the window—such a nice target.

He has a rifle. Why does he stand there watching quietly?

He has no orders.

Perhaps he was a teacher in a small town during his civilian life, or a notary, a street cleaner in Leipzig, a waiter in Cologne?

What would he do if I were to nod my head at him?

Give him a friendly wave?

Perhaps he does not even know that things are as they are. It could be that he just arrived yesterday from far away. . . .[28]

Compare the way Antoni Dzymanowski, Janina Bauman, and Janusz Korczak viewed the perpetrators? What differences seem most striking? Why do you think Bauman calls them "hunters"? Why did Korczak choose to focus on a single German? How would you answer the questions he raises? How do you think the other two might answer them?

In August of 1942, a Catholic underground group called "Front for Reborn Poland" published 5,000 copies of a leaflet entitled "Protest" by Zofia Kossak-Szatkowska. It is addressed to bystanders:

> The world looks at this crime, worse than anything history has experienced so far, and—remains silent. Millions of defenseless humans are slaughtered in the midst of a general sinister silence. The henchmen are silent. They do not brag about their deeds. England and America do not raise their voices; even the influential international Jewish community, so sensitive in its reaction to any transgression against its people earlier, is silent. Poland, too, is silent. The Christian Poles, the political friends of the Jews, confine themselves to a few newspaper reports; the Polish enemies of the Jews express a lack of interest in this matter that is foreign to them. The dying Jews are surrounded by a host of Pilates who are washing their hands in innocence. . . . we do not want to be Pilates! Actively, we can do nothing against the German slaughter, we cannot help, can save no one—but we protest from the depth of the hearts of those who are gripped by compassion, indignation and horror. God demands this protest from us, God, who does not permit killing. Our Christian conscience demands it. Every being who thinks of himself as human has a right to charity. The blood of the helpless cries to the heavens for revenge. Those who do not support us in this protest are not Catholic.[29]

Pontius Pilate was the official in the Roman Empire who sentenced Jesus to death. According to many historians and theologians, he was an exceptionally cruel man. Yet according to the Gospels written by John, he is portrayed as wanting to release Jesus but giving in to the pressure of the crowds in Jerusalem. Yet before giving the order, he washed his hands as a sign that he was ridding himself of responsibility for Jesus's fate. Whom does Zofia Kossak-Szatkowska view as "Pilates"? Why do you think she referred to this particular New Testament story in a pamphlet urging aid for Jews?

In a part of the protest not quoted above, Zofia Kossak-Szatkowska writes:

> Our feelings towards the Jews have not changed. We still consider them to be political, economic, and ideological enemies of Poland. What is more, we are aware that they consider us to be responsible for their misfortune. Why, on what grounds—that is a mystery of the Jewish soul, but it is a fact that is being confirmed again and again. The awareness of these feelings, however, does not relieve us of our duty to condemn the crime.[30]

Kossak-Szatkowska later organized Zegota, a special section of the AK that tried to help Jews in an organized way. Why would someone who viewed Jews as "enemies of Poland" want to save their lives? Protest crimes against them? How do her views complicate our thinking about human behavior?

Buried Treasure

A few days after the Aktion began, Emmanuel Ringelblum and other members of Oneg Shabbat decided it was time to hide the thousands of documents they had been collecting.

Documents were buried in milk cans as well as boxes. These cans were dug up after the war.

Israel Lichtenstein, a member of Oneg Shabbat, and his two young assistants packed the archives into crates. Before they sealed the boxes, each slipped in his own testament. Then the three men buried their treasure. Eighteen-year-old Naum Grzywacz wrote:

> We have decided to describe the present times. Yesterday we sat up till late in the night, since we did not know whether we would survive till today. Now I am in the midst of writing, while in the streets the terrible shooting is going on . . . . Of one thing I am proud, that in these grave and fateful days I was one of those who buried the treasure. . .In those days when they were shooting. . . in order that you should know of the tortures and murders of the Nazi tyranny. . . .[31]

David Grober, who was just one year older than his friend, wrote:

> We must hurry, because we are not sure of the next hour. . . . Yesterday we worked till late in the night. I want the coming generations to remember our times so that in a free and socialistic world our pains and turmoil may be recalled, so that it will be remembered that in such a time of ruin, there were people who had the courage to do such work. . . .
>
> With what ardor we dug the holes for the boxes. . . with what joy we received every bit of material. We felt our responsibility and we were not afraid of any danger,

we were well aware of the fact that we were creating a piece of history and that this was more important than a few individual lives, this burying of the treasure. . . we would rather have cut off our limbs than betray our secret. . . How I would like to live to the moment when the treasure is dug out and the whole truth proclaimed. . . . BUT WE CERTAINLY WILL NOT LIVE TO SEE IT. . . .

Therefore, I write this testament. May this treasure come into the right hands, may it live in better times, may the world be aroused to know that such things could have happened in the 20th century! . . . Now we can die in peace, we have fulfilled our mission![32]

CONNECTIONS

What was the treasure the two men buried? Why were they willing to risk their lives to keep it safe? Was their work an act of resistance?

Elie Wiesel wrote that "Emmanuel Ringelblum and his hundred scribes have but a single thought: to gather and bury as many documents as possible—so much suffering, so many trials must not be lost to History. Since European Jewry is doomed, it becomes imperative to at least preserve the scorched vestiges of its passing. Poems, litanies, plays: to write them, Jews went without sleep and bartered their food for pencils and paper. They gambled with their fate. They risked their lives."[33] Why does Wiesel consider it "imperative to at least preserve the scorched vestiges" of the passing of European Jewry? For whom were Jews preserving those vestiges? After reading excerpts from a few of the documents that Ringelblum and his scribes saved, what do you think of their work? What does it reveal that other documents do not tell?

Fateful Choices

As the Great Aktion continued, more and more Jews were aware that deportation meant death. And so, individually, and as families, they made fateful choices.

Martin Gray was among those who made important decisions in the summer of 1942. Although he continued to run out into the streets each day, he hid his mother and two young brothers in a cupboard. He brought them food late at night when the roundups ended for the day. After a while, he writes, the days blended together, but one day stood out from all the rest.

> It must have been around mid-August, I was on my way home, when I heard singing. Soon I saw them, neat and clean, holding each other's hands: the children from the orphanage. Led by Dr. Korczak, the children were off to the *Umschlagplatz*. I'd applauded at their recitals, the entertaining scenes they'd enacted in charity shows at the Femina Theater. I'd been a regular contributor to the orphanage. Now they were off to the *Umschlagplatz*.
>
> Dr. Korczak was striding forward with a fixed look, holding two small expressionless boys by the hands. I walked along beside him whispering, "Doctor, Doctor." I pleaded with him but he didn't answer, as if he hadn't recognized me. I walked to the barriers with them and watched them enter the *Umschlagplatz*. The cattle cars were lined up alongside the platforms and the little SS man was smiling.
>
> "Come on." It was my father. He seized me by the arm and dragged me towards Mila Street.
>
> "Korczak didn't want to frighten them. He's going with them."
>
> I didn't answer. How could he have consented, not tried to hide the children? Why offer himself as a sacrifice?
>
> "Don't judge him. Don't judge anyone. He's trying to save them, to protect them, in his own way."[34]

By September, Martin Gray's father had been deported. And Martin's struggle to keep his mother and brothers alive was becoming more and more difficult. Then one terrible day, he stood on a rooftop looking down at the street only to see his mother and brothers being led to the *Umschlagplatz*. Their hiding place had been discovered. He slowly climbed down from the roof and joined them:

> "Don't cry, Mother."
>
> I went over to her, and one by one took away the clothes she was clutching to her chest as if they were her most treasured possessions. I made a bundle of them. I patted my brother's heads. . . .
>
> So we set off along Zamenhofa Street. Goodbye, Mila Street, goodbye Zamenhofa Street. We were walking on torn clothes, scattered books; we were avoiding smashed furniture; we were treading on what had been the lives of tens of thousands of our people, the things for which they'd toiled, we were trampling on our own lives. The warm sun, still amazingly strong for September, beat down on our backs. I was walking behind my people, steering them so that they weren't driven to the edge. By this time we'd reached Dzika Street and I could see the Umschlagplatz and the hospital. . . .

By now I could see the cattle cars, the Jewish police ferreting about in the columns lined up in front of the doors, some people trying to slip away. The little SS man was still there, lash in hand. . . .

We weren't even taken to the hospital. They needed heads. They were nearing the end of their task, they wanted to keep going, there wasn't a "left" or a "right" anymore, we all got into the cattle cars. I managed to help my people up into one which was only half full; so we all remained together, but by the time they'd shut the door we were in the middle, surrounded, and it was hopeless trying to get near a side. . . .

We were waiting, suffocating; the wails, screams, pleas for help.

Then the cattle car moved off and at once I started talking, trying to convince my neighbors of the possibility of escape, sometimes shouting, but I wasn't on my own this time, I was wedged there in the middle determined not to leave my brothers, my mother. . . So I stopped talking. . . .

The train was heading for Treblinka.[35]

Not long after Martin Gray and his family were deported, the Great Aktion ended. On September 12, 1942, nearly two months after the deportations began, the Germans ordered Jewish policemen and their families to the *Umschlagplatz*. Alexander Donat writes:

So did the Germans reward their faithful service. A crowd of thousands looked on in stony silence as the policemen with heads bowed walked to the loading platforms to share the fate they had so zealously handed out to others. Of the nearly 2,000 policemen on the force before the deportations began, only 240 were left. . . .

In a period of eight weeks, more than 300,000 people had been deported in cattle cars to the extermination chambers and mass graves of Treblinka. There was now no further doubt about the destination or its purpose: the incredible was a matter of fact. One of those who had miraculously escaped from the death factory at Treblinka was a man who had formerly been the janitor of the building we lived in on Orla Street, and we had the story from his own lips. The nation of Kant and Goethe was deliberately and systematically murdering defenseless men, women, and children in its gas chambers. There were now 30,000 "legal" inhabitants in the Ghetto, legality meaning that they possessed German documents giving them the right to live. Nearly as many "wild ones" were hidden.[36]

CONNECTIONS

In his autobiography, Yitzhak Zuckerman wrote, "We were witness to a heroic stance of Jews who resisted the Germans on numerous occasions. They are the unknown who appear in the files as "5,394, shot," reported in the official German accounts of the "resettlement" action." Why did Zuckerman call those "unknown" Jews "heroic"? In what sense were their actions heroic? What about Israel Lichtenstein, Naum Grzywacz, David Grober, and other members of Oneg Shabbat (Reading 10)? Were they also heroic? How would you characterize the actions of young men and women like Martin Gray who refused to let their families go to Treblinka alone or of older people like Janusz Korczak who tried desperately to keep faith with the children under their care as they went to their deaths?

How would you answer the questions Martin Gray asks about Korczak and the children? How did he answer those same questions when he saw his mother and young brothers being led to the *Umschlagplatz*? Martin Gray was the only member of his family to survive the Holocaust.

Nachum Remba was in the *Umschlagplatz* the day Korczak and his orphans were deported. In a report smuggled out of the ghetto, he wrote:

> I'll never forget the sight to the end of my life. It wasn't just entering a boxcar—it was a silent but organized protest against the murderers, a march like which no human eye had ever seen before. The children went four-by-four. Korczak went first with his head held high leading a child with each hand. The second group was led by Stefa Wilczynska [Korczak's assistant]. They went to their death with such a look of contempt for their assassins. When the ghetto policemen saw Korczak, they snapped to attention and saluted. "Who is that man?" asked the Germans. I couldn't control myself any longer, but I hid the flood of tears that ran down my cheeks with my hands. I sobbed and sobbed at our helplessness in the face of such murder.[37]

Why were observers so moved by the deportation of Korczak and the orphans? Why did Remba describe the event as "a silent but organized protest against the murderers, a march like which no human eye had ever seen before"? In what sense was it a protest?

Many people claimed that Jews went to the *Umschlagplatz* like "sheep to slaughter." The phrase comes from Isaiah: "He was oppressed and he was afflicted, yet he opened not his mouth; he is brought as a lamb to the slaughter, and as a sheep before her shearer is dumb, so he openeth not his mouth." What does the passage mean? Why did it take on special meaning to the Jews of Poland in 1942?

Abba Kovner used the phrase as part of a call for armed resistance in Vilna in January of 1942. Long after the war, he told an audience that it was meant "to shake ghetto inhabitants out of their conviction that they were standing before a situation of total destruction." He went on to say, "I never thought afterwards that a woman whose child has been taken out of her arms had gone to her death like 'a sheep to the slaughter.' There was only one occasion, or type of occasion, afterwards when I thought that, and it was during the fighting when there might have been sheep. But that was a different occasion altogether, and I have never thought the sheep had anything to be ashamed of."[38] How do the accounts included in this reading explain why Kovner insisted that he never thought the "sheep had anything to be ashamed of"?

Michel Mazor writes:

> The twentieth century witnessed a new sort of crime, committed not by criminals or mobs of gangsters, but by the state; a state had perpetrated the most horrible of crimes—the annihilation of whole peoples—genocide. The first example of such a crime was the massacre of the Armenians by the Turks in 1915, in the course of the First World War.
> During the terrible days of July and August 1942, we often spoke of the fate of the Armenians; most of us knew [Franz] Werfel's book, *The Forty Days of Musa-Dagh*, and we often recalled an episode in it—the arrival of French warships bringing aid to the Armenians. "But," we said, "we unfortunately cannot count on any aid, we are doomed, and no one's going to try to rescue us." This was in the period when Hitler occupied Europe from the Pyrenees to the Volga; thousands of kilometers separated us

from the free world, delivering us defenseless to the Nazi monster. Free humanity had not fulfilled its duty to the Armenian martyrs; it had forgotten about this unprecedented crime and by this fact, had fatefully committed a sin against itself. And perhaps, if at the end of the First World War, a [tribunal] had convened at Istanbul, the gas chambers and crematoria of Auschwitz and Treblinka would not have come into being.[39]

What does Mazor believe was the duty of "free humanity" to the Armenians? How does he link that failure to the plight of the Jews in Europe during World War II? What is he suggesting about the future? If individuals who perpetrated such crimes in the name of their state are not held accountable, who can be judged? What happens to a history that has not been judged or even acknowledged?

To those who wonder why the Jews did not simply run away, Primo Levi replied in his book *The Drowned and the Saved*: "In what direction could they flee? To whom could then turn for shelter? They were outside the world, men and women made of air. They no longer had a country." In what sense were Jews "outside the world"? In what sense did they no longer have a country?

Treblinka Means Death

Martin Gray, his mother, and brothers were among the over 300,000 Jews shipped to Treblinka in the summer of 1942. Almost all of them were murdered there. Gray was among the very few who survived.

In his autobiography, Martin Gray tells of how he was separated from his mother, his two young brothers, and a friend soon after the family's arrival at Treblinka. He writes of his first two days in the camp.

This was the start of a new era. All I knew about Treblinka was the name but I knew that those I loved were going to die there.

SS men, Ukrainians holding lashes, cudgels poised to land on heads and backs. A loudspeaker, a cool voice repeating, "Men to the right, women and children to the left."

My head down to avoid the blows, I could see a small railway station, read the usual signs: Buffet, Waiting/Room, toilets, Ticket Office. Everything was spick and span as a stage set. Then further on I saw barbed wire covered with pine branches.

Goodbye, my family. They'd already disappeared into the huddled mob: gray hair, fair hair, curly hair: my mother, Rivka, my brothers. I knew, heart swelling up into my throat, they they would never come back. That I wouldn't be able to hold them an arm's length from death any longer. . . .

I edged forward, to gain a few seconds in which to understand, so as to choose my fate instead of submitting. Around us were prisoners, hunched, their heads disappearing between their shoulders, rushing in all directions, picking up the luggage, shoving us forward. One of them bumped into me. I caught him.

"What's going on here?"

He pulled away sharply, gave me a shove.

"Never mind, don't worry, just do as you're told."

I dodged blows, followed the line. Some old men were shown to an entrance with a red cross above it: "Lazarett," The loudspeaker went on giving orders:

"Get undressed. Have a shower. Then you'll be moved to your new work sites."

I looked at the barbed wire, the cattle cars returning empty, the silent, anonymous prisoners. Here waited an unknown death.

"Take your valuables and your papers. Don't forget your soap."

I walked on into an open space where some men were already naked, and that was when I heard a loud, rhythmic sound, like a heavy engine with a dull throb, sometimes dragging, as if making an effort to turn over; an impersonal, monotonous beat: the pulse of the camp, which even the shouts of the SS couldn't drown.

Whips in hand, wearing black, SS men were walking among the naked, catching some by the arm and making them dress again. I still had my clothes on, so I eased over to them, pushing aside men who were having difficulty removing their shoes. I was being driven towards them by some force inside me shouting, "Go on, Martin. Go on, Mietek. That's where life is. Go on."

One of the SS men tapped me on the shoulder with his lash, singling me out.

I began to run along after the rest, carrying bundles of clothes to the sorting lot, helping to make up piles. Running head down borne forward by those clothes, all that remained of men's lives. More cattle cars had arrived, the last section of our train, and the changing lot was deserted where, barely an hour before, there'd been a throng of naked men; the place where my mother, my brothers, and Rivka had been, before disappearing into the hut. The loudspeaker again. I ran off again with heavy loads, as fast as I could.

With every step I came to know Treblinka: its yellowish sand, its all-pervading stench, its voices, its pulse: the engine pounding away in the northeast corner of the camp where, at the far end of an avenue of small dark pine trees, scarcely taller than a man, a brick building lay half-concealed behind a bank with barbed wire on top: a camp within a camp. On the sorting lot, I made separate piles of children's clothes, men's hats, spectacles, overcoats: every object had its pile and you had to rush from one pile to the next. The Ukrainians lashed out with their whips, and at times an SS man shot someone, or killed someone with his rifle butt. I scurried around stooping.

"Mind your face," a prisoner had whispered to me.

Then the breeze, bringing the sound of the engine closer. Over in that other camp they were raking sand. I could clearly hear metal prongs clawing at the ground. They were forever digging over there. We were assembled on a large open space, between the huts. The SS passed in front of us, the Ukrainians at our sides like dogs. And there were dogs too, huge ones, straining at their leashes. The SS pointed to men who then left the ranks and went off flanked by Ukrainians. Then we heard shots. We lined up for mess cans of water containing a few potatoes, and were shoved into one of the huts.

I was still alive. The stench in the hut was intolerable. Men were groaning, others prayed. I was sitting next to a man who was trembling, his eyes fixed, his fists and jaws clenched. He was wearing a red badge: a veteran of the camp.

"Where do they go, the rest of them from the train?"

"The gas chambers."

"Where?"

"To the lower camp, that other camp."

I huddled against the wooden wall. My people, thousands of them. Warsaw! And I was still alive. . . .

In the morning four bodies were dangling from the beams. We were lined up on the parade ground and Lalka, the doll, the SS man, harangued us: we were nothing, less than dogs, we were worth less than the soil they'd bury us in, we were vermin. He was of the race of kings.

My first morning in Treblinka, and already the past was receding, already my time in the ghetto was merging with "before." Before the war, before my birth. By the second I found out about life and death in Treblinka. I saw the lepssudra: men who'd been struck in the face, whose welts meant death. They were taken from the ranks and marked for the Lazarett, the "hospital." I saw prisoners killed with shovels. I saw dogs attack inmates. I knew why you had to walk with your head down, why you always had to run, do better, go faster: because the SS and the Ukrainians killed us to spur us on. There wasn't any shortage of us. The cattle cars arrived twenty at a time: three sections of twenty, a train. And the others, like Rivka, my mother, my brothers. . . were shoved onto the platform, split up, men to the right, women and children to the left; stripped. And we helped them.

"What's going on here?" they asked.

"Nothing, it's all right, all right," we said.

I collected pairs of shoes: I gathered up clothes that reeked of sweat, I ran. I learned how to run my hands quickly through the pockets, find biscuits and sugar, put them in my mouth and swallow those crumbs of life without even chewing them. A twitch of the lips or the jaw and it was death in the Lazarett, or a bullet in the back of the neck. Or death from rifle butts or whips. I went down that avenue, that lovely avenue lined by black pine trees, which lead to the Himmelstrasse, "road to Heaven," to pick up objects which some of them had dropped, to make the avenue attractive, welcoming, peaceful. I went and cleaned the filth from the walls and floors of the cattle cars. In the evening, on the parade ground, I saw more lepssudra leave the ranks for the Lazarett; I saw men even with unmarked faces picked at random with a glance and sent to their deaths. Death reaped our ranks constantly. Slowing down at work: death. Carrying too light a load: death. Chewing a bit of food: death. They wanted to terrorize us. We had to feel their power bearing down on us as if from mysterious gods. They were our fate.[40]

Gray survived only because he escaped from the camp by strapping himself to the underside of a truck. Others were not as fortunate. Only a tiny remnant survived Treblinka and the other death camps. Many years after the war was over, journalist Gitta Sereny interviewed Franz Stangl, the commandant of the death camp at Sobibor and later at Treblinka. She spoke to him not long after his arrest in Brazil in 1971 and his subsequent trial. She asked:

"Would it be true to say that you finally felt they weren't really human beings?"
"When I was on a trip once, years later in Brazil," he said, his face deeply concentrated, and obviously reliving the experience, "my train stopped next to a slaughterhouse. The cattle in the pens, hearing the noise of the train, trotted up to the fence and stared at the train. They were very close to my window, one crowding the other, looking at me through that fence. I thought then, 'Look at this; this reminds me of Poland; that's just how the people looked, trustingly, just before they went into the tins. . . .'"
"You said tins," I interrupted. "What do you mean?" But he went on without hearing, or answering me.
". . . I couldn't eat tinned meat after that. Those big eyes. . . which looked at me. . . not knowing that in no time at all they'd all be dead." He paused. His face was drawn. At this moment he looked old and worn and real.
"So you didn't feel they were human beings?
"Cargo," he said tonelessly. "They were cargo." He raised and dropped his hand in a gesture of despair. Both our voices had dropped. It was one of the few times in those weeks of talks that he made no effort to cloak his despair, and his hopeless grief allowed a moment of sympathy.
"When do you think you began to think of them as cargo? The way you spoke earlier, of the day when you first came to Treblinka, the horror you felt seeing the dead bodies everywhere—they weren't 'cargo' to you then, were they?"
"I think it started the day I first saw the Totenlager [death camp] in Treblinka. I remember [Christian] Wirth [the man who set up the death camps] standing there, next to the pits full of blue-black corpses. It had nothing to do with humanity—it couldn't have; it was a mass—a mass of rotting flesh. Wirth said, 'What shall we do with this garbage?' I think unconsciously that started me thinking of them as cargo."
"There were so many children, did they ever make you think of your children, of how you would feel in the position of those parents."
"No," he said slowly, "I can't say I ever thought that way." He paused. "You see," he then continued, still speaking with this extreme seriousness and obviously intent on

finding a new truth within himself, "I rarely saw them as individuals. It was always a huge mass. I sometimes stood on the wall and saw them in the tube. But—how can I explain it—they were naked, packed together, running being driven with whips like . . ." the sentence trailed off.

"Could you have changed that?" I asked. "In your position, could you not have stopped the nakedness, the whips, the horror of the cattle pen?"

"No, no, no. This was the system. Wirth had invented it. It worked. And because it worked, it was irreversible."[41]

CONNECTIONS

Martin Gray writes that he needs "another voice, other words" to describe Treblinka. Primo Levi, an Italian Jew deported to Auschwitz in 1944, believes that our understanding is hampered by the way everyday words took on new meanings in the camps.

Just as our hunger is not the feeling of missing a meal, so our way of being cold has need of a new word. We say "hunger," we say "tiredness," "fear," "pain," we say "winter" and they are different things. They are free words, created and used by free men who lived in comfort and without suffering in their homes.[42]

Levi believed that if the war had lasted longer "a new, harsh language would have been born" and only this language could express what it means to have "in one's body nothing but weakness, hunger, and knowledge of the end drawing near." What does this reading suggest about the way that language was learned?

In the introduction to this chapter, Abba Kovner recalls that he was once "shown a model of the Treblinka death camp, and told that it was an 'accurate and authentic picture' of Treblinka. But it was not; it was the buildings without the anguish and the horror. Treblinka was not the buildings and the fence; without the horror, it was just another youth camp." How does Gray's account help us confront the anguish and the horror of Treblinka? What does the interview with Stangl add to our understanding of Treblinka and other death camps?

Let the World Know!

The Great or Grosse Aktion began on July 22, 1942 and continued with occasional pauses until September 12, 1942. In August, during one of those "pauses," two prominent Jews met with a courier for the Polish underground and begged him to alert the world to what was happening to the Jews of Poland.

Jan Karski was a young Pole who carried information to and from the Polish government-in-exile in London and the Polish resistance movement in Nazi-occupied territory. Just before he left Poland on a mission to the West, he met secretly with two Jews, one a Zionist leader and the other a Bundist. In a book written just two years later, in 1944, Karski described that secret meeting and its outcome:

It was an evening of nightmare, but with a painful, oppressive kind of reality that no nightmare ever had. I sat in an old, rickety armchair as if I had been pinned there, barely able to utter a word while the torrents of their emotion broke over me. They paced the floor violently, their shadows dancing weirdly in the dim light cast by the single candle we could allow ourselves. It was as though they were unable even to think of their dying people and remain seated. . . .

. . . . The Bund leader spoke first, resting his hands on the table as though it helped him to concentrate on what he was about to say.

"We want you to tell the Polish and Allied governments and the great leaders of the Allies that we are helpless in the face of the German criminals. We cannot defend ourselves and no one in Poland can defend us. The Polish underground authorities can save some of us but they cannot save masses. The Germans are not trying to enslave us as they have other people; we are being systematically murdered."

The Zionist broke in.

"This is what people do not understand. That is what is so difficult to make clear."

I nodded my assent. The Bund leader continued:

"Our entire people will be destroyed. A few may be saved, perhaps, but three million Polish Jews are doomed. This cannot be prevented by any force in Poland, neither the Polish nor the Jewish Underground. Place this responsibility on the shoulders of the Allies. Let not a single leader of the United Nations be able to say that they did not know that we were being murdered in Poland and could not be helped except from the outside."

This was the solemn message I carried to the world. They impressed it upon me so that it could not be forgotten. They added to it, for they saw their position with the clarity of despair. At this time more than 1,800,000 Jews had been murdered. These two men refused to delude themselves and foresaw how the United Nations might react to this information. The truth might not be believed. It might be said that this figure was exaggerated, not authentic. I was to argue, convince, do anything I could, use every available proof and testimonial, shout the truth till it could not be denied. . . .

They offered to take me to the Warsaw ghetto so that I could literally see the spectacle of a people expiring, breathing its last before my eyes. They would take me into one of the many death camps where Jews were tortured and murdered by the thousands. As an eye-witness I would be much more convincing than a mere mouthpiece. At the same time they warned me that if I accepted their offer I would have to risk my life to carry it out. They told me, too, that as long as I lived I would be haunted by the memory of the ghastly scenes I would witness. . . .

Two days later I went to the Warsaw ghetto with the Bund leader and another member of the Jewish Underground. . . .[43]

At one point during Karski's visit to the Ghetto, his two escorts rushed him into an apartment building so that he could witness an "event" that he would not have believed had he not seen it for himself. They called it "the hunt." From an upper-story window that faced the street, he saw two boys dressed in the uniform of the Hitler Youth.

They wore no caps and their blond hair shone in the sun. With their round, rosy-cheeked faces and their blue eyes they were like images of health and life. They chattered, laughed, pushed each other in spasms of merriment. At that moment, the younger one pulled a gun out of his hip pocket and then I first realized what I was witnessing. His eyes roamed about, seeking something. A target. He was looking for a target with the casual, gay absorption of a boy at a carnival.

I followed his glance. For the first time I noticed that all the pavements about them were absolutely deserted. Nowhere within the scope of those blue eyes, in no place from which those cheerful, healthy faces could be seen was there a single human being. The gaze of the boy with the gun came to rest on a spot out of my line of vision. He raised his arm and took careful aim. The shot rang out, followed by the noise of breaking glass and then the terrible cry of a man in agony.

The boy who had fired the shot shouted with joy. The other clapped him on the shoulder and said something to him, obviously complimentary. They smiled at each other and stood there for a moment, gay and insolent, as though aware of their invisible audience. Then they linked their arms and walked off gracefully toward the exit of the ghetto, chatting cheerfully as if they were returning from a sporting event.

I stood there, my face glued to the window. In the room behind me there was a complete silence. No one even stirred. I remained where I was, afraid to change the position of my body, to move my hand or relax my cramped legs. I was seized with such panic that I could not make the effort of will to take a single step or force a word out of my throat. It seemed to me that if I made the slightest movement, if a single muscle in my body so much as trembled, I might precipitate another scene such as I had just witnessed.

I do not know how long I remained there. Any interval could have passed, I was so completely unconscious of time. At length I felt someone's hand on my shoulder. Repressing a nervous start, I turned around. A woman, the tenant of the apartment, was standing there, her gaunt face the color of chalk in the dim light. She gestured at me.

"You came to see us? It won't do any good. Go back, run away. Don't torture yourself any more."[44]

Karski left the Ghetto soon after the incident but returned a few days later. He also paid a similar visit to what he thought was Belzec, a death camp. Historians later discovered that he was actually at Izbeica Lubelska, northwest of Lublin. It was a holding camp for Jews destined for Belzec which lay forty miles to the southeast. Just a few days later Karski left the country to report what he had seen and heard to the Polish government-in-exile, officials in the British and American governments, and Jewish leaders in the United States and England. He also related his experiences to some of the world's most famous writers including H.G. Wells and Arthur Koestler. He hoped to convince them to tell the story with "greater force and talent" than he possessed. Yet everywhere, he encountered disbelief. Karski recalled:

> No one was prepared to grasp what was going on. It is not true, as sometimes has been written, that I was the first one to present to the West the whole truth of the fate of the Jews in occupied Poland. There were others. . . . The tragedy was that these testimonies were not believed. Not because of ill will, but simply because the facts were beyond human imagination.
>
> I experienced this myself. When I was in the United States and told [Supreme Court] Justice Felix Frankfurter the story of the Polish Jews, he said, at the end of our conversation, "I cannot believe you." We were with the Polish ambassador to the US, Jan Ciechanowski. Hearing the justice's comments, he was indignant. "Lieutenant Karski is on an official mission. My government's authority stands behind him. You cannot say to his face that he is lying." Frankfurter's answer was, "I am not saying that he is lying. I only said that I cannot believe him, and there is a difference."[44]

CONNECTIONS

Write a working definition of the word *bystander*. What responsibilities do bystanders have to the victims? In 1942, were the Allies—Britain, the United States, and the Soviet Union— bystanders to mass murder? Can a nation be a bystander?

What is the significance of the "hunt"? Why did it paralyze Karski for a few moments? How did the incident underscore the message he had received from the two leaders?

Think about Frankfurter's statement. What is the difference between saying that someone is lying and saying that you cannot believe what he or she is saying? Why do you think he chose not to believe?

Historian Leni Yahil divides knowledge into three parts: receipt of information, acknowledgment of that information, and action based on the information. What facts would have been hardest for a Polish Catholic like Karski to accept? What facts would be hardest for an American Jew of German descent like Frankfurter to accept? What do you think you personally would have had the most difficulty acknowledging: laws that set Jews and others apart as the "enemy," the creation of the Warsaw Ghetto, the mass deportations, or the death camps? How does Yahil's division of knowledge apply to the way people in recent years responded to the murders in Bosnia or Rwanda? How does it apply to catastrophes in other parts of the world? Do people *know*? Have they *acknowledged* the information? Have they *acted* on that knowledge?

Many people did hear what Jan Karski and others had to say. And some wanted to help but thought it was impossible to do so in time of war. Elie Wiesel has long disagreed. How would you answer the questions he raises? To what extent was the failure to act a failure of "the human imagination"?

> I know that many will say: "It was impossible to send anything from outside. . ." Impossible? No one even tried! Had there been a hundred attempts, one might have succeeded. Can it be argued it was less dangerous for the ghetto-couriers to travel

from one ghetto to another (to warn, to organize resistance, to bring assistance) than it would have been to travel to Budapest from Istanbul, and from there to Warsaw?[46]

After the war, a Polish woman recalled two occasions when she turned away rather than help someone from the Warsaw Ghetto. Wondering if the outcome would have been different if she and others had followed their conscience, she concludes, "Possibly, even if more of us had turned out to be more Christian, it would have made no difference in the statistics of extermination, but maybe it would not have been such a lonely death." Every major religion teaches that we are indeed "our brothers' keepers" and yet much of history describes the way neighbors have turned against or simply away from their neighbors in times of trouble. What can history teach us about the value of our neighbors? About the way people everywhere are linked?

[1] Michel Mazor, *The Vanished City: Everyday Life in the Warsaw Ghetto*, trans. by David Jacobson (Marsilio Publishers, 1993), 19.

[2] Quoted in *The Holocaust as Historical Experience*, ed. by Yehuda Bauer and Nathan Rotenstreich (Holmes & Meier), 251.

[3] Michel Mazor, *The Vanished City*, 113-123.

[4] Lawrence Langer, *Versions of Survival: The Holocaust and the Human Spirit* (State University of New York Press, 1982), 74.

[5] Philip Zimbardo, "The Pathology of Imprisonment" *Societies*, April 1972, 109.

[6] Halina Birenbaum, *Hope Is the Last to Die: A Personal Documentation of Nazi Terror*, trans. by David Welsh (Twayne Publishers, 1971), 8-9.

[8] Alexander Donat, *The Holocaust Kingdom* (Holt, 1965), 12.

[9] Cited in Yisrael Gutman, *The Jews of Warsaw 1939-1943: Ghetto, Underground, Revolt* (Indiana University Press, 1982), 64.

[10] Abraham Lewin, *A Cup of Tears: A Diary of the Warsaw Ghetto*, ed. by Antony Polonsky and trans. by The Institute for Polish Jewish Studies (Basil Blackwell, 1988), 62-64.

[11] Martin Gray, *For Those I Loved* (Little Brown, 1971), 51-54.

[12] Michel Mazor, *The Vanished City*, 42.

[13] Quotes in *A Holocaust Reader*, ed. by Lucy S. Dawidowicz (Behrman House, 1976), 207-208.

[14] *Notes from the Warsaw Ghetto: The Journal of Emmanuel Ringelblum*, ed. and trans. Jacob Sloan (Schocken, 1974), 125-126.

[15] Ibid., 329.

[16] Paul Trepman, *Among Men and Beasts*, trans. Shoshana Perla and Gertrude Hirschler (A.S. Barnes and Bergen-Belsen Memorial Press, 1978), 189.

[17] Janina Bauman, *Winter in the Morning: A Young Girl's Life in the Warsaw Ghetto and Beyond 1939-1945* (Free Press, 1986), 55-56.

[18] Elie Wiesel, *One Generation After*, 55-56

[19] Adina Blady Szwajger, *I Remember Nothing More: The Warsaw Children's Hospital and the Jewish Resistance*, trans. Tasja Darowska and Danusia Stok (Pantheon, 1990), 44-46

[20] Ibid.

[21] David Wdowinski, *And We Are Not Saved* (Philosophical Library, 1985), 53.

[22] Ibid., 54.

[23] Zivia Lubetkin, *In the Days of Destruction and Revolt*, trans. Ishai Tubbin (Ghetto Fighters' House, 1981), 88-89.

[24] Yitzhak Zuckerman, *A Surplus of Memory: Chronicle of the Warsaw Ghetto Uprising*, trans. and ed. by Barbara Harshav (University of California Press, 1993), 150.

[25] Vladka Meed, *On Both Sides of the Wall: Memoirs from the Warsaw Ghetto*, trans. Dr. Steven Meed (Holocaust Library, 1979), 15-16.

[26] Quoted in *The Warsaw Ghetto: A Christian's Testimony* by Wladyslaw Bartoszewski. Trans. by Stephen G. Cappellari (Beacon Press, 1987), 21-22.

[27] Janina Bauman, *Winter in the Morning*, 67-68.

[28] Quoted in *The Warsaw Ghetto: A Christian's Testimony* by Wladyslaw Bartoszewski, 32-33.

[29] Ibid., 31-32

[30] Quoted in Andrzef Bryk, "The Hidden Complex of the Polish Mind," in *My Brother's Keeper? Recent Polish Debates on the Holocaust*, ed. by Antony Polonsky (Routledge, 1990), 167.

[31] Quoted in *Martyrs and Fighters: The Epic of the Warsaw Ghetto* by Philip Friedman (Praeger, 1954), 134-135.

[32] Ibid., 135.

[33] Elie Wiesel, *One Generation After* (Pocket Books, 1965), 52.

[34] Martin Gray, *For Those I Loved*, 108.

[35] Ibid., 123-124.

[36] Alexander Donat, *The Holocaust Kingdom*, 94-95.

[37] Quoted in *The Warsaw Ghetto: A Christian's Testimony*, 33-34.

[38] Quoted in *The Holocaust as Historical Experience*, ed. by Yehuda Bauer and Nathan Rotenstreich (Holmes & Meier), 252.

[39] Michel Mazor, The Vanished City, 136.

[40] Martin Gray, *For Those I Loved,* 126-131.

[41] Gitta Sereny, *Into That Darkness* (Pan Books, 1977), 200-202

[42] Primo Levi, *Survival in Auschwitz*, trans. S. Woolf (Collier, 1993), 123.

[43] Jan Karski, *Story of a Secret State* (Houghton Mifflin, 1944), 322-325.

[44] Ibid., 332-333.

[45] Quoted in Macief Kozlowski, "The Mission That Failed: A Polish Courier Who Tried to Help the Jews," in *My Brother's Keeper? Recent Polish Debates on the Holocaust*, 87-88.

[46] Elie Wiesel, Introduction to *On Both Sides of the Wall* by Vladka Meed, 5-6.

6. The Warsaw Ghetto Uprisings

The question is not why all the Jews did not fight,
but how so many of them did.
Tormented, beaten, starved,
where did they find the strength—spiritual and physical—to resist?

Elie Wiesel

As the Great Aktion drew to a close in the fall of 1942, some Jews in Poland believed that the task ahead was "to keep alive the remnants" so that there would be "witnesses to this great crime." Others, like Emmanuel Ringelblum, cried out for revenge:

> Whomever you talk to, you hear the same cry: The resettlement should never have been permitted. We should have run out into the streets, have set fire to everything in sight, have torn down walls, and escaped to the other side. The Germans would have taken their revenge. It would have cost tens of thousands of lives, but not 300,000. Now we are ashamed of ourselves, disgraced in our own eyes, and in the eyes of the world, where our docility earned us nothing. This must not be repeated now. We must put up a resistance, defend ourselves against the enemy, man and child.[1]

Resistance was not a new idea. Jews had been defying the Nazis since the war began. But they had always rejected the notion of an armed uprising, because even the smallest action was likely to provoke massive German retaliation. But after the Great Aktion, a growing number of Jews came to believe that only by fighting back could they "preserve Jewish honor" and "die with dignity." On April 19, 1943, they opened fire on German soldiers as they entered the ghetto for yet another round of deportations. Twenty-five years later, Yitzhak Zuckerman reflected on what people might learn from that revolt.

> I don't think there's any need to analyze the uprising in military terms. This was a war of less than a thousand people against a mighty army, and no one doubted how it would turn out. This isn't a subject for study in a military school. Not the weapons, not the operations, not the tactics. If there's a school to study the *human spirit*, then it should be a major subject. The really important things were inherent in the force shown by Jewish youth, after years of degradation, to rise up against their destroyers and determine what death they would choose: Treblinka or Uprising. I don't know if there's a standard to measure *that*.[2]

This chapter explores the choices he and other Jews made before, during, and after the uprising. It considers not only the legacies of their choices but also those that bystanders made in Poland and in countries around the world. In May of 1942, even as the Germans were announcing that Warsaw Ghetto was "no more," a Polish Girl Scout named Maria Kann worried about those legacies in a pamphlet she entitled "An Appeal to the Conscience of the World:"

> A people was murdered before the eyes of the world, before our eyes, before the eyes of our youth. We watched inactively. In spite of all our indignation we grew accustomed to the idea that killing is permissible, that you can build crematories for living human beings. The idea that there are different kinds of people takes seed in the minds of children. "Master," "servants," and finally "dogs" that you can kill without punishment. This is the horrendous legacy left by the bloodthirsty Fuerher . . . .

Sometime the world will cease to be a slaughterhouse. Order and peace will return. And many years later a child will ask: Did they kill a human being or a Jew, Mother?[3]

Alfred Kazin, an American Jew, expressed similar feelings when he noted, "Where so great a murder has been allowed, no one is safe." As you read about the uprising in the Warsaw Ghetto, keep in mind the words of Marion Pritchard, who rescued Jews in the Netherlands. She warns that it is a "dangerous oversimplification" to "divide the general population during the war into a few 'good guys' and many 'bad guys.' [There] were indeed some people who behaved criminally by betraying their Jewish neighbors and thereby sentenced them to death. There were some people who dedicated themselves to actively rescuing as many people as possible. Somewhere in between was the majority, whose actions varied from the minimum decency of at least keeping quiet if they knew where Jews were hidden to finding a way to help them when they were asked."[4]

Elie Wiesel reminds us that what we know about the uprising comes mainly from survivors. And he writes, "Of necessity [their stories are] fragmentary, they do not reflect the whole but are part of it. In fact, this can serve as a general rule: every witness expresses only his own truth, in his own name. To convey the truth of the Holocaust in its totality, it is not enough to have listened to the survivors, one must find a way to add the silence left behind by millions of unknowns. That silence can have no interpreter."[5]

Finding Common Ground

Not long after the Nazis occupied Poland, many Jews began to realize that the political, social, and religious differences that separated them before the war were no longer meaningful. As Emmanuel Ringelblum reminded them, "The Germans did not distinguish between the Zionists and the Bundists. They hated the former and the latter as one, and wanted to annihilate them both." Although Jews in Warsaw and other cities agreed on the need to oppose the Germans, they disagreed on the "right" way to do so.

No issue divided the Warsaw Ghetto more deeply than the question of armed resistance. On July 23, 1942, the second day of the Great Deportation, sixteen Jews met secretly in the ghetto. They represented political and religious groups ranging from the Orthodox Agudat Israel to the Communists. Among them were a number of individuals who did not represent a particular group but were known and respected by almost everyone in the community. In his autobiography, Yitzhak Zuckerman recalled the meeting:

> First, they talked about the question of what could be done. Should we defend ourselves? Presenting the problem like that required dealing with it. [Historian Yitzhak] Schipper, for example, said he had information that [the deportation] concerned taking only 80,000 Jews! He spoke of historical responsibility: it's true, he said, these people might be executed, but can we endanger the lives of all the other Jews? Schipper was a good speaker. He said that there are periods of resignation in the lives of the Jews as well as periods of self-defense. In his opinion, this wasn't a period of defense. We were weak and we had no choice but to accept the sentence.
>
> .... I proposed that those present and their comrades, the community leaders (we could assemble a few hundred Jews) demonstrate in the streets of the ghetto with the slogan: "Treblinka Is Death!" Let the Germans come and kill us. I wanted the Jews to see blood in the streets of Warsaw, not in Treblinka.... That was the direction of my thought. I explained it like this: we have no choice. The world doesn't hear, doesn't know; there is no help from the Poles; if we can't save anyone—at least let the Jews know! So they could hide. I also said that we had to attack the Jewish police. If we had worked in this spirit, we might have prolonged the process, made it hard for the Germans to carry it out....
>
> Alexander-Zysze Friendman, one of the leaders of Agudat Israel, was weeping as he said words of love and respect to me: "My son, the Lord gives and the Lord takes." Since we couldn't save anyone, perhaps, that should have been our answer too, since in the situation the Jews were in, what difference did it make who went to his death first? But we thought we could save some. We thought that if people saw blood, if they knew that going meant death, murder, and if they knew it not from afar, not behind fences, but if they saw it with their own eyes, they wouldn't go willingly...[6]

In the end, Zuckerman reported that the group chose to take no action. Instead they "pleaded for patience and held that we should still wait. How long then? Until the situation was clarified." Zivia Lubetkin, a leader of Dror, writes:

> We saw that we were facing an impenetrable wall. Again we asked ourselves: "What can we do?"... We made another attempt. We called a meeting of [the Zionist workers'] parties ... and the Bund Socialist Party.... Yitzhak Zuckerman outlined the sit-

uation, presented the information we had at our disposal and proposed the formation of a Jewish Fighting Organization. . . . When Yitzhak finished speaking, Maurici Orzech, the well-known Bund leader, rose to his feet, looked disdainfully at him and replied: "You're still a very young man, and your evaluation of the situation is too hasty. The Germans simply wouldn't be able to destroy all of us—three-and-a-half million Polish Jews. You're an alarmist. Thousands of Poles . . . are being killed as well. We have to wage our struggle together with the Polish working class for a better world, for the redemption of mankind. We will not participate in an all-Jewish organization."[7]

The leaders of the pioneering Zionist youth groups decided to meet on their own. Six days after the deportations began, they agreed "to organize for defense and struggle for our honor and the honor of the Jewish people." But they disagreed on other issues, including where the fighting ought to take place. Some argued that from a military point of view, the ghetto was no place to wage a war against the Nazis. They wanted to join the partisans, fighters who hid in the forests and harassed the enemy. Zuckerman, Lubetkin, and others agreed that the ghetto was not the ideal place to wage guerrilla warfare. But they feared that if they left, there would be no one to defend the ghetto. They asked, "Could we abandon our parents, our children, the helpless among us, our ill, the place where we were formed? May we leave them helpless and defenseless in order to seek out a war where there are better chances for life and victory and where there is a chance for greater contact with non-Jewish movements?"

In the end, the majority decided to remain in the ghetto and organize the Jewish Fighting Organization. The ZOB, the initials in Polish of the new group, would consist of Jewish soldiers led by Jews fighting in and for the Jews of the ghetto. Mordecai Anielewicz of Hashomer Hatzair was the commander of the ZOB and Yitzhak Zuckerman second in command. But in reality, no one person was in charge. Decisions were made jointly by representatives of the various youth groups.

CONNECTIONS

How did those who attended the various meetings in July answer the question of whether to resist? What attitudes, values, and beliefs do their answers reflect? What did you have to believe in order to favor armed resistance in July of 1942? To what extent did those who attended the meeting make a "choice-less choice?" These are decisions made in the "absence of humanly significant alternatives—that is, alternatives enabling an individual to make a decision, act on it, and accept the consequences, all within a framework that supports personal integrity and self-esteem."

Elie Wiesel has written, "The question is not why all the Jews did not fight, but how so many of them did. Tormented, beaten, starved, where did they find the strength—spiritual and physical—to resist?" How might Zuckerman and Lubetkin answer Wiesel's question? How do you answer it? Some have called resistance a choice Jews made about how to die rather than about how to live. Others argue that resistance is more about the will to live and the power of hope than it is about death. Which view is closest to Zuckerman's or Lubetkin's thinking? Which view is closest to your own?

Building a Movement

In time, other Zionist parties, the Bund, and the Communists joined the Jewish Fighting Organization, or the ZOB. Each group formed and trained its own "battle units." These units were later united and placed under the command of the ZOB (the initials in Polish of the Jewish Fighting Organization). The Zionist Revisionists did not join the new group but did cooperate with resistance efforts. Its members formed their own group, the ZZW, (the initials in Polish of the Jewish Military Union).

The first step in armed resistance is to obtain weapons. While some members of the ZOB gathered arms, others decided to work with the resources it had on hand. Zivia Lubetkin described the night of the ZOB's first operation on August 20, 1942:

Zivia Lubetkin and Yitzhak Zuckerman were among the leaders of the ZOB.

> We separated into groups. One group was to burn deserted buildings and warehouses filled with loot [the Germans had stolen from the Jews], another was to post announcements on billboards and buildings, and one of us was going to kill [Jozef Szerynski, the head of the Jewish police]. Our hearts pounded as we went out into the street, carefully checking that there were no German, Polish or Jewish policemen in the vicinity. We slowly made our way along the sides of the buildings until we reached our destination. . . . We collected mattresses and furniture, anything flammable, piled them together and set them on fire. Success! . . . We rejoiced as we saw the reflection of the revenge that was burning inside us, the symbol of the Jewish armed resistance that we had yearned for, for so long.
>
> . . . . We completed our assignments and returned to Dzielna. We all arrived safely, there were no casualties. Only one person was missing, Israel Kanal. We began to worry. He might have been caught. We sat there tense and apprehensive and then we heard the secret whistle. Israel was now on the way. For a moment we stood there in shock. He looked and acted as if nothing had happened. He might have had second thoughts. We knew that he dreaded the idea of having to kill a man! This was to be the first time he had ever fired a gun. We stood there in suspense. Then he turned to us and said in a quiet voice, "It's all right." We felt relieved.
>
> He later told us that he had shot Szerynski once. When he went to fire a second time, the gun jammed. The shot was heard by all the Jewish policemen in the area who came running to capture him. He pointed the faulty weapon and threatened to kill anyone who approached. The policemen were frightened and he managed to escape. . . .

Our joy was great that evening at Dzielna, but it reached its climax when an air-raid alarm pierced the air, followed by the thunderous echo of bombs. The Soviets were bombarding the city of Warsaw for the first time! It was a sign: the flame that we had struck this evening against the enemy had flown up and reached our allies. . . .

Grey and overcast days followed that evening of celebration. Jewish Warsaw had been frightened by our posters and fires. People asserted that they were nothing but a German provocation designed to bring further tragedy to the remaining Jews in Warsaw. Our comrades returned from an operation in tears. They had been caught pasting wall-posters by a group of Jews and beaten. . . . The Jews had been pleased by the [shooting of Szerynski], but they had falsely credited it to the PPR [the Polish Socialist Party]. They didn't believe Jews capable of such an operation. . . . [8]

Despite such disappointments, the ZOB managed to acquire a few weapons: five pistols and eight hand grenades. Still, Zuckerman recalled, "bad luck seemed to jinx our activities." Two small groups went into the forests outside the city to organize resistance. Both groups perished. Then on September 3, 1942, the Gestapo arrested a key member of the ZOB and shot another in the street. That very evening, the Nazis found the group's small arsenal of guns and ammunition. On September 13, the last night of the Aktion, the ZOB's leaders gathered to mourn their losses. Zuckerman described the evening:

In gloomy silence, we ate the meager dinner. The young people in the group went into another room. The older ones were left. We were alive. We had to know what to do tomorrow. I don't remember who spoke first, Arye [Wilner] or Zivia [Lubetkin]. The words were bitter, heavy, determined. There would be no Jewish resistance. . . . When there were hundreds of thousands in Warsaw, we couldn't organize a Jewish fighting force—will we succeed now, when only a few tens of thousands are left? We didn't win the trust of the masses. . . . The people are destroyed, honor is trampled. . . .Come on let's go out to the streets tomorrow, burn down the ghetto and attack the Germans. We'll be liquidated. . . . But honor will be saved. In days to come, they will remember: youth rose up for that helpless people and saved as much honor as they could.

Other comrades spoke. Everyone in his own way. The meaning was the same. Despair was the dominant feeling. Feelings demanded action.

In an atmosphere of total despair, it was hard to say anything else. Even though one of the comrades [Zuckerman] grew bold and said, more or less: . . . The crisis is great and the shame is great. But the act proposed is an act of despair. It will die with no echo. . . . We have to start all over. . . . Arye must go back to the "Aryan side." We have to look for new contacts. We shall raise money in the ghetto and buy weapons from private dealers. We have to fight the Jewish scoundrels to the bitter end. If not for Jewish treason, the Germans wouldn't have ruled so fast and so easily in the ghetto. . . .

The discussion was sharp. But gradually, sober voices of calm were heard. The atmosphere cooled off. . . . This was the most fateful night for the Jewish Fighting Organization. We decided to take heart and start rebuilding the Jewish fighting force with all means and forces at our disposal, with superhuman means. [9]

Yitzhak Zuckerman and Zivia Lubetkin were Zionists committed to socialist principles. What values and beliefs seem to have shaped the choices they made and the positions they support in this reading? How do they define their "universe of obligation"— the individuals and groups toward whom they have responsibilities, to whom they believe society's rules must apply, and whose injuries call for amends?

Zuckerman describes himself, Lubetkin and other leaders of the ZOB as the "older ones." They were in their twenties. The "younger ones" were in their teens. How do you think the youth of its members affected the choices the group made and the risks individuals were willing to take?

Alexander Donat writes of "a new type" in the ghetto: "Jewish young people who held their heads high, prepared for anything that might happen. Rightly or wrongly, sensibly or not, faithful to Jewish tradition or against it, this portion of the Ghetto youth had come to a decision: they had taken enough; they would take no more."[10] What set these young people apart? Were they a "new type"? Zivia Lubetkin reflected on that question:

> It was not because we were wiser or more intelligent, but because we were part of a movement, which even in better days had demanded our complete devotion, a pioneer-youth movement which was based on each individual working for the common ideals through his own actions, and not merely by words. . . If during normal times this attitude was expressed by doing manual labor, by a personal revolution in the way of life of Jewish youth, now in these troubled times, it was expressed by our struggle to live, to preserve the honor of our people and our human dignity, our Jewish pride. Today self-realization meant to stand up with a gun in one's hand.[11]

Not everyone in the ZOB was a Zionist, but many were idealists. What is an idealist? What qualities do idealists share? What distinguishes them from realists? From optimists?

The first act of the ZOB was "to fight the Jewish scoundrels." Historian Yisrael Gutman describes that decision as a "necessity." Armed resistance would be impossible as long as there were people in the ghetto prepared to collaborate with the Germans. In response to those who claim the ghetto police had no choice, Zuckerman writes:

> Of course they had no choice—from the moment they decided to be policemen. There were different kinds of policemen, more brutal ones and less brutal ones. There were those who took bribes and those who thought they had to excel. . . . They served the German occupier, willy-nilly, and thought they could save their lives and their families like that.[12]

For Elie Wiesel, those who cooperated with the Nazis "arouse pity more than contempt. The weak, the cowardly, all those who sold their soul to live another day, another anxious night, I prefer to include them in the category of victims. More than the others, they need forgiveness. More and in other ways than their companions, they deserve compassion and charity."[13] Why is it difficult to judge those who cooperated? What does your answer suggest about the complexity of human behavior?

Zuckerman asked: "When a person decides to commit suicide, does he decide that in a moment of heroism or of weakness?" He thought perhaps it was "out of both heroism and weakness." But he argues that such an action would have "no resonance, no influence." How would you answer the question he raises? How would you answer the question he implies but does not ask directly: How does a group take action in ways that make a difference?

In Search of Hiding Places

Although the leaders of the ZOB and ZZW urged young people to "climb the walls, to defend themselves," they did not expect everyone to fight. Yitzhak Zuckerman explains: "We didn't tell [Jews]: 'To the barricades!' But rather, we said: 'Hide, hide your children, don't believe the temptations of the Germans! Go to the Aryan side! Make shelters!'"

Hiding anywhere in occupied Europe was extraordinarily difficult and Warsaw was no exception. Those who wanted to "go to the 'Aryan side'" needed help. Even if they had "Aryan looks" and spoke Polish without a trace of a "Jewish accent," they needed identification, a job, a place to live. And if they looked or sounded "too Jewish," they had to find someone willing to hide them until the war was over and the danger had passed.

As in other parts of Nazi-occupied Europe, most Christians in Poland did not want to endanger their own lives or the lives of loved ones by "getting involved." Of those who were willing to take risks, some made it their business to turn in Jews. Others were willing to shelter Jews for a price. A very few—about one to two percent of the population— hid friends, co-workers, even strangers out of compassion, religious conviction, or patriotism. How could someone trapped in the ghetto find those individuals? Some did so painfully through trial-and-error. Others relied on friends, the ZOB, or the ZZW to help them find a safe place.

As the need for hiding places increased dramatically in the summer and fall of 1942, during and immediately after the "Great Deportations," a few Poles joined with representatives from the Jewish underground to start a new organization, later known as the Council for Aid to Jews or Zegota. It set out to save as many Jews as possible, particularly Jewish children. The group placed over 2,500 youngsters in homes, convents, and orphanages in the Warsaw area alone. A former member of the Polish underground estimated that another 2,500 children were sheltered by individuals and independent groups.

Some Poles were willing to assist Jews by providing housing, food, clothing, and false documents. Others helped indirectly by keeping silent when they saw a stranger's face in an attic window or heard the cry of a child in the apartment of a childless couple. In some places and at some times, hiding Jews became so dangerous that individuals could not stay in any one place for more than a week. Wladyslaw Bartowszewski described a few of the challenges that he and other rescuers faced in their work:

> At the very least a person living in hiding had to possess a birth certificate, a work permit, and a so-called identity card, a necessary legal document in occupied Poland. The birth certificates could easily be obtained through priests, who, in filling out the documents, used the names of deceased persons whose deaths had not been entered in the parish registers. The identity cards and work permits were obtained as followed: an assumed "Aryan" name was inserted into a blank form that had been stolen by a Polish civil servant for a Jew hiding outside of the ghetto. In case of a random identity check on the street—and bear in mind that these checks were everyday occurrences in Poland at the time—these documents were usually sufficient, especially in the case of women.[14]

It was even more difficult to find hiding places for Jews. Sheltering a Jew was punishable by death in Nazi-occupied Poland. And the Nazis carried out frequent house-to-house searches in cities like Warsaw. When they found a hidden Jew, the consequences were tragic for everyone involved.

Poles who hid Jews faced agonizing choices. So did the Jews they hid. Few Poles were willing or able to hide an entire family. So many Jewish parents had to entrust their children to strangers. Some were unwilling to do so. One such parent was Manya Ziegelboim. She had asked Vladka Meed, a courier for the ZOB, to find a place for her child on the "Aryan side." But at the last minute, Ziegelboim refused to let her little boy go: "Together we have endured all this misery and misfortune. Without me, he would perish." Meed writes:

What could I say to Manya? What assurances could I offer? I wanted to persuade her that Artek would be safer beyond the wall than with her in the ghetto. But I could not speak. [Abrasha Blum, a leader of the Bund], more composed than I, tried to persuade her that the ghetto was becoming more dangerous each day, that it was on the verge of a bloody battle. He urged her to think the matter over and send her son over the wall, where he would have a good chance of surviving.

Manya heard him out in silence, the battle between emotion and reason mirrored in her pale, drawn face. I tried my best to describe the place we had found for her son, with an honest, trustworthy Polish railroad employee who had been recommended to us by a co-worker.

"No, I cannot do it." The decision seemed wrenched from her by a force she could no longer fight. "Whatever my fate, it shall also be the fate of my son. We've been through so much together. Perhaps we'll succeed in surviving after all. If not, at least we'll perish together."

And so, Manya Ziegelboim did not part from her son. Both of them were to die in the ghetto uprising.

The truth was that we could never be sure of what would happen to the children we smuggled over to the "Aryan side." There was always the danger that they would say or do something to give them away, or that the Poles who had agreed to take them in would go back on their promise at the last moment.[15]

Other parents made different choices. Many would have given anything to secure a hiding place for their children on the "Aryan side." Those who could not get out or chose to stay with their families now searched for "bunkers" or hiding places within the ghetto. If they could not find one, they built one. Alexander Donat explains:

Shelters were dug under courtyards where garbage cans were kept, under courtyard toilets, and other places normally so repulsive as to offer security. Secret rooms were built in apartments with entrances through large armoires—there were no built-in closets in Poland—or by swinging a big tile stove aside on hidden hinges. Entrance might be through coal bins. Many shelters were simply walled-up alcoves consisting of space hollowed out between two apartment walls. . . .

Another category of shelters was the nest-type, built in attics and giving builders a free field for fantasy. Our bunker was of this kind and came into being when the carpenter who lived above us reminded me one night in November [of 1942] that everyone was building a hide-out and suggested we do likewise. I agreed and we set to work. . . .We planned it for fifteen persons and it seemed to us foolproof. All users-to-be shared equally in financing the project.

Besides building shelters, people were also frantically making passageways between rooms, apartments, staircases, cellars, attic, linking houses until eventually we could move around an entire residential block without once going into the street. By that means the Ghetto became an enormous honeycomb connected by invisible arteries.[16]

One of the many hiding places in the Warsaw Ghetto.

CONNECTIONS

In the introduction to this chapter, Marion Pritchard of the Netherlands is quoted as saying it is a "dangerous oversimplification" to divide the general population during the war into a few "good guys" and many "bad guys." Why do you think she sees "oversimplification" as dangerous? Would Wladyslaw Bartowszewski agree?

Alexander Donat and his wife Lena faced a similar dilemma to one that Manya Ziegelboim confronted, but they made a different choice. They sent their young son to the "Aryan side" to live among strangers. Historian Deborah Dwork views both decisions as "an overwhelmingly painful form of courage and resistance. It cannot be stressed too fervently that it was the parents who took the first step and the most terrifying step in the protection of their children, as it was they who had to determine whether it was best to send them into hiding, to try to smuggle them out of the country, or to keep them at their side."[17] How does Dwork define courage and resistance? How does she help us understand the choices both Ziegelboim and Donat made?

As a courier for the ZOB on the "Aryan side" of Warsaw, Vladka Meed had to conceal her true identity. So she understood the problems Jewish adults and children faced on the "Aryan side" where even a small mistake could have tragic consequences. She later wrote:

> One had to be wary of each movement, each word, to avoid giving oneself away. The Poles had no difficulty in recognizing Jews. Lately, having become aware that some Jews were escaping from the ghetto, young Poles had lost no time in capitalizing on this knowledge through *szmalcowe*—blackmail. The moment they came upon a Jew, they demanded money and, if they failed to find enough, stripped the victim of his overcoat, shoes, or anything else of value he happened to have on his person. These *szmalcownicy* were to be found everywhere. They haunted the residential quarters, prowled the streets and factories, looking for victims.[18]

How do her comments explain why she could not promise Manya Ziegelboim that her child would be safe?

The ZOB and other resistance groups in the ghetto used young Jews with an "Aryan appearance" to distribute information to other ghettos, make contact with the Polish underground, and buy arms. How did these young people take advantage of German stereotypes of "the Jew"? What do Meed's comments suggest about the other qualities those couriers needed to survive on the "Aryan side"?

To what extent were the bunkers Alexander Donat describes an act of resistance? To what extent were they a conscious, even a creative, choice at a time when meaningful choices were disappearing?

Gay Block and Malka Drucker interviewed and photographed over 100 individuals from ten countries, including Poland, for their book, *Rescuers: Portraits of Moral Courage in the Holocaust*, (Holmes and Meier, 1992). Malka Drucker writes that these women and men "serve to give a different face to the word 'hero' than the one to which we are accustomed. They challenge our ideas about what we think heroes look like: they aren't all square-jawed, broad-shouldered handsome men with unwavering eyes, nor do these faces necessarily project conventional images of serenity and wisdom. These people look like us, like ordinary people." How do you define the word *hero*? What characteristics do heroes share?

A Turning Point

As 1942 ended and a new year began, more and more Jews believed it was only a question of time until the Germans mounted a new Aktion. Members of the ZOB and the ZZW gathered arms and planned their strategies. Almost everyone else looked for hiding places. Yet when the Aktion began, it caught most people in the ghetto by surprise.

Before daybreak on the morning of January 18, 1943, German soldiers and SS troops quietly surrounded the ghetto as they prepared for yet another Aktion. This time, however, they encountered armed resistance. One group led by Mordecai Anielewicz, the commander of the ZOB, opened fire on the Germans as they herded Jews to the Umschlagplatz. Although all of the Jewish fighters except Anielewicz were killed in the skirmish, the battle itself electrified the ghetto. As Tuvia Borzykowski recalled, "For the first time since the occupation, we saw Germans clinging to walls, crawling on the ground, running for cover, hesitating before making a step in the fear of being hit by a Jewish bullet."

There were other acts of resistance as well. When the Germans entered one apartment building, a group under the leadership of Yitzhak Zuckerman greeted the soldiers with bullets and homemade bombs. It was the first of four battles that raged within apartment complexes. There was also at least one battle in a German-owned factory. And some young Jews defied the Nazis even after they were captured. When sixty Bundists was ordered onto cattle cars, they refused to go. An SS commander shot and killed all of the resisters on the spot. Still Marek Edelman, a Bundist leader and a member of the ZOB command, believed that the group's action "served as an inspiration that always, under all circumstances, one should oppose the Germans."[19]

Zivia Lubetkin, who was also part of the ZOB command, recalled her own excitement and that of other young ghetto fighters at the end of the first day of the Aktion.

> No more did the Germans shout as they had before. They went by stealthily, one by one, close to the walls of the houses. Before going into a house they sent the Jewish police in as cover, and even then entered only with the greatest care. Their searches were more hurried and less painstaking—they were trembling with fear of our deadly bullets, and they seemed to sense that there were ambushes everywhere.
>
> Our spirits rose. No more did we feel the worry, the anguish of the days that had gone before. We felt redeemed—we felt our lives were again useful. . . .Tens of thousands of Jews were in hiding that night, trembling with fear. But they lived because a few of us had dared to oppose the invaders. [20]

On the first day of the *Aktion*, Shmuel Winter, a member of Emmanuel Ringelblum's Oneg Shabbat group, hid in a bunker. That night, he wrote in his diary:

> Rumors have reached me that Jews—members of Hashomer Hatzair and [other] pioneering movements—put up a fight on Niska and Zamenhofa streets. They are idealists. What cause are these idealists serving? What evil will they bring down upon us? I believe that from the viewpoint of history, and for the sake of posterity, the work of the historical committee, "Oneg Shabbat," is more important than their Jewish war. Today 3,000 Jews were removed from the Warsaw ghetto.[21]

The next day Winter wrote, "Combat groups went out to war again, at Mila 34. Today they took a thousand plus a few hundred more Jews. Blessed be those youngsters."[22] On the third day of the Aktion, he noted, "A few hundred Jews were taken today. The Jews are hiding [and] the Germans are afraid to go into cellars and hideouts."[23] On the fourth and final day, Winter wrote, "The Germans retreated and left the ghetto. I believe that the war of the youngsters forced them to do that."[24] In assessing the ZOB's role in the Nazis' retreat from the ghetto, Edelman notes that even though about 80 percent of its fighters were killed, their resistance had an impact not only on people within the ghetto but also on those outside the walls of the ghetto:

> Public opinion, Jewish as well as Polish, reacted immediately to the ghetto battles. For now, for the first time, German plans were frustrated. . . . For the first time, the Jews in the street realized that it was possible to do something against the Germans' will and power. The number of Germans killed by ZOB bullets was not the only important thing. What was more important was the appearance of a psychological turning point. The mere fact that because of the unexpected resistance, weak as it was, the Germans were forced to interrupt their "deportation" schedule was of great value.[25]

CONNECTIONS

What distinguishes a "turning point" from other events? Why do you think Marek Edelman called the January uprising "a psychological turning point"? What changed as a result of the uprising? How important was that change?

During the January uprising, the ZOB and ZZW learned a number of important lessons. According to Yitzhak Zuckerman, one lesson was that "we can fight; we know how to fight." What else do you think the groups learned from their first battles with the Germans? What do you think other Jews in the ghetto learned from those battles?

How do you account for the change in Shmuel Winter's views? What does your answer suggest about the way the ZOB won the support of many people in the Ghetto?

Yechiel Gorni, a Jew in the Warsaw ghetto during the January *Aktion,* wrote in his diary:

> Yesterday, on January 22, 1943, I overheard the following . . . : "If at the beginning of the deportation in July, 1942, the Jews had armed, had attempted to resist, and had killed a number of Germans and forced the Jewish [police] to refrain from taking an active role [in the operation] thousands would undoubtedly have been cut down by German bullets, and other Jews would have said: What happened is the fault of their foolish heroism. . . . Today, when 6,000 Jewish Deportees [cost the lives of] 1,000 Jews and twelve Germans, the public has finally understood the heroism of the 'foolish youngsters.'"[26]

How do you explain the change in attitude Gorni describes? What did Jews know in January of 1943 that they did not know or were not prepared to acknowledge six months earlier?

In Search of Weapons

Although the January uprising strengthened the morale and the resolve of the Jews in the Warsaw Ghetto, it also revealed how weak the ZOB and ZZW truly were. Both desperately needed more weapons. And they needed them as quickly as possible. Time was running out. It was only a matter of days before the Germans returned and many feared that the next Aktion would be the last.

Immediately after the uprising in January of 1943, the ZOB received a small shipment of arms from the Armja Krajowa (AK), the "official" Polish underground army. When Polish leaders refused to send more, the ZOB decided to buy weapons "on the street." Zivia Lubetkin explained how they raised the money to do so:

> It cost millions of zlotys to arm five hundred fighters. In the beginning, we set up a sub-committee to solicit contributions. . . . When this proved insufficient, we started to impose taxes. We began with the public organizations, the Judenrat treasury and the ghetto bank, which was guarded by Polish policemen. One fine day, we went in with pistols and took all the money from the bank. We emptied the Judenrat treasury in a similar manner. Later on, when these funds proved to be insufficient, we levied taxes on rich Jews, particularly those who maintained ties with the Germans. It went very easily at first. We would send a notice from the Jewish Fighting Organization: "You are required to pay, etc.," and we would receive the money straight away. They obviously thought it was the fearsome gentiles who were demanding the money. When they learned who was really responsible. . . they refused to pay. Although we knew only too well that all the Jews would eventually be murdered and their money stolen, we could not kill Jews for not fulfilling their obligations.
>
> Preserving the high moral level of our fighters was always a primary considera- tion for us. . . . Even when we had millions of zlotys, the food supplies for the Jewish Fighting Organization were meager. We did not go hungry, but we made do with a modest portion of dry bread. . . . We had no desire to enjoy the money collected from our brothers, nor did we want to kill Jews for refusing to contribute even if the funds were to be used in the fight against the Germans. The Jews knew how to exploit this weakness. . . . We would negotiate for hours and in the end they would hide their money to avoid handing it over to the Jewish Fighting Organization. The armed guards we sent to search houses had little effect and we finally had to set up our own jails where we detained those who refused to help us financially. We imposed our taxes only on the rich whose source of income was definitely known to be corrupt.[27]

Money was not the only problem the ZOB faced in securing weapons. Vladka Meed writes that whenever she and other couriers met, their "conversations invariably centered on the crucial question: How? How, as strangers among the Poles, in the guise of ordinary Polish citizens, were we to conduct traffic in such forbidden, scarce com- modities as weapons and explosives?"

In time, the couriers learned where to go and whom to contact. They bought stolen arms from guards at army dumps, German soldiers short of cash, and Poles who worked in gun factories. They explored every possibility and tracked down every lead. Not long after the January uprising, Michal Klepfisz, a young Bundist, came up with an idea for building bombs rather than trying to buy them. Meed liked the idea but had a few concerns:

> [Where] would we find the chemicals and where would we work with them? After a few days, we had collected only a small quantity of the necessary ingredients. We did our mixing secretly whenever our Gentile landlords happened to be out.
>
> Once our bottles were ready and the fuses in place, a new problem arose—where could we test our new weapon? After all, there was bound to be a big explosion, and this could not easily be hidden from our neighbors. Michal managed to bribe his new landlord into permitting him to perform his experiment.
>
> Late that night, Michal tested his weapon in the deserted lime kiln of the factory where [his landlord] lived. With a powerful explosion the bottle shattered and the liquid inside burst into a blinding flame. We had scored a success! Michal was delirious with joy. Later on, he admitted that he had performed this same experiment in secret once before, but that it had failed miserably. But now, at last, we had hope of producing homemade bombs.[28]

An expert on explosives in the Polish underground taught Klepfisz how to perfect his bombs. He also showed him how to make a "Molotov cocktail" [a bomb in a bottle]. Before long, Klepfisz was back in the ghetto organizing a "bomb factory." Meed writes:

> Our job on the "Aryan side" was to acquire the necessary chemicals and smuggle them into the ghetto for processing. It was difficult to get the gasoline, acid, and potash we needed. In order not to attract attention, we purchased the "merchandise" from suppliers in various parts of the city, and occasionally had to run the risk of transporting the ingredients across Warsaw by horse-cart. If we were discovered, it would mean death. Until they could be smuggled into the ghetto, the bags and boxes of chemicals were hidden under our own beds.[29]

Michal Klepfisz's homemade bombs did not eliminate the need for guns and other weapons, even other explosives. The search continued. The man who led that search was Arye Wilner, the ZOB's main contact to the AK.

Henryk Wolinski, the official in charge of Jewish affairs for the AK, liked and respected Wilner, but he was appalled at the risks his friend took. He feared Wilner's arrest might jeopardize both Jewish and Polish resistance efforts. Wilner told Wolinski that he had to buy from strangers despite the risks. How else was he to supply the ghetto with arms? The ZOB also urged Wilner to be careful. "But of course," Zuckerman notes, "he wouldn't allow himself to give up even one source that came his way."

On March 6, 1943, Arye Wilner took one risk too many. He was arrested on the "Aryan side" after purchasing weapons from a woman who betrayed him. His arrest posed a serious problem for both the ZOB and the Polish underground. The AK cut off all contact with the ZOB. Many years after the war, Wolinski explained why in an interview, "We had an unwritten law that if someone got arrested, he had to keep silent for at least three days. After that, if he was broken, nobody would blame him for that." But to the surprise of many, Wilner never cracked. Wolinski recalled, "They tortured . . . Wilner for a month, and he gave not a thing away—no contacts, no addresses, although he knew plenty of them, both on the Jewish side and on the 'Aryan side' as well."

Wolinski and others in both the Polish and Jewish resistance movements managed to get Wilner released through a combination of bribes and luck. They had to secretly carry him out of a labor camp because he was unable to walk. The Gestapo had tortured him by placing white-hot iron bars on the soles of his feet. Although a number of Poles offered to hide him until the war was over, he insisted on returning to the ghetto. A few days after his release, the Poles resumed contacts with the ZOB. Yitzhak Zuckerman took Wilner's place. He left the ghetto on April 13, 1943—just a week before the final *Aktion*.

CONNECTIONS

The Polish underground was no more united than the Jewish underground. Most Polish resisters belonged to the *Armja Krakowia* (AK), the Polish Home Army which had ties to the Polish government-in-exile. Others joined the smaller *Armja Ludowa* (AL), the People's Army with ties to Russia's Communist party. Although both groups had members of almost every political persuasion, each viewed the other with suspicion. The ZOB, which relied on both groups for help, often found itself in the middle. Before the January uprising, the AK refused to give the Jews more than a handful of weapons because its leaders believed that the guns would be wasted; Jews wouldn't fight and if they did fight, they couldn't win. After the uprising, the AK gave the ZOB a small cache of weapons as a sign of "good will." Its leaders refused to give more because the Jews were accepting help from "Moscow." What do these incidents suggest about the way divisions in the Polish underground hampered Jewish efforts to buy weapons and secure other help? Some Jews in Warsaw thought the issue had little to do with the struggle between the AK and AL and everything to do with antisemitism. What experiences might support that view? What experiences might call it into question?

After the uprising in January, 1943, Bernard Goldstein, a Bundist leader (Chapter 4), wrote, "All eyes in the ghetto looked to the underground organizations, to the coordinating committee, and to the Jewish fighting organization. . . . The 'all-powerful' Judenrat was now ignored. . . . When the Germans asked [the new head of the Judenrat] to help carry out the evacuation of the factories, he answered that he had no influence in the ghetto, that power resided in other hands."[30] How do you account for the change Goldstein describes? What was the source of the ZOB's power? How did it use that power? What were its goals?

In his autobiography, Zuckerman acknowledges that he and others made mistakes. He writes, "Those were extraordinary times. If every commander takes stock, he will find, in hindsight, that this or that person would have survived if he hadn't done what he did." What does he mean by the term "extraordinary times"? What things are demanded in "extraordinary times" that are "unthinkable" in "ordinary times"?

The Limits of Persuasion

Soon after the January uprising, Heinrich Himmler, the head of the German SS, ordered the "liquidation" of the Warsaw ghetto. This time, however, the Nazis did not immediately send in troops. They relied instead on German factory owners to carry out the order.

On February 16, 1943, Walther C. Toebbens, the largest German industrialist in the ghetto, announced that he and other German manufacturers were moving their operations to two labor camps. Alexander Donat who now worked in a print shop owned by Toebbens, described one of the meetings the industrialist held with workers:

> By order of Himmler, Toebbens told "his Jews"—in a kindly, paternal tone—Warsaw was to be made Judenrein, literally cleansed of the Jews. We were not, however, for a moment to suppose this meant Treblinka or Maidanek. Instead, all machinery and personnel were to be shifted to Poniatow and Trawniki, labor camps in the Lublin district. There, Jewish workers, their wives, and children could live out the war safely in the wholesome country air. All German ghetto shop owners personally addressed their Jewish workers, swearing that no harm would come to a single Jew.[31]

But many Jews were no longer willing to trust the Germans. Donat recalls:

> When the Germans actually began to dismantle the machinery in some shops, there was sabotage. Shops and warehouses were destroyed or badly damaged. Underground activists beat up a number of the foremen, and one manager who collaborated with the Nazis was shot dead in the street in broad daylight. On the walls of buildings the inscription "Poniatow and Trawniki equals Treblinka!" was scrawled and the ZOB issued a proclamation warning that the new program was simply a continuation of the planned extermination of the Jews. "Hide your wives and children and take up arms!" the underground advised, "Only resistance can save the remnants of the ghetto's people!"[32]

On March 20, Donat was told to set in type Toebbens' appeal "To the Jewish Munitions Workers of the Jewish Quarter!" Copies of the appeal were signed by Toebbens and then posted throughout the ghetto alongside the proclamations of the ZOB. The appeal stated in part:

> Jewish armament workers! Do not believe those who are trying to mislead you. They want to incite you so that they can force the consequences that will inevitably ensue.
>
> The "shelters" offer no security whatsoever, and life in them is intolerable. The same is true on the "Aryan" side. . . . I ask you: Why are wealthy Jews coming to me, from the "Aryan" side of their own accord, and asking to be among those shipped out [to Trawniki]? They have enough money to keep them going on the "Aryan" side, but they couldn't bear it.
>
> With a clear conscience, I can only advise you again: Go to Trawniki, go to Poniatow, for you have a chance to live there; you can sit out the war there! The Kommando of the Fighting Organization does you no good, and its promises are meaningless. . . .
>
> Place your faith solely on the heads of the German firms who, together with you, want to transfer the production to Poniatow and Trawniki.[33]
>
> Take your wives and children with you, for they will also be looked after.

Toebbens offered to meet with the leaders of the ZOB, but they refused. Instead, they urged Jews to prepare for the "liquidation" of the ghetto. This time they were believed. Some people found places on the "Aryan side." Those who could not escape, Donat writes, "dreamed only of getting weapons. It became an obsession: people would part with everything they owned to get hold of a pistol or a single hand grenade." And everywhere, people were saying, "'Let's give them some of their own back' 'One German, at least, for every Jew.' 'This time we won't give up so easily.'"[34]

CONNECTIONS

The object of propaganda is to persuade. Adolf Hitler believed that propaganda has little to do with truth. To be effective, "it must be limited to a very few points and must harp on these in slogans until the last last member of the public understands what you want him to understand by your slogan." Look carefully at examples of propaganda in this reading. Use those examples to help you define the term. How do dictionaires define the word? What is the difference between persuasion in advertising and propaganda?

What was the message of the ZOB's proclamation? At whom was it directed? What emotions did it evoke? What actions did it encourage? What did it assume its audience knew? What did it assume people feared? Reread Toebbens' letter and answer those same questions. What images does it use to arouse emotions? To encourage action?

Toebbens and other German industrialists came to Poland to make money. Their businesses earned extraordinary profits, because they relied on slave labor. But for a few businessmen, that wealth came at too high a price. In Krakow, when the Nazis tried to close Oskar Schindler's plant and ship his workers to Auschwitz, he refused to let them go. He used his money and influence to transport over 1100 workers to a new factory in Czechoslovakia. How do you account for the stand Schindler took?

In January of 1943, at a time when many Jews were looking for a "place" on the "Aryan side," Donat writes of a young woman who returned to the ghetto.

> "I'd rather die with you here," she repeated, over and over, in the face of her parents' pleas and despair. She was only fifteen years old and Aryan-looking. By March she informed her parents that she had joined the ZOB. Her father did everything he could to dissuade her, in vain. "I should think you'd be proud of me, give me your blessing," she told him, "not mourn the loss of a daughter. We're all going to die anyway. I should think you'd be happy I've earned such an honor." At this, her father, Josef, burst into tears, took Ada into his arms and crying all the while, recited the Hebrew blessing over her. . . .[35]

Ada was not alone. A number of other young people refused to leave the ghetto or returned because they believed that "to save one's life under the circumstances was worse than selfishness: it was treachery." All they asked for was weapons.

On the Eve of Passover

Just after midnight, on April 19, 1943, the Polish police surrounded the ghetto. For weeks, Jews in Warsaw had been preparing for their arrival.. Yet, Zivia Lubetkin recalled, "even though we were prepared . . . . a tremor of joy mixed with a shudder of fear passed through all of us. But we suppressed our emotions and reached for our guns." The final "liquidation" of the ghetto was about to begin on the eve of Passover.

Over 2,000 German soldiers, including SS troops, entered the ghetto early on the morning of April 19. According to historian Martin Gilbert, they came with 13 heavy machine guns, 69 hand-held machine guns, 135 submachine guns, several howitzers and other artillery pieces, and 1,358 rifles. The Jews had about 500 pistols and a few submachine guns. Their main weapons were fire bombs and "Molotov cocktails."

Young ZOB runners raced from building to building, alerting people to the danger. In the still, dark hours of the morning, many quickly dressed and then made their way to their hideouts. In Alexander Donat's bunker "everyone was silent, caught up in his own bleak thoughts, drawing up the balance sheet of his life. We had to prepare to meet our deaths."

At 8 am, Donat heard the first shots ring out. Zivia Lubetkin, who led a band of thirty fighters, described her first glimpse of the enemy.

> We could see from afar large forces of the German army advancing towards the ghetto as if it were a real battle-front. We had planted mines connected to electric currents under the main streets of the ghetto, where the Germans would have to pass. . . . . We were the first to welcome the German murderers into the ghetto. Hundreds of polished and light-hearted German soldiers marched in close order singing a military march. They were on their way to the "last battle" with the Jews. They were taken by surprise as a burst of hand grenades and bombs showered down from above, and they scattered in confusion.[36]

That day, in his daily report to his superiors in Germany, SS General Jurgen Stroop noted that he had lost six SS men and six Ukrainian auxiliaries.

At sunset, Passover began. Alexander Donat writes, "Although we did not observe the holiday in full ritual, its spirit was very much with us. No one could remain unaware that Passover commemorated the freeing of the Jews from slavery in Egypt and many of the verses of the *Haggadah* had immediate and special meaning for us in the Ghetto."[37] One fighter, Tuvia Borzykowski, forgot about the holiday as he set out that evening to find batteries. As he made his way through the passageways that connected one building to the next, he found himself in the apartment of Rabbi Eliezer Yitzhak Mayzel. He later wrote:

> The apartment was in a state of chaos. Bed linens were spread all around, chairs turned upside down, various household items were strewn on the floor, and all the window panes were smashed into little bits. During the daytime, while the members of the family had sought shelter in the bunker, the house had become a mess; only the table in the middle of the room stood: festive, as if a thing apart from the other furniture.
>
> The redness of the wine in the glasses which were on the table was a reminder

of the blood of the Jews who perished on the eve of the holiday. The *Haggadah* was recited while in the background incessant bursts of bombing and shooting, one after the other, pounded through the night. The scarlet reflection from the burning houses nearby illuminated the faces of those around the table in the darkened room. . . .

The mood of the room went up and down, depending on the shooting and fires; when they eased off, it went down, when they increased, it improved. In a moment of surging desire the rabbi expressed his hope for a miracle, as in ancient days in Egypt. But a wave of despair drowned his last hope, and we felt that our inexorable fate was to perish one by one to the last.

The more the rabbi read from the *Haggadah,* the more depressed he became. . . . He was sitting at the table, yet the spirit of the holiday hardly touched him. . . . He wanted to hear some words of solace and asked about the Fighting Organization, about the course of the first day's fighting, and about our plans for the next day and the near future.

When I departed, the rabbi very warmly wished me success.

"I have lived my life," he said, "but you youngsters—do not flinch, fight on and may God be on your side."

The rabbi walked me to the door and gave me a few packages of matzos for my unit. "Should we be lucky enough to live till tomorrow," he added, "come over and bring Zivia with you." And so I did. The next day, on the second seder night, both of us, Zivia and I, visited the rabbi.

Returning to my friends I found myself in a different world. I again enjoyed the warm, comradely atmosphere and the indomitable spirit with which trouble and misfortune were faced head on, tearlessly. In this strong spirit lay the main power of the Organization. It lifted one above the waves of despair, and encouraged one to hold fast and fight the enemy.[38]

CONNECTIONS

In the days before the *Aktion,* many Jews looked forward to Passover. Tuvia Borzykowski writes, "Matzos were baked (out of dark flour—with the permission of the rabbis), wine was prepared for the seder; also there was spring housecleaning, special cleaning of dishes, and everything else, as in natural times. The houses and courtyards looked festive and gay." A seder is more than a holiday meal. It is a time when family and friends gather to retell the story of the exodus from Egypt. At a seder, every song, every tale, every dish on the table, even the wine itself has meaning. How might each of those symbols have taken on new meaning in the Warsaw ghetto?

At Rabbi Mayzel's request, Borzykowski brought Zivia Lubetkin to the second seder. The rabbi blessed both her and Borzykowski that night. What do you think their coming meant to the rabbi and his family? To Borzykowski and Lubetkin?

Women made up over one-third of the ZOB's members. From the start, they played an active role in the organization. General Jurgen Stroop noted in a report to his superiors in Berlin:

During the armed resistance the women belonging to the battle groups were equipped the same as the men; some were members of the *Halutzim* [pioneer] movement. Not infrequently, these women fired pistols with both hands. It happened again and again that these women had pistols or hand grenades concealed in their bloomers up to the last moment to use against the men of Waffen SS, Police or Wehrmacht.

Why was Stroop so surprised? What stereotypes did the women shatter?

The Ghetto in Flames

When General Jurgen Stroop sent his troops into the ghetto on April 19th, he expected the operation to be over by the following day, Hitler's birthday. Nearly a month later, the fighting continued. The young fighters in the Warsaw Ghetto had held off the Germans longer than the French army did in 1940.

The Nazis set fires to force Jews out of their hiding places.

After the first week of fighting, General Stroop made an important decision:

> The resistance put up by the Jews and bandits could be broken only by relentlessly using all our force and energy by day and night. . . . I therefore decided to destroy the entire Jewish residential area by setting every block on fire, including the blocks of residential buildings near the armament works. One [building] after the other was systematically evacuated and subsequently destroyed by fire. The Jews then emerged from their hiding places and dug-outs in almost every case. Not infrequently, the Jews stayed in the burning buildings until, because of the heat and the fear of being burned alive they preferred to jump down from the upper stories after having thrown mattresses and other upholstered articles into the street from the burning buildings. With their bones broken, they still tried to crawl across the street into blocks of buildings which had not yet been set on fire or were only partly in flames. Often Jews changed their hiding places during the night, by moving into the ruins of burnt-out buildings, taking refuge there until they were found by our patrols. Their stay in the sewers also ceased to be pleasant after the first week. Frequently from the streets, we could hear loud voices coming through the sewer shafts.[39]

After the war, Simha Rotem, a member of the ZOB, described the decisions he made in the last days of the uprising. He told filmmaker Claude Lanzmann:

During the first three days of fighting, the Jews had the upper hand. The Germans retreated at once to the ghetto entrance, carrying dozens of wounded with them. From then on, their onslaught came entirely from the outside, through air attack and artillery. We couldn't resist the bombing, especially their method of setting fire to the ghetto. The whole ghetto was ablaze. All life vanished from the streets and houses. We hid in the cellars and bunkers. From there we made our sorties. We went out at night. The Germans were in the ghetto mostly by day, leaving at night. They were afraid to enter the ghetto at night. . . .

Besides fighting the Germans, we fought hunger and thirst. We had no contact with the outside world; we were completely isolated, cut off from the world. We were in such a state that we could no longer understand the very meaning of why we went on fighting. We thought of attempting a breakout to the Aryan part of Warsaw, outside the ghetto.

Just before May 1 Sigmund and I were sent to . . . Aryan Warsaw. . . .Our job was to contact Yitzhak Zuckerman to try to mount a rescue operation, to try to save the few fighters who might still be alive in the ghetto. We managed to contact Zuckerman. We found two [Polish] sewer workers. On the night of May 8-9 we decided to return to the ghetto with another buddy, Ryszek [a Polish socialist who helped the ZOB] and the two sewer men. After the curfew we entered the sewers. We were entirely at the mercy of the two workmen, since only they knew the ghetto's underground layout. Halfway there they decided to turn back, . . . and we had to threaten them with our guns. We went on through the sewers until one of the workmen told us we were under the ghetto. Ryszek guarded them so they couldn't escape. I raised the manhole cover to go up into the ghetto.

At bunker Mila 18 [the headquarters of the ZOB] I missed them by a day. . . . The Germans found the bunker on the morning of the eighth. Most of its survivors committed suicide, or succumbed to gas in the bunkers. I went to bunker Francziskanska 22. There was no answer when I yelled the password, so I had to go on through the ghetto. I suddenly heard a woman calling from the ruins. It was darkest night, no lights, you saw nothing. All the houses were in ruins, and I heard only one voice. . . . I didn't find her.

I was alone all the time. Except for that woman's voice and a man I met as I came out of the sewers, I was alone throughout my tour of the ghetto. . . .[40]

Among the dead at Mila 18 were Mordecai Anielewicz and Arye Wilner. But other fighters were still alive. In a report he wrote in 1944, Rotem recalled:

At 4 o'clock I returned to the sewer. I closed the manhole cover behind me. "Let's go," I shouted in an inhuman voice to Ryszek and the sewer workers; "there's nobody." We began walking back. We were soaked to the skin because all cisterns and sluice gates were closed. The water comes up to our waist. We walk and I signal with my flashlight in the hope that, nevertheless, there would be someone. I shouted, "Jan! Jan!"— the password of the fighters. Suddenly, a group of 10 fighters bursts out of a side channel. Tearfully we greet one another. In a few words I learn everything that had happened during my absence. Help was late in coming. By one day! We had no choice but to save those who remained. Two fighters return to the Ghetto to take those who are left. Meanwhile, we advance slowly toward Prosta Street. We post scouts along the way, a few dozen meters apart.[41]

In the ghetto, Zivia Lubetkin, Marek Edelman, and a few other survivors prepared to leave the burning ghetto. On the "Aryan side," Rotem made arrangements for their rescue. He and several other men commandeered trucks to transport the group to a nearby forest early in the morning. But the first truck did not show up at 5 AM as scheduled. By the time it did arrive, it was too late to take people out of the sewers without attracting a crowd. But if they didn't get out, they would die from the toxic fumes in the sewers. So as soon as the first truck arrived, Rotem and his comrades cordoned off the street and began pulling people out of the sewer and into the vehicle as quickly as possible. When several minutes passed without anyone leaving the sewer, he gave the order to move out. As the truck pulled away, he learned that fifteen people had been left behind. They were in another part of the sewer.[42]

When Rotem went back, he discovered that the Germans had shot both the men who stayed behind and fifteen fighters who had been left in the sewers. At the same time, the Germans sealed the sewers and blocked all of the tunnels. They also cut off the ghetto's electricity and its water supply. The few people still in the ghetto continued to fight but were running out of food and ammunition.

On May 16, Stroop announced that his mission had been accomplished: the ghetto was "no more." But in fact, the Germans reported fighting in the ghetto throughout the spring and summer of 1943. Jan Pika, the commander of a ZZW group, held out until June 5. The ZOB unit under the command of Zachariah Artstein fought until July 3 or 4 when it disappeared "without a trace." And there were reports of battles with several "wild groups" throughout the months of August and September.

Most of the other survivors were now in hiding on the "Aryan side." Some joined partisan groups in the forests. Others, including Zuckerman, now focused on rescue. With money from Jewish groups abroad, they worked with Zegota to support as many hidden Jews as possible. In a report Zuckerman and Adolf Berman sent to Zionist leaders abroad, they wrote, "We go about in disguises. We feel like tightrope aerialists performing over an abyss. Night and day we hover between life and death. Every day we work is a miracle. But we do not cease."

CONNECTIONS

Zivia Lubetkin wrote of a decision the fighters made the night they left the ghetto:

> It was hard to depart from the ghetto, from the dead, the fallen friends. And above all, we were tortured by the thought of having to leave the other fighters in Zachariah [Artstein's] and Joseph Ferber's units behind. We decided on a meeting with them tomorrow, after all. It was dawn; there was no possibility of reaching them: if we went to them in open daylight we would betray both ourselves and them to the enemy. Our souls were torn: what should we do? Logic stated categorically that nothing could be done, we should leave. But our consciences did not give us peace. How could we go without them? These were stormy moments. Several of our comrades said, "We will not move from here. If even a single person remains in the Ghetto, all of us will remain with him." They lay motionless on the ground; many even threw away their ammunition pouches, renouncing salvation under those circumstances. But finally, with heavy hearts, we descended into the sewers.[43]

What values shaped their choice in the end? Why did the decision give them no peace? Was it a choice-less choice?

After the war, Abba Kovner, a leader of the resistance in Vilna, said:

> The destruction that we, for lack of any other word, call "the Holocaust," brings every rational one of us back to the basis of human existence. There is no understanding. . . . We are talking about the total defeat of man, the total defeat of civilization. It is not just certain places where certain individuals failed, but a total defeat such as never happened before. And we are part of that defeat. Only if we realize that, can we begin climbing up out of the abyss.[44]

How do his comments help us understand the pain of the choices like those Lubetkin and her comrades made on their last night in the ghetto?

Lubetkin wrote that when she and the others reached the forest, she was moved to tears:

> It had been so long since we had known the fragrance of a forest, of spring, of the sun. We were moved to our very depths. Everything that had been locked away for so many years, petrified deep within me, suddenly broke loose and I burst into tears. Many were the times "there" that I had wanted to weep and relieve the burden, but my heart had turned to stone. It was forbidden to cry. It was shameful to shed a tear. And now all the pain seemed alleviated.[45]

How do you account for her sadness? Her feelings of guilt? For whom was she crying? Why didn't she allow herself to cry "there"?

Both Lubetkin and Marek Edelman were distraught when they discovered that fifteen people had been left behind. They wanted to return to the sewer immediately, but Simha Rotem refused to let the truck turn back. Over 30 years later, Edelman told an interviewer that he still received phone calls from Rotem saying the deaths were all his fault. Edelman tells him "that's not true, that 'Kazik' [Rotem's cover name] performed marvelously, and that the only one responsible was he himself, since it was he who told the others to move away from the outlet in the first place. At which point Kazik, still from his city three thousand kilometers away, says, 'Stop it. After all, it's the Germans who were responsible.'"[46] In his autobiography, Rotem recalled that Zivia Lubetkin believed that the fault was hers and threatened to shoot him if he did not let her go back. Who, if anyone, was at fault? Why did the incident haunt the survivors long after the war ended?

Polish Responses

On April 23, 1943, soon after the uprising began, Yitzhak Zuckerman and other members of the ZOB on the "Aryan side" issued a statement to "Poles, citizens, freedom fighters!" It informed them that "a battle is being waged for your freedom as well as ours. For your and our human, civic, and national honor and dignity. We shall avenge the crimes of Auschwitz, Treblinka, Belzec, Majdanek! Long live the brotherhood of arms and blood of fighting Poland! Long live freedom!"

Although many Poles admired the stand the Jews were taking, few came to their aid. Among those who did were people like Wladyslaw Bartoszewski and his associates at Zegota. They tried not only to find hiding places for Jews who fled the ghetto but also to influence public opinion in Poland and abroad. Bartoszewski recalled that in radiograms, bulletins, and other reports:

Mordecai Anielewicz, the commander of the ZOB.

> We stressed the important historical and moral meaning of the ghetto uprising: this was, after all, the first rebellion of a city in the history of the European resistance movement, the first mutinous battle in the center of a major city where there was a contingent of several tens of thousands of German troops. And finally, this uprising was also a turning point in the history of the Jewish people under the occupation. A phenomenon that even surpassed the goals and expectations of the organizers and leaders of the fight themselves.[47]

The Polish underground publicized the uprising. There were broadcasts on the radio and longer accounts in newspapers and bulletins. One of the most widely reprinted documents was a letter that Yitzhak Zuckerman received from Mordecai Anielewicz, the commander of the uprising. It was written on the fifth day of the fight.

> I don't know what to write you. Let's dispense with personal details this time. I have only one expression to describe my feelings and the feelings of my comrades: things have surpassed our boldest dreams: the Germans ran away from the ghetto twice. One of our units held out for forty minutes, and the other one for more than six hours. The mine planted in the Brushmakers' area exploded. So far, we have had only one casualty: Yehiel, who fell as a hero at the machine gun.
>
> Yesterday, when we got information that the PPR [Polish Socialist Party] attacked the Germans and that the radio station *Swit* broadcast a wonderful bulletin about our self-defense, I had a feeling of fulfillment. Even though there's still a lot of work ahead of us, whatever has been done so far has been done perfectly.
>
> From this evening, we are switching to a system of guerrilla action. At night, three of our units go out on missions: an armed reconnaissance patrol and the acquisition of weapons. Know that the pistol has no value, we practically don't use it. We

need grenades, rifles, machine guns, and explosives.

I can't describe to you the conditions in which the Jews are living. Only a few individuals will hold out. All the rest will be killed sooner or later. The die is cast. In all the bunkers where our comrades are hiding, you can't light a candle at night for lack of oxygen. . . .

Of all the units in the ghetto, only one man is missing: Yehiel. That too is a victory. I don't know what else to write you. I imagine you have many questions. But for now, be content with this.

The general situation: all the workshops in the [Central Ghetto] and outside it were closed, except for Werterfassung, Transavia, and Daring. I don't have any information on the situation in Schultz and Toebbens. Contact is cut off. The Brushmakers' workshop has been in flames for three days. I have no contact with the units. There are many fires in the ghetto. Yesterday, the hospital burned. Blocks of buildings are in flames. The police force was dismantled. . . . Not many people have been taken out of the ghetto, but that is different in the shops. I don't have the details. During the day, we sit in hiding places. Be well, my friend. Perhaps we shall meet again. The main thing is the dream of my life has come true. I've lived to see a Jewish defense in the ghetto in all its greatness and glory.[48]

Although Zuckerman and others tried desperately to get the AK to send more weapons to the ghetto and actively aid the fighters, they received only "moral support." On May 5, 1943, then prime minister of the government-in-exile, General Wladyslaw Sikorski, told the nation:

We are witnesses to the greatest crime in human history. We know that you are giving all the help you can to the tortured Jews. For that, my countrymen, I thank you in my own name and in that of the government of Poland. I ask you to continue to grant them any conceivable help and at the same time to put a stop to this inhuman cruelty.[49]

Although the statement heartened members of the ZOB, it did nothing to change the outcome of the uprising. Yitzhak Zuckerman expressed his personal disappointment, when he assessed the value of the aid the ghetto fighters received from the Poles:

Any operations that were done were simply humanistic gestures. They didn't change the struggle in the ghetto one iota; it didn't create an opening for rescue.. . . . So even if something was done, it was only symbolic, an expression of the brotherhood of Polish people, and not an act by an organized Polish force coordinated with the Jewish fighters. . . . [The AK's] behavior was deliberate and conscious. . . . By the AK, I mean the big social and military force, the leadership, the people who decided in cold blood not to help. Let's be objective about this. I'm not talking about antisemites or about those who sympathized with us. The AK always made its own . . . accounting, which told them that, if our uprising spread beyond the wall, Polish Warsaw would be prematurely inflamed by an uprising doomed to failure because the Germans would easily put it down.

In general, . . . all those I talked with were full of admiration and goodwill; but nothing came of it. History requires facts, and even good intentions don't leave traces. The intention was expressed but not carried out. . . .

From our perspective, the act of Stefan Sawicki, the young gentile who simply went and joined the Jewish Fighting Organization, was infinitely more important than all the good wishes that accomplished nothing. When I talk about the sympathetic Polish street, I mean the simple man, the head of a household, who walks in the street and sees the fire, the smoke; he's a human being, and he expresses that—sometimes with a tear, sometimes with a good word, an expression of identification. But that doesn't obligate him to anything. Organizational force is something else.[50]

CONNECTIONS

How did each of the following individuals and/or groups define their "universe of obligation": the ZOB, the Polish underground, Wladislaw Bartowszewski and his associates? How was Poland's "universe of obligation" defined in the prime minister's speech? Does he view the "tortured Jews" as fellow citizens or as outsiders?

Many years after the war, Abba Kovner, a leader in the Vilna Ghetto, told a group of scholars that "it is not a question of when [people] knew or what they knew; it was a question of what they should have done with what they knew. What were the alternatives? What conclusions can be draw when there was no choice?" Kovner was speaking of Jews. How do his remarks apply to the Christian Poles Zuckerman describes?

Yitzhak Zuckerman writes that "history requires facts, and even good intentions don't leave traces." What "facts" does he spell out? What were the "good intentions" that failed to leave traces?

Zuckerman distinguishes between expressions of sympathy and "organizational force." What difference does he see? How do those differences apply to events in the world today? For example, which did the world show in Bosnia or Rwanda in the 1990s?

The introduction to this chapter quotes from Maria Kann's "Appeal to the Conscience of the World." Who is the "we" in her remarks? What is the danger she describes? What does she see as the possible legacy of silence and of the failure to take action?

The World Is Silent

In December of 1942, six months before the uprising in the Warsaw ghetto, the Allies issued a joint declaration acknowledging that the Germans were "now carrying into effect Hitler's oft-repeated intention to exterminate the Jewish people in Europe." But they took no other action. They did nothing to stop the killings or rescue Jews. Their leaders insisted that the "most effective relief which can be given victims of enemy persecution is to insure the speedy defeat of the Nazis."

On April 28, 1943, the Polish underground, which was among the first to alert the world to the Holocaust, sent a radiogram to the Allies. It stated:

> The attitude of the defenders is creating admiration among the population of the country and humiliation and anger among the Germans. . . . Immediate successful help is now exclusively in the power of the Allies. In the name of the millions of Jews who have already been killed, in the name of those who are now being exiled and massacred, in the name of the heroic combatants, and of all of us condemned to die, we call on the whole civilized world: the mighty blow of the Allies against the blood-thirsty enemy should be dealt now in the only understandable language of revenge, and not at some time in the misty future.[51]

Neither the United States nor Britain responded to the message. The Soviet Union was also silent. Writer Alfred Kazin commented in his journal in spring, 1943:

> The *New York Times* notes in an easy-to-miss corner of a back page that on May 12, in London, the Polish Jew Shmuel Ziegelboim, who represented the Jewish Workers Bund in the Polish cabinet-in-exile, was found dead by his own hand in a London flat. His wife and child had been murdered by the Nazis. [See Reading 3.]

Ziegelboim's letter was addressed to the president of Poland and to Prime Minister Wladyslaw Sikorski.

> I take the liberty of addressing to you my last words, and through you to the Polish government and to the Polish people, the governments and peoples of the Allied states— to the conscience of the world. From the latest information received from Poland, it is evident that the Germans, with the most ruthless cruelty, are now murdering the few remaining Jews in Poland. Behind the ghetto's walls the last act of a tragedy unprecedented in history is being performed. The responsibility for this crime of murdering the entire Jewish population of Poland falls in the first instance on the perpetrators, but indirectly is also a burden on the whole of humanity, the people and the governments of the Allied states which thus far have made no effort toward concrete action for the purpose of curtailing this crime.
>
> By the passive observation of the murder of defenseless millions, and of the maltreatment of children, women, and old men, these countries have become the criminals' accomplices.
>
> I must also state that although the Polish government has to a high degree contributed to the enlistment of world opinion, it has yet done so insufficiently. It has not done anything that would correspond to the magnitude of the drama being enacted now in Poland. From some 3,500,000 Polish Jews and about 700,000 other

Jews deported to Poland from other countries—according to official statistics provided by the underground Bund organization—there remained in April of this year only about 300,000. And this remaining murder still goes on.

I cannot be silent—I cannot live—while remnants of the Jewish people of Poland, of whom I am a representative, are perishing. My comrades in the Warsaw Ghetto took weapons in their hands on that last heroic impulse. It was not my destiny to die there together with them, but I belong to them, and in their mass graves. By my death I wish to express my strongest protest against the inactivity with which the world is looking on and permitting the extermination of my people. I know how little human life is worth today; but as I was unable to do anything during my life, perhaps by my death I shall contribute to breaking down the indifference of those who may now—at the last moment—rescue the few Polish Jews still alive from certain annihilation. My life belongs to the Jewish people of Poland and I therefore give it to them. I wish that this remaining handful of the original several million of Polish Jews could live to see the liberation of a new world of freedom, and the justice of true socialism. I believe that such a Poland will arise and that such a world will come. I trust that the President and the Prime Minister will direct my words to all those for whom they are destined, and that the Polish government will immediately take appropriate action in the fields of diplomacy. I bid my farewell herewith to everybody and everything dear to me and loved by me.

The *Times* added: "That was the letter. It suggests that possibly Shmuel Ziegelboim will have accomplished as much in dying as he did in living." At Kazin's request, the *New Republic* reprinted Ziegelboim's last message. Under it, Kazin wrote:

Something has already been done—by us the bystanders as well as by the Nazi killers—and that will never be undone. Hitler will leave hatred of the Jews as his last political trick, as it was his first. The people who have been most indifferent to the massacre of the Jews will be just those who wonder why all the pacts and all the formal justice will have done so little to give them their prewar "security" again.

You who want only to live and let live, to have the good life back—and think you can dump three million Jews into the furnace, and sigh in the genuine impotence of your undeniable regret, and then build Europe back again! Where so great a murder has been allowed, no one is safe.[52]

CONNECTIONS

In December, Ziegelboim said on British radio: "It will actually be a shame to go on living, to belong to the great human race if steps are not taken to halt the greatest crime in human history." For the next five months, he tried desperately to awake the conscience of the world and failed. What did he hope to accomplish through his death that he had failed to accomplish in his life? Did he succeed?

What does Kazin think will be the legacy of the world's silence? Compare his predictions with those of Maria Kann in the introduction to this chapter. What similarities seem most striking? Did the world turn out much the way they predicted? Have we learned the lesson they hoped we might learn?

For Your Freedom and Ours

*Many Jews in Eastern Europe heard about the uprising in the Warsaw Ghetto over illegal
radios hidden in the ghettos. The news also spread by word of mouth to the partisans in the
forests and even to Jews in the death camps.*

Shmerl Kaczerginski, a poet in Vilna, recalled the day when an incredible message
flashed over the secret radio of his partisan group: "Hello, hello, the survivors in the
Warsaw Ghetto have begun an armed resistance against the murderers of the Jewish people. The Ghetto is aflame!"

> Two short lines conveyed the flaming news. . . . We knew no other particulars yet. . .
> but we suddenly saw clearly the flames of the Warsaw Ghetto and the Jews fighting
> with arms for their dignity and self-respect. Restless days. Sleepless nights. We armed
> ourselves. The news of the uprising lifted our spirits and made us proud. . . and
> although we were in agony at their unequal struggle. . . we felt relieved. . . our hearts
> became winged.[53]

The spirit of the uprising inspired other revolts among the handful of Jews who
remained alive in Poland. That summer, there were revolts in Vilna, Krakow, Kovno,
Bialystok, Bedzin-Sosnowiec, and other cities. Jews even managed to mount a rebellion
in Treblinka that August. About 150 prisoners escaped. The rest were murdered, but not
before they killed 16 guards. By the end of September, Treblinka was closed. Armed
revolts also took place at Sobibor and Auschwitz.

The spirit of the uprising also remained alive in Warsaw. When the Polish
underground began its own rebellion on August 1, 1944, hundreds of Jews volunteered
to fight. Among them were the inmates from Birkenau and Majdanek whom the
Germans had ordered to clear the ruins of the ghetto. Another group of volunteers was
commanded by Shmuel Kenigswein who had been a boxer in the Maccabi games before
the war. Now he led a unit that included over 40 former inmates of a labor camp the
Poles liberated soon after the uprising began. Yet another unit, led by Yitzhak
Zuckerman, was made up of the remnants of the ZOB. On August 3, Zuckerman issued
the following appeal to them and other survivors of the Warsaw ghetto:

> TO THE DEFENDERS OF THE WARSAW GHETTO! TO THE JEWS WHO REMAIN ALIVE!
> The population of Warsaw has been conducting an armed struggle against the
> German invaders for the last three days. This is our struggle, too. A year has passed
> since we raised the flag of the famous revolt in the Ghettos and labor camps, since we
> began the battle for our lives and honor, and we again join the entire Polish nation in
> the fight for freedom. Hundreds of Jewish youths and members of the Jewish
> Fighting Organization stand shoulder to shoulder with their Polish comrades at the
> barricades. We send our greetings to the fighters.
>
> Together with the rest of the Polish nation we are, today, struggling for freedom.
> All of the members of the Jewish Fighting Organization who have survived and all
> Jewish youths capable of fighting are hereby called on to continue the struggle. No
> one should stay behind. Join the ranks of the rebels. Through war we shall achieve
> victory, and a free, sovereign, strong and just Poland![54]

Zuckerman writes, "We went to that war of our own will, and we wanted to be in it as Jews." Tuvya Borzykowski recalled with pride, "The members of the Jews of the Jewish Fighting Organization in the Old City were the only Jews in the Warsaw uprising who fought officially as Jews in a Jewish fighting group."[55]

The ZOB joined the AL, recalls Vladka Meed "not primarily because these Jews were Socialists or Communists, but because the [AK] was filled with antisemitic agitators. Even while fighting the Nazis, the Jewish insurgents in the Armja Krajowa units suffered persecution from their Polish comrades. The Poles assigned them the most dangerous missions and the most difficult tasks—and on occasion shot them in the back." A number of Jews were murdered by Poles during the uprising. Among them were two volunteers still in concentration-camp clothes.

It took the Germans two months to crush the revolt. By the time it ended, one out of every three people in Warsaw was dead and the city itself had been reduced to rubble. Of the thousand Jews who took part in the uprising, 500 were dead. The survivors, including Yitzhak Zuckerman and Zivia Lubetkin, either escaped to the countryside or hid in bunkers. Many believed it was only a matter of days until the Russians liberated the city. The war was finally was coming to an end.

The Russians arrived in the city on January 17, 1945. Zuckerman later recalled that he, Lubetkin, and a wolfhound they acquired after its owners were killed "went out to the square and saw Soviet tanks, tank drivers with soot-blackened faces, joyful; and *suddenly, for the first time—I started weeping.*"

> [For] me, January 17, the day the Soviet forces entered Warsaw, was one of the saddest days of my life. . . . I saw the masses shouting for joy, when I was there with Zivia and the dog, suddenly the knowledge that there was no Jewish people sliced through me like a knife. That feeling rose in me as the tank drivers kissed the crowd and flowers flew in the air; that jubilation in contrast to our loneliness, we the orphaned, the last ones—what joy could we have? I was thoroughly crushed and broken. Until then, I had had to hold onto myself tightly, but now I could cry, be weak. Suddenly I asked: what am I and what is my strength? Ultimately, my own struggle for life had a limit. And not only for me, everybody. There had always been a sense of mission that gave us strength; but now, it was over, as it were.[56]

Of the 3.3 million Jews of Poland, ninety percent were murdered in the Holocaust.

CONNECTIONS

The uprising in the Warsaw Ghetto ended tragically. Why then did it inspire other uprisings?

Zuckerman says of the ZOB's participation in the Polish Uprising:

> Our group wasn't important in terms of quantity, but symbolically, it made an extraordinary impression. To this very day, the Poles mention that. There was something strange in it and, perhaps, in fact, not so strange. Between 1.4 and 1.5 million Jews fought in World War II in the Allied armies; I'm talking about the participation of the Jews in the war. And what remains of that in history? The Warsaw Ghetto Uprising! Because it was done under a Jewish banner. In the ranks of the Polish Uprising, there were perhaps a hundred or two hundred times more fighters, but our small group of

less than twenty people was what inserted the Jewish banner into the Polish revolt. The Poles themselves note that. And we appeared there, from the first moment, as Jews. Although I wasn't known as a Jew, here and now, in this Uprising, I wanted them to know I was a Jew.[57]

How do you account for the impact the ZOB had on the Poles? Why might people be more likely to recall the uprising in the Warsaw Ghetto than other Jewish participation in the war?

How do you explain the persistence of antisemitism in Poland despite heroic efforts by individuals and groups in Poland to save as many Jews as possible?

In reflecting on the history you have been studying, Elie Wiesel wrote:

Heroes and martyrs became the pride of their people by fighting with a weapon in their hand or a prayer in their soul. In a thousand different ways, each proclaimed that freedom alone gives meaning to the life of an individual or a people.

For a people—that is, for a social, ethnic, or religious group—the problem and its solution are both simple. When a people loses its freedom, it has a right, a duty, to employ every possible means to win it back. But resistance can be expressed in nonviolent ways too.

The Jews who lived in the ghettos under the Nazi occupation showed their independence by leading an organized clandestine life. The teacher who taught the starving children was a free man. The nurse who secretly cared for the wounded, the ill, and the dying was a free woman. The rabbi who prayed, the disciple who studied, the father who gave his bread to his children, the children who risked their lives by leaving the ghetto at night in order to bring back to their parents a piece of bread or a few potatoes, the man who consoled his orphaned friend, the orphan who wept with a stranger for a stranger—these were human beings filled with unquenchable thirst for freedom and dignity. The young people who dreamed of armed insurrection, the lovers who, a moment before they were separated, talked about their bright future together, the insane who wrote poems, the chroniclers who wrote down the day's events by their flickering candles—all were free in the noblest sense of the word, though their prison walls seemed impassable and their executioners invincible. . . .

Do not misunderstand me: I am in no way trying to minimize the Nazis' evil power. I am not saying that all prisoners succeeded in opposing them by their will to be free. On the contrary—locked in a suffering and solitude unlike any other, the prisoners generally could only adapt to their condition—and either be submerged by it or swept along by time. The apparatus of murder was too perfect not to crush people weakened by hunger, forced labor, and punishment. But I am saying that the executioner did not always triumph. Some victims managed to escape and alert the public in the free world. Others organized a solidarity movement within the inferno itself. One companion of mine in the camps gave the man next to him a spoonful of soup every day at work. Another would try to amuse us with stories. Yet another would urge us not to forget our names—one way, among many others, of saying No to the enemy, of showing that we were free, freer than the enemy.[58]

What does Elie Wiesel suggest we can learn from this history? What lessons have you learned from it? What would you want others to know about it?

1 *Notes from the Warsaw Ghetto: The Journal of Emmanuel Ringelblum*, ed. and trans. by Jacob Sloan (Schocken Books, 1974), 326.

2 Quoted in *A Surplus of Memory: Chronicle of the Warsaw Ghetto Uprising* by Yitzhak Zuckerman, trans. and ed. by Barbara Harshav. (University of California Press, 1993), xiii.

3 Quoted in Wladyslaw Bartoszewski, *The Warsaw Ghetto: A Christian's Testimony*, trans. by Stephen G. Cappellari (Beacon Press, 1987),93.

4 Quoted in *Rescuers: Portraits of Moral Courage in the Holocaust* by Gay Block and Malka Drucker, 32-33.

5 Elie Wiesel, *One Generation After* (Pocket Books, 1970), 55-56

6 Yitzhak Zuckerman, *A Surplus of Memory*, 193-194.

7 Zivia Lubetkin, *In the Days of Destruction and Revolt*, trans. by Ishai Tubbin (Ghetto Fighters' House, 1981), 93-94.

8 Ibid., 115-117.

9 Quoted in Yitzhak Zuckerman, *A Surplus of Memory*, 214-215.

10 Alexander Donat, *The Holocaust Kingdom* (Holt, 1965), 107-108.

11 Zivia Lubetkin, *In the Days of Destruction and Revolt*, 123-124.

12 Yitzhak Zuckerman, *A Surplus of Memory*, 207.

13 Elie Wiesel, *One Generation After*, 55-56

14 Wladyslaw Bartoszewski, *The Warsaw Ghetto: A Christian's Testimony*, 50-51.

15 Vladka Meed, *On Both Sides of the Wall*, trans. Dr. Steven Meed (Holocaust Library, 1972), 111.

16 Alexander Donat, *The Holocaust Kingdom*, 111-112.

17 Deborah Dwork, *Children with a Star* (Yale University Press, 1991), 255.

18 Vladka Meed, *On Both Sides of the Wall*, 89-90.

19 Marek Edelman, "The Ghetto Fights," in *The Warsaw Ghetto: the 45th Anniversary of the Uprising* (Interpress Publishers, 1988), 38.

20 Quoted in *The Fighting Ghettoes*, trans. and ed. by Meyer Barkai (Lippincott, 1962), 23.

21 Quoted in Yisrael Gutman, *The Jews of Warsaw 1939-1943: Ghetto, Underground, Revolt* (Indiana University Press, 1982), 317.

22 Ibid.

23 Ibid., 317-318

24 Ibid., 318

25 Marek Edelman, "The Ghetto Fights" in *The Warsaw Ghetto: the 45th Anniversary of the Uprising*, 38.

26 Quoted in Yisrael Gutman, *The Jews of Warsaw 1939-1943*, 309-310.

27 Zivia Lubetkin, *In the Days of Destruction and Revolt*, 166-168.

28 Vladka Meed, *On Both Sides of the Wall*, 125.

29 Ibid., 126.

30 Bernard Goldstein, *The Stars Bear Witness*, trans. and ed. Leonard Shatzkin (Viking Press, 1949), 184.

31 Alexander Donat, *The Holocaust Kingdom*, 131.

32 Ibid.

33 Quoted in Yisrael Gutman, *The Jews of Warsaw 1939-1943*, 334-335.

34 Alexander Donat, *The Holocaust Kingdom*, 133.

35 Ibid., 133.

36 Zivia Lubetkin, *In the Days of Destruction and Revolt*, 180-181.

37 Alexander Donat, *The Holocaust Kingdom*, 138-139.

38 Quoted in *The Fighting Ghettoes*, trans. and ed. by Meyer Barkai, 49-51.

39 Quoted in Nora Levin, *The Holocaust Years* (Krieger Publishers, 1990), 259-260.

[40] Quoted in Claude Lanzmann, *Shoah: An Oral History of the Holocaust* (Pantheon, 1985), 198, 200.

[41] Quoted in Simha Rotem, *Memoirs of a Warsaw Ghetto Fighter,* trans. and ed. Barbara Harshav (Yale University Press, 1994), 166.

[42] Ibid., 166-167.

[43] Zivia Lubetkin, *In the Days of Destruction and Revolt,* 243-244.

[44] Quoted in *The Holocaust as Historical Experience,* ed. by Yehuda Bauer and Nathan Rotenstreich (Holmes & Meier, 1981), 251.

[45] Zivia Lubetkin, *In the Days of Destruction and Revolt,* 255.

[46] Quoted in *Shielding the Flame: An Intimate Conversation with Dr. Marek Edelman* by Hanna Krall, trans. by Joanna Stasinska and Lawrence Weschler (Henry Holt, 1977), 76.

[47] Wladyslaw Bartoszewski, *The Warsaw Ghetto: A Christian's Testimony,* 79.

[48] Quoted in Yitzhak Zuckerman, *A Surplus of Memory,* 357.

[49] Quoted in Wladyslaw Bartoszewski, *The Warsaw Ghetto: A Christian's Testimony,* 79-80.

[50] Quoted in Yitzhak Zuckerman, *A Surplus of Memory,* 374-375.

[51] Ibid., 77.

[52] *A Lifetime Burning in Every Moment: From the Journals of Alfred Kazin,* 19-21.

[53] Quoted in Ruth Rubin, *Voices of a People: The Story of Yiddish Folksong* (Jewish Publication Society, 1979), 453.

[54] Quoted in T*he Fighting Ghettoes,* trans. and ed. by Meyer Barkai, 97.

[55] Quoted in *Martyrs and Fighters: The Epic of the Warsaw Ghetto* by Philip Friedman (Praeger, 1954), 309-310.

[56] Yitzhak Zuckerman, *A Surplus of Memory,* 557-558.

[57] Ibid., 528.

[58] Elie Wiesel, *From the Kingdom of Memory: Reminiscences* (Schocken, 1990), 221-223. Originally published as "What Really Makes Us Free?" *Parade Magazine,* December 27, 1987.

7. Legacies

Being human is a surprise, not a foregone conclusion.
A person has the capacity to create events. . . .
Indeed the enigma of a human being is not in what he is
but in what he is able to be.

Abraham Joshua Heschel

Chapter 1 explored the idea that each of us is an individual with a unique identity. That chapter and the ones that followed focused in particular on the meanings people have attached to a Jewish identity at various periods in history. At times, Jews and other minorities were welcomed and encouraged to take an active part in the larger society. At other times, they were subject to discrimination, separation, isolation, and ultimately annihilation. As Martha Minow, a legal scholar, has pointed out, "When we identify one thing as like the others, we are not merely classifying the world; we are investing particular classifications with consequences and positioning ourselves in relation to those meanings. When we identify one thing as unlike the others, we are dividing the world; we use our language to distinguish—to discriminate."[1]

In reflecting on the history outlined in this book, one student noted that "no one could imagine anything worse than each unfolding stage of the Holocaust. So it was in some ways a failure of people's imagination that escorted them to tragedy." The student went on to say that "because of this course, I can imagine. So I will try to do the right thing." Good citizenship is a creative act—a work of the imagination. Writer Julius Lester, an African American and a Jew, defines the word *imagination* as "that ability to experience another in myself, to experience another as myself." He goes on to explain the relationship between imagination and a study of the past:

> As a human, I am more than I have experienced directly. If this were not so, literature, poetry, film, drama, and so on, would not communicate to anyone except their creators. If I were no more than my experience, I could not communicate with anyone else, or they with me. Imagination is the wings of the soul, carrying me from the singularity of personal existence across the void of Time and Space to alight in that realm where each of us is the other and God is One.
>
> But we seldom give the imagination a place in our reflections on history and ourselves. We seldom include it as integral to history. We ignore that the Nazis did what they did to the Jews because of whom they imagined Jews to be.
>
> When I confront the Holocaust, I use the faculty of imagination. . . .[2]

This chapter considers the ways a few individuals have used their imagination to not only confront the past but also build a more just society. As Benjamin R. Barber, a professor of political science, reminds us, it is through the imagination that we come to see others as "sufficiently like ourselves for them to become subjects of tolerance and respect if not always affection." A number of readings in Chapter 7 describe efforts to bridge the gap between "ourselves" and "others," end reliance on stereotypes, and honestly confront the issues that may divide us. This chapter also offers insights into the process of growth and change. That process reminds us that the mystery, or enigma, of a human being is not in what he or she is but in what he or she is able to be.

The Persistence of Hatred

In the spring of 1945, the Allies finally defeated the Nazis and brought the war to an end. But as historian Martin Gilbert points out, "Too many scars had been inflicted, too much blood had been spilled, for 8 May, 1945 to mark the end of the story, or the end of tragedy for the two hundred thousand survivors of the ghettos, camps and death marches."

On May 20, 1945, less than two weeks after the war, 25 young Jews returned to their hometown—Dzialoszyce, Poland. "We thought to ourselves," Henry Slamovich later recalled, "we had survived. We are alive. We are going to enjoy freedom."[3] But within just days of their arrival, four were killed by antisemites. Slamovich and the other survivors decided there was no place for them in Poland. They would rebuild their lives elsewhere.

There was anti-Jewish violence in other Polish cities as well: in Krakow on August 20, 1945, in Sosnowiec on October 25, and in Lublin on November 19. On February 1, 1946, the *Manchester Guardian* in England noted that "Polish thugs" had murdered 353 Jews since the end of the war. "Unfortunately," it added, "antisemitism is still prevalent in spite of the Government efforts to counteract it."[4]

In the spring of 1946, Joseph Tenenbaum, the president of the World Federation of Polish Jews, returned to the land of his birth to help survivors of the Holocaust. In 1919, at the end of World War I, he had described a civil war in eastern Galicia as a "bloody conflict" between "3,293,023 Ukrainians who hated the Poles, a minority of 1,349,626 Poles who in turn despised the Ukrainians, and 658,722 Jews thrust between them."[5] (See Chapter 3.) Twenty-seven years later, he found Poland in the midst of a similar conflict, this time between Communist and anti-Communist factions. And once again, the Jews were "thrust between them."

Tenenbaum was not the only one stunned by the anti-Jewish violence. Professor Olgierd Gorka, the head of the Jewish Department in Poland's Foreign Office and a leader of the newly formed League to Combat Racism, was also deeply concerned. Together, the two men, one a Jew and the other a Pole, arranged a meeting with Cardinal August Hlond, the head of Poland's Catholic Church on June 3, 1946. Tenenbaum later described the visit:

> I said I was glad to convey to [the Cardinal] the appreciation of the Jewish people for his activities on behalf of the Jews during the German occupation in France. These sentiments stimulated him into a long account of his exile and imprisonment by the Nazis and of his and the French Cardinal's efforts to rescue Jews from deportation. During his residence at Lourdes, he had certified many Jews for Catholic identification papers. He had induced the French Cardinal to issue orders to the monasteries to safeguard Jewish children. . . .
>
> I took the first opportunity that offered itself to state the purpose of my visit. I said that the Jewish people were aware of his activities in France, and were grateful for these acts of Christian mercy, but the more so are they bewildered with regard to the present attitude of the Church in Poland. They could not help but wonder at the silence of the Church in respect to the antisemitic outrages. . . . He stared at me in bewilderment.

I became more explicit. "Your Eminence," I said, "it is my conviction from what I have seen in the two months that I have spent in Poland, that the Church is the most important institution in molding the minds and hearts of the Polish people. A strong appeal from Your Eminence, and this terrible crime would cease at once."

He began his reply by agreeing that what I had said about the influence of the Church was accurate, but then followed a series of disheartening evasions. To my assertion that a thousand Jews had been killed since the liberation, he began by denying knowledge of this fact, and then countered by saying these were political rather than racial murders, that over 100,000 Christians had been killed, that entire villages were being destroyed by the Communists. For a moment, he lost his equanimity. "Jewish Communists are running this country. Why does world Jewry allow them to take over the government and oppress the Christian people?" . . .

"Your Eminence," I finally managed to put in a word, "Jews, like other people belong to different classes and different parties. There are Communists among them. But Jews have as much a right to be Communists as they have to be capitalists. In the second place," I assured His Eminence, "the pitiful remnants of Nazi destruction have necessarily but little interest in anything except the mere preservation of their lives and to rehabilitate themselves after the terrible Nazi ordeal. They have little interest in any of the political 'isms' that agitate Polish public opinion, and, certainly, they are not in the least responsible for the acts of the few individual Communists of Jewish extraction, who are in the Government."

Professor Gorka forcibly supported my arguments. But the Cardinal insisted: "These Jewish Communists in the Government are at the root of all evil."[6]

Tenenbaum and Gorka wanted the Cardinal to issue a statement condemning the murders. The Cardinal refused, insisting that the killers "do not murder Jews as Jews. They just retaliate for the murder of the Christian population by the Jewish Communist-run Polish Government." In reply, Tenenbaum showed him an invoice prepared by the Krakow Community Administration for burial expenses in the month of May. It listed the victims by name and age. Tennenbaum told the Cardinal:

"Your Eminence, you have among others the names and ages of two small children, one a mere infant and the other a few years older. Now, can anyone think that these children were killed by the bandits because they were Communists? Or is the common procedure of pulling suspected Jews out of trains and buses and stripping them to see if they are circumcised, and if proven to be so, murdering them on the spot, while non-Jews are returned to the train with apologies; is this political murder, or murder of Jews because they are Jews?" The Cardinal took the bill for "investigation."

I pressed again the matter of the pastoral letter. "Well," said the Cardinal, "the Church has no influence on the [right-wing extremists]." "That may be so," I said, "but such murders are possible only in an antisemitic atmosphere. It could not happen on so large a scale, if the populace were not infected with so much poisonous propaganda, and to eliminate the poison from the population is clearly the duty of the Church. . . ."[7]

At the end of the meeting, the Cardinal assured Tenenbaum and Gorka that "justice will be done." Yet just a few weeks later, on July 1, 1946, historian Martin Gilbert writes, "an eight-year-old Polish boy from Kielce, Henryk Blaszcyk, disappeared from his home."

Two days later he returned, claiming that he had been kept in a cellar by two Jews who had wanted to kill him, and that only a miracle had enabled him to escape. In fact, he had been to the home of a family friend in a nearby village. The friend had taught him what to say after his return.

On July 4 a crowd of Poles, aroused by rumors of Jews abducting Christian children for ritual purposes, attacked the building of the Jewish Committee in Kielce. Almost all the Jews who were inside the building, including the Chairman of the Committee, Dr. Seweryn Kahane, were shot, stoned to death, or killed with axes and blunt instruments. Elsewhere in Kielce, Jews were murdered in their homes, or dragged into the streets and killed by the mob.

Forty-one Jews were killed in Kielce that day. Two, Duczka and Ada Fisz, were children. Four, Bajla Gerntner, Rachel Zander, Fania Szumacher and Naftali Teitelbaum, were teenagers on their way to Palestine. Three, Izak Prajs, Abraham Wajntraub and Captain Wjanreb, were officers in the Polish army. Seven could not be named. One of those whose name was unknown was a survivor of Birkenau, a fact disclosed by the tattoo number of his arm, B2969.

The Jews of Kielce published the names of the dead in the one surviving Polish-Jewish newspaper, in a black border. The name of the Jew who had been in Birkenau was never found. The numbers B2903 to B3449 had been given to those Jews in a train from Radom on August 2, 1944 who had been "selected for the barracks." Radom and Kielce are only twenty-five miles apart.

Following the Kielce "pogrom," one hundred thousand Polish Jews, more than half the survivors, fled from Poland seeking new homes in Palestine, Western Europe, Britain, and the United States, Latin America and Australia.[8]

Who were the Jews who remained in Poland? Some were too old, too weak, too tired to try to put down roots in another land. Most, however, were young men and woman who were sympathetic to Poland's new Communist regime. A few had been members of the Communist party for many years and actively supported the changes the Russians were bringing to Eastern Europe. Others thought of themselves as Poles. They were eager to channel their talent, energy, and knowledge into rebuilding the country of their birth, the place where their ancestors lived and died. Although they were not Communists, they were confident that a Communist government would never tolerate antisemitism. Many recalled the support they received from Polish Communists during the war.

Within a few years, these Jews discovered that Communist leaders were as willing as right-wing leaders to use antisemitism to acquire and maintain power by turning neighbor against neighbor. In the 1950s, Joseph Stalin launched a campaign against Jews in Russia. Thousands were imprisoned. Countless others were forced from public life. In 1968, party officials in Poland responded to demands for reform with a similar campaign. Soon after it began, more and more Jews left Poland. Those who remained were careful not to call attention to their Jewish identity.

CONNECTIONS

A stereotype is a judgment about an individual based on real or imagined characteristics of a group. Stereotyping fosters prejudice and discrimination, because it reduces individuals to categories. What does the encounter between Joseph Tenenbaum and Cardinal

Hlond suggest about the power of stereotypes? How can such stereotypes be broken?

In response to the pogrom at Kielce, Polish sociologist Stanislaw Ossowski wrote:

> A more far-sighted, more cynical or more willful person, or someone with greater historical knowledge might have recalled that sympathy is not the only reaction to the misfortune of others. . . . He might also recall that if one person's tragedy gives someone else an advantage, it often happens that people want to convince themselves and others that the tragedy was morally justified. Such persons as owners of former Jewish shops or those who harass their Jewish competitors can be included in this group. And perhaps by citing a whole array of historical examples, I could express my doubt as to whether the reaction against the Nazi achievements will, in the short run, root out the influences of the Nazi spirit which, within the course of a few years, attained so much and which led human awareness to become inured to certain offensive slogans because of their frequent repetition.[9]

What does Ossowski mean when he writes that "sympathy is not the only reaction to the misfortune of others"? What other reactions have you experienced or read about? How does Ossowski account for such responses? How do you explain them?

In July of 1996, on the 50th anniversary of the pogrom at Kielce, Dariusz Rosati, Poland's Foreign Minister, sent a letter to the World Jewish Congress asking "your forgiveness" on behalf of his country. Some Poles objected to the apology, citing evidence that the Communists were responsible for the incident that set off the pogrom. Poland's president, Aleksander Kwasniewski, sharply criticized them. Why do you think he might have done so? Why is it hard for individuals to admit they did something wrong? Why might it be even harder for them to admit that their nation was at fault? How important are formal apologies?

In 1943, Maria Kann, a young Polish Girl Scout, wondered about the legacies of hatred. Her words are quoted in the introduction to Chapter 6. What did she fear would be the legacy of the war? To what extent did events after the war support those fears?

Wislawa Szymborska, a Polish poet who won the Nobel Prize for Literature in 1996, reflected on the power of hatred in a poem that is reprinted in Chapter 2, Reading 9. What does she mean when she writes that hatred "gives birth to the reasons that give it life"? What does she think it takes to keep any feeling or emotion alive? Why does she believe that only "hatred has what it takes"? How do events in Poland after the war support that belief?

In February, 1946, four Jewish delegates traveling to a convention in Krakow were murdered on a train from Lodz. Poland's communist government offered to give them a state funeral as "victims of anti-Communist forces." The organizers of the convention refused, saying, "They died as Jews, not in the fight for Communism." In the 1990s, Joseph Brodsky, a Russian poet, wrote that "whenever one pulls the trigger in order to rectify history's mistake, one lies. For history makes no mistakes, since it has no purpose. One always pulls the trigger out of self-interest and quotes history to avoid responsibility or pangs of conscience."[10] How do Brodsky's comments apply to the murders on the train? How do they apply to the Cardinal's insistence that the killers "do not murder Jews as Jews" but as Communists or to those who say the victims "died as Jews, not in the fight for Communism"?

Faith and Dialogue

Elie Wiesel has asked, "If Auschwitz didn't eliminate antisemitism, what will? If Treblinka didn't eradicate hatred, what will? If those places didn't teach our generation at least, and the ones to come, of the necessity, the urgency to bring people together as we usher in a new century, what will?"

On October 11, 1962, Pope John XXIII opened the first session of the Ecumenical Council, part of Vatican II. It re-examined the Church's relationships with other faiths, including Judaism. As Catholic religious leaders tried to define those relationships, they consulted a number of scholars including Abraham Joshua Heschel, a professor of religion and ethics at the Jewish Theological Seminary in New York. From 1962 to 1965, he offered advice, provided scholarly insights from a Jewish point of view, and encouraged the Church to take a strong stand against antisemitism.

Progress on an official statement was slowed for a time by the death of Pope John XXIII. But after a new pope was named, the document slowly began to take shape. It was revised again and again as Catholic leaders struggled to find common ground. At one point, Heschel learned that a new draft proclaimed that "the Church expects in unshakable faith and with ardent desire . . . the union of the Jewish people with the Church." Outraged, Heschel explained why he and other Jews would find such a statement offensive.

> Jews throughout the world will be dismayed by a call from the Vatican to abandon their faith in a generation which witnessed the massacre of six million Jews and the destruction of thousands of synagogues on a continent where the dominant religion was not Islam, Buddhism, or Shintoism.
>
> It is noteworthy that the Vatican document on [Muslims] makes no reference to the expectation of the Church for their conversion to the Christian faith. Is one to deduce . . . that Islam offers a more acceptable way to salvation than Judaism?
>
> Our world, which is full of cynicism, frustration and despair, received a flash of inspiration in the ecumenical work of Pope John XXIII. For a few years all men of good will marveled at the spiritual magnificence which he disclosed, and were touched by his reverence for the humanity of man. At a time of decay of conscience he tried to revive it and to teach how to respect it. Mutual reverence between Christians and Jews began to fill the hearts. We ardently pray that this great blessing may not vanish.[11]

The sentence Heschel objected to was dropped from the final draft of the document known as *Nostra Aetate*. And Heschel took pride in the fact that it was "the first Christian discourse dealing with Judaism—which is devoid of any expression of hope for conversion."[12] To some Catholics, he seemed overly sensitive. After all, the Church was not calling for forced conversion. Susannah Heschel suggests one reason for her father's sensitivity:

> Words, he often wrote, are themselves sacred, God's tool for creating the universe, and our tools for bringing holiness—or evil—into the world. He used to remind us that the Holocaust did not begin with the building of crematoria, and Hitler did not

come to power with tanks and guns; it all began with uttering evil words, with defamation, with language and propaganda. Words create worlds, he used to tell me when I was a child. They must be used very carefully. Some words, once having been uttered, gain eternity and can never be withdrawn. The Book of Proverbs reminds us, he wrote, that death and life are in the power of the tongue.[13]

The *Nostra Aetate* did not end antisemitism, prejudice, or discrimination, but it was an important step on a longer journey. The document inspired other steps, more statements of principle, and further dialogue. At a meeting in 1985 to mark the twentieth anniversary of the document, Pope John Paul II, the first Polish-born pope, stated:

Jews and Christians must get to know each other better. Not just superficially as people of different religions, merely coexisting in the same place, but as members of religions which are so closely linked to one another. This implies that Christians try to know as exactly as possible the distinctive beliefs, religious practices, and spirituality of the Jews, and conversely that the Jews try to know the beliefs and practices and spirituality of Christians. . . . Jewish-Christian relations are never an academic exercise.[14]

In 1990, on the twenty-fifth anniversary of the *Nostra Aetate*, Poland's bishops reflected on the relationship between Christians and Jews in Poland:

We Poles have particular ties with the Jewish people from as early as the first centuries of our history. Poland became for many Jews a second fatherland. The majority of Jews living the world today are by origin from the territories of the previous and current Polish commonwealth. Unfortunately, in our century this particular land became the grave for several million Jews. Not by our wish, and not by our hands. . . .

Many Poles saved Jews during the last war. Hundreds, if not thousands, paid for this with their own lives and the lives of their loved ones. For each of the Jews saved there was a whole chain of hearts of people of good will and helping hands. The express testimony of that help to Jews in the years of the Hitler occupation are the many trees dedicated to Poles in Yad Vashem, the place of national memory in Jerusalem, with the honored title, "The Just Among the Nations" given to many Poles. In spite of so many heroic examples of help on the part of Polish Christians, there were also people who remained indifferent to this incomprehensible tragedy. We are especially disheartened by those among Catholics who were in some way the cause of the death of Jews. They will forever gnaw at our conscience on the social plane. If only one Christian could have helped and did not stretch out a helping hand to a Jew during the time of danger or caused his death, we ask for forgiveness of our Jewish brothers and sisters. We are aware that many of our compatriots still remember the injustices and injuries committed by the postwar communist authorities, in which people of Jewish origin also took part. We must acknowledge, however, that the source of inspiration of their activity was clearly neither their origin nor religion, but the communist ideology, from which the Jews themselves, in fact, suffered many injustices.

We express our sincere regret for all the incidents of antisemitism which were committed at any time or by anyone on Polish soil. We do this in the deep conviction that all incidents of antisemtism are contrary to the spirit of the Gospel and—as Pope John Paul II recently emphasized—"remain opposed to the Christian vision of human dignity."

In expressing our sorrow for all the injustices and harm done to Jews, we cannot forget that we consider untrue and deeply harmful the use by many of the concept of what is called "Polish antisemitism" as an especially threatening form of that anti-semitism; and in addition, frequently connecting the concentration camps not with those who were actually involved with them, but with Poles in a Poland occupied by the Germans. Speaking of the unprecedented extermination of Jews, one cannot forget and even less pass over in silence the fact that the Poles as nation were one of the first victims of the same criminal racist ideology of Hitler's Nazism.

The same land, which for centuries was the common fatherland of Poles and Jews, of blood spilled together, the sea of horrific suffering and of injuries shared—should not divide us but unite us. For this commonality cries out to us—especially the places of execution and, in many cases, common graves. We Christians and Jews are also united in our belief in one God, the Creator and Lord of the entire universe, who created man in his image and likeness. We are united by the commonly accepted ethical principles included in the Ten Commandments, crowned by the love of God and neighbor. We are united in our respect for the biblical books of the Old Testament as the word of God and by common traditions of prayer. Last, we are united in the common hope of the final coming of the kingdom of God. . . .

The most important way to overcome the difficulties that still exist today is the establishment of a dialogue will lead to the elimination of distrust, prejudices and stereotypes, and to mutual acquaintance and understanding based on respect for our separate traditions as well as opening the way to cooperation in many fields. It is important, moreover, that while doing this, we learn to experience and appreciate the proper religious contexts of Jews and Christians as they are lived by Jews and Christians themselves.[15]

CONNECTIONS

When asked on what basis do people of different religions come together, Rabbi Heschel replied: "First and foremost, we meet as human beings who have much in common: a heart, a face, a voice, the presence of a soul, fears, hope, the ability to trust, a capacity for compassion and understanding, the kinship of being human."[16] How are his views of interfaith encounters similar to those of Pope John Paul II? Why do you think both stressed the importance of coming together as individuals rather than as representatives of groups?

Why did Rabbi Heschel believe so strongly in the power of words? What kinds of words "once having been uttered, gain eternity and can never be withdrawn"? How are those words reflected in the document prepared by the Polish bishops? In what words do they take pride? What words do they find hurtful, even offensive? Keeping in mind that a dialogue is not a debate, if you were to enter into the kind of dialogue the bishops call for, what would you like them to know? What would you like to learn? What questions might you ask of them?

In 1990, Pope John Paul II stated:

One of the more important tasks of the Church is the education of a young generation in a spirit of mutual roots, and our common tasks in the contemporary world. But [the Church] must also bring up the young generation to learn about their own distinctiveness and identity. I heartily bless all the efforts which serve this goal.[17]

What kind of experiences would promote that kind of education for young Catholics? What experiences would you add or delete in educating young Jews, Protestants, and Muslims?

Rabbi Heschel once said, "In our age, antisemitism is anti-Christianity and anti-Christianity is antisemitism." How does he regard the relationship between Christians and Jews? What does his statement mean for Jews? What does it mean for Christians?

In 1995, on the 50th anniversary of the liberation of Auschwitz, Pope John Paul II reflected on "one of the darkest and most tragic moments in history."

> God forbid that tomorrow we have to weep over other Auschwitzes of our time. Let us pray and work that this may not happen. Never again antisemitism! Never again the arrogance of nationalism! Never again genocide! May the third millennium usher in a season of peace and mutual respect among peoples.[18]

How do the Pope's remarks reflect Heschel's belief that words are "God's tool for creating the universe, and our tools for bringing holiness—or evil—into the world"?

Shortly before his death in 1972, Abraham Heschel attended a conference of religious leaders. Each day the group opened its meetings with prayers. On the day Heschel led those prayers, he told the group, "It is important for me to remember now, that while I have prayed from the heart for the Muslims all my life, I have never prayed with them before, or been face-to-face to talk about God. This is so important. We must go further."[19] What was he suggesting unites people of different faiths? Why does he stress the importance of opening a dialogue with what people have in common rather than on the issues that divide them? The word *ecumenical* comes from a Greek word meaning "of the whole world." Why is that an appropriate name for interfaith dialogues?

"And You?"

Religious leaders are not the only ones who have reflected on questions of questions of guilt and responsibility, the duty to remember and the longing to forget, and, most of all, prevention. Ordinary citizens also think about such questions.

James Carroll is a Catholic who was born in the United States during World War II. A few years ago, he inherited a clock that his mother bought in Germany after the war. He writes:

> I love the clock for the carved mahogany case, the rhythm of the ticking, the dependable consolation of the musical strokes—and the reminder of my stalwart mother.
>
> But lately the clock has come to mean something else as well. I have found it impossible to keep from wondering whose clock it was before my mother found it in a rough warehouse near the Rhine River in Wiesbaden. Recent news stories have systematically revealed how the possessions of Europe's annihilated Jews found their way into the homes of respectable people; their savings accounts in the general funds of impeccably credentialed Swiss banks; their gold and jewels into the vaults of prestigious institutions from Spain to Argentina; their art onto the walls of great museums, including the Louvre—all without compensation to anyone.
>
> In Paris, apartments and houses that once belonged to Jews are now known to have been efficiently appropriated by others, again without purchase. These revelations underscore the great but still largely unaddressed fact of the Holocaust—that while small minorities of Europeans either actively cooperated in the anti-Jewish genocide or actively resisted it, the vast majority not only looked the other way, but in subtle ways benefited from the disappearance of the Jews.
>
> Now I find myself staring at my mother's clock, half hypnotized by the swinging pendulum, the metronome click of which seems to ask a question: And you? Who are you to assume complete innocence?
>
> I was born in 1943, the year the jurist Raphael Lemkin coined the word "genocide." Already, by then, most of the murders of Jews had been carried out. People of my generation have viewed the Holocaust from the moral high ground as a crime for which we bear no responsibility.
>
> Yet the Holocaust was not simply what happened to Jews between 1933 and 1945. It involved not only the 6 million, but the tens of millions of their lost progeny. Imagine the music they would be composing, the science they would be discovering, the books they would be writing, the neighbors they would make. It is the absence of that Jewish legion that the world has come increasingly to feel as a real presence.
>
> History must name forever the perpetrators of the Final Solution, and the particular crime of Nazis must never be generalized. I am not asserting the properly derided theory of "corporate guilt," because it is true that if all are guilty, no one is. Nevertheless, the broader culture within which the genocide occurred is morally polluted by what happened. That is what the endless revelations of at least passive complicity are telling us.
>
> Who benefited? The Holocaust must continue to put its question to individuals, institutions, and nations. What about the unclaimed money in Switzerland, not

in 1945, but now? What about Picasso's "Head of a Woman," known to have been in the private collection of one Alphonse Kann, but now hanging in the Pompidou Center? What about the unfinished moral legacies of universities, churches, and nations?

And, yes, what about my mother's clock? Unlike meticulously recorded bank accounts, famous art works, or real estate, the provenance of this lovely but finally ordinary timepiece can never be established. That means that I can never know that it was stolen from a Jewish family, and, equally, that I can never know that it wasn't. In that way, my mother's clock has taken on a new character as a chiming icon—"And you?"—of this century's final question.

In an era of mass murder massively exploited and massively denied, why shouldn't the conscience of the West still be uneasy?[20]

CONNECTIONS

Carroll writes that "it is the absence of that Jewish legion that the world has come increasingly to feel as a real presence." What does he mean? In what sense can people who are absent be "a presence"?

Why does Carroll believe that this century's final question is "And you?" What did that question mean during the Holocaust? In the 1970s, three million Bangladeshis and over a million Khmers in Cambodia were victims of mass murder. In the 1980s the Chinese were accused of genocide in Tibet. The same charge was leveled in both the Balkans and Rwanda in the 1990s. What did the question mean then? What does it mean today?

Why does Carroll sees his mother's clock as a legacy of the Holocaust? What kind of legacy is it? How would you answer the question he asks in his closing paragraph? How might the religious leaders described in the previous reading answer it?

Judgment

In 1939, as Hitler planned the invasion of Poland, he asked, "Who after all, speaks today of the annihilation of the Armenians?" During World War I, Turkey, which then ruled the Ottoman Empire, turned against the Armenians, a Christian minority that had lived for generations within the empire. Accused of divided loyalties, the Armenians became the century's first victims of genocide. It was a crime that was never judged or acknowledged.

Toward the end of World War II, as rumors of Nazi atrocities were confirmed, the leaders of the United States, Britain, France, and the Soviet Union decided that this time they would try the individuals responsible for crimes against humanity before an international court. This time, the perpetrators would be held accountable for their actions.

On November 14, 1946, the Allies brought to trial twenty-two Nazi leaders accused of one or more of the following crimes: conspiracy to commit crimes; crimes against peace; war crimes; crimes against humanity. The defendants were the most prominent Nazis the Allies could find at the time. Many of the best-known Nazis, including Adolf Hitler, were not tried at all. They committed suicide in the final days of the war. Others, like Adolf Eichmann, disappeared during the confusion that marked Germany's defeat.

That trial was the first of thirteen separate trials held in Nuremberg, Germany, between 1946 and 1950. John Fried, the Special Legal Consultant to the United States War Crimes Tribunals, said of them, "The story of the Nuremberg tribunals offers a concrete instance in which an individual's responsible for a terrible crime is examined before the world. Not an abstract debate, but a life and death matter for the defendants, those age-old questions converged in the city of Nuremberg, and the standards established in that trial have become part of the unwritten law of nations ever since."21

Each of the four Allied nations that occupied a part of Germany immediately after the war held its own war-crimes trials in its zone of occupation. Together, Britain, France, and the United States convicted over 5,000 Nazis and sentenced 800 to death. The Soviets held similar trials but did not release statistics. Trials also took place in nations once occupied by Germany. The Poles and the Czechs, for example, convicted and executed Jurgen Stroop, the SS leader who "liquidated" the Warsaw Ghetto; Rudolf Hoess, the commandant of Auschwitz; and Arthur Greiser, the man who set up the first death camp at Chelmno.

By the 1950s, the trials seemed to be over, even though a number of Nazi war criminals were still at large. Most countries were eager to put the war behind them. Only Israel, which became an independent nation in 1948, remained committed to bringing every perpetrator to justice. The Israelis were particularly eager to capture Adolf Eichmann, Hitler's "expert" on the "Jewish Question." He was the one who set up the ghettos. And later he was the one who arranged for the deportation of hundreds of thousands of Jews to the death camps. Much of Eichmann's work took place behind the scenes. As a result, the Allies knew little about him. While they were trying top Nazi officials at Nuremberg, Eichmann was hiding in a prisoner-of-war camp. In 1950 he managed to emigrate to Argentina. Using the name "Ricardo Klement," he traveled on a passport issued by the Vatican to "displaced persons."

In May of 1960, the Israelis found Eichmann and smuggled him out of Argentina to stand trial in Jerusalem. In February, 1961, he was indicted on fifteen counts, including "crimes against the Jewish people," "crimes against humanity," and "war crimes." In his opening statement, Gideon Hausner, Israel's chief prosecutor, told the court:

> As I stand here before you, Judges of Israel, to lead the prosecution of Adolf Eichmann, I do not stand alone. With me, in this place and at this hour, stand six million accusers. But they cannot rise to their feet and point an accusing finger towards the man who sits in the glass dock and cry: "I accuse." For their ashes are piled up on the hills of Auschwitz and in the fields of Treblinka, or washed away by the rivers of Poland; their graves are scattered over the length and breadth of Europe. Their blood cries out, but their voices are not heard. Therefore it falls to me to be their spokesman and to unfold in their name the awesome indictment.[22]

As the trial unfolded, Hausner examined the history of Nazi Germany, from Hitler's rise to power through the planning and implementation of the Holocaust. He entered 1,600 documents into evidence including Jurgen Stroop's own account of how the Nazis put down the uprising in the Warsaw Ghetto. Hausner also called over one hundred witnesses, many of them survivors. Among those who testified were Yitzhak Zuckerman, Zivia Lubetkin, David Wdowinski, and Abba Kovner. (See Chapters 4-6.) At earlier trials, prosecutors had relied on the documents the Nazis left behind to prove their case. These documents were so detailed that Holocaust survivors were rarely asked to testify. Now for the first time, they were encouraged to tell the world what the Nazis had done to them, their families, friends, and neighbors.

Eichmann's lawyer, Robert Servatius, did not dispute the testimony of the survivors or the accuracy of the documents offered in evidence. Instead, he defended Eichmann as a man who was merely "following orders." The court disagreed. It ruled that "obedience to orders" does not relieve an individual of moral responsibility. Eichmann was sentenced to death.

Throughout the trial, Israelis stood silently in the streets and listened as loudspeakers broadcast the proceedings. People in other countries also followed the trial. No group was more deeply affected by the trial than Holocaust survivors. For the first time, many heard someone tell their story in a court of law. In his memoirs, Hausner described the mail he received from survivors:

> Some sent in the yellow badges of ghetto days which they had kept all these years. A man sent me a picture of three little children riding ponies, and wrote: "This is their last picture, from summer 1939. They were all killed in Treblinka, and against the laws of nature I, their father, survived them. I empower you to charge Eichmann also on behalf of these three innocent children.". . .
> "When I was discharged from Bergen-Belsen as a girl of fourteen," wrote a woman of Jerusalem, "I always hoped that one day I would be able to avenge the loss of my parents and of my whole family, though I did not know what revenge was. I could do nothing all these years, but now, having listened to the trial, I feel some relief."
> There were other letters laden with emotion. "I kept my tears back all these years. I can weep now," wrote a woman saved as a child from the Kovno ghetto. "Our neighbors here will now stop wondering how we managed to survive," wrote a couple in a joint letter.
> "I was ten years old when I was liberated," wrote a member of a kibbutz. "Fourteen years of life in this country have corrected much of my distorted childhood,

but I had to live and see this trial to relive all the horror, to be able to live it down."

"I relive with you the tragic days," a schoolteacher wrote to me. "I was nine years old that summer in 1942 when my despairing parents, who were about to be deported, delivered me to their Christian neighbors. With their help I survived," wrote a woman who signed with initials only. "I saw and passed through a lot, and later related these things, without ever shedding a tear. It was only when listening to your opening address that the clock was put backward and the tears of the small orphan girl came out now, after nineteen years. Thank you for helping me to cry."[23]

CONNECTIONS

What is the purpose of a trial: Is it to judge the guilty, avenge the victims, or warn those who might commit similiar acts in the future?

When Hitler asked, "Who after all, speaks today of the annihilation of the Armenians," what was he saying about war? Some Armenians believe that if the perpetrators of the Armenian Genocide had been prosecuted and punished after World War I, the trial might have served as deterrent for the Holocaust. Do you agree?

Was Israel right to kidnap and try Eichmann or should some other nation have assumed responsibility? How would your answer change if no other country was willing to do so?

The Eichmann trial was the first to make extensive use of the testimony of survivors. What might their words add to the trial that official reports, memos, letters, and other evidence cannot provide? How do you account for the response of survivors to the trial? What happens to a history that is not judged or acknowledged?

Education and Memory

Rose Murra is a Holocaust survivor who now lives in the United States. She recalls that after the Nazis murdered her father, brother, and uncle, her mother told her repeatedly, "Don't ever forget to tell the story." Rose Murra never forgot her mother's words, but for many years, few people were willing to listen to her story or those of other survivors.

In bringing Adolf Eichmann to trial, Israeli leaders hoped to not only punish him for his crimes but also educate people about the Holocaust. To a large measure, they succeeded. "The period of amnesia ended with the Eichmann trial," recalls an American Jew. "The trial brought to the surface a lot of things that people had suppressed, ripped that all wide open. A nation was suddenly riveted." Gideon Hausner, the chief prosecutor at the trial, described the letters people sent him:

Many writers, especially from Africa and the Far East, who sounded as if this were the first time they had heard of the Jewish disaster, expressed their intense indignation and dismay. People would give vent to their emotions in different ways, ranging from a few words scribbled on a simple piece of paper in remote Finland to a long cable dispatched from New York. They felt a need and a desire to identify themselves with us and give some expression to their feelings. . . .

The greater part of these letters, over five thousand of them, arrived from Israel. It was the overwhelming popular reaction of a nation shocked to the core. Many, notably youngsters, too ashamed to reveal themselves but still wishing to react somehow, expressed their emotions in various ways. . . .

A girl wrote saying she had no uncles and aunts to visit on Saturdays and holidays, like other children, but had never understood before why they were all dead.

"The trial explained to me the behavior of the six million from a human point of view," wrote a youngster of fifteen from Haifa. A girl of seventeen from Ramat Gan went further. "I could not honor all my relatives about whom I heard from my father. I loathed them for letting themselves be slaughtered. Thank you for opening my eyes to what had really happened."[24]

Young American Jews had similar reactions. One man recalled the day the principal of his Hebrew School told of his experiences during the Holocaust. As the students listened spellbound, "Rabbi Aidelson went on to tell us that when he first came to America, he never talked about these experiences because no one wanted to hear about them. 'No one wanted to touch the wounds,' was the way he put it. But even though I was only a kid of ten or eleven when I heard his story it touched me in a way the made-for-television movies never had."[25]

Another Jew remembers being uncomfortable with stories about the Holocaust. "When I found out what happened, I was ashamed. I wondered how the Jews could have let the Nazis do that to them. I thought the Germans couldn't have killed that many if the Jews didn't cooperate. . . . I was embarrassed that these people who marched to their deaths without fighting were my people. I was a tough kid, and if somebody tried to do something to me I fought back."[26] Max Wechsler had similar views of the Holocaust until he became friends with a survivor. He recalls:

I was minding my own business on a Sunday afternoon, listening to the Yankee game on the radio, when my sister's current boyfriend came into my room. He had been going with her for a few weeks and was a refugee—thin, bent, broken. He spoke with a thick accent. I'd always thought of the DPs [Displaced Persons], those former concentration camp inmates, with a little bit of contempt. How could they have let what happened happen? The few times antisemitic slurs had been hurled at me, I always fought back. But from what I had learned about these people, they went like sheep to be slaughtered. That was something I could not understand.

Now this guy was in my room—hovering over me, intruding, switching the station on my radio to some classical music. There were a few brief moments of objection on my part. Then my mother intervened: "He's a guest. Let him listen to whatever he wants."

He might have been a guest, but he was an unwelcome one. And someone whom I had absolutely nothing in common with. Baseball was what you listened to on the radio. You didn't listen to classical music.

Yet somehow, in the weeks and months that followed, this man and I developed a relationship. He told me about the Nazi sadists and a German nation that went mad. He spoke about people losing all their dignity, having their heads shaved, forced to work in subzero temperatures with the thinnest of clothing.

The whole subject began to take on a personal dimension. The names of the camps and their commandants, the maps of Poland, Germany, and Czechoslovakia formed and reformed in my mind just like the makeup of the baseball teams and their rosters. Only baseball was such an upside to my teenage life whereas his chilling testimony cited horror after horror. I learned what a ghetto was, what it was like to have to wear the yellow star, what it was like to have German shepherds nip at your fingers and your knees, what it was like to be separated, cut up, carved up from those you loved, what it was like to see your family die.

Hundreds of hours of conversation with him changed my macho American-Jewish boy stance, made me see and feel the enormity of what had happened. The shame I felt about the European Jews not fighting back was gone. In its place was compassion and sympathy for all of their losses and a rage and fury at the Nazi murderers.[27]

CONNECTIONS

Why were American and Israeli Jews reluctant "to touch the wounds"? What did they fear?

The son of Holocaust survivors told an interviewer, "We talk about the Holocaust; we memorialize it. But on some level, I don't think we comprehend the way our Jewish identity has been shaken and obliterated." Why did many American and Israeli Jews feel embarrassment or shame about the Holocaust? What were they embarrassed about? What were they ashamed of? What prompted some to revise the way they felt? How does the Holocaust affect the ways Jews you have met or read about define their identity? How does it affect the way you see yourself and others?

In "I Dream in Good English Too," Donia Blumenfeld Clenman, a survivor who now lives in Canada, writes of her children's inability to understand her history. What does she suggest they fear? How was that fear reflected in this reading? Why might it be even greater for children or grandchildren of survivors? How do your answers explain why she finds it difficult to be a "normal Canadian mother"?

Sometimes
I am a stranger to my family
for I bring Europe's ghosts
into the well-lit living room
of Canadian internationalism
and mobile,
passionately objective youth.

My scars are nicely healed,
and my concerns properly intellectual,
yellow with the stamp of legality
of naturalization papers
twenty years old.
Yet somehow
the smoke of the past
darkens Heinz's clear consommé
and, though only a witness,
I spread fear
by my very presence,
a living fossil
at a table worshipping the "Now."

They love me deeply
and tenderly,
yet would exorcise a part of me,
dreading an eruption of memory
no matter how oblique
to force them
into captive partnership.

This is my past
not theirs,
their hostile glances shout.
We are all descendants of Adam.
Why bring Abraham
into happy Canadian homes?

I was no child on arrival
and yet, so well assimilated,
even my verses are native,
and I dream in good English too.
So I put on the ointment of reason
and tape heartbreak with Band-Aids
and they are relieved,
and reassured,
to get back
their normal Canadian mother.[28]

In "Those Who Remain," Rachel Goldstein, the daughter of Holocaust survivors, also writes of fear. Whose fears does she describe? How might those fears shape the way she views the past and the present?

> They name their children
> for the dead,
> tie red ribbons on their wrists
> to keep away the "evil eye,"
> carry extra fruit and sandwiches
> in old cloth sacks, just in case.
> Over pots of warm tea and honey
> they unfurl stories about
> the lost villages of their hearts,
> and sing to their children,
> "You were not there, you were not there."[29]

Monuments and Memorials

Anniversaries, birthdays, and holidays are ways of remembering the past. So are photos, diaries, and poems. Some memorials are monuments— structures that tell of acts of courage or recall great tragedies. Each aims to preserve the collective memory of the generation that built the monument and shape the memories of generations to come.

After the Holocaust, some survivors returned to their former homes only to find strangers living in their houses. Their synagogues were destroyed and their cemeteries in ruins. In many places, the Nazis had machine-gunned the tombstones and then ground the broken slabs into dust. In other places, the stones were used to pave roadways, sidewalks, and courtyards. Even those tombstones left untouched had crumbled from years of neglect or were choked by tall weeds, twisted vines, and thick grass.

A number of survivors tried to reconsecrate their cemeteries. Sometimes this meant gathering up the broken gravestones and piling them into great heaps. In a few places, people built pyramids and obelisks from the broken fragments of the tombstones. According to James E. Young, these memorials are a reminder that "memory is never seamless but always a montage of collected fragments, recomposed by each person and generation."

Five years after the uprising in the Warsaw Ghetto, Jews around the world contributed to a memorial to mark both the heroism of Jewish resistance to the Nazis and the destruction of the Jews of Eastern Europe. The sculptor, Natan Rapoport, was a Jew from Warsaw who fled to Russia just three months before the Germans invaded Poland in 1939. He was living in Siberia when he heard about the uprising. Deeply moved by the story, he told friends that he lived only to create a monument to the fighters.

Today Rapoport's monument stands in the midst of a well-kept square surrounded by apartment buildings. In 1948, when it was unveiled, it was the only standing structure in "a moonscape of rubble." The seven heroic men and women on the monument's western wall appeared to be fighting their way out of that rubble, out of the burning ghetto. The monument is dedicated "To the Jewish People—Its Heroes and Its Martyrs." But at first glance, viewers see only heroes. The martyrs are on the opposite side of the monument. They are represented by twelve stooped and huddled figures, one for each of the twelve tribes of Israel. They seem to be marching from right to left across the monument before disappearing into the granite. Three Nazi helmets and two bayonets in the background suggest their

Natan Rapoport's monument to the Warsaw Ghetto uprising.

fate. Eleven of the twelve trudge along with their eyes to the ground. The twelfth is a rabbi holding a Torah scroll in one arm. He alone looks up to the heavens as if to beseech God.

In 1964, the Poles dedicated yet another memorial to Jewish victims of the

Holocaust; this one was at Treblinka, the Nazi death camp where 850,000 Jews were murdered, many of them from Warsaw. In a nation now nearly empty of Jews, sculptor Franciszek Duszenko and architect Adam Haupt created a memorial that resembles a huge graveyard. They set 17,000 granite shards in concrete and then inscribed several hundred of the stones with the names of *shtetlach,* Jewish villages, destroyed during the Holocaust. At the center of the shattered landscape is a 40-foot obelisk that is split from top to bottom. A menorah, a candelabra with seven branches, is carved into the top of the structure. At the base is a stone tablet with the words "Never Again" in Yiddish, Russian, English, French, German, and Polish.

A memorial to Jewish victims of the Holocaust at Treblinka.

CONNECTIONS

Every memorial tells a story. What is the message of the Warsaw Ghetto memorial? Who is the messenger? Who is the audience—that is, at whom is the message aimed? What is the message of the memorial at Treblinka? Who is the messenger? Who is the audience?

Before World War II, Jews made up about 10 percent of Poland's population. Today only a few thousand Jews live in the country. Whose memory is being shaped by memorials like those described in this reading?

When asked why his monuments feature individuals rather than abstract symbols, Nathan Rapoport replied, "Could I have made a stone with a hole in it and said, 'Voila! The heroism of the Jews'?" How would you answer the questions he raises? Does a monument have to be lifelike to show heroism?

Only one of the sharp-toothed granite stones at Treblinka is inscribed with a person's name. In 1978, on the hundredth anniversary of Janusz Korczak's birth, a stone carved with his name was set among the others. Every year on the anniversary of his deportation, people leave freshly-cut flowers and wreaths on that stone. Sometimes the note that accompanies the flowers is written in Hebrew and sometimes in Polish. Review the readings that focus on the life of Janusz Korczak in Chapters 2-5. Why do you think he was singled out?

Monuments tell a story in symbols rather than words. Every detail, even the location of the memorial, contributes to that story. As people walk through the monument they make meaning of their experience. The poem and the paragraph that follow it were written by individuals who visited memorials at Auschwitz and Treblinka. What meaning does each find in the memorial? How does each help us understand why "memory is never seamless but always a montage of collected fragments, recomposed by each person and each generation"?

In the Museum at Auschwitz

I stare at shoes. I cannot move
away from them, abandoned
pressed against the glass between us,
thousands of separated
pairs, some curled as if still
running, some crushed
beneath the weight of
those above them,
some try to reach heaven.

The sign reads:
Shoes Collected from the Inmates.
Which shoes did
my grandfather wear?

My father hardly spoke
of him, or maybe I don't remember.
Perhaps the one with the buckle
loosely hanging on,
or the one with twisted straps,
like barbed wire.
I keep staring,
but all that is revealed
is my own reflection
laced in wordless prayer.
I am what remains.[30]

Rachel Goldstein

Then I saw a bird. I remembered the poem "The Birds Don't Sing in Treblinka." Not knowing why, my feet followed this bird as it took flight. Suddenly, the bird disappeared. Awakened to my surroundings, I gasped: the stone in front of me was quite large, and it read "Opoczon." This is it, this was my grandparents' home town. For the first time in my life, I felt connected. I came from somewhere. I belong. I am alive. And though the birds don't sing, and the stones stand silently for the world to see, I remember, and so should we all.[31]

Anabela Moskovitz

In 1996, 4000 people in Warsaw attended the opening of a photography exhibition entitled "And I Still See Their Faces."[32] It featured pictures of Jewish life in Poland from the late 1800s to the Holocaust. The organizers of the exhibit found the pictures by placing ads in Polish newspapers and magazines asking for old photos of Jewish life. They received over 8,000 pictures from which they chose 400 for display. Some people sent in snapshots in the hope that a face would be recognized or that, perhaps, a friend had somehow managed to survive.

Why do you think so many people saved photographs of Jews? Why do you think so many others were drawn to pictures that show "assimilated, observant, modern, and traditional Jews, rich and poor, the influences of Yiddish and Hebrew, Socialism and Zionism, all creating an exuberant and forceful world, now lost"?

If you were to create a memorial to the Holocaust, what would you want visitors to remember? What would your memorial look like? Where would you want it placed?

Politics and Memory

Over the years, the memorial to the uprising in the Warsaw Ghetto has been the center of a struggle for memory in Poland. In 1983, that struggle revealed some of the links between the past and the present.

In 1980, a group of Polish workers at a shipyard in Gdansk formed a union known as Solidarity. Their calls for democratic reform inspired other protests, other demands for change. Poland's communist leaders responded to Solidarity's growing popularity by outlawing the union. When the protests continued and even grew, the government placed the entire nation under military rule. Countries around the world condemned the action. In an effort to improve their image abroad, the Communists decided to hold a special ceremony to mark the 40th anniversary of the Warsaw Ghetto uprising in the spring of 1983. They invited dignitaries from all over the world to participate.

Among the invited guests was Marek Edelman of the Bund. In 1983, he was one of the very few surviving leaders of the uprising and the only one to make his home in Poland. He was now a cardiologist in Lodz. In public letter dated February 2, 1983, he explained why he would not take part in the official ceremonies:

> Forty years ago we fought not only for our lives. We fought for life in dignity and freedom. To celebrate our anniversary here where social life is dominated throughout by humiliation and coercion would be to deny our fight. It would mean participating in something contrary to its ideals. It would be an act of cynicism and contempt. I shall not participate in such arrangements or accept the participation of others who do so, regardless of where they come from or whom they represent. Far from these manipulated celebrations, in the silence of the graves and in people's hearts, there shall live the true memory of the victims and the heroes, the memory of the eternal human striving for freedom and truth.[33]

The Communists went ahead with their plans for a commemoration on April 19 without Edelman. Just days before it was to take place, they learned that Solidarity intended to hold its own rally at the Warsaw Ghetto Memorial. Government officials immediately placed Edelman under house arrest and jailed the union's top officials, but they could not stop the rally itself. Several hundred people gathered at the monument to hear Janusz Onyszkiewicz, a spokesperson for the union. He read a message from union leaders declaring that the ideals that motivated Solidarity were similar to those that had prompted the uprising in the Warsaw Ghetto. As soon as he finished the statement, he too was arrested. Another member of the union then stepped forward and read a letter from Edelman praising Solidarity and its ideals. Journalist Hanna Krall later reflected on Edelman's stand:

> His decision not to participate in the official commemoration in 1983 seemed to me at first dubious; I felt that over those ashes there should be a moment of silence amidst all that political noise. But after everything that happened on April 17th, the rally and Onszkiewicz's speech and all—I understood for the first time that the Ghetto uprising had now become a Polish thing. Because the truth is there had always been the main road of the Polish resistance movement, and alongside it there had run this honored though seldom-used path (because who ever traveled it?) of the

fight of Jews. Thanks to the commemoration organized by Solidarity about which everybody soon knew, thanks to Edelman, and thanks to the regime, which precisely on the 40th anniversary of the uprising greeted its leader with a house-arrest, this Jewish path became for a while part of this whole Polish war story. And when Edelman was sitting in his house surrounded by the police cars, . . . not even for a moment did he have the feeling that he was alone. On the contrary, he had the feeling of belonging to the world, to that world of fair and brave people, and beautiful, and calm.[34]

CONNECTIONS

What were the ideals of the Warsaw Ghetto Uprising? Did Edelman uphold those ideals by refusing to participate in the commemoration or should there have been "a moment of silence amidst all that political noise"? Edelman's statement was widely reprinted abroad. He had hoped that it would persuade Jews and Jewish organizations to boycott the official ceremony. Some Jews stayed home, but several thousand chose to attend. Were they right to do so?

How important was it that "this Jewish path became for a while part of the whole Polish war story"? What does your answer suggest about the power of memory? James E. Young says that "memory is never seamless but always a montage of collected fragments, recomposed by each person and generation." How do his words apply to the ceremonies marking the 40th anniversary of the uprising in the Warsaw Ghetto?

Reclaiming a Heritage

In 1989, Poland's communist government collapsed. The people of Poland replaced it with a democracy. With freedom, a growing number of Jews in Poland have begun to reclaim their identity. The same has been true of Jews in other parts of Eastern Europe. Once again, Eastern European Jews are organizing religious schools, lighting Sabbath candles, and celebrating Jewish holidays.

On a visit to Poland in the early 1990s, journalist Jonathan Kaufman was impressed by the vibrancy of the Jewish community emerging in a place where he and others had come to believe that there was no Jewish life. After commenting on a nursery school founded by Jews in Warsaw, Kaufman reported, "Dying communities, a friend of mine observed wryly, do not open nursery schools."[35]

Under communist rule, few Eastern European Jews were willing to call attention to their Jewish identity. It was safer to keep quiet in a region where the Communists maintained power by turning neighbor against neighbor. Yet even before the fall of communism, a few Polish Jews were beginning to publicly reclaim their Jewish identity. For some, it was a way of defying the government.

In 1983, Iwona Irwin-Zarecka, a sociologist and a Jew reared in Communist Poland, visited the nation. She was surprised to discover "young people, mostly in their thirties, who, together, with their children, celebrate Shabbat and Jewish holidays, who gather to learn and discuss Jewish history and Jewish philosophy, who avidly read books by and about Jews, written in French and English and acquired by whatever means possible." She went on to note:

> These young Jews have much more in common with young and not-so-young Jews in [North] America or France than they have with the older generations of Polish Jews. . . . They do not speak Yiddish, nor are they trying to learn it, Hebrew being their first choice as a link with Jewish culture. Avid readers, they are more versed in modern Jewish philosophy and theology than they are in the Torah. And those few who made their return to Jewishness a return to Judaism were following a highly individualized and highly intellectual road, one in which they have little in common with those who never left. Their religious observance does not easily fit into any existing categories. If they were in America, they would probably feel most at home within the Reform movement. This suggestion, however, is sheer speculation, for they do live in Poland where there is not much room for other than relatively orthodox forms of worship. . . .

According to Irwin-Zarecka, the younger generation was not alone in its return to Judaism. A number of older people were also rejoining the Jewish community. Many were Communists and communist sympathizers who had become disillusioned after the government launched its antisemitic campaign in 1968. She describes these older Jews as drawing "on memories of a traditional Jewish life, colored with much nostalgia." It is a nostalgia that their children and grandchildren do not share or even understand.

That kind of generation gap is not unique to Poland or to Eastern Europe. Many young Jews in the West also face a generation gap, but there are significant differences. Perhaps the most important in Irwin-Zarecka's view is that almost all young

Polish Jews are the children and grandchildren of Holocaust survivors. She compares and contrasts them with their counterparts in the West:

> It appears that while the individual stories vary, the majority of survivors [in the West] adopted silence as a way of sheltering their children from the horrors they experienced. Often, only the concentration camp number, tattooed on the arm, spoke of the past. Growing up not only without one's grandparents, aunts and uncles, but without the memory of their life and death, combined with a strong sense of being different from one's peers, would produce a great deal of anxiety, feelings of isolation and the need to know. Growing up laden with so much hope and importance by parents who had lost everything created a heavy psychological burden. It was difficult to break the silence, to start asking questions. It is still difficult for the "children of the Holocaust" to come to terms with their own experience and the experience of their parents.
>
> The story of Poland's "children of the Holocaust" is remarkably different; in contrast to those in North America, they grew up sharing in collective mourning, as it were. Many of their peers, Jews as well as non-Jews, came from families who had lost someone during the war, or from families with survivors of labor and concentration camps. . . . In short, being a "child of the Holocaust" and living in Poland carried little if any of the isolation and strangeness it would in America. It also meant being a part of a whole generation, the one born after the war and instilled with special hopes. The whole country and not the Jews alone, would be healing wounds and rebuilding life on the ruins.
>
> Yet if sharing in grief spared Poland's "children of the Holocaust" from feeling alone, it also made it difficult for them to approach the Holocaust as a uniquely Jewish experience. This perception is changing, but the change is a part of the general shift towards a recognition of the uniqueness of the Holocaust. For a child—and I am now speaking about myself as well—hearing stories of the often miraculous survival of the Jews was not sufficiently different from learning in school or watching a movie about the risky escapades of the resistance, for example. . . .
>
> What makes the experience of Poland's "children of the Holocaust" truly different, though, is the quality of the silence they grew up with. More generally, what makes these young Jews different from their Western counterparts is the sheer length of their return journey. For some, the starting point consists of a realization that Jewishness does matter. For others, it was the discovery often fairly late in life, that they were Jewish at all. . . .
>
> [As] I talked with these young "return" Jews," I came to realize that the biggest step they have taken so far has been the very acknowledgment of their Jewishness, an acknowledgment to themselves and to the outside world. . . .
>
> Set on being highly visible as Jews, they have not abandoned or even diminished their commitment to the cause of democratic Poland. In a way, theirs is a struggle reminiscent of the early nineteenth century plight of Jewish assimilationists, a struggle for a Poland where one could be a good Jew and a good Pole at the same time. The main difference, however, is that these young Jews now have a better grasp of Polish patriotism than they have of Jewish tradition—a reverse of the assimilation story. . . . They also have, (naturally enough, considering their upbringing within Polish culture and Polish values), an outlook on the world and ethic which are essentially Polish. . . .
>
> When I first heard of this small group of young Jews celebrating their Jewishness again—in early 1983, at the height of Polish media interest in things Jewish—my first reaction was a mixture of disbelief and awe at the sheer and irrational strength of the nearly undefinable bond of "feeling Jewish." When I first met them in the fall of that

year, I was touched to see children again singing Hebrew songs by Shabbat candles in Poland. Neither I nor my Warsaw companions would have thought it possible even in 1973. . . .

This is not to say that their experience was problem-free. . . . But for all its psychological difficulties. . . , this rediscovery of Jewish heritage did not appear to . . . make these young people suddenly strange or unacceptable. In fact, as I was to find out, their new Jewishness proved, if not fully comprehensible, at least quite attractive to their gentile friends. In some cases, it was because of the direct prompting and curiosity of their gentile friends that the search for some substance to "being Jewish" began. . . .

And today, while the observance of Shabbat and Jewish holidays might indeed be reserved for the Jewish members of the group, the work on projects in Polish Jewish history, the public and private discussions and the very active interest in things Jewish involve both young Jews and non-Jews. More importantly, perhaps, they involve a set of common questions about Poland and its Jewish heritage. Many a touchy question and many a blank spot is not only something they can share with each other, but something they can and do share in large part with their non-Jewish friends. . . .

Finally, and this is perhaps most important, the interest in things Jewish is very much a part of the larger struggle for a democratic Poland. A young Jew who was not always involved in the opposition, but now does so more and more as a Jew, is not abandoning his old ideals or his old friends. His journey might indeed be a very private affair, his experience of Jewishness of necessity different from interest alone, but his questions about the Jewish heritage are at the very center of a very wide and public debate on democracy, pluralism and "Polishness." He can and often does feel that what is at stake is the future of Poland. Paradoxically, his efforts to be more Jewish may be rendering him more Polish at the same time, or at least more committed to a Poland where his personal choices would indeed become a matter of personal choice.[36]

CONNECTIONS

In writing of the young Polish Jews who discovered their Jewish identity in the 1980s, Iwona Irwin-Zarecka emphasizes the importance of friendships in their journeys of discovery. How does being among friends make it easier to embark on a search for one's identity?

Early on the morning of February 26, 1997, Warsaw's only remaining synagogue was firebombed. To some it seemed as if the past were repeating itself. Yet there were important differences. Within hours of the incident, leaders in the Jewish community announced plans for an ecumenical service in the synagogue. Among those who came were the mayor of Warsaw, Poland's deputy prime minister, the American ambassador to Poland, and the president of the Gypsies. The Catholic Church made a public offer to repair the damage. Why do you think Jewish leaders arranged the ecumenical service? What message did they hope it would send? At whom was that message directed? What message were those who attended the service sending? At whom was their message directed? What message was the Church sending? At whom was it directed? How important was each of these messages?

In 1997, U.S. Secretary of State Madeleine Albright learned that even though she was raised as a Catholic, her parents were Jews who fled Czechoslovakia in 1939, just days after the Nazis occupied the country. After the war, they returned to Czechoslovakia but left again when the Communists took power in 1948. On a visit to the country of her birth in July of 1997, she reflected on what her newly discovered Jewish identity meant to her: "To the many values and many facts that make up who I am, I now add the knowledge that my grandparents and members of my family perished in the worst catastrophe in human history. So I leave here tonight with certainty that the new part of my identity adds something stronger, sadder, and richer to my life." How is Albright's journey of discovery similar to the ones described in this reading? What differences seem most striking?

Madeleine Albright's story is not unique. She is one of many people from Eastern Europe who have only recently become aware of their Jewish ancestry. After the war, some survivors of the Holocaust abandoned their Jewish identity in an effort to break with their painful past and ensure a safer life for their children. Albright said of the choice her parents made in 1939, "They clearly confronted the most excruciating decision a human being can face when they left members of their family behind even as they saved me from certain death. I will always love and honor my parents and will always respect their decision, for that painful of choices gave me life a second time." Why does she call their decision "the most excruciating" a human being can face?

Irwin-Zarecka writes of her disbelief and awe "at the sheer and irrational strength of the nearly undefinable bond of 'feeling Jewish.'" Why is she amazed at its strength? What does that strength suggest about the future of Judaism in Eastern Europe?

Restoring the Life That Was

In 1997, a Jewish woman in Poland told an American reporter, "My father didn't fight for being Jewish. He was just a Jew. You have to go to your roots and you have to check your history and bring the pieces of the broken glass and . . . try to put it together, but it will never become a mirror. You have to build your new image from the old pieces."[37] Jews in Poland are not alone in their efforts to put together the pieces of their heritage. Jews all over the world have been engaged in that process in the years since the Holocaust.

In a book written twenty-five years after the Holocaust, Elie Wiesel described a service he attended one Sabbath in a small shtibel, or prayerhouse, in New York. The Jews who gather there are Hasidim. Many of them are also survivors of the Holocaust. Wiesel writes:

> Attended yesterday, Saturday, an unexpected reception in honor of a young professor who comes to this shtibel for the same reasons I do: he loves and admires these miraculous survivors of another age who have remained steadfast in their fight against oblivion and sadness.
>
> The officiant had already started the service when one of the worshippers went up to the leader of the small community—Reb Leibele Cywiak—and whispered into his ear: "They say our young visitor is getting married this week."
>
> The service comes to a halt and the Hasidim flock around the bridegroom-to-be to congratulate him and offer their good wishes. Gruffly, Rabbi Cywiak pretends to be offended: "Why didn't you say anything? First of all, tradition requires that you be called to the Torah. Secondly, if I had known, I would have prepared a reception, a true-to-form Kiddush. But you wished to deprive us of that pleasure. That is not nice, young man, not nice at all."
>
> "Oh, you know . . . Why trouble you? After all. . ."
>
> "Trouble us, you say? Do you hear him, friends? He deprives us of a good deed and expects us to thank him! It is by taking us unawares, that you trouble us. . . Not nice, I tell you, not nice at all. . ."
>
> "Forgive me. . . Not important. . . Dislike receptions. . ."
>
> "How selfish can you be? You only think of yourself! What about us? Don't we count any more? It is written. . ."
>
> "It is written nowhere that the bridegroom must be entertained before the wedding. During and after—yes. Not before."
>
> From the privacy of my corner, I observe the young man. He is moved, but his emotions are under control. He seems shy, intimidated, that's all. Embarrassed. In the face of the rabbi's exuberance, he makes an effort not to blush. He blushes anyway.
>
> I notice the famous thinker A. J. Heschel. He too is watching the bridegroom.
>
> "Why so melancholy?" I ask him.
>
> "I look at this young man and I see him elsewhere. If not for the war. . ."
>
> "If not . . ."
>
> ". . . I know, I know. But sometimes, in my dreams, I put out the fire in time. I rediscover myself as I was before. And I remember. The customs of long ago. The Saturday preceding the wedding the whole town escorted the young man to the synagogue. He was treated like a prince and given the place of honor. As he was called to

the Torah, the congregation rose. And after he had recited the traditional prayers, he was showered with nuts, raisins and other sweets: symbols of abundance and good wishes. Then he was escorted home with great pomp. For hours and hours, there would be singing and dancing and drinking in his honor. The old men told stories, the troubadours composed songs. While now. . ."

"What do you expect?" I say, answering for the young man. "Times have changed, so have customs. We have unlearned the art of inviting joy and fervor."

We both fall silent. We know the young professor lost his parents. It is probably best to leave him to his thoughts.

Meanwhile, it is getting late. The service has been resumed. But Reb Leibele Cywiak and his friends are conferring in a corner.

"What? Let him leave like that, without anything?

"Empty-handed?"

"Inconceivable. . ."

"Inadmissible. . ."

"Let's arrange. . ."

". . . a reception? In one hour? And on Shabbat, no less? Impossible. . ."

"Even so. . ."

The young visitor is not one of the regulars; but his new status entitles him to full consideration and honors.

All of Israel's children are equal; one must love them equally and, if need be, prove it to them.

"All right," says the rabbi, "don't worry. We'll manage. It will not be said that we are giving up our traditions."

He quickly removes his ritual shawl and disappears behind the door leading to his private quarters. A half hour later he is back, more radiant than ever.

He catches up with the service; in the meantime we have reached the reading of the Torah. A conscientious stage director, the rabbi manages to communicate his secret instructions to the congregants without attracting the groom's attention.

The young man is the last to be called to the *bimah*. He is reciting the closing benediction when, suddenly, in response to the rabbi's signal, the other men take several steps backwards. Suddenly he finds himself alone. At first he looks lost and frightened. Then his face reflects profound and painful surprise, as nuts and raisins rain down on him, as in years gone by, as though he were still living in a world protected by his father.

I watch him close his eyes and I see the trembling. Through the ripped veil, no doubt, he is seeing the same things my own imagination is retrieving out of the irrevocable past. No doubt he grasps the distance separating him from that past. Any second he will give in: the tears he has held back so long will be allowed to flow.

But no, not here, not now, he seems to be telling himself, I must not let go. Not here, not anywhere, not ever. Think of something else, turn back to the present. You cannot let go. Be careful. Clench your fists until they ache, bite your lips until they bleed: not one tear must be shed. After all, you didn't train your will all these years just to come to this? And with an effort he hopes will go unnoticed, he reads the Haftorah and chants the benedictions; his voice does not betray him a single time.

His duty done, he withdraws into a corner for the second half of the service. More alone than ever, he seems even paler.

But the story does not end here. Reb Leibele Cywiak has further surprises in store: everybody is invited to an improvised reception. No sooner are seated than we are served wine, liqueurs, vodka and everything else one may expect to find at a Hasidic celebration.

Someone calls out: "Rabbi Cywiak, we didn't know you could work miracles!"

And our host, proud of his exploit, responds: "The continuation of a tradition, that is the true miracle!"

We fill the glasses, we drink to the young man's health and future happiness, we intone one song and then another. Almost like before, almost like over there, on the other side of war. And still the young man remains silent and aloof, breathing deeply, heavily, as if to calm his pounding heart. He gasps for air; his forehead is bathed in perspiration. I know his thoughts are with those who are absent, for his face, his eyes are clouded. If only he knew their resting place, he would follow tradition and go anywhere at all, to invite them to his wedding. But there is no place to go.

At the table, the guests make every effort to cheer him; some try to change his mood by teasing him, others speak to him in whispers.

Reb Leibele Cywiak calls for silence: "One day the Gerer Rebbe, may his sainted memory protect us, decided to question one of his disciples: How is Moshe Yaakov doing?—The disciple didn't know.—What! shouted the Rebbe, you don't know? You pray under the same roof with him, you study the same texts, you serve the same God, you sing the same songs, and you dare tell me you don't know whether Moshe Yaakov is in good health, whether he needs help, advice or comforting?

"Therein lies the essence of Hasidism," concludes our host, "it requires that every man share in every other man's life and not leave him to himself in either sorrow or joy."

A furtive glance toward the guest of honor; never have I seen him so tense. The basement is only dimly lit but dark glasses shield his eyes. His drawn features betray his turmoil. His lips open and close without sound. How much longer until his strength gives out?

Other speakers take the floor. In accordance with custom, we now sing the bridegroom's praises. Does he even hear what is being said? The qualities attributed to him? The wishes being expressed? His eyes, what do they see at this very moment? What images do they call forth and from what depths? And why does he feel this oppressive desire, this need to weep? And why is he not weeping? Whom is he defying by holding back his tears? His head bowed low, he is sitting among us against his will, dazed and ill at ease, a stranger at his own feast.

Sensing his distress, I want to touch his shoulder and say: Chase away your sadness, lift your eyes and look at the friends surrounding you, don't reject them. But out of discretion, I keep my place and my role.

Professor Heschel, though, takes the initiative by turning toward the guests: "What! Don't you people know how to dance?"

The Hasidim ask for nothing better. Quickly they move tables and benches out of the way. No sooner has a circle been formed than a powerful song rises from the entire congregation: a rapid, torrential song, full of rhythm and fire, a dizzying call to fervor, a song so vital it imposes its mark on the earth. They dance, hand-in-hand, shoulder-to-shoulder, their faces aflame, their hearts filled with joy. The circle gets larger and smaller in turn. The dancers part, come close again, lose and rediscover each other: they become one with the song, they become song. Song has won a victory over silence and solitude: we exist for others as well as for ourselves. And so we sing to cover the noise of all those years reverberating in our memories. And also to show our ancestors: Look, the chain has not been broken. We take up the same song ten times, a hundred times, so as not to leave it, so as not to leave each other. The way it was in Wiznitz and in Sighet. And the Hasidim dance the way they danced in Ger. Louder, faster! May the song become dance, and motion become song. May joy come to orphans and their friends, a joy at once ancestral and personal, violent and serene, a joy that announces and is part of creation.

Since I have remained on the sidelines because of a fractured leg, I am free to watch the participants. From the very beginning of the festivities, the young man has often closed his eyes. Even now he is staring at the floor, his teeth are clenched while he allows the Hasidim to encircle and pull him into their frantic rounds. Does he know what he's doing or where he is? Suddenly I am drawn into the vision: we are in another town, another synagogue, surrounded by other guests. He recognizes them, he knows them: parents, uncles, cousins, teachers, fellow students, friends. And all murmur: Thank you for inviting us, thank you for allowing us to celebrate this Shabbat with you; we shall come to your wedding.

And that is when, for the first time the defenses fall. Everything is spinning around him, inside him. There is no more reason to feel shame or fear remorse. Through his eyelids, closed as though forever, he feels the flow of his first adult tears: they flow and flow and scorch his face.

And I wonder about his eyes. Whether they are still the same.

CONNECTIONS

The Jewish woman quoted in the introduction to this reading says that despite efforts to put together the pieces of broken glass, "it will never become a mirror. You have to build your new image from the old piece." What is she suggesting about the effects of the Holocaust on Jewish life today? What is she suggesting about the future of Judaism? Would Reb Cywiak agree?

Why do you think Reb Cywiak regards the continuation of tradition as a "true miracle"? In what sense is it miraculous? How do you explain his insistence on honoring the young man even though it is clear to everyone that being singled out is making the bridegroom miserable? Was Reb Cywiak right to insist on a celebration or should he have ignored the occasion? What is the moral of the story he tells at the reception? Why does he regard it as the "essence of Hasidism"? Is it also the essence of Judaism and of humanity?

How do you explain what happens as the men dance at the reception? What meaning does Wiesel find in their dance? What meaning do you find?

Why did the bridegroom cry? What do his tears represent? How would you answer the question Elie Wiesel raises at the end of the story. Are the young man's eyes still the same?

Imagination and Possibility

In the late 1800s, many Eastern European Jews settled in the United States in the hope that in America everyone would be equal. Whenever they encountered prejudice or discrimination, many believed that as Jews, they had a responsibility to speak out. For some Jews, writes Jonathan Kaufman, "there was a line that ran from Kishinev—site of the Russian pogroms in the twentieth century—through Auschwitz to Birmingham." Birmingham, Alabama was the site of a major struggle in the fight for civil rights.

The Civil Rights Movement in the 1950s and 1960s included black and white Americans, rich and poor, Republicans and Democrats, old and young, Christians and Jews. Among those who worked for equal rights was an immigrant from Poland, an Orthodox Jew with a white beard and a yarmulke. His name was Abraham Joshua Heschel. He explained what drew him to the movement in a telegram to President John F. Kennedy in June of 1963:

> I look forward to privilege of being present at meeting tomorrow at 4 p.m. Likelihood exists that Negro problem will be like the weather. Everybody talks about it but nobody does anything about it. Please demand of religious leaders personal involvement not just solemn declaration. We forfeit the right to worship God as long as we continue to humiliate Negroes. Churches, synagogues have failed. They must repent. Ask of religious leaders to call for national repentance and personal sacrifice. Let religious leaders donate one month's salary toward fund for Negro housing and education. I propose that you Mr. President declare a state of moral emergency. A Marshall Plan for aid to Negroes is becoming a necessity. The hour calls for high moral grandeur and spiritual audacity.[38] [Rabbi Heschel wrote at a time when the word *Negro* was the preferred way of referring to an African American. He also used the word *man* to refer to both men and women. Today people would substitute words like humanity or humankind.]

The Marshall Plan provided funds for rebuilding war-torn countries in Europe and later Asia. Heschel was suggesting that it be expanded to help African Americans recover from centuries of discrimination. His telegram reflected a religious commitment to building a just society. Not surprisingly, when Dr. Martin Luther King, Jr. asked members of the clergy to come to Alabama in 1965 to support voting rights for African Americans, Heschel was among the first to arrive. He locked arms with King and the two men led a parade of rabbis, ministers, priests, nuns, and ordinary citizens across the Pettus Bridge toward Montgomery, Alabama. For Heschel, the march was a religious moment. He wrote, "I thought of my having walked with Hasidic rabbis on various occasions. I felt a sense of the Holy in what I was doing."

Although Jews make up less than five percent of the population in the United States, about half of the white Americans who participated in the Civil Rights Movement in the South during the 1950s and 1960s were Jewish. Jonathan Kaufman explains what motivated them to take a stand:

> With the exception of rabbis like Heschel, few Jews cast their involvement in the movement in overtly Jewish terms. . . . Henry Schwartzchild, a refugee from Nazi Germany, told friends he dated his involvement in the Civil Rights Movement from

the years following World War II. Returning to Germany to help the American army interrogate Germans, Schwartzchild resolved he would never be a "good German" standing by in the face of evil. "There was no doubt in any of our minds that we were risking our lives to achieve the very American goal of integration because our kinsmen had been slaughtered in Lithuania, Poland, and Germany," wrote Paul Cowan, a Jew from a highly assimilated family, reflecting on his family's commitment to civil rights. But most Jews spoke of their involvement as Carolyn Goodman had spoken of her son Andrew's. . . : They were liberals; it was the right thing to do.

Yet while these Jews did not get involved because they were Jewish, there was something very Jewish about their getting involved.[39]

CONNECTIONS

What do the terms *moral grandeur* and *spiritual audacity* mean? To what extent was the Holocaust due to people's failure to exhibit "moral grandeur"? To what extent was it due to a lack of "spiritual audacity"?

Elie Wiesel writes, "The more Jewish the poet, the more universal his message. The more Jewish his soul, the more human his concerns. A Jew who does not feel for his fellow Jews, who does not share in their sorrows and joys, cannot feel for other people. And a Jew who is concerned with his fellow Jews is inevitably concerned with the fate of other peoples as well."[40] What is Wiesel suggesting about the relationship between one's own particular history and the world as a whole? How did Rabbi Heschel's participation in the Civil Rights Movement reflect that relationship?

After marching with Dr. Martin Luther King, Jr. in Alabama in 1965, Heschel wrote: "I felt again what I have been thinking about for years—that Jewish religious institutions have again missed a great opportunity, namely, to interpret a civil-rights movement in terms of Judaism. The vast number of Jews participating actively in it are unaware of what the movement means in terms of the prophetic traditions."[41] After participating in the Polish Uprising in 1944, Yitzhak Zuckerman (Chapter 6) wrote:

> In the ranks of the Polish Uprising, there were perhaps a hundred or two hundred times more fighters, but our small group of less than twenty people was what inserted the Jewish banner into the Polish revolt. The Poles themselves note that. And we appeared there, from the first moment, as Jews. Although I wasn't known as a Jew, here and now, in this Uprising, I wanted them to know I was a Jew.[42]

Both Zuckerman and Heschel believed it was important for Jews to participate in the larger events of their day not just as individuals but as Jews. How does each define his universe of obligation? How is that definition similar to the one Wiesel implies when he writes, "The more Jewish the poet, the more universal his message. The more Jewish his soul, the more human his concerns"?

The Importance of Not Coming Too Late

Rabbi Abraham Heschel was seven years old when he encountered the biblical story of Abraham's sacrifice of Isaac for the first time. Years later, he could still recall how his heart beat faster and faster as he read of Isaac making his way to Mount Moriah with his father. He remembered trembling as he imagined Isaac lying bound on the altar, waiting to be sacrificed. Then just as Abraham lifted the knife, the voice of an angel was heard: "Abraham, lay not thine hand upon the lad, for now I know thou fearest God." It was at this point in the story that young Heschel began to sob. When his teacher asked why he was crying, the child replied, "Suppose the angel had come a second too late." The rebbe comforted the boy by saying that an angel cannot come late. In retelling the story as an adult, Heschel would add, "An angel cannot come late, my friends, but we, made of flesh and blood, we may come late."

In 1994, the people of Billings, Montana, discovered the importance of not coming too late. The Associated Press reported:

> When swastikas appeared here in Montana's largest city, Chief Wayne Inman was determined to halt the hatred early. As a police officer in Portland, Ore., in the late 1980s, he had watched skinhead racism and antisemitism mushroom and turn deadly.
>
> "Hate crimes are not a police problem," Chief Inman said. "they're a community problem. Hate crimes and hate activity flourish only in communities that allow it to flourish."
>
> So he and others stirred the city to a level of outrage that at least for now appears to have cowed the racist groups.
>
> The first signs of bigotry came last year when fliers started showing up in mailboxes on doorsteps, under windshield wipers, vilifying Hispanic Americans, Indians, blacks, homosexuals, lesbians, and welfare recipients. The fliers reserved special venom for the 48 Jewish families among the city's 81,000 residents.
>
> Then in January, people attending a Martin Luther King, Jr. Day observance returned to find their parked cars papered with Ku Klux Klan material.
>
> In the spring, skinheads began showing up in twos and threes at Wayman Chapel African Methodist Episcopal Church, glowering in the back pews.
>
> In August, a black swastika painted on white poster board was nailed to the door of Beth Aaron Synagogue, and tombstones were toppled in its cemetery.
>
> In October, swastikas and racial slurs were spray-painted on the home of a husband and wife of different races.
>
> Chief Inman recognized an emerging pattern: hate literature to intimidation to vandalism to personal attacks. In Portland that evolution culminated in the November 1988 beating death of Mulugeta Seraw, a young Ethiopian, by three skinheads returning from a meeting with recruiters from a white supremacist group.
>
> "I saw the emergence of the hate groups and a community's denial, and I saw a wake-up call that was the death of a black man . . . because he was black," Chief Inman said. "That's what it took to wake up Portland. We didn't have go through that here to get the wake-up call."
>
> The 100,000 people living in the Billings area reacted swiftly in unison.
>
> "There was not silence," Chief Inman said, "There was community outrage, saying, 'If you harass and intimidate one member of this community you are

attacking all of us.'"

And the resistance was more than bluster. Within five days of the spray-painted vandalism, 27 volunteers from Painters Local 1922 swarmed over the defaced house and obliterated the slurs in 45 minutes.

Bigotry resurfaced the next month. On Nov. 27, a beer bottle was hurled through a glass door at the home of Uri Barnea, conductor of the Billings Symphony. Five nights later, a cinder block thrown through a window sent shards of glass flying over the bed of 5-year-old Isaac Schnitzer.

Both houses were decorated with Hanukkah menorahs, and in both houses baby sitters were watching children.

The city reacted immediately. Christian churches distributed photocopies of menorahs. The Billings Gazette published a black-and-white picture of a menorah with an editorial, then a full-page version in color. Several businesses began providing paper menorahs.

Within days, the nine-candled symbol of Jewish perseverance and resistance was displayed in thousands of windows across the city.

The menorah idea started with Rev. Keith Torney of the First Congregational Church and Margie MacDonald of the Montana Association of Churches.

"This was just getting to be too much," Mr. Torney said. "First the gays, then the black community, but it seemed to me, they kind of hit their stride in the Jewish community. It's like they're searching around to get attention."

Civic leaders, churches and businesses declared their revulsion. The Universal Athletics Company replaced its billboard display on a busy thoroughfare with this message: "Not in Our Town! No Hate. No Violence."

But the hatemongers returned. In December, they broke windows at two Jewish homes and two churches that displayed menorahs, shot bullets through windows at Billings Central Catholic High School and stomped and battered six vehicles at homes displaying menorahs, telling two owners in phone calls, "Go look at your car, Jew-lover."

The spasm of hate created more resistance. Many more people put menorahs in their windows.

"It became physically impossible for the hate groups to harass and intimidate thousands and thousands of Billings citizens," Chief Inman said.

On Dec. 10, about 100 people attended a Hanukkah service at Beth Aaron Synagogue. Outside, neighbors discreetly stood vigil in the dark.

The city is not proclaiming victory, but Chief Inman thinks the hate groups have backed off. No vandalism has occurred since the incidents in December, and the literature and the anonymous calls have diminished.

"I would hate to predict we have stopped the influence and impact of hate crimes, but something appears to be working," he said.

A grimmer outlook comes from Clinton Spies, a former skinhead who did time for assault, armed robbery and burglary, and now runs a program to help youngsters leave racist groups. He said, "A year from now, we're going to have racial assaults, vandalism, all kinds of violence."

But Sheriff Charles Maxwell of Yellowstone County remains optimistic. "It may happen again," he said. "But the reaction will remain the same."[43]

Six months later, another reporter visited Billings to see how the town was faring. After interviewing a number of townspeople, he noted that many in the community were reexamining their attitudes and beliefs as a result of the menorah campaign.

Wayne Inman admits that it took a long while for his own sense of social justice to develop. As a child in Plains [a small town in Montana], he saw no African Americans, no Jews and only a few Hispanic migrant workers. "We grew up calling blacks 'niggers.' It was as common as the sun coming up in the morning. Nobody ever confronted the issue. It was 'normal.' But when I got out into the larger world, I found that it wasn't normal, or if it was normal, it should be opposed. When you have a person present, not just a word, you see that you're talking about a human being whose skin is black. I saw that once for myself. I saw the hurt and pain in his eyes. It became a very personal issue for me."

People are also wondering if the strong community response to the Schnitzers would have been accorded a black or Hispanic family. The Schnitzers are Jewish, but they are also respected white, middle-class citizens. Some people feel that it was relatively painless for the community to rally behind them. Others simply believe that the timing of the menorah movement was propitious and that people were lucky to have a dramatic visual symbol to substitute for more layered, and perhaps more contradictory, thoughts.

Others wonder among themselves if the town was opposing violence or hatred. . . .In recent years, there have been more fights in bars and incidents of vandalism that have no connection with hate crimes. Like most cities, the town is fed up. Even a *Gazette* editorial titled "Violence Begets Violence" asked: "In the long run does it matter" whether the smashing of the high school "Happy Hanukkah" sign was a hate crime or vandalism?

And there is discussion, as well, about the difference between encouraging diversity in the community and opposing bigotry. Several evangelical churches did not participate in the menorah movement because it was led by the Human Rights Coalition, whose support of homosexual rights they do not endorse. . . . "Once there was a visual act of bigotry, it was easy to get people involved," [Kurt] Nelson says. "Personal tolerance is harder to achieve. . . ."[44]

Sarah Anthony, a member of the Human Rights Coalition, reflected on the struggle and why it matters to her. She told the reporter:

> I believe in this community because of what it gives back to me. When someone tells a story of pain, a lot of people in Billings think, "Your pain is my pain." And when people decide to alleviate someone's pain, there's something very serious happening. I can't put my finger on it, but it's there.
>
> I mean, what have we done so far? Come up with a plan. Make a few phone calls. Put up menorahs. That's all we did. Pretty simple stuff, actually. But you have to build the sentiment, to forge the real feeling that goes deep. We did something right here, and we will do it again if we have to. If we don't, there are people who would break every window in Billings, and we would look in those windows and see ourselves.[45]

CONNECTIONS

What is the moral of the story retold in the introduction to this reading? How does it apply to events in Billings? How did Chief Inman learn the lesson Heschel preached? Look through newspapers or magazines for other examples of people who have discovered the importance of not coming too late.

How does Chief Inman define the term hate crime? How do you define the term? After a rock was thrown through the window of a Vietnamese family's home, Deputy Superintendent William Johnston of the Boston Police Department noted that the rock did more than shatter glass. It also shattered a family. What do you think he meant? How do his words apply to Billings?

Martin Niemoller was a Protestant minister in Germany. In 1933 he voted for the Nazi party. By 1938, he was in a concentration camp. After the war, he is believed to have said, "In Germany, the Nazis came for the Communists, and I didn't speak up because I wasn't a Communist. Then they came for the Jews, and I didn't speak up because I wasn't a Jew. Then they came for the trade unionists, and I didn't speak up because I wasn't a trade unionist. Then they came for the Catholics, and I didn't speak up because I was a Protestant. Then they came for me, and by that time there was no one to speak for me." How do his remarks apply to Billings? To other communities you have read about or visited?

Since 1994, the people of Billings have participated in a video made to spread the word about the importance of speaking out against hate crimes. It is called Not in Our Town and is available from the Facing History Resource Center. The video has inspired several communities to speak out against racism and antisemitism. In 1997, *Parade* Magazine reported:

> In Cedar Rapids, Iowa, . . . the Faith United Methodist Church has used the Not in Our Town video to encourage community groups to speak out against public events sponsored by the Iowa Militia. "We did not want the militia to be the only loud voices talking to our children," said Tom Mohan, who works through the Methodist church. "We watched the program so the people could talk about what happened in Billings and what we can do here. Doing something that you know others are doing all over the country makes you feel stronger."
>
> In Bloomington, Il., "Not in Our Town" became the town motto: An official road sign was erected with a red circle containing a slash over the word "racism," followed by the phrase "Not in Our Town." Last year, nearly 1000 people signed a pledge against intolerance. Police officers wore "Not in Our Town" buttons on their lapels as they joined the mayor in a protest against racial hatred and church burnings around the country.[46]

What does the response to Billings suggest about the way people get involved in a movement? What does it suggest about the way one act leads to another and yet another?

What does Sarah Anthony mean when she says "We did something right here, and we will do it again if we have to. If we don't, there are people who would break every window in Billings, and we would look in those windows and see ourselves"? Would she agree with observation that the silence of good people can be as damaging as the actions of bad people? With the view that silence cannot only be damaging but also dangerous? Do you agree?

Education and the Future

Confronting the past is not always easy, but it is important work. By denying people access to a difficult history, we fail to honor their potential to confront, to cope, and to make a positive difference today and in the future.

A principal sends the following letter to teachers on the first day of the school year:

Dear Teacher:

I am a survivor of a concentration camp. My eyes saw what no man should witness:

Gas chambers built by learned engineers.

Children poisoned by educated physicians.

Infants killed by trained nurses.

Women and babies shot and burned by high school and college graduates.

So, I am suspicious of education.

My request is: Help your students become human. Your efforts must never produce learned monsters, skilled psychopaths, educated Eichmanns.

Reading, writing, arithmetic are important only if they serve to make our children more humane.[47]

In a television interview given shortly before his death, a reporter asked Rabbi Abraham Heschel what advice he would give young people. He replied:

[Let] them remember that there is a meaning beyond absurdity. Let them be sure that every little deed counts, that every word has power, and that we can, everyone, do our share to redeem the world in spite of all absurdities and all the frustrations and all disappointments. And above all, remember that the meaning of life is to build a life as if it were a work of art. You're not a machine. And you are young. Start working on this great work of art called your own existence.[48]

CONNECTIONS

What does it mean to build a life as if it were a work of art? What individuals that you have read about or know have built lives that are works of art?

What would you include in a curriculum that addresses the concerns expressed in this reading and in this course as a whole? What readings would you require? What films would you show? What speakers would you invite? What would you omit and what would you add? How would you begin the course and how would you end it?

In designing a curriculum, decisions have to be made. Whose history should be included? Whose might be left out? If everyone's history is included, what may be lost? How do you discover universal lessons from a particular history?

The title of this course is "Facing History and Ourselves." What does that title mean to you? How has it been reflected in this course? In the way you have come to perceive the past? In the way you approach the future?

1 Martha Minow, *Making All the Difference: Inclusion, Exclusion, and American Law* (Cornell University Press, 1990), 3

2 Julius Lester, *Falling Pieces of the Broken Sky* (Little, Brown, 1990), 263-264.

3 Quoted in Martin Gilbert, *The Holocaust* (Holt, 1985), 812.

4 Ibid., 817.

5 Joseph Tenenbaum, *In Search of a Lost People: The Old and the New Poland* (Beechhurst Press, 1948), 11.

6 Ibid. 236-237.

7 Ibid., 238-239.

8 Martin Gilbert, *The Holocaust*, 819.

9 Quoted in Antony Polonsky, "Introduction," to *My Brother's Keeper?* ed. by Antony Polonsky (Routledge, 1990), 4.

10 Joseph Brodsky, "Blood, Lies and the Trigger of History," *New York Times*, August 4, 1993, Op-Ed page. Copyright © 1993 by The New York Times Company. Reprinted by Permission.

11 Quoted in *Abraham Joshua Heschel and Elie Wiesel: You Are My Witnesses* by Maurice Friedman (Farrar, Straus & Giroux, 1987), 82-83.

12 Ibid., 159.

13 Susannah Heschel, "Introduction" in *Moral Grandeur and Spiritual Audacity*, ed. by Susannah Heschel (Farrar, Straus, Giroux, 1996), viii-ix.

14 Quoted in *Spiritual Pilgrimage: Texts on Jews and Judaism, 1979-1995,* compil. by the Anti-Defamation League and ed. by Eugene J. Fisher and Leon Klenicki (Crossroad Publishing, 1995), 52.

15 Quoted in *Dignity & Defiance: The Confrontation of Life and Death in the Warsaw Ghetto* (Simon Wiesenthal Center, 1993), 89-91.

16 Abraham Joshua Heschel, "No Religion Is an Island," in *Moral Grandeur and Spiritual Audacity*, ed. by Susannah Heschel, 238.

17 Ibid., 151-152.

18 Quoted in *Spiritual Pilgrimage: Texts on Jews and Judaism, 1979-1995*, compil. by the Anti-Defamation League and ed. by Eugene J. Fisher and Leon Klenicki, 210.

19 Quoted in Samuel H. Dresner, "Heschel the Man," in *Abraham Joshua Heschel: Exploring His Life and Thought* ed. by John C. Merkle, 7.

20 James Carroll, "My Mother's Old Clock," *Boston Globe*, February 4, 1997, op. ed.

21 John Fried, *Trial at Nuremberg: Freedom and Responsibility* (National Project Center for Film and Humanities and the Research Foundation of the City University of New York, © 1973).

22 Gideon Hausner, *Justice in Jerusalem* (Harper & Row, 1966), 323-324.

23 Ibid., 434-435.

24 Ibid., 433-434.

25 Quoted in *Growing Up Jewish in America* by Myrna Katz Frommer and Harvey Frommer (Harcourt Brace, 1995), 132.

26 Ibid., 125.

27 Ibid, 126-127.

28 Donia Blumenfeld Clenman, "I Dream in Good English Too," *Poems* by Donia Blumenfeld Clenman (Flowerfield and Littleman, 1988).

29 Rachel Goldstein, "Those Who Remain." © 1997 by Rachel Goldstein.

30 Rachel Goldstein, "In the Museum at Auschwitz. © 1997 by Rachel Goldstein.

31 Quoted in *Liberating the Ghosts* by Raphael Shevelev with Karine Schomer (Lens Work Publishing, 1996), 68.

32 Jane Perlez, "Poland Turns Out for Glimpse of a Lost World," *New York Times*, May 19, 1996, p. 8.

33 Quoted in Anna Krall, *Shielding the Flame: An Intimate Conversation with Dr. Marek Edelman*, trans. by Joanna Stasinska and Lawrence Weschler (Henry Holt, 1986), 119.

34 Ibid., 119-124.

35 Jonathan Kaufman, *A Hole in the Heart of the World: Being Jewish in Eastern Europe* (Viking, 1997), 304.

36 Iwona Irwin-Zarecka, *Neutralizing Memory: The Jew in Contemporary Poland* (Transaction Publishers, 1990), 75-82.

37 Miriam Gonczarska. 1997. Interview by Martha Teichner. Sunday Morning. CBS, Inc. April 13.

38 Quoted in in *Moral Grandeur and Spiritual Audacity,* ed. by Susannah Heschel, vii.

39 Jonathan Kaufman, *Broken Alliance: The Turbulent Times Between Blacks and Jews in America* (Simon & Schuster, 1988, 1995), 99.

40 Quoted in *Abraham Joshua Heschel and Elie Wiesel: You Are My Witnesses* by Maurice Friedman, 202.

41 Quoted in *Moral Grandeur and Spiritual Audacity*, ed. by Susannah Heschel, xxiii-xxiv.

42 Ibid., 528.

43 Copyright © 1994 by the Associated Press. Reprinted by permission.

44 From "Their Finest Minute" by Roger Rosenblatt. *The New York Times Magazine,* July 3, 1994. Copyright © New York Times Company. Reprinted by permission.

45 Ibid.

46 Colin Greer, "We Won't Tolerate Hate," *Parade* Magazine, February 23, 1997, 6.

47 Haim Ginott, *Teacher and Child* (Macmillan, 1972), 317.

48 "Carl Stern's Interview with Dr. Heschel" in *Moral Grandeur and Spiritual Audacity*, ed. by Susannah Heschel, 412.

bar mitzvah (n.) (1) Literally "a son of the Commandment"; a Jewish boy who has reached his thirteenth birthday and is therefore responsible for his own deeds and religious obligations. (2) The ceremony that marks a boy's reaching the age of bar mitzvah. To commemorate the occasion, he is called to the altar of the synagogue to participate in the reading of the Torah. A "daughter of the Commandment" is called a bat mitzvah. (p.18)

Chanukah (n.) The Feast of Lights, observed in December for a period of eight days; a holiday commemorating the Jews' victory over their Syrian rulers in 168 B.C.E. They were fighting for the right of Jews to worship in their own way.

chuppa (n.) A bridal canopy. A Jewish marriage ceremony takes place under a chuppa. (p. 11)

Gentile (n.) One who is not of the Jewish faith. (p. 2)

goy, pl. **goyim** (n.) (1) (Heb.) Nation or people. (2) (Yid.) Gentile

Haftorah (n.) A selection from the biblical books of the Prophets that is chanted along with the Torah reading on the Sabbath and other holidays. The Haftorah is related in content to the lesson contained in the Torah reading. (p. 18)

Hasidism (n.) Jewish reform movement that spread through Eastern Europe in the eighteenth century. Hasidism teaches that the divine presence is everywhere, in everything. Followers therefore try to live a life of total dedication to God.

hasid, pl. **hasidim** (n.) A follower of Hasidism.

hazan (n.) Cantor or prayer leader. Although many synagogues today have a full-time cantor, any Jew familiar with the prayers and the order of the prayer service can serve as a cantor. (p. 57)

Hebrew (n) (1) The language of the ancient Hebrews. (2) The language Jews traditionally use in prayer and study. (3) The official language of the State of Israel. (p.3)

Hebrew school (n.) A school that teaches Jewish children the Hebrew language and the customs and traditions of their faith. (p. 3)

heder (n.) The Yiddish word for Hebrew school. (p. 3)

High Holy Days (n.) Rosh Hashanah and Yom Kippur.

kiddush (n.) A blessing recited over a cup of wine; a blessing said to consecrate the Sabbath or a holiday. (p. 7)

kosher (adj.) Describes foods and other items that meet Jewish ritual requirements. Kosher food is prepared according to the dietary laws, which are based on restrictions in the Book of Leviticus. (p. 6)

mezuzah (n.) A tiny wooden, metal, or glass case that is placed on the door post of a Jewish home. Inside the case is a tiny parchment containing verses from the Book of Deuteronomy. The first sentence is the watchword of the Jewish people: "Hear O Israel, the Lord is our God, the Lord is One." (p. 3)

mikvah (n.) A pool for ritual purification; a ritual bath. (p. 30)

mitzvah, pl. **mitzvot** (n.) The Hebrew word for commandment; a good deed. (p. 17)

Passover (n.) A spring festival traditionally observed for eight days. Passover commemorates the escape of the Jewish people from slavery in Egypt; the English translation of the Hebrew word *Pesach*. (p. 53)

Pesach (n.) (Heb.) Passover. (p. 8)

rabbi (n.) Literally a teacher. Traditionally, a rabbi is not only a teacher but also a spiritual leader. Rabbis minister to the needs of their congregations by preaching, overseeing ritual observances, administering religious education, and supervising ceremonies associated with birth, marriage, and death. (p. 6)

Rosh Hashanah (n.) The Jewish new year which falls in September or October. The holy day, which is celebrated for two days, marks a period of divine judgment–a time when Jews believe they are called to account for their actions by God. Rosh Hashonah is the beginning of the ten most solemn days in the Jewish calendar. They are days of repentance and resolution to make amends. The period ends on Yom Kippur. (p. 6)

seder (n.) A ceremony traditionally held at home on the first two nights of Passover. At a festive meal, the story of the exodus of the Jewish people from slavery in Egypt is told in words, songs, and symbols. (p. 7)

Shabbat (n.) The Sabbath; observed from just before sundown on Friday until just after sundown on Saturday. On Shabbat, religious Jews refrain from all work. They spend the day in prayer, relaxation, study, and enjoyment of family and friends. (p. 6)

Shema (n.) The prayer religious Jews recite three times a day: "Hear O Israel, the Lord is our God; the Lord is One." The prayer is an affirmation of faith. (p. 30)

shofar (n.) A ram's horn that is sounded on Rosh Hashanah and the end of Yom Kippur. The horn is a reminder of the ram offered to God by Abraham in place of his son Isaac (Gen 22:13). The shofar is a symbol of revelation and redemption. (p. 6)

shtetl pl. **shtetlach** (n.) The Yiddish word for a village or small town in Eastern Europe. (p. 10)

shul (n.) The Yiddish word for "synagogue." (p. 7)

synagogue (n.) Jewish house of prayer. Traditionally, a synagogue is also a house of study. (p. 18)

tallis (n.) A shawl with four fringes or tassels sewn at each corner of the garment. A tallis is worn during morning prayers. (p. 18)

Talmud (n.) A word that means study or learning. The Talmud has two main components: the Mishnah, which summarizes the laws Jews have developed over thousands of years (from ancient times to the beginnings of the Middle Ages); and the Gemarah, the commentaries on the Mishnah. Together, they are a collection of law, legend, and philosophy, a blend of logical and practical solutions to problems, of history and science, of anecdotes and humor. (p.10)

tefillin (n.) Two small leather boxes attached to long leather straps. Observant Jews wrap tefillin around the forehead, over the heart, and around one arm to focus their entire being on God as they recite morning prayers. Each tiny square-shaped box (about two fingers in width) contains a prayer that urges Jews to love God and subject every part of their life—thoughts, feelings, and actions—to His service. Tefilin are worn only on week-day mornings. On the Sabbath and holidays, Jews have no need of a spe-cial reminder. The day itself serves that function. (p. 69)

Torah (n.) The Hebrew Bible; the Five Books of Moses. A portion of the Torah, beginning with the book of Genesis, is publicly read at morning and afternoon services every Sabbath and Fast Day. A portion is also read during the morning service on every holiday, the first day of each month, and every Monday and Thursday. In the course of a year, the entire Torah is read aloud. (p. 3)

tzadaka (n.) Literally "righteousness;" charity, the striving to be a zaddik through deeds. According to the Talmud, tzadaka is one of three central principles in life. The other two are Torah or learning and service of God. (p. 6)

Yiddish (n.) The everyday language of the Jews of Eastern Europe; a Germanic language that contains many Hebrew and Polish words. (p.6)

Yom Kippur (n.) The day of atonement; a fast day devoted to prayer. Yom Kippur marks the end of the ten most solemn days in the Jewish calendar, which began with Rosh Hashonah. (p. 6)

zaddik (n.) A righteous person; one whose life exemplifies the ideals of Judaism. (p. 45)

Zionism (n.) The belief that Jews must become a nation with a land of their own in Palestine. (p. 6)

Abel, Theodore, 72
Abelard, Peter, 27
African Americans, 29-31, 65, 107, 255
Agudat Israel, 89, 91, 95-96, 189
Akiva, 99, 162. *See also* **Youth Groups.**
Albright, Madeleine, 13, 14, 15, 249
Aleichem, Sholem, 69-70, 76-77
Alexander II, tsar of Russia, 53
Allies. *See* names of individual countries.
Alter, Abraham Mordecai, 95-96, 252
Altman, Rachel, 9-11
American Jewish Committee, 86
American Joint Distribution
    Committee, 133
American Red Cross, 135
American Revolution, 73
Americanization, 13-14
Anarchist movement, 8, 77
Anielewicz, Mordecai, 190, 199,
    210, 213-214, 213 (photo)
Anthony, Sarah, 258
Anti-Judaism, 26-28, 35-38, 39-40,
    42-43, 58-59, 61-64, 170; efforts to
    combat, 228-230. *See also*
    Antisemitism.
Antisemitism, 29; after the Holocaust,
    224-226; after World War I, 81,
    83-84, 224-226, 229-230; and the
    Communists, 226, 227, 246; and
    economic competition, 104-105; and
    the Holocaust, 150, 170; and Jewish
    emigration, 70, 107, 111-112,
    224-226; and Jewish identity, 13-14,
    16-17, 54, 61-63, 63-64, 101-103,
    108, 117, 136-137, 246-248; and
    nationalism, 73-74, 76-77; and peace
    treaty of 1919, 86-87; during World
    War I, 78-79; fears of, 13-14; in
    Billings, MT, 256-258; in Poland in
    1920s and 1930s, 86-87, 89-91,
    101-103, 104-105, 106-107; in
    Russian Poland in 1800s, 53-54,
    58-59, 60-64; spelling of, 77. *See also*
    **Anti-Judaism, Pogroms, Violence
    against Jews.**
Appiah, Anthony, 15
Arbeiter Ring. *See* **Workmen's Circle.**

Arendt, Hannah, 81
Armenian Genocide, 80, 83, 175-176,
    234
Armenians, during World War I, 80, 83,
    175-176; in Polish Commonwealth, 42
Armja Krajowka (AK), 167, 170,
    182-183, 201, 203, 213-215, 219.
    See also **Polish underground.**
Armja Ludowa (AL), 203, 219. *See also*
    Polish underground.
Army, Polish, Jews in, 117-118, 122;
    Russian, and antisemitism in, 79-80;
    Russian, Jews in, 53, 78-79; U.S., Jews
    in, 24
Arrenda system, 42
Ashkenazic Jews, 37
Assimiliation, 13-14, 48-50; and Jewish
    tradition, 51, 52-53; efforts to halt,
    95-96
Auerbach, Rachel, 155
Auschwitz, 147, 218; 50th anniversary of
    liberation, 231; memorials at, 242-243.
    See also **Death camps.**
Austria, 35, 111-112. *See also* **Austro-
    Hungarian Empire.**
Austro-Hungarian Empire, 50 (map),
    72, 78
Azenberg, Manny, 6-7

Baal Shem Tov. *See* **Ben Eliezer**, Israel.
Balfour, Arthur James, 86
Balkans, conflict in 1990s, 75, 84-85
Bartowszewski, Wladyslaw, 196, 213
bar mitzvah, 7, 18, 21
Barber, Benjamin R., 223
Bauman, Janina, 117-118, 159, 168
Beit Yakov, 95-96. *See also* **Education.**
Bell, Daniel, 1
Bedzin-Sosnowiec, 218
Belkhatov, 104-105
Belorussians, 89
Belzec, 147, 182
Ben Eliezer, Israel, 44-45, 45-46
Berger, Gottlob, 167
Berkovitz, Eliezer, 1
Bessarabia, 61
Betar, 162. *See also* **Youth Groups,
    Zionism.**

Beth din, 30
Bially, Rosa, 81, 83
Bialer, Tosha, 142-143
Bialystok, Poland, 123, 218
Bilgoray, Poland, 93-94
Billings, Montana, 256-258
Birenbaum, Halina, 125, 151-152
Block, Gay, 198
Blonder, Steve, 16-17
Bloomington, Illinois, 259
Bohemia, 35
Boleslaw, prince of Kalisz, 35-36
Bookbinder, Paul, 147
Borzykowski, Tuvia, 206-207
Brandeis, Louis, 88
Britain: and Holocaust, 182-183; and
    nationalism, 73; and Nuremberg trials,
    234; and peace treaty after World War
    I, 86; and refugees in the 1930s,
    111-112; and World War I, 72
Brosky, Joseph, 75, 84-85
Bronowski, Jacob, 9
Bukovina, 78
Burlington, Vermont, 6
Buell, Raymond, 96
Bund: after World War I, 95, 98; and
    Kishinev pogrom, 61-63; and efforts to
    combat antisemitism, 108-110;
    defined, 61; during the Holocaust,
    128-129, 136-137, 138-139, 165-166,
    181-182, 189-190, 199

Carroll, James, 15, 232-233
Cedar Rapids, Iowa, 259
Chagall, Bella, 70
Chagall, Marc, 70
Charters, medieval, 35-36
Chelmno, 147, 163
Chernovitz, 96
Chmielnicki, Bogdan, 43
Christians: and economic competition
    with Jews, 104-105; and the
    Holocaust, 182-183, 184; and violence
    against Jews 26-27, 60-64, 83-84,
    89-91, 98, 108-110, 224-226; divisions
    among, 27-28, 42-43; relations with
    Jews during the Middle Ages, 26-28,
    36-37, 39-40, 41, 42-43; relations with
    Jews in Nazi-occupied Poland, 125,
    126; relations with Jews in the Polish

Republic, 98, 101-102, 106-107;
    relations with Jews in post-war Poland,
    224-226, 229-230; relations with Jews
    in Russian-occupied Poland, 49-50,
    52-54, 56-59, 60-64 relations with
    Jews today, 2-3, 21-22, 24, 24-25; in
    Warsaw Ghetto, 151-152. *See also*
    **Protestantism, Roman Catholic
    Church.**
Ciechanowski, Jan, 183
Civil Rights movement (U.S.), 29,
    254-255
Clenman, Donia Blumenfeld, 238-239
Collective Responsibility: and Jewish
    resistance, 136-137; and the Nazis,
    128-130
Commission for Polish Relief, 135
Commonwealth of Poland-Lithuania,
    74. *See also* **Poland, Lithuania**
Communism, 76; in Eastern Europe
    after World War I, 83; in Hungary
    after World War II, 13-14; in Poland
    after World War II, 224-226, 246-248
Communists, in Poland, after World
    War II, 224-226, 227, 246-248; and
    the Warsaw Ghetto Memorial, 244-
    245; during World War II, 203, 219
Conservative Judaism, 29
Conversion: and the Haskalah, 53-54;
    and medieval charters, 36; in Nazi-
    occupied Europe, 125; to Christianity,
    13-14, 15, 48, 54; to Judaism, 29-31
Cossacks, 62, 78
Council for Aid to Jews. *See* **Zegota.**
Craven, Carolyn, 29-31
Crusades, 26
Culture, Jewish: and art, 70; and
    Hasidism, 44-46; and the Haskalah,
    48-49, 51, 52-54; and literature,
    69-70, 72, 93-94; and theatre, 93; in
    the Pale of Jewish Settlement, 56-59;
    in Poland during the Middle Ages,
    35-37; in the United States, 16-17
Czechoslovakia, 13, 88; invasion of, 117
Czerniakow, Adam, 128-129, 165, 166

Davies, Norman, 74, 78
Dawidowicz, Lucy, 51, 55
Day of Atonement. *See* **Yom Kippur.**

Death camps, 147, 177-179. *See also* names of individual camps.

Democracy: Henry Morgenthau on, 83 in Poland after World War I, 89; loss of, in Poland in 1935, 91; struggle for, in Poland, in 1980s, 244-245, 246-248

Deutsch, Helena, 101

Diaspora, defined, 107

Dmowski, Roman, 73-74

Doeblin, Alfred, 100

Donat, Alexander, 122-123, 125, 133-134, 152, 174, 197, 204-205, 206

Dror, 138, 163, 189. *See also* Youth Groups, Zionism.

Drucker, Malka, 198

Dzialoszyce, Poland, 224

Dzymanowski, Antoni, 167

East St. Louis, Illinois, 65

Eastern Europe: after World War I, 72, 83; and Communism, 226, 246; and growth of hasidism, 45-46; and peace treaty after World War I, 86-87; collapse of empires in, 72

Eban, Abba, 7

Edelman, Marek, 199, 200, 210, 212, 244-245

Education: after World War I, 93-94; and discrimination, 108, 110; and the Enlightenment, 48-49; and nationalism, 100; and Polish resistance to Russia, 49-50; and resistance to the Nazis, 138; and women, 9-10, 46-47, 52-54, 95-96; and youth groups, 99; in Russian-occupied Poland, 53-54; Jewish, cultural, 7-8; Jewish, religious, 3, 6, 95-96

Education, Polish Ministry of, 108

Eichmann, Adolf, 234-235; trial of, 235-236, 237-238

Einsatzgruppen, 147

Emigration: from Pale of Jewish Settlement 58, 69-70; from Poland in the 1930s, 107; from Poland in 1939, 122-124; from Poland after the Holocaust, 226; from Poland in the 1960s, 226; from Western Europe during the Middle Ages, 26-27

Enlightenment: and Jews, 48-49, 52-54; and social change, 33-34; defined, 33;

in Poland, 43. *See also* Haskalah.

Erikson, Kai, 40-41

Evian, France, conference in, 111-112

Families, Jewish: and the Haskalah, 48, 52-54; and resistance, 205; and return to Judaism in present-day Poland, 246-247; choices after the Nazi occupation, 140-141; choices during the Holocaust, 196-197, 205; generation gap in, 9-11, 99, 246-248; in North America, 2-3, 6-7, 16-17; in the Warsaw Ghetto, 151-152, 155-156, 157, 160-161, 173-174, 177-179, 196-197, 205; traditions of, 11, 21

Fiddler on the Roof, 70

Fink, Ida, 116

"Flying University," 49. *See also* Education.

Folkist Party, 89

Forced labor, 131-132

Forward, 65

France: and the Enlightenment, 33; and the French Revolution, 73; and nationalism, 73; and the Nuremberg trials, 234; and World War I, 72, 78

Frankfurter, Felix, 183

Freemen, Jews as, 36-37

French Revolution, 73

Fried, John, 234

Friedman, Alexander-Zysze, 189

Friedman, N.M., 78, 79

Galicia: civil war in after World War I, 81-83; during World War I, 78

Gaon of Vilna. *See* Zalman, Elijah ben Saloman.

Gates, Henry Louis, Jr., 14, 25, 65-66

General Government, 135

General Union of Jewish Workers in Lithuania, Poland, and Russia. *See* Bund.

Genocide, 80

Gerer Rebbe. *See* Alter, Abraham.

German Anthropological Society, 73

Germans: in Polish Commonwealth, 42; in Second Polish Republic, 89-91. *See also* Germany.

Germany: and collective responsibility, 128-129; and the Holocaust, 116,

125-126, 128-130, 131-132, 146-147, 155-156; and invasion of Poland, 116, 117-118, 119-120; and invasion of Russia, 147; and Kristallnacht, 112; and medieval charters, 35-36; and pact with Soviet Union, 122; and rise of Nazis in, 111; and social aid, 135; and World War I, 72; Jews in, 112, 118. *See also* **Holocaust.**

Gestapo, 128-129, 202

"Ghetto Benches," 108-110

Ghettos: and the Nazis, 142-143; compared, 146, 148-149; defined, 27; in Western Europe, 27; lack of in Poland, 39; and the Russians, 53. *See also* **Pale of Jewish Settlement, Warsaw Ghetto.**

Gilbert, Martin, 225-226

Goldman, Joey, 18-19

Goldsmith, Suzanne, 41

Goldstein, Bernard, 129, 132, 136-137, 138-139, 140, 141, 203

Goldstein, Rachel, 240, 242-243

Goldszmit, Henryk, 49-50, 106-107, 126, 169, 173, 175, 242

Goldszmit, Hirsh, 48

Goldszmit, Jakub, 48-49

Goldszmit, Josef, 48-49

Goodhart, Arthur, 101

Goodman, Andrew, 255

Goodman, Carolyn, 255

Gordon, Judah Leib, 51

Gorka, Olgierd, 224, 225

Gorni, Yechiel, 200

Gorky, Maxim, 64-65

Grabowski, Heniek, 162

Gray, Martin, 119-120, 125-126, 155-156, 173-174, 177-179

Greater Poland, 37

Greece, 35

Greek Orthodox Church, 42-43

Greenberg, Blu, 21

Greenberg, Irving, 21

Grober, David, 171

Grojanowski, Yakov, 163

Grossman, Vladimir, 78-79

Gruenbaum, Yitzhak, 89

Grynszpan, Herschel, 112

Grynszpan, Zindel, 112

Gutman, Israel, 132, 166, 193

Gwiazda, 98

Hanover, Nathan, 42-43

Hartglas, Apolinary, 126

Hashomer Hatzair, 162, 190, 199. *See also* **Youth Groups, Zionism.**

Hasidic tales, 45

Hasidim, 44-46, 52, 81

Hasidism, 44-46, 53, 95-96, 97

Haskalah, 48-50; and women, 52-54. *See also* **Enlightenment.**

Haupt, Adam, 241

Hausner, Gideon, 235, 235-236, 237

Hautzig, Esther, 5

Hay, Malcolm, 28

Hebrew School, 3, 6, 16-17, 57, 96. *See also* **Education.**

Hecht, Avrohom, 6

Heder. *See* **Hebrew School.**

Herzl, Theodore, 77

Heschel, Abraham Joshua, 31, 228-229, 231, 250, 254, 254-255, 256, 260

Heschel, Susannah, 228-229

Heydrich, Reinhard, 147

Hillel, rabbi, 135

Himmler, Heinrich, 167, 204

Hirshaut, Hanna, 101-102

Hitler, Adolf, 111, 116, 177, 137, 162, 234

Hlond, August, Cardinal, 108, 224-225

Holidays, Christian: and antisemitism, 58, 61-62, 226; and Jewish identity, 21. Jewish: celebration of today, 6, 7, 11, 18, 53; celebration of in Warsaw Ghetto, 138, 206-207. *See also* names of individual holidays.

Holocaust: and world opinion, 216-217; defined, 147; legacies of 9-11, 13-14, 16-17, 187-188, 223, 232-233, 237-238; news of and Polish underground, 167, 181-183, 213-215, 216; news of and outside world, 181-183; news of and Warsaw Ghetto, 162-163; witnesses to, 167, 171-172. *See also* **Death camps.**

House Committees. *See* **Tenants' Committees.**

Hovevei Zion, 65, 76. *See also* **Zionism.**

Hungary, 13-14, 444

Identity (chart), 3-4

Identity, Jewish: and antisemitism, 13-14, 16-17, 54, 61-63, 63-64, 101-103, 108, 117, 136-137, 246-248; and "belonging," 21-22; and conversion, 29-31; and the Eichmann trial, 235-236, 237-238; and faith, 6, 16-17, 21, 29-31; and the Haskalah, 48-50, 51, 52-54; and the Holocaust, 9-11, 13-14, 16-17; and Israel, 20; and Jewish traditions, 7, 9-11, 30-31; and minority rights, 87; and Nazi occupation, 155-156; and pogroms, 61-64; and prejudice, 2-3, 24-25; and resistance to the Nazis, 193; and socialism, 7-8, 18-19; and stereotyping, 2-3, 21-22, 22, 24, 24-25; and Yiddish culture, 7-8; and Zionism, 6-7; the hiding of, 13-14, 246-248; in Poland after World War II, 224-226, 246-248; pride in, 5-6, 6-7, 60-61, 69-70; secret of, 13-14

Immigration: to Palestine, 107, 111; to Poland, 35-37; to Soviet territory in 1939, 122-124; to the United States, 1, 8, 9, 111-112, 224-226

Industrial Revolution, 34

Inman, Wayne, 256-258

Irwin-Zarecka, Iwona, 246, 247-248

Ish-Kishor, Sulamith, 28

Islam, 26

Israel, 7, 11, 20, 29, 234; and Eichmann trial, 234-236. *See also* **Palestine, Zionism.**

Israelis, and Eichmann trial, 235-236, 237

Isserles, Moses, 37

Italy, 35

Jewish American Princess (JAP), 22

Jewish Fighting Organization, 195; and April uprising, 206-207, 209-211; and January uprising, 199-200; and Polish uprising, 218-219; and self defense, 195; assessment of, 187; debates among members, first operation of, 191-192; founding of, 190; initial setbacks, 192; power of, 204-205; relations with Polish underground, 201-202, 203-204, 213-215; search for weapons, 201-202

Jewish Military Union, 191, 195, 201

Jewish Theological Seminary, 228

Jewish Welfare Society, 134, 135

Jews. *See* particular topics.

Jews, German, 118

Jewish Society of Social Welfare, 134

"Jewish street," in Poland, 37

John XXIII, pope, 228

John Paul II, pope, 229, 230-231

Judaism, 1; and Hasidism, 44-46, 95-96, 97; and memory, 1; and women, 9-11, 93-94, 95-96; Ashkenazic, 37; Conservative, 29, Orthodox, 6, 30, 53, 89, 95-96, Reform, 29, 53; return to in Poland, 246-248; role of rabbis in, 41; Sephardic, 37. *See also* **Zionism.**

Judenrat, 128-129; and deportations, 165; and forced labor, 132; and Jewish underground, 201, 203; and self help, 133. *See also* **Kehillah.**

Kabbalah, 52

Kaczenrginski, Shmerl, 218

Kadare, Ismail, 75

Kanal, Israel, 191

Kann, Maria, 187-188

Kaplan, Chaim, 122, 140, 143, 146

Karski, Jan, 181-183

Katyn Massacre, 124

Kaufman, Jonathan, 246, 254

Kazin, Alfred, 188, 216, 217

Kehillah, 37, 43, 128. *See also* **Judenrat.**

Kennedy, John F., U.S. President, 254

Kielce, Poland, pogrom in, 225-226, 227; apology for, 227

Kiev, Russia, 60

King, Martin Luther, Jr., 255

Kishinev, Russia, pogrom in, 61-63

Klepfisz, Michal, 201-202

Koestler, Arthur, 183

Korczak, Janus. *See* **Goldszmit, Henryk.**

Kosciuszko, Tadeusz, 48

Kossak-Szatkowska, Zofia, 169-170

Kot, Andrej, 129

Kovner, Abba, 147, 149, 162, 164, 175, 212, 235

Kovno, Poland, 218

Krakow, Poland, 37, 96, 218

Krall, Hanna, 244-245
Kristallnacht, 112
Kushner, Tony, 1
Kwasniewski, Aleksander, 227

Labor Zionists. *See* Paolei Zion.
Langer, Lawrence, 149, 152, 164
Lanzmann, Claude, 209
Lazowert, Henryka, 157
Lemberg. *See* Lwow.
Lester, Julius, 12, 223
Levi, Primo, 176, 180
Lewin, Abraham, 107, 153, 154
Lichtenstein, Israel, 171
Lifton, Betty, 48-49
Lithuania: and Kingdom of Poland, 37;
    and Russian rule, 53, 78-79; united
    with Poland, 42
Lithuanians, in Polish Commonwealth,
    42
Little Poland, 37
Lodz, Poland, 125
Lubetkin, Zivia, 163, 189-190, 191
    (photo), 191-192, 193, 199, 201, 206,
    207, 210-211, 211, 212, 219, 235
Ludmir, Poland, 37
Luria, Solomon, 41
Luther, Martin, 27
Lutheran Church, 28
Lvov, Poland, 37, 110, 123
Lwow, Poland, 81; civil war in, 81,
    83-84; in World War I, 78

Mabovitch, Golda. *See* Meir, Golda.
Mabovitch, Sheyna, 60-61
Maccabi games, 98, 218
Maidanek, 204, 218
Marranos, 27, 35, 54, 140
Marriages, Jewish, 9-10, 250-253
Marshall, Louis, 86
Masaryk, Thomas, 88
maskilim, 48-50, 51
Mazor, Michel, 135, 146, 148-149,
    156-157, 161, 175-176
Mayzel, Eliezer Yitzhak, 206-207
Meed, Vladka, 165-166, 196-197,
    197-198, 201-202
Meir, Golda, 7, 60, 61, 112
Merton, Kati, 13-14
mikvah, 30, 37

Milejkowski, Israel, 152
Minorities: attitudes toward in Poland,
    49-50, 83-84, 89-91; attitudes toward
    in the Second Polish Republic, 89-91;
    protection of after World War I,
    86-87; rights of, 86-87
Minorities Treaty (1919) , 87
Minow, Martha, 12, 84, 223
Mitnagim, 45, 52, 95, 96
Mizrachi, 93, 97. *See also* Zionism.
Moneylending: and the Church, 27,
    39-40, 43; and Jews, 27, 39-40
Montefiore, Moses, 49
Monuments, to the Holocaust, 241,
    242-243
Morgenthau, Henry, 83-84, 84 (photo),
    86, 87, 88, 101
Moskovitz, Anabela, 243
Mosse, George, 73, 80
Motol, Russia, 56-59
Mutual Aid. *See* Self-Help.

Nachman, of Bratislav, 47
Narutowicz, Gabriel, 90
Nation, defined, 73
National Democrats, 89
National Minorities bloc, 89-91
Nationalism: and education, 100; and
    "race," 73, 11-112; and World War I,
    72; defined, 72; Jewish, 59, 60-61, 65,
    76-77; Polish after World War I, 81,
    83-84, 100; Polish in 1700s and
    1800s, 48-50, 73-74; Polish in 1930s,
    101-103, 104-105, 106-107, 108-110;
    Polish under Russian rule, 49-50. *See
    also* Zionism.
Newspapers: and Kishinev pogrom,
    62-63; antisemitic, 61; during World
    War I, 80; for children, 101; Jewish in
    Nazi-occupied Poland 138-139;
    religious, 95; socialist, 95; Yiddish in
    U.S., 65
Niemoeller, Martin, 259
Nostra Aetate, 28, 228-229
Nuremberg, Germany, trials of Nazis in,
    234

Oneg Shabbat, 144, 171-172, 199
Onyszkiewicz, Janusz, 244
Orphanages, 106-107

Orthodox Judaism, 6, 30, 53, 89, 95-96
Ottoman Empire, 76, 80, 81, 83
Ozrech, Maurici, 190
Pale of Jewish Settlement, 50 (map), 56, 78, life in, 56-59
Palestine, 37; and Jewish immigration, 98, 107, 111; and Turkish authorities 65, 76-77; and Zionists, 59, 60, 61; as a Jewish homeland, 76-77. *See also* Israel, Zionism.
Paolei Zion, 61, 62 (photo). *See also* Zionism.
Paris, France, 112
Parliament, Polish. *See* Sejm.
Partisans, 190; Jewish, 190, 218
Passover: and assimilated Jews in St. Petersburg, 53; in Warsaw Ghetto, 206-207
Peretz, Y.L., 46, 72
Pilsudski, Jozef, 73-74, 83-84, 87, 90, 91, 106
Pinsk, Poland, 60, 83
Pinsker, Leon, 76
Pogroms: and Nazis, 116, 136-137; defined, 54; in Kiev, 60; in Kishinev, 61-64; in Poland after World War I, 81, 83-84; in Poland after World War II, 225-226, 227; in Pryztyk, 108, 109; views of Jozef Pilsudski on, 83
Poland: and "Flying University," 49; and Minorities Treaty of 1919, 87-88; and nationalism, 49-50, 73-74, 81, 83-84, 89-91; and passports, 112; and Russian occupation, 56, 122-124; arrenda system in, 42; arrival of Jews in, 33, 35; as Catholic country, 42; charters in, 35-36, 39; civil wars in after World War I, 81, 83-84; during the Middle Ages, 35-37, 39-40; emigration from, 8, 10-11; ethnic diversity in, 42, 89; expansion into Ukraine, 42; fight for independence in the 1800s, 48, 49-50; in World War I, 78-79; in World War II, 116, 117-118, 119-120, 122, 129; kingdom of, 37; origins of name, 35; partition of, 33, 43, 50 (map); Second Polish Republic, 82 (map), 89-91, 98, 101-103, 108-110, 117; under Russian occupation, 52-54, 56-59; united with Lithuania, 42; visits to, 9

Police: German, 153-154, 168-169; Jewish, 158-159, 167, 174, 191-192, 193; Polish, 98, 153, 155, 201; Russian, 60-61, 62
Polish Boy Scouts, 162
Polish Girl Scouts, 187-188
Polish-Jewish relations: after the collapse of communism, 248, 249, 250; after World War I, 81, 83-84; after World War II, 224-226; during the Nazi occupation, 120, 125, 136-137, 139, 169, 182-183, 184, 195-196, 198, 201-203, 211, 213-215, 218-219; during the 1920s and 1930s, 89-91, 98, 101-103, 108-110, 117; during World War I, 78-79; under communist rule, 226, 244-245, 246-247
Polish nobles: in Ukraine, 42-43; relations with Jews, 36, 42-43, 49, 50, 58-59
Polish underground, 144, 169, 181-183, 201-203, 213-215
Politcal Parties, in Second Polish Republic, 89-91, 98
Pomerantz-Meltzer, Roza, 89
Power and powerlessness: during the Middle Ages in Poland, 35-37, 39-40; in Nazi-occupied Poland, 150, 153-154, 158-159, 160-161, 165-166, 167-169, 181-183; under Russian rule, 51-54
Poznam, 37
Prejudice: and stereotypes, 4-5, 24, 24-25; defined, 2; effects of, 2-3, 24-25, 60-64, 89-91, 98, 101, 103, 104-105
Press. *See* Newspapers.
Pritchard, Marion, 188
Propaganda: and German factory owners in the Warsaw Ghetto, 204-205; and the Nazis, 119, 136-137, 142; and Polish attitudes toward Jews in 1930s, 105, 106; antisemitic, 61, 105, 119
Protestant churches, 27-28
Przytyk, Poland, pogrom in, 108-109

Rabinovich, Sholem. *See* Aleichem, Sholem.
"Race," 15; and citizenship, 111-112; and nationalism, 73; in Nazi Germany, 111

Radio: and antisemitism, 103; and German invasion, 119-120; and Henryk Goldzmit, 106-107; and nationalism, 106-107; and news of the Holocaust, 216-217; and Polish underground, 213

Rapoport, Natan, 241

Red Russia, 37

Refugees, Jewish: during Nazi occupation, 122-124, 140; during World War I, 78-79; from Communism, 13-14; in the 1930s, 111-112. *See also* **Emigration, Immigration.**

Reform Judaism, 29, 53

Remba, Nachim, 175

Rescue, during the Holocaust, 195-197, 198, 211, 213

Resistance, Jewish: against the Nazis, 136-137, 138-139, 174, 175, 201-202, 210-211; to Russian antisemitism, 49-50, 60-61. Polish: against Russia, 48, 49-50; to antisemitism after the Holocaust 224-226; to discrimination against Jews in the 1930s, 107, 108, 110; to Nazi antisemitism, 126. *See also* **Jewish underground, Polish underground, Zegota**, names of individual groups.

Ringelblum, Emmanuel, 133, 138, 147, 158, 159, 171, 172, 187, 189

Roman Catholic Church: after World War II, 224-225; and the *Nostra Aetate*, 28, 228-230; and relations with Jews, 36, 39-40, 43, 58, 108, 110, 224-225, 228-230; during the Holocaust, 169-170, 224; in Communist Hungary, 13; in Poland, 42, 229-230, 248

Romans, 26

Roosevelt, Franklin D., 113

Roosevelt, Theodore, 79

Rosati, Dariusz, 227

Rosenberg, Elsa, 2-3

Rosenthal, A.M., 75

Rotem, Simha, 140-141, 209-210, 211, 212

Rubenstein, Richard, 136

Russia: and Jews in the 1800s, 52-54; and Jews during World War I, 78-79; and Katyn Massacre, 124, and liberation of Warsaw in 1945, 219, and pact with Germany in 1939, 122; and partition of Poland, 33; and Polish Jewish refugees, 122-124; and rule of Poland, 49; collapse of empire, 73, 81; during World War I, 78-79. *See also* **Soviet Union.**

Sabbath: and Jewish workers in Poland, 104-105; celebration of, 6, 7, 11; protection of after World War I, 87; protection of by Jewish deputies in the Sejm, 89; protection of in medieval charters, 36

St. Petersburg, Russia, 53, 79

Sanacja, 91

Sarajevo, Austria-Hungary, 72

Saskatoon, Saskatchewan, 2-3

Sawicki, Stefan, 214-215

Schenirer, Sarah, 95, 96

Schindler's List, 68

Schoem, David, 59, 103

Schipper, Yitzhak, 189

Schoenberger, Chana, 24-25

Schools: colleges in United States, 16-17, 18-19, 21-22; in Russia in the late 1800s, 54, 63, 93-94; Jewish in Poland after World War I, 87; religious in North America, 3, 6; segregated in Poland, 108-110; Yiddish in United States, 7-8. *See also* **Education.**

Schwartzchild, Henry, 254-255

Sejm: in Kingdom of Poland, 37; in Second Polish Republic, 89-91

Self-defense, Jewish: during World War I, 79; in Galicia after World War I, 81, 83; in Poland in the 1920s and 1930s, 93, 98, 108-110, 109 (photo); in response to Kishinev pogrom, 62-63, 63-64; in response to Nazi occupation, 136-137

Self-Help, Jewish, 133-134

Sephardic Jews, 37

Serbia, 72

Sereny, Gita, 179-180

Servatius, Robert, 235

Shapiro, Lauren, 21-22

Shema Yisrael, 29, 30, 160-161

Shtetl: and Haskalah, 49, 53; in 1600s, 42-43; legacies of, 17; life in, 10, 48,

56-59, 69-70

Shulhan Arukh, 37

Singer, Isaac Bashevis, 93-94

Sigismund III of Poland, 42-43

Sikorski, Wladyslaw, General, 214

Smuggling, during World War II, 124, 140-141, 153-154, 155, 157

Sobibor, 147, 218. *See also* Death camps.

Social Structure: and the Englightenment, 33, 34; in Poland, during Middle Ages, 35-37; in Pale of Jewish Settlement in the late 1800s, 58-59, 69-70

Socialism, 60-61, 76

Socialists, 60-61, 108-110. *See also* Bund, Zionists

Socialist-Zionist movement, 60-61

Solidarity, 244

Solomon, Robert Bailey, 24

Soviet Union, 122-124, 226, 234. *See also* Russia.

Spain, 27, 35

Spanish Inquisition, 27

Spielberg, Steven, 68

Sports and Jewish Youth, 98, 99 (photo)

Stalin, Joseph, 226

Stangl, Franz, 179-180

Stendhal, Krister, 26

Stereotyping, of Jews: and separation, 27; definition of, 4; of Jewish women, 22; of Jews in Canada in 1930s, 2-3; of Jews in Poland after World War II, 226-227; of Jews in Poland in the 1920s and 1930s, 89-91, 98, 101-102, 106-107; of Jews in the United States, 21-22, 24, 24-25; religious, 24-25, 39-40

Stroop, Jurgen, SS General, 206, 207-208, 209, 211, 234, 235

Survivors, of the Holocaust, 11, 160; and Eichmann trial, 235-236; children of, in Poland, 246-248; children of, in United States, 9-11, 13-14, 238-240

Szerynski, Jozef, 158, 191-192

Szezawinska, Jadwiga, 49

Szwajger, Adina Blady, 123-124, 133-134, 160-161

Szymborska, Wislawa, 67-68

Talmud, 10

Tannen, Deborah, 4

Tartars, in Polish Commonwealth, 42

Tenants' Committees, 133-134, 135

Tenenbaum, Joseph: after World War I, 81, 83-84; after World War II, 224-225

Terror, Nazis, and collective responsibility, 128-130; and forced labor, 131-132; during Holocaust, 150; in the Warsaw Ghetto, 153-154, 165-166, 167-168

Thompson, Dorothy, 111

Thon, Osias, 92

Toebbens, Walter C., 204-205

Tolstoy, Leo, 64

Tradition, Jewish: 6-8, 21; after the Holocaust, 250-253; and family, 21-22; and German occupation, 133-134; and men, 18-19; and women, 9-11; breaks with, after World War I, 93-94, 95-96;

Treblinka, 147; as a death camp, 177-180, 189, 204; memorial at, 241, 243. *See also* Death camps.

Trepman, Paul, 158-159

Tsene-Urene, 46-47

Turkey, 35. *See also* Ottoman Empire.

Turks, 65, 80

Ukraine: and growth of Hasidism, 44; in World War I, 78; Polish conquest of, 42; uprising in, 42-43

Ukrainians: after World War I in Galicia, 81, 83; in Polish Commonwealth, 42-43; in Second Polish Republic, 89-91

Umschlagplatz, 165, 167, 168, 173, 174, 175

Unions, 104-105. *See also* Bund.

United States: and citizenship, 73; and Holocaust survivors, 9-11; and Kishinev pogrom, 65; and news of the Holocaust, 182-183; and Nuremberg trials, 234; and refugees in 1930s, 111-112, 113; and World War I, 80, 83, 86-87

Vaad Arba Aratzot (Council of Four Lands), 37, 43

Vatican, 228-229

Vienna, Austria, 96

Vilna, 5, 123, 147, 212; destruction of Jews in, 162-163; uprising, 218

Violence, against Jews: after World War I, 83, 86; in Russia, 67-68. *See also* **Antisemitism, Holocaust, Pogroms.**

Vitebsk, Russia, 70

Volhynia, 36, 37

Wagner, Eduard, Colonel, 116

Wallenberg, Raoul, 14

Warsaw, 63; and German invasion, 116, 117-118; and German occupation, 125-126, 136-137, 140-141, 195-196; division of city by Nazis, 142-143; growth in 1800s, 49; in 1920s and 1930s, 101-102, 108-110; in World War I, 78-79; seige of, 119-120; uprising in, 218-219

Warsaw Ghetto, 146 (map); and reaction to news of the Holocaust 162-163; April uprising, 199-200; armed resistance in, 187; bunkers in, 197; contrasts in, 156, 156-157; creation of, 142-143; death rate in, 152 (chart); description of, 148-149; great deportation from, 165-166, 167-169, 173-174, 181, 187; hiding places in, 197; hunger in, 151-152, 156; in flames, 209-211; January uprising, 199-200; memorial to uprising in, 241-243; need for papers in, 165-167; propaganda in, 204-205; sealing of, 143, 148; search for unity in, 189-190; smuggling in, 153-154, 155-156

Warsaw Ghetto Memorial, 241; and Solidarity, 244-245

Wasiutynska, Helena, 101

Wdowinski, David, 130, 132, 160, 162-163, 235

Wechsler, Max, 237-238

Weichert, Michael, 135

Wengeroff, Pauline, 52-54

Weinberg, Arthur, 7-8

Weinryb, Bernard, 39, 40

Weizmann, Chaim, 7, 56-59, 63, 64, 65

Wells, H. G., 183

Western Europe: and migration from, 26-27; anti-Judaism in, 26-27; Enlightenment in, 33; Industrial Revolution in, 34

White Russia, 56

White Russians: in Polish Commonwealth, 42; in Motol, 56-59

Wiesel, Elie, 44-45, 45-46, 147, 159, 164, 172, 183-184, 188, 190, 193, 220, 250-253, 255

Wilner, Arye, 192, 202-203, 210

Wilson, Woodrow, 80, 83, 86

Winter, Shmuel, 199-200

Wistrich, Robert S., 26, 28

Wolinski, Henryk, 202-203

Women, Jewish: and education, 46, 94, 95-96; and Hasidism, 46; and Haskalah, 52-54; and marriage, 9; and resistance to Nazis, 139, 207-208; and *Tsene-Urene*, 46; as revolutionaries, 60-61; as Zionists, 60-61; in Jewish tradition, 9-11; stereotyping of, 22

Workmen's Circle, 7-8

Workers, Jewish: and socialism, 61-63; and unions, 104-105; in Warsaw Ghetto, 165-166, 204-205; ingenuity during Nazi occupation, 140-141

World Federation of Polish Jews, 224

World War I: and change, 93; and collapse of empires, 72, 81; and Jews, 78-79; and nationalism, 72; casualties, 72; outbreak, 72

World War II: outbreak, 116, 117-118; post-war trials, 234; refugees, 122-124; seige of Warsaw, 119-120. *See also* **Germany, Holocaust, Poland.**

Yahil, Leni, 183

Yiddish, language: historical development of, 40; in the United States, 6, 6-7, 7-8; newspapers, 62, 65, 95, 138-139; Polish influence on, 40; teaching inUnited States, 5, 7-8

Yiddish culture. *See* **Culture.**

Yismakh, Borukh, 98

Yom Kippur: a Hasidic tale about, 45; in Motol, 57; in the Warsaw Ghetto, 138, 142

Yoselovich, Berek, 48

Youth, Jewish: and economic competition, 104-105; and generation gap, 10-11; and Jewish tradition, 95-96; and Kishinev pogrom, 61-63; and protests in Poland in 1930s, 108-110;

and sports, 98; in 1920s-1930s, 7-8,
93-94, 95-96, 98, 99; in 1940s in U.S.,
6-7; in 1960s in U.S., 6, 10-11; in the
Warsaw Ghetto, 151-152, 155-156,
157, 160-161, 189-190, 191-192, 193;
in Russian Poland, 54, 60, 61; stereotyping of, 24-25; today, 16-17, 18-19,
21-22. *See also* **Education, Identity,
Youth Groups.**

Youth Groups: and awareness of
Holocaust, 162-163; Christian, 98,
162, 187; religious, 96; socialist, 98,
108, 189-190; Zionist, 98, 99,
138-139, 189-190, 191-192. *See also*
**Jewish Fighting Organization, Jewish
Military Union,** and names of individual groups.

Zable, Arnold, 33, 35
zaddik, 45
Zalman, Elijah ben Solomon, 45
Zegota, 170, 195, 211
Ziegelboim, Manya, 196-197
Ziegelboim, Shmuel, 128-129, 216-217
Zimbardo, Philip, 150
Zionism: and Jewish identity, 6-7,
8; after World War I, 86-87, 93-94, 98,
107; origins of, 59, 60-61, 76-77
Zionists: and antisemitism, 63-64, 76;
and the Holocaust, 181-182; and
peace conference after World War I,
86-87; and resistance to the Nazis,
189-190; camp for, 6-7; during Nazi
occupation, 138-139; in Russian-occupied Poland, 60-64; in the Sejm,
89-91; in the United States, 6-7;
youth groups, 99
Zionists Revisionists, 191
ZOB. *See* **Jewish Fighting Organization.**
ZTOS. *See* **Jewish Welfare Society.**
Zuckerman, Yitzhak, 126, 127, 164,
166, 174, 187, 188, 189, 189-190,
191 (photo), 192, 193-194, 213,
214-215, 218-219, 219-220, 235, 255
ZZW. *See* **Jewish Military Union.**